# The Complete Guide to Autism Treatments

## A parent's handbook: make sure your child gets what works!

### S.K. Freeman, Ph.D.

**Library of Congress Control Number: 2006904196**
**Library and Archives Canada Cataloguing in Publication**

Freeman, Sabrina Karen, 1958-
   The complete guide to autism treatments. A parent's handbook:
   make sure your child gets what works! / Sabrina Freeman.

Includes bibliographical references and index.
ISBN 978-0-9657565-5-6

         1. Autism in children--Treatment. 2. Autism--Treatment. I. Title
RJ506.A9F725 2007         618.92'85882'06         C2007-900064-9

Published by:

SKF Books USA, Inc.
413 19th St. #322
Lynden, WA  98264

SKF Books, Inc.
20641 46th Avenue
Langley, BC  V3A 3H8

Printed in the U.S.A.
First Edition

# Contents

## Section Two: How Do We Know What Works and ... What Doesn't

# Introduction

*The Complete Guide to Autism Treatments* was inspired by parents of children afflicted with autism. I have spoken to thousands of parents about various treatments and answered the same questions over and over again. Many times I gave tutorials to individual parents. I realized that parents need a clear way to understand how science works so they can make appropriate treatment decisions for their children.

In addition, professionals and paraprofessionals need to have a better understanding of the scientific method so they do not inadvertently recommend a treatment with no science behind it to the parents of the children they work with. It is crucial that professionals remember that they hold considerable status and legitimacy in the eyes of parents, and with that legitimacy comes responsibility — a responsibility *to not* inadvertently send parents down the road of quackery in autism treatments.

Currently, many parents find it difficult to evaluate autism treatments for their child. They are forced to rely upon experts who may or may not know enough about the science to provide accurate information. Therefore, in a sense, parents need to become experts themselves. Fortunately, the scientific method is not difficult to understand. It simply needs to be laid out in a form that is understandable. All parents, professionals and paraprofessionals alike need to know how to make informed choices about which therapies to use to treat the child's autism. After reading this book, my sincere hope is that everyone will be able to evaluate the next, new purported treatment or cure that comes along. It is very important to be able to ask the right questions and to find the flaws in the science behind the purported treatment, or to find the evidence that, in fact, the treatment is effective.  At a minimum, understanding the scientific method will protect thousands of children from quackery and, hopefully, provide parents and professionals with the tools to find treatments that are effective for autism.

I must apologize in advance to many deceased philosophers of science insofar as I am going to make short shrift of most of their concepts; however, parents of children with autism and the professionals they rely upon only need to know enough about scientific theories and theoretically motivated research to protect their children from quackery and the vendors of "snake oil" treatments for autism.   Parents of children with autism are better off when they understand statistics and how they are used to report study findings.  Only then will consumers be able to evaluate claims about autism treatments that are supported through the use (or misuse) of statistics.  In short, this book is designed to give those who care about the futures of children with autism the information they need to make sure their child "Gets What Works!"

The book is organized into two sections.  In Section One, we scrutinize the range of treatment options offered to parents of children with autism and use the tools of the scientific method to evaluate each treatment to help create informed consumers of autism treatment services.  Section Two is designed to provide a background in science for parents or professionals who are newcomers to the scientific method.  This section is a must-read for consumers who plan to independently scrutinize the next autism treatment introduced into the marketplace.  For those who may not have a background in science, I suggest that Section Two be read first as a primer, prior to reading about specific autism treatments.  Otherwise, the first section is best read by topic, as a reference, or sequentially as a comprehensive guide to autism treatments.

# Section One

## What Works and What Doesn't?

This section groups similar autism treatment approaches together.  Although the typology may not be perfect because some treatments do not easily lend themselves to a specific orientation, this categorization is probably the easiest way for readers to wade into the deep, murky world of available autism treatments (I use the word "treatment" very loosely for some of these methods).

When reading a section on a particular method, I have introduced the method with no editorializing.  In other words, I present the treatment method in the clearest way available based upon what the treatment professional has said about his or her method.  No matter how wild or wacky an idea may sound, we must look at the data rather than rely on our intuition to determine if the treatment method is absurd or sensible.

After introducing the method, I then look at the evidence that supports the claims made by those who teach or practice the method.  In this subsection, I highlight concerns about the studies and then give readers a chance to evaluate my comments.   Finally, I provide a "Bottom Line" regarding each treatment.

Science is defined by debate; therefore, I welcome readers to disagree with me regarding my evaluations based on the scientific evidence.  The goal of this book is to have consumers critically evaluate autism treatments so they are 100 percent informed about a treatment before they attempt it on a vulnerable child.

## Cost of Autism treatment

Because I am also a parent (and an ethical human being), I refuse to evaluate a treatment based on economics.  There is a very serious political debate raging among policy makers about the number of resources children with autism should receive relative to other children with special needs.  Aside from the draconian and heartless nature of these debates, the arguments are also flawed because this group of children needs to be treated and educated rather than warehoused.  Unfortunately, highly bureaucratized systems concerned with short-term budgeting (civil servants forgetting their primary function), regularly attempt to provide children with treatments that are economical rather than effective, as a means to ration resources.

In addition, there is a trend to ration treatment based upon an autistic child's functioning level.  It is particularly disturbing to see a child with severe autism not given the intervention required due to the degree of severity.  As a result of treatment rationing, much litigation takes place revolving around treatment for children with autism.  This book does not enter the turbulent treatment rationing debate, although it is self-evident that as advocates for their children, parents need to fight for the most appropriate treatment available, regardless of cost to the health care or educational systems.

## Half-baked Research

One of the primary shortcomings of most research in the autism field is that researchers tend to apply their findings prematurely on children.  It seems as though an autism treatment researcher or practitioner need only develop an interesting idea and desperate parents are happy to volunteer their children to receive the treatment.  Unfortunately, much of this research is still very much in the experimental stage (and lacks evidence that it is effective).  Well-meaning parents and professionals who are uninformed how research must proceed to determine a treatment's effectiveness often recommend this experimental treatment to parents of autistic children.  This observation is particularly true in the area of biomedical therapies for autism.

In this section, I have included every treatment offered to parents, irrespective of whether it has been discredited, is still in the experimental stage (half-baked), or whether it is considered best practice.  After evaluating the data, it is up to consumers — the parents — to decide whether or not to experiment with their child.  However, it is very  important to note that some of the unsubstantiated treatments may actually be harmful for the child.  Some caution is advisable.  As will become evident throughout Section One, I strongly recommend against pursuing these potentially harmful treatments.

# Behavioral Therapies                    Section 1.1

▷ *Home-based Intensive Behavioral Treatment*

▷ *School-based Intensive Behavioral Treatment*

▷ *Offshoots of Intensive Behavioral Therapies*

# Behavioral Therapies

## What is Behaviorism as it Applies to Autism?

In the world of autism therapies, there is a considerable amount of research conducted on various types of behaviorism. Behavioral methods or schools of thought may be different in terms of their goals for the child (e.g., which behaviors they would like to increase or decrease or which skills they would like the child to acquire).  However, keep in mind that the actual method they are relying upon has the same origin. *It all flows from the work of B.F. Skinner, the grandfather of behaviorism.*

Behavioral intervention for individuals with autism involves behavior modification based on B.F. Skinner's principles of operant conditioning, used to decrease undesirable behaviors and to teach and encourage new and desirable behaviors.  Behavioral practitioners and theorists analyze human functioning based *only* on those behaviors that are overt and observable, as opposed to making inferences about internal mental states.[1]  Behavioral theory proposes that the use of reinforcement and punishment techniques to eliminate non-functional or destructive behavior, while building up the frequency and variety of alternative behaviors, will provide a basis for aiding development.

## What is Applied Behavior Analysis?

When it comes to autism, over the last forty-five years behaviorists have taken lessons from research done on animals, and have *significantly* modified those techniques for use with many people, including those with autism.  The techniques that this field has established are not simply to teach people with a wide variety of problems how to "behave;" rather, through behavioral techniques that originate in the field of Applied Behavior Analysis (ABA), treatment professionals are able to change self-destructive or maladaptive behaviors so that persons afflicted with autism can attain a large repertoire of important life skills, including communication, academic, social, self-help, and foundation skills which promote independence.

The field of Applied Behavior Analysis is very broad:  the treatment of autism is only a small but growing part of this field.  The certifying body, the Behavior Analyst Certification Board defines ABA as follows:  "Applied behavior analysis is a well-developed discipline among the helping professions, with a mature body of scientific knowledge, established standards for evidence-based practice, distinct methods of service, recognized experience and educational requirements for practice, and identified sources of requisite education in universities."[2]  In terms of autism, government agencies occasionally attempt to define the field of ABA as a young, emergent field that has insufficient data on efficacy[*] or, conversely, that there is not enough data on the application of ABA principles for children with autism six years of age and older.  This is categorically untrue, as is evident by hundreds of studies conducted from 1980 to the present done in this field, most of which were conducted with adults, not children.[3]

It is important to understand that not all those certified in Applied Behavior Analysis necessarily have the expertise to design and implement an intensive behavioral treatment program for children with autism.  Before parents set up an intensive behavioral treatment program with a behavior analyst, they need to make sure that this professional has the requisite experience with a range of autistic children.

---

[*]For more information on the way the governments have warped and distorted the field of ABA to avoid paying for treatment for children with autism, I encourage you to read, *Science for Sale in the Autism Wars*.[4]

# What is Intensive Behavioral Treatment?

Intensive Behavioral Treatment (IBT) for children with autism is centered on the idea that the use of behavioral principles in a highly intensive manner (e.g., forty hours per week of treatment) is effective in ameliorating the symptoms of autism.  Researchers have found that the global development of children with autism can be influenced through the use of 1) operant conditioning, 2) techniques researched and applied from the field of behavior analysis, and 3) findings from the literature on child development.  In other words, since autism is a Pervasive Developmental Disorder, IBT can be used to intervene positively in the outcome of autistic disorder by forcing development that is not occurring naturally.  It was hypothesized, and later supported, by research that the child's delay or disorder in language, social development, cognition, and overall functioning can be mitigated or eliminated with early IBT.  Although some describe IBT as devoid of developmental influences from the theories of child development, this is, in fact, not the case.

## Is the IBT Program Home-based or Center-based?

According to practitioners of IBT, when done competently, treatment should take place during every waking hour of the child's life in order to maximize the child's developmental window.  Whether a child participates in a home-based behavioral treatment program or a center-based treatment program is generally a decision made by the child's parents.  There are differences in philosophy regarding these two options when it comes to integration versus segregation. The data generated by home-based programs is more plentiful and generally stronger than that of center-based  programs.  This may have less to do with comparative effectiveness of the two program approaches, but rather reflects the prolific nature of those researchers who conduct studies on home-based treatment programs.  In the next few pages, I will introduce the traditional home-based and school-based intensive behavioral treatment programs, and then discuss autism treatment offshoots from the behaviorism field.

# Behavioral Therapies:  Home-based Intensive Behavioral Treatment

## What is Home-based Intensive Behavioral Treatment?

The pioneer in treating children with autism in a home-based milieu is Dr. O. Ivar Lovaas of the University of California at Los Angeles (UCLA), with the work he initiated in the 1960s and 70s at the Young Autism Project.  Many worldwide sites were originally established to replicate the ground-breaking autism treatment work of Lovaas first published in 1987.  Today, intensive home-based treatment programs for children with autism are now quite popular. Although there are many reputable practitioners who never trained at either the Young Autism Project or associated replication sites, as a result of the treatment protocol developed and tested by Lovaas and colleagues, home-based IBT programs have come to be referred to by parents as "The Lovaas Method" of Applied Behavior Analysis, or "Lovaas-type ABA."* Unfortunately, there is at this time no systematic way to differentiate those practitioners who are doing a competent job of programming for an Intensive Behavioral Treatment program from those who are unqualified, much to the frustration of both parents and

---

*This branding is disturbing to many reputable academics[1] because they are concerned about a focus or overreliance on specific techniques rather than the use of data-driven changes based on the principles of ABA.  They are also concerned that branding precludes new science-based advances.  Although these are legitimate concerns, consumers (the parents making crucial treatment decisions for their children) find that branding provides some protection from every Tom, Dick or Harry who wants to hang out his shingle and claim he knows how to create, maintain, and supervise a science-based behavioral treatment program.  Many critics of branding claim that certification in ABA should be sufficient to protect parents from incompetent or unqualified providers.  I disagree as there are Board Certified Behavior Analysts who create programs exclusively relying on certain techniques that are without sufficient evidence of efficacy. It is my view that the ethical guidelines of the self-policing board certifying body is not sufficient protection for consumers when it comes to efficacy.  Hopefully, one day there will be a Board Certified Behavior Analyst specialization in autism and branding will fall out of favor.  However, until that time, I predict that parents will continue to brand and use this shortcut to refer to the home-based Intensive Behavioral Treatment program that originally created the results from the landmark 1987 Lovaas study, even though many of the techniques have been refined and improved since the 1970s and 80s.

ethical academics in this field. In the field of intensive behavioral treatment in general, but home-based treatment in particular, it is still very much a case of *caveat emptor*.

Early behavioral treatment for children with autism applies behavior modification principles to teach children with autism in their homes and communities under the watchful eye of their parent or caregiver. This intervention identifies skill deficits (areas of weakness) which have resulted in the child's lack of success in typical learning situations, and targets them for "manual" acquisition of the necessary skills. The difficulty that children with autism typically have in learning naturally from the environment is targeted by breaking down skills and instructions into their smallest components. The child first acquires each step separately, then chains them together and eventually masters the entire skill. To make the skill acquisition process easier, several methods are used. Currently, the common structures in competent IBT programs include: direct instruction (the child being directly taught the part of the skill by a therapist); 1:1 therapist to student ratio (one adult to one child); discrete trial training (a therapist-led, highly structured teaching technique); discrimination training (another highly structured technique that teaches through direct comparison); prompting and fading strategies (a technique that helps the child learn by prompting or giving hints for the correct answer and then fading the prompts or hints once the learning has taken place); shaping (a technique which takes the skill level of the child and, through well-planned reinforcement, teaches the child to improve his or her skill level); and chaining (a technique by which a complex skill is taught by teaching a number of simple skills and connecting these simple skills to master the complex skill); and using a variety of reinforcement strategies (a technique to reward the child for the correct response). The basic curriculum includes imitation skills, receptive language skills, toy play, and self-help skills. Once these components have been mastered, the more advanced curriculum includes expressive language skills, abstract language and interactive play (with other children). Further advancement has the child overcome deficits in both the home and school environments where the curriculum includes pre-academic and academic abilities (such as weather and calendar skills), socialization skills, cause-effect learning and observational learning. The goal of this stage is to prepare these children to learn "naturally" from the school environment. Intensive Behavioral Treatment programs follow a basic hierarchy of skills; however, they are highly individualized and flexible based on the skill level of each child.

Importantly, in Intensive Behavioral Treatment programs, non-learning behaviors (e.g., self-destructive or maladaptive) are targeted for elimination using a variety of behavioral techniques. Originally, the treatment protocol employed extinction (ignoring the behavior), time-out (removing the child from the situation for a short period of time), physical restraint (holding the child's hands if he or she were hurting him or herself), verbal reprimands (telling the child "no" or "stop"), types of differential reinforcement (e.g., rewarding the child for not engaging in a particular behavior), and redirection (involving the child in another activity to interrupt a nonfunctional behavior). Many of these techniques are used today; however, time-outs and physical restraint have fallen out of favor with many practitioners.

## What evidence do practitioners have that this really works?

Our wide literature search netted over 100 articles on comprehensive IBT programs. Most of the publications were commentaries about the original studies and the replications of Lovaas' work. In terms of peer-reviewed articles presenting data on IBT, there were fourteen (14) articles. In each and every study where the treatment fidelity was high,[2,3,4,5,6,7,8,9,10] children in the experimental group significantly improved over children in the control group. Even in some of the parent-directed groups,[9,11] the children in the experimental group fared much better than the control group that did not receive the intensive treatment. There are a few studies in which the parent-directed therapy was not sufficiently rigorous, and therefore, the children did not make substantial gains.[13,15,16] The above articles will be now presented and discussed.

The original Lovaas study (1987), showed extremely promising results for treatment efficacy. The outcomes indicated that 47% of the experimental group (n=19) achieved normal functioning, 40% were assigned to classes for the language delayed and 10% were assigned to classes for the autistic/retarded. In contrast, only 2% of the control group (n=40) achieved normal functioning. Forty-five percent were placed in classes for the language-delayed with the other 53% placed in classes for the autistic and mentally retarded.[15] The experimental group made average IQ gains of over 30 points. These treatment gains were assessed five years later and found to be maintained, with the exception of two children.[5] One of these children moved back into a language delayed class; however, another child joined a mainstream class and, therefore, outcome percentages remained stable.

Smith and colleagues (1997), undertook a replication of these results through archival data; however, they used participants who were in the lowest functioning range. Their results confirmed that treatment gains were achieved, even with the most challenging population of autistic children. Average IQ gains made were ten points on average (+/-2) for the experimental group, versus an average three point decrease in the control group. At intake, no child in either the experimental or the control group had any speech; however, at follow-up, ninety-one percent (10/11) of the experimental group used spoken words functionally, versus twenty percent (2/10) in the control group. It is important to note that the Smith et al. (1997) study selected children with diagnoses of autism *and* severe mental retardation, making these results that much more impressive. As mentioned earlier, there are several other designs replicating the results of Intensive Behavioral Treatment.[3,4,7,8,9,10,11,12,13,14] Although most of the above studies were home-based, even those studies where the children were in a pre-school,[7,8] showed a significant component of home-based treatment.

The majority of studies that attempt to replicate Lovaas' original work generally use control groups, creating a between-subjects design. Anderson (1987) is an exception: they used a within-subjects design with fourteen children receiving treatment. Between-subjects designs (using a control group) are often used to control for confounding variables which could influence the outcome or results of the studies (see the next section of the book for a discussion on the role of a control group). The one methodological problem which exists in the studies was the absence of random assignment to the experimental and control groups. Due to parental protest at the time Lovaas conducted his original study, he was unable to use randomization to assign children to groups. The National Institutes of Health (the funding source of the study), gave their blessing to Lovaas to use a different technique to assign children to groups. To diffuse parental concerns, Lovaas assigned children to experimental condition based on funding and distance from the UCLA clinic. In addition, he matched children in the control and experimental groups to guarantee that the two groups were similar at intake.[*]

---

[*]Baer (1993) referred to this technique as functionally random assignment and argued that it could be equally as convincing as random assignment providing the researchers did not control the way the children were assigned. Baer explains that because assignment to control or experimental group was based on resources, a variable out of the experimenter's control, there is no reason why this procedure could not have created true randomization. He states: "the child's status as a best-potential case or a worst-potential case, even if perceptible to the clinician, could not have affected the availability of those resources at the moment that the child was available for assignment, and so, in my judgment, the assignment was functionally random."[17]

In addition to matching, Lovaas (1987) varied treatment intensity between the control and experimental groups to determine whether high-quality, low intensity treatment would have positive effects. It did not.

None of the replications of the original study randomly assign children to groups because it is ethically impossible to do so due to the original data which shows the effectiveness of the treatment. In order to overcome this problem, Sheinkopf and Siegel (1998) used matched pairs assignment. The Smith et al. (1997) article examined archival records and attempted to match the groups based on age, IQ, diagnosis, language and behavior. Each study used a variety of widely-accepted measures of the dependent variable, autism.

Results indicate significant improvement for the experimental group in all home-based behavioral intervention studies. As mentioned above, the most dramatic results came from the study by Lovaas (1987), which reported an average of thirty point IQ gains in the experimental group. This program also had the highest intensity of treatment at forty hours per week for two or more years. The McEachin (1993) study is a follow-up on the children from the Lovaas (1987) study, which shows that these children maintained their gains and subsequent school placements. In addition, the Sallows et al. (2005) study not only replicated the original Lovaas (1987) study demonstrating that the experimental group significantly improved over the control group, but showed the level of improvement of the children in the experimental group rivals that of the Lovaas best outcome children. An additional study, Cohen et al. (2006) used a quasi-experimental design with twenty-one-age and IQ-matched children in a community-based setting over a three-year period. They found that the children who received IBT based on the UCLA protocol fared significantly better than the matched children attending special education classes.[10] One study that requires particular mention is the Howard et al. (2004) study in which IBT was contrasted with high quality, intensive eclectic programming. The Howard et al. study clearly demonstrates that eclectic treatments for autism are not as effective as IBT based on the principles of Applied Behavior Analysis.

## What does the therapy actually look like?

Since the data demonstrate[2] that an average of thirty to forty hours per week of intensive intervention is crucial for best outcome to be achieved, the ideal therapy program will have the child engage in therapy forty hours per week. The rationale for this level of intensity comes from typically developing children. Children without autism engage in at least forty hours per week of active learning; however, for them it is a naturalistic, incidental type of learning. Since autistic children do not generally learn useful skills or information naturally from their environment during their free time, this learning needs to be facilitated, and is best done through structured learning for approximately the same amount of time as that which occurs for their typically developing peers. The UCLA protocol starts therapy in an intensive one to one intervention in which skill acquisition occurs using highly structured forms of learning. The therapy first takes place in the home, typically with young college students trained as therapists, and eventually progresses into the preschool setting. As the child's abilities increase, the structure of the teaching decreases and learning begins to happen more naturalistically. The eventual goal for children who have gone through the program is to achieve independent learning, from their environment, in the same manner as occurs with typically developing children. In good IBT programs, naturalistic learning is programmed for children only once they are ready, and not before. The ideal scenario occurs when the autistic child is able to enter kindergarten independently and learn naturalistically in the same manner as that child's peers.

## Would I try it on my child?

Yes, I would and I did.  My child began an intensive, home-based behavioral treatment program based on the work of Dr. Lovaas when she was four years old.  I chose this method before it became popular (approximately 1992) because it was the only treatment that had any high quality between subject-designed studies to evidence the effectiveness of the treatment.  My decision was based on science, which indeed bore fruit as my daughter did make incredible gains.  It is important to remember, though, that my anecdotal reporting regarding my child's gains should not sway you to use this method.   Anecdotal reports are unreliable to use when making the important decision about treatment methods to use with your child, even if the anecdote comes from someone who respects science.  What should convince you, when choosing one method over another, is the abundance of *scientific* evidence behind the method.  It was scientific evidence that led me to choose IBT for my child.

## What else do I think?

Although it is very frustrating to parents, the lack of any known cause of autism makes the behavioral treatment approach ideal because its effectiveness does not depend on an underlying theory of cause.  Based on the evidence provided by this group of studies, it can be concluded that home-based behavioral intervention, using the best practices models that can be found in the UCLA protocol and its close approximations, is an effective method for the treatment for autism.  As is illustrated by the Smith (1997) study, this intervention is effective, even for the autistic and severely mentally retarded population which, in my opinion, presents the greatest challenge before us as parents and professionals.

What I find particularly appealing about home-based IBT is that the parent is the case manager. In other words, the child is under the watchful eye of those who love him or her. In addition, the concept that my toddler or pre-schooler is able to enjoy all the experiences of typically developing children, with a therapist helping to facilitate this interaction, rather than the child being segregated from the earliest age (to access more expertise), is very appealing. After speaking to thousands of parents, I found that the philosophy of integration and normalization is a philosophy that is more comfortable for a parent of a newly-diagnosed child to accept. Although this philosophy may or may not be a contributing factor for the effectiveness of a behavioral treatment protocol, it is fortunate when the treatment protocol naturally accommodates inclusion and integration, and avoids stigmatization.

One issue that parents should be aware of in running home-based IBT programs is that if the fidelity of the treatment is not sufficiently high (i.e. the program is not "tight" or implemented correctly), some of the data indicate that the child's gains will suffer. That said, the parent-directed group which received three hours of supervision every other week in the Sallows and Graupner (2005) study was of such high quality that their children fared as well as the clinic-directed children.[18] This finding was unexpected and important, though, because it demonstrated that parent-directed treatment programs with minimal supervision (six hours a month) can produce excellent outcomes.

Critics of IBT (and there are many), claim that this treatment is a mechanistic program which essentially turns children into robots. These programs are also criticized because some claim that the children do not generalize their skills from the therapy sessions into the natural environment. As I previously mentioned, a good behavioral intervention program must be individually designed and customized for each child. The program grows and is modified with the child's developing skills  and, as a result, the program becomes increasingly less structured as the child becomes better able to learn in that format.  Generalization of skills is programmed into any quality behavioral intervention program to ensure that skills taught "at the table" will also be taught to be useful for the child in their everyday living.  This is widely recognized in the field of IBT as a key goal for programmers.   In short, good IBT programs do incorporate generalization and do not create "robots."  Critics also charge behavioral therapists as being abusive to children through the use of verbal and physical aversives. Fortunately, the use of physical aversives[*] and other techniques, such as physical restraints, are not part of the home-based treatment protocol (and have not been for over twenty years).

In the original Lovaas study (which began in the early 1970s), a mild physical aversive (a slap on the thigh) was used with a small subset of the children. This physical aversive was dropped from the protocol approximately twenty-five years ago.  Currently, the Lovaas Institute For Early Intervention (LIFE) uses the techniques of extinction, redirection, differential reinforcement and teaching alternate forms of behavior.  The use of physical aversives no longer occurs through practitioners from the institute or at any of the treatment sites affiliated with the UCLA Young Autism Clinic, or by any *reputable* independent practitioners using the UCLA protocol.

## What additional studies would I like to see the researchers do in this field?

At this point, there are a large number of IBT research replication sites, both in the United States and throughout the world (www.Lovaas.com lists the worldwide

---

[*]Today, if physical restraints are to be used (which may be necessary if the child is severely self-injurious), they are generally used only as needed, in highly controlled institutional settings such as hospitals, where there is video monitoring, precise data collection and, depending upon jurisdiction, judicial surveillance.

replication sites). The replication sites are designed to do exactly what their name implies: replicate the original study published by Lovaas and associates in 1987. These replication sites use the original protocol from the Lovaas (1987) study with a few exceptions. Replicating the treatment protocol utilizing rigorous scientific method is crucially important for our children. Unfortunately, the randomization to either a control or experimental condition increasingly becomes problematic because the more evidence that is gained regarding the effectiveness of this method, the more unethical it becomes to have a control group of children who do not receive an intensive amount of this type of treatment. Due to the relentless rationing of health care[*] and education for children with autism, continued replication of the Lovaas' initial landmark study (Lovaas, 1987) by independent investigators is particularly important concerning the politics of autism policies rather than the science of autism treatment.

## Who else recommends for or against home-based behavioral treatment as a method for the treatment of autism?

There is a large number of reputable organizations that have conducted independent reviews endorsing IBT as best practices. The New York State Department of Health's clinical practice guidelines (1999) regarding the use of IBT as a treatment for autism, was based largely on five studies, all conducted by Lovaas and colleagues, or from partial replications of the protocol developed by Lovaas and colleagues. Largely based on these five studies, the New York Report concludes: "It is recommended that principles of applied behavior analysis

---

[*]The incorporation of Intensive Behavioral Treatment will be fought by those in the autism industry offering competing treatments and by governments and their policy analysts who do not want to pay for this treatment. They are attacking the science behind IBT purely because they are self interested. The more evidence that is published about the efficacy of IBT, the less likely it is that they will be able to continue to deny children with autism best practices treatment.

(ABA) and behavior intervention strategies be included as an important element of any intervention program for young children with autism."[19]   In addition, a U.S. Surgeon General, Dr. David Satcher, had the following to say about Lovaas' work: "Thirty years of research demonstrated the efficacy of applied behavioral methods in reducing inappropriate behavior and in increasing communication, learning, and appropriate social behavior. A well-designed study of a psychosocial intervention was carried out by Lovaas and colleagues (Lovaas, 1987; McEachin et al., 1993).  Up to this point, a number of other research groups have provided at least a partial replication of the Lovaas model."[20]  It is important to remember that this report was published in 1999 prior to the publication of additional studies replicating these results.  Additional organizations endorsing IBT include the American Academy of Pediatrics (2001),[21] the National Research Council (2001),[22] and the American Academy of Child and Adolescent Psychiatry.[23]

## So you're still on the horns of a dilemma?

If you are still thinking about whether or not to set up a home-based behavioral treatment program for your child, you might want to read Lovaas (2003),[24] Maurice et al. (1996),[25] and Leaf et al. (1999)[26] to gain an in-depth understanding of how home-based treatment programs are administered.  In addition, I encourage you to view the videotape, "Behavioral Treatment for Children with Autism" available in most university libraries or to be purchased on-line at the Cambridge Center for Behavioral Studies.[27]  This videotape chronicles Lovaas' research from the late 1960s to the late 1980s and provides an overview of the original treatment protocol.

## What's the bottom line?

Based on the scientific research to date, there is substantial evidence that home-based Intensive Behavioral Treatment is effective for children with autism. In addition, treatment gains appear to be long-term and for a broad range of functioning levels.

# Behavioral Therapies: School-based Intensive Behavioral Treatment

School-based Intensive Behavioral Treatment shares many of the components of home-based Intensive Behavioral Treatment programs except that these programs are based in preschool settings, which are often segregated or integrated with a high ratio of autistic children to typically developing children. The main issue with school-based IBT programs is treatment fidelity. In other words, how much of the day is the child actually receiving quality autism treatment, and how much of the day is the child only receiving care-giving. Although this characterization may appear somewhat blunt, this is indeed a concern with many school-based programs. Below we will highlight three programs that produced data and discuss each program separately.

## What does school-based IBT look like?

## Princeton Child Development Institute

The Princeton Child Development Institute (PCDI) is a nonprofit society that runs a preschool, a school and two teaching homes. In addition, they offer supported employment and career development for adults.[1] The PCDI is not affiliated with a university; however, research is conducted with some of the children enrolled in the PCDI and findings are published in peer-reviewed journals. Programs are individualized for each child based on that child's skills and deficits. Each child's curriculum is implemented using the principles of applied behavior analysis. A curriculum for a student at the PCDI would typically include nonverbal and verbal imitation, receptive instructions, toy play, receptive and expressive language skills, reading and academic programs and social initiations. These programs are delivered using a variety of techniques, which include discrete trial training, incidental teaching, use of time delay, visual schedules and video modeling, as appropriate.  Direct instruction is used at the PCDI, using a teacher-to-student ratio that ranges from one-to-two to one-to-five.  Problematic (i.e. maladaptive) behaviors are targeted for elimination using a variety of well-established behavioral strategies that originate from the rich field of applied behavior analysis.

## Douglass Developmental Disabilities Center

The Douglass Developmental Disabilities Center (DDDC) is a therapeutic, experimental preschool which is affiliated with the Department of Psychology at Rutgers University and is located on the university campus.  The DDDC is designed to research the treatment and education of children with autism; accordingly, staff and doctoral students in psychology administer the center.  The DDDC has organized the preschool into three classrooms, each grouping children based on ability.  One of the goals is to move the children from a small group into a larger group setting *once the child can function in that setting*.  A typical curriculum at the DDDC includes the following:  expressive and receptive language skills (teaching the child to communicate as well as understand what is being said to him); gross and fine motor skills (working on the child's coordination with his entire body as well as using his fingers and hands on smaller tasks); affect (understanding and expressing emotion); self-help (daily living skills to promote independence); cognition (teaching concepts that are pre-academic or academic in nature); socialization (which includes interacting with others, promoting a concept of self, and controlling and promoting various behaviors).  In this broad curriculum, the various teaching programs or units are taught using direct instruction with one teacher to one child, or in a group setting.  Each child receives between thirty-five and forty-five hours of instruction per week, twelve months per year.[2]

## LEAP Program for Preschoolers

The LEAP program (Learning Experience Alternative Program for Preschoolers and Parents) for preschoolers with autism promotes an integrated early childhood education occurring across home, school and community settings.  LEAP uses behavioral practices and developmentally appropriate strategies to implement the curriculum.  A component of the LEAP philosophy is to teach a child with autism to learn from his peers.[3]  Within the curriculum, children are taught to transition from one activity to another, select play, and follow routines and group activities. Independent play is taught through: 1) having the child model peers; 2) breaking the task down into smaller more manageable parts; 3) direct teaching (instruction); 4) cuing the child to the correct answer (prompting), and 5) rewards or reinforcements.  Social interaction is taught by creating a structured environment, using peers, teacher involvement, rewards and role-playing scripts.  Language is taught using "milieu teaching" (which includes incidental teaching) and direct instruction at the beginning.  Teaching style is both child and teacher directed. The classroom has three teachers to sixteen children, (ten typical children and six children with autism). Problematic behaviors are dealt with by using preventative and positive strategies.  To prevent poor behaviors, LEAP employs class rules, daily schedules, activities, instructional materials, staff assignments and choice-making. They also use something they term "Individualized Preventative Strategies," such as opportunities for adult or peer attention, waiting activities, choices and decreasing task demands.

## What evidence do the practitioners have that school-based IBT really works?

The literature on school-based autism programs is replete with descriptions of programs that have very little data supporting them.  The exception to this is represented by five articles that report significant gains with children who have attended school-based IBT programs.[4,5,6,7,8]  Fenske et al, (1985) published an outcome study for eighteen subjects, nine under age five, nine over age five at the PCDI.  Of the nine students under age five, six of them indicated a positive outcome as a result of the intervention.  Of the nine students over age five, only one indicated a positive outcome.  Positive outcome for this study was measured by whether the child could live at home and attend a public school or whether the child continued to require treatment services.[*]  Positive outcome is defined very strictly and does not include the gains of those who required ongoing treatment (and, therefore, remained in treatment at the institute).  This group's gains were not reported as they were in the negative outcome group based on living arrangements (which is an indirect way to measure progress).  In addition, the study compared older children with younger children:  there was no control group for comparing results of no treatment or a different treatment, to the one being offered to both groups of children in this study.  Fortunately, these results are similar to those of many of the home-based behavioral treatment studies (which use very similar techniques).  Therefore, we have some confidence that the outcome of the children from the study conducted at the PCDI was a result of the curriculum and not a result of the children simply getting older and  maturing.

Three outcome studies published by the DDDC provide data on the individuals enrolled in their programs.[5,6,7]  Methodological weaknesses do exist in all three studies. The Harris et al. (1990) study compares three groups of children assigned to different types of classrooms (ten children with autism - five per group, and four typical peers).  Classroom assignment is based on severity of behavior, which is problematic because it introduces a relevant variable to autism —

---

[*]These findings were significant at a level of $p < .02$; please see Section Two for a discussion on the meaning of significance levels.

behavior. The authors themselves categorize this study as a "quasi-experimental design."[9] They found that the children did make gains in language development. They also found that integration versus segregation did not influence rate of development; however, due to the design flaws of this study, the data regarding integrated versus segregated settings must be viewed as tentative.

Unlike the Harris et al. 1990 study, the other two studies — Handleman et al. (1991) and Harris et al. (2000) — do not state the criteria by which participants were assigned to classrooms. Due to this missing information, we do not know which classroom is responsible for the gains the children made. In other words, is there an effect created by an integrated or segregated classroom or is this variable irrelevant? Second, can the improvements seen be attributed to the original functioning level of the children, or are they due to the techniques used in the classrooms themselves? Put another way, if the subjects assigned to the integrated classroom have more skills that make them capable of learning in a group setting, how representative are they of the autistic population or how similar are they to the other group which is comprised of children with less skills? The ability to learn in a group is an important goal for all autistic children; however, a large amount of one-on-one teaching or intervention is very often required before a child can actually learn in a group setting. Specifically, in order for a child with autism to learn from a group, that child needs to be able to first learn through observation and then understand group instruction.

The Harris et al (1990) study indicates that their subjects, as a group, could be characterized as "high-functioning."[10] Unfortunately, the lack of representation of the population of children with autism as a whole makes it difficult to generalize the results, and the fact that the varied groups of children did not have different forms of treatment (or no treatment), makes it difficult to judge whether or not the treatment is responsible for the gains. Fortunately, in the later study the researchers did publish the children's pre-and post IQ scores, which indicate that some of the children did improve significantly (using a within-subjects design for the study).

The Harris et al. (2000) study follows the original 27 children who spent time at the DDDC between 1990 and 1992. Therefore, I will focus on this latest study as it encompasses the long term results of children who purportedly made gains at the DDDC using widely acceptable IQ measures. These researchers studied the relationship between the age and IQ of the children when they entered the DDDC program and their eventual school history. The researchers found that those children who entered the program prior to their fourth birthday were more likely to be in regular education than children who entered the program at a later age. In addition, the intake IQ of these children influenced their eventual educational outcomes. Fortunately, the researchers used a few different tests to measure improvement in the children (including widely accepted IQ measures[*]), which provides the reader with a good degree of confidence that the gains observed did, indeed, occur.

There is one study with outcome data from the LEAP preschool model. The data showed that children made gains in eight out of eight areas measured.[8] These eight areas — fine motor manipulation and writing, language comprehension and labeling, cognitive counting and matching, and gross motor object and body movement[12] — were measured using only one assessment of the dependent variable: the Learning Accomplishment Profile (LAP). Unfortunately, the LAP is not an assessment measure that has been widely proven to be reliable and valid and is not widely used by psychologists in testing children with autism.

---

[*]The Harris et al study (2000) reports IQ testing using the Stanford-Binet test which is widely accepted. They also use the CARS and the LAP which are less widely accepted measures. In previous studies, however, children were tested using the Peabody Picture Vocabulary Test-Revised (PPVT-R)[6] and the Vineland Adaptive Behavior Scales: Survey Form.[11]

In addition, there was no blind, independent evaluator measuring these eight dependent variables. The assessments were performed by the teacher, which introduces rating bias; consequently, it is unwise to trust the results of the LAP.

Unfortunately, there are several other methodological weaknesses which do not allow the conclusion that the LEAP model is an effective intervention for children with autism. The study design lacked a control group. The various tests were not done independently prior to and after the study, and commonly accepted psychometric measures were not used. Consequently, it is very difficult to know whether the gains made were a result of the intervention or simply due to the child growing older.

Regarding the children in the study, only six children were involved, and the diagnosis for these children was "autistic-like." An additional concern regarding the study was that the diagnosis of the children was not made by an independent clinician. These children were labeled "autistic-like" simply based on observations along the following criteria: self-stimulation; minimal or no functional speech; prolonged tantrums; minimal or no positive interaction with peers; mild to severe range of mental retardation based on McCarthy Scales of Children's Abilities (MSCA).[13] It is not stated in the article, who it is that made the observation or administered the MSCA. This lack of rigor in research could result in bias in the classification of the participants as autistic or autistic-like and could also result in errors in diagnosis, e.g., that these children may have been PDD or PDD-NOS but were erroneously labeled "autistic-like." Therefore, the participants were not representative of the typical autistic population. The Diagnostic Statistical Manual (DSM - III or IV) would have been a more reliable measure.

## What does the therapy actually look like?

IBT is often run in a preschool or school setting; however, the PCDI also runs two teaching homes.  Their preschool and school programs are limited to twenty-five students at any given time and services are provided in-home and community settings as well.  Staff are initially trained by the PCDI and regularly evaluated.  The various school and teaching home programs are integrated to foster consistency and resources are shared between programs.  Progress is assessed in areas of behavior, instructional procedures and family satisfaction.

Staff at the DDDC use a variety of teaching techniques depending on the level of the child and the content being taught.  They instruct using discrete trial training, incidental teaching and communication training.  Discrete trial training is a very efficient, systematic, behavioral teaching technique where a child works with a teacher one-on-one, breaking down concepts to make it easier to teach.  In contrast, incidental teaching is a method which attempts to teach a child by focussing upon the information the child needs to learn when he or she has the opportunity to learn it naturally.  The belief is that the concept will be more meaningful when it is relevant to the child.   The third teaching technique, communication training, uses comprehensive speech and language instruction implemented by a teacher, following the recommendation of the speech therapist.[14]

Problematic behaviors are targeted for elimination using the typical, scientifically-substantiated behavioral techniques customized to the child.  Examples of these methods include a variety of techniques such as time-outs, verbally reminding the child and overcorrection.  Every two weeks a speech and language pathologist assesses the progress of each child.  In addition, children's progress is measured by using a variety of psychometric tests such as the Stanford-Binet IV, the Battelle Developmental Inventory and the Learning Accomplishment Profile.

The LEAP preschool model is applied for fifteen hours per week, twelve months per year. Students with autism are integrated with typical peers in a classroom setting. In the study by Hoyson, Jamieson and Strain (1984), there were sixteen students in the classroom, ten typical students and six students with autism. The curriculum is individualized for the student, and parents are viewed as partners in the "educational" process. They use a method of individualized group instruction termed *TRIIC*, the acronym for "[Tri-I (Innovative, Integrative, Individualized) Curriculum] for mainstreaming."[15] In this form of instruction, each child is given individual objectives in three skill areas, and the teacher designs and implements a group lesson plan that meets the needs of all the children in the group.

## Would I send my child to a school-based Intensive Behavioral Treatment program?

The decision to send one's toddler off to a treatment facility, even if it is in a preschool, is a difficult one. I would be very careful to establish how much of the day is treatment-based and how much is preschool. If I had lived in New Jersey when my child was very young, I would have thought very seriously about sending my child to the PCDI. However, I would have been vigilant to make sure that the child received treatment every minute of every day. As a parent, I've seen too many preschools that claim they are providing treatment, when in fact they are providing childcare. This is a serious problem. Government or university affiliation is no guarantee that the autism expertise is sufficient to run a treatment program. Among the worst preschool programs that actually claim to be "therapeutic," are government-funded and staffed programs with a price tag of $2.5 million dollars to treat twenty-five (25) children!

In interviewing the school staff, I would need to know how the school program and home program are coordinated and monitored. In addition, I would need to see evidence that the ratio of one teacher to more than one student is effective. This is particularly important at the beginning of treatment when most children with autism do not have the skills to pay attention, understand instructions or sit at a table. I would also have questions about how the skills learned at school are going to be generalized across settings (i.e., school to home) for children who are not receiving any therapy outside the classroom. If these questions were answered to my satisfaction, then I might have enrolled my child. Most importantly, I would need to know when the child is destined to leave the therapeutic program and is slated to be integrated with his typically developing peers.

My child required one-on-one treatment from the outset, as she did not have any skills that would have allowed her to learn in a group setting. Therefore, as long as she could be placed initially in the preparatory classroom (with one teacher to one child), I would have considered the DDDC program. I would be quite nervous about my child moving to learn in a group-setting to the exclusion of one-on-one teaching which is, in my view, much more efficient than group teaching. Eventually, we want and need our children to learn in a group setting; however, it may take the preschool some years to achieve that goal. I would require assurances that it is my decision when she is ready for the group setting and that the decision was only motivated by what is best for my child, rather than some budgetary constraints requiring more "efficiency" and, therefore, moving her away from a one-on-one treatment setting.

Although the LEAP curriculum sounds like an acceptable curriculum for children with autism, there is not enough evidence that the children make substantial gains; therefore, I would not enroll my child in a LEAP program. The integrated classroom is an interesting idea since it makes sense that a child with autism should be with typically developing children. However, I would like to see a child with autism learn a number of skills prior to integration, in order for integration to be worthwhile. If my child needed to be mainstreamed, I would prefer to mainstream the child into a setting that was not therapeutic in nature but rather was the kind of setting where parents would send their typically developing children. Once my child were taught to learn through modelling the behaviors of others, the last thing I would desire is for her to be exposed to (and possibly model) *other* autistic children who might engage in repetitive, self-stimulatory or other maladaptive behavior.

## What else do I think?

What is particularly compelling about the PCDI is that although they concentrate on early intervention, if the child has not graduated from the preschool into a kindergarten for typically developing children, then that child continues in a treatment program. The parents are not suddenly left with the impression that they are on their own because their child is already too old to be in an intensive, behavioral treatment program. The aging out issue is a criticism of many IBT programs that tend to concentrate on the younger children and wash their hands of the older children even though these children may require more treatment. It's a particularly common occurrence among government-funded programs worldwide, where the sooner the children can graduate from IBT, the less money the government has to spend.

With respect to the measure used by LEAP – the Learning Accomplishment Profile (LAP) – this measure does not give a comprehensive assessment of all relevant areas of development and, therefore, does not adequately assess its own intervention strategies. Specifically, issues such as IQ and behavioral change are not assessed, and language assessment is limited to naming and comprehension. In addition, LEAP claims to target social interaction, independent play, functional skills and peer teaching; however, none of these content areas are assessed in the outcome study. The only areas assessed by the LAP are the eight areas that they identify (fine motor writing and manipulation, gross motor object and body movement, cognitive matching and counting, and language naming and comprehension). This measure excludes some very important skill deficit and behavioral excess areas. Furthermore, there is no evidence that self-stimulatory or other maladaptive behaviors are targeted for elimination. While LEAP uses strategies to prevent such behaviors, there is no mention of how behaviors are targeted when they occur. Due to the nature and frequency of these non-learning behaviors, it is essential that behaviors which obstruct learning are controlled and, ideally, eliminated.

## What kind of study would I like to see the school-based IBT researchers do?

There are several important factors I would like to see in future outcome studies on school-based IBT programs. More data is required to compare the progress of subjects in experimental versus control groups, creating groups with varied types and intensity of intervention. The dependent measure of positive versus no positive outcome needs to be defined and operationalized more explicitly. Specifically, the additional use of IQ and language assessment indicators would be helpful in further examining outcome, particularly in groups of different ages. A measure which indicates the amount of progress being made, even by those individuals who require continued treatment, must be incorporated in future research. These variables would ideally be measured by at least one independent evaluator who is blind to the assignment of subjects to groups. In addition, factors such as treatment intensity (home and school), student-to-teacher ratio, dual diagnoses and age at treatment initiation need to be controlled more stringently in order to determine the many factors which influence treatment outcome.

In terms of LEAP specifically, new outcome data is required before any conclusions can be made about the LEAP model and its efficacy. The Scientific Review of Mental Health Practice had the following to say about LEAP: "Although certain aspects of the LEAP program appear promising, the paucity of the available research, and especially the absence of controlled research, preclude judgments about its usefulness."[16] Of the utmost importance is the need for a control group in any further investigations. This is required in order to determine the source of the changes found in the results. Also, it would be necessary to provide an experimental design which includes a larger subject pool of children diagnosed with autism by an independent source. Ideally, these children would be assessed for baseline levels of ability using various measures including IQ, behavior and more extensive language measurement. These assessments should also be administered by independent evaluators who have no knowledge of the experiment, rather than teachers or other individuals directly involved with the experiment.

## Who else recommends for or against the School-Based IBT for the treatment of autism?

There are many organizations that recommend ABA throughout the child's life and in every setting. The Association for Science in Autism treatment describes ABA as being effective across a variety of settings including school and home.[17] In addition, the Behavior Analyst Certification Board uses children in school settings as an example of the application of ABA.[18] After examining the data, no bona fide scientist would disagree with the delivery of school-based behavioral treatment to treat the condition of autism. The question, however, is whether treatment should be designed by the school-based or home-based professionals consulting with the parent.

## So you're still on the horns of a dilemma?

If the question is where to enroll the child — in an ABA school or a home-based program — the answer depends upon where the child can receive the best program. The parent needs to determine whether the ABA school in the area (if it exists) is of a high quality. If not, then a home-based program may be the only option, bringing in competent professionals from the community or, if that is impossible, then flying in professionals from a different region, or in some cases, another country.

## What's the bottom line?

The scientific research to date collected on children who attend *high quality,* school-based, Intensive Behavioral Treatment programs provides evidence to conclude that their condition improved in school-based treatment settings and that although the most significant gains were made by those children who began treatment before the age of five, older children made significant gains as well.

# Offshoots of Intensive Behavioral Therapies: Pivotal Response Training and the Natural Learning Paradigm

## What is Pivotal Response Training/the Natural Learning Paradigm?

Pivotal Response Training/the Natural Learning Paradigm (PRT/NLP) is a technique to motivate individuals with autism to respond to multiple cues. PRT/NLP targets an autistic person's lack of motivation and tendency to concentrate on one stimulus at the expense of other stimuli or "the big picture" (termed stimulus overselectivity) by targeting these two areas which are considered pivotal. These behaviors are considered to be pivotal because the theory is that changing them results in a change in many other behaviors.[1] The goal of the intervention is to provide an easy-to-implement strategy which can also be used in the community.[2] PRT uses *some* principles of behavior modification to teach the person with autism. The components of the intervention are: 1) ensuring attention; 2) interspersing maintenance tasks (tasks that have already been mastered); 3) allowing the child to lead; 4) giving the child multiple cue instructions; 5) providing reinforcement immediately; 6) providing reinforcement contingently (rewarding the person based on their answer); 7) providing reinforcement that is directly related to the behavior or task, and 8) providing reinforcement for any goal-directed *attempt* at responding. PRT is designed to discourage the individual from engaging in aggressive, self-injurious, self-stimulatory and ritualistic behaviors; however, how these behaviors should be dealt with is not specified. The Natural Learning Paradigm encompasses the philosophy of Pivotal Response Training, which defines the learning as child-led in a non-demanding setting where Pivotal Response Training occurs.

## What evidence do the practitioners have that this technique works?

PRT/NLP relies upon literature which studies the lack of joint attention behaviors characteristic of children with autism[3] and the ramifications of the lack of joint attention on the development of speech and language.[4]  Although there has not been a *single* study comparing children in a comprehensive Pivotal Response Training program to a well-settled behavioral treatment program (such as Lovaas and colleagues created), Pivotal Response researchers have found a positive relationship between very targeted interventions and an increase in speech.[5] Although there are dozens of articles which relate to naturalistic teaching and, by extension Pivotal Response Training, there are currently twelve peer-reviewed journal articles providing outcome data on individuals with autism who have been treated using PRT/NLP.[4,6,7,8,9,10,11,12,13,14,15, 16]  These twelve studies concentrate on encouraging language through play, encouraging social behavior and/or sociodramatic play or comparing the natural language paradigm versus a more structured adult led approach, which they refer to as analog teaching.  In almost all the studies, the sessions were videotaped and subsequently coded by different researchers whose coding was compared to ensure consistency.  This safeguard was important because in some of the studies, peers or parents, not professionals, were involved in sessions with the autistic child.  In most of the studies, the interobserver agreement (the agreement between those researchers who coded the sessions) was relatively high, i.e., in Laski et al. the interobserver agreement did not drop below seventy-seven percent (77%) and at times was as high as ninety-eight percent (98%).[17]

Eleven of the twelve studies were single-subject case designs (see the next section for an in-depth discussion on SSCD) utilizing a small number of children (with the largest study involving ten children), most of whom had a diagnosis based on a version of the Diagnostic Statistical Manual (DSM). Over the last eighteen years, proponents of PRT/NLP have published data on a total of fifty-one children who were involved in very short term and/or low intensity experiments (often lasting no more than thirty minutes a week over three months and often less than that). The majority of children in these studies were over three years of age, with many between the ages of five and ten years, some of whom were very high functioning.[15,16] Based on these children, results have been reported that children with autism utilizing PRT/NLP have more prosocial behavior, improvements in social skills (and play), and an improvement in speech and language. Although these results sound encouraging, the studies as a whole have several serious drawbacks. Due to the complexity of the studies and the various claims made, each claim will be discussed separately.

## Is Pivotal Response Training/Naturalistic Learning Paradigm more effective for language acquisition?

PRT/NLP researchers and proponents claim that naturalistic teaching, when used for speech and language, is more effective than the traditional research supporting discrete-trial training.[16,17,18,19,20] This may have occurred with the subjects in their experiments; however, this claim cannot be generalized to the population of children with autism for two reasons: 1) the small number of children per study (usually two or three children in each design) is too few children to make generalizations about the effectiveness of PRT/NLP for the overall autistic population and none have any follow-up after the study to see whether the observed gains were permanent;[*] 2) the data from PRT/NLP is based on children with varying degrees of language impairment who have had discrete trial training

---

[*]There is one study where the researchers retrospectively studied intervention data from children who did well or poorly in prior treatment. Unfortunately, they used retrospective pre-intervention archival data and compared it to the postintervention data rather than following the children from their study longitudinally.

learning histories prior to being part of these studies.  Naturalistic or incidental learning is predicted to be more efficient for children who had achieved some competency in language and/or who had extensive amounts of past treatment using discrete trial training.  The reasoning here is the child has already achieved the skills needed to learn in a more natural setting.[15]  This is an important point because the suggestion that comes out of the PRT/NLP literature is to abandon one of the most important techniques for some children in the ABA toolbox -- discrete trial training.  This would be a severe mistake with a child who *appears* to be completely unteachable (which is common for children with autistic disorder), and for which discrete trial training may be the only option at the beginning of a treatment program.

One study[4] compared naturalistic teaching with more structured teaching to determine which was more efficient.  They found that naturalistic teaching was much more motivating than structured teaching.  However, this study has a fundamental flaw which seriously undermines the results of the study.[*]  In the naturalistic condition, the clinician used highly-motivating three-dimensional items to teach the target sounds; whereas, the analog condition used picture cards with the items on the cards to teach the same sounds, and then praised the child and reinforced the child's correct response with food or a desired object.  This research demonstrates that using a desired object to teach a sound (or any concept for that matter) will be more powerful because what is being taught is intrinsically rewarding.  However, it does not demonstrate that naturalistic teaching is more efficient.  This study needs to be done with the clinician in both conditions using the highly-reinforcing three-dimensional items to teach, in both

---

[*]The way analog vs. naturalistic teaching is defined confuses the fundamental differences.  In Koegel, Koegel and Carter (1999), they define the difference between naturalistic and analog teaching very strictly, making the point that in analog teaching the child has no choice.[14]  There is, however, no contradiction between analog teaching and giving a child a choice of the activity he or she would like to do first.  The difference has more to do with the child-led versus adult-led nature of the *actual* teaching trial.

the structured (analog) and naturalistic conditions.   Otherwise, the differences in teaching techniques are being confused with differences in: 1) degree of reinforcement, and 2) the relevance of the reinforcer to what is being taught.[*]

## Do children with autism emit less disruptive behaviors with PRT/NLP?

The second claim made by proponents of PRT/NLP is that children emit less disruptive behaviors using the naturalistic teaching paradigm.[21]  It is plausible that initially there would be a difference between adult-led and child-led therapy in terms of disruptive behavior.  It makes perfect sense that behavior will not be a concern if no demands are made of a child.  However, the real question is whether these children will progress to the point where they can cope in situations where their ideas or way of doing things is not adopted, and be able to learn to do what others require of them without emitting disruptive behavior, as all typically developing children are expected to learn from an early age.  Another point worth emphasizing is that in good analog teaching, disruptive behaviors should not occur on a regular basis even when demands are placed on the child. I suggest that the researchers have inadvertently compared a naturalistic learning environment to a poor analog teaching environment where the reinforcement levels are insufficient.  In other words, the two different types of programs were of a different quality.  They compared a high-quality naturalistic-teaching program with a very poor-quality adult-led analog program.

As previously mentioned, the learning histories (previous types of treatments) of these children need to be taken into account.  One set of researchers describe

---

[*]For this study to be valuable, there should be four conditions: 1) analog condition, relevant reinforcer; 2) analog condition, irrelevant reinforcer; 3) NLP condition, relevant reinforcer, and 4) NLP condition, irrelevant reinforcer.  Although we can predict that condition four will be the least successful, it is not clear whether condition one or three will be more efficient.  In short, the variable of reinforcer needs to be controlled.

a child who actually says "No cards."[22] This indicates to me that this child has experienced poorly delivered therapy which has created an aversion to learning. A poor therapy experience prior to the current study may have seriously biased the results of that study as would any child's prior learning history (one of the issues researchers using single-subject case designs studies must address).

## Do children with autism increase their social and play skills with PRT/NLP?

There have been a few studies[8,9,10,11,12,16] which attempt to use PRT/NLP to increase the ability of autistic children in these areas.  One study has been published in two separate articles, one concentrating on language and toy play,[11] the other observing social behavior.[12]  Both of these articles appear to be a replication of the earlier published findings.[8]  This study, conducted on two children with autism, and two typically developing peers, reports positive changes in social language and play skills.  The children were ten years old and had language abilities over three years of age prior to entering the study.  Although their language ability is not at age level, it is at a degree much higher than many young children with autism, so their skills might not be representative of children with classic autism. This was also the case of a more recent study which used two children who were eight and nine years of age[16] (treatment programs for children with autism typically begin in the toddler years).

An additional question concerns the validity of findings regarding play.  These children with autism may have memorized repertoires that they learned from typically developing children when in therapy, and then use when playing with another group of children.  In other words, creative pretend play does not occur. Although this criticism may seem hypercritical, and I think that children with autism may benefit by memorizing a number of scripts to use while playing with peers, it is important to differentiate whether the child is reproducing play repertoires or whether he or she is truly engaged in pretend play (the two can be differentiated by the uniqueness of each session without peer prompting). Two alternative hypotheses to explain the results are that: 1) an autistic child may be incorporating a peer into rigid, role playing, which is not about joint attention or true social engagement, but simply the use of a peer as a "tool" for a higher level of self-stimulatory or repetitive behavior, or 2) the child may be using memorized scripts which are activated when particular toys are present. In addition, one study counted the number of play date invitations made after the intervention. This measure may have more to do with the parent's ability to be reinforcing to the typical peers than any actual increase in friendship.[16]

Another article published by Stahmer[10] was far superior to the above studies and allows us to unravel the complexity of the findings on play. This study used a control group who provided language training, had more extensive dependent measures, made sure the observers were "blind" to the condition of the participants and reported the statistical significance of the results (a "p" value). An important contribution of this study is the researcher's honesty when she suggests that for individuals without a certain level of language ability, the intervention may not be developmentally appropriate.[23] Stahmer discusses one child whose stereotyped play interfered with his learning and noted that the "children with the best language skills were the most creative and spontaneous during play."[24] This is an illuminating point because this data demonstrates that if Pivotal Response Training does ameliorate autism, it is only so for a high-functioning subset of children or a subset of children who have reached a certain level with well-settled IBT programs. Stahmer's research is important because it introduces the concept that PRT/NLP may be useful for a certain subset of children with autism but not effective (or premature) for another group of children who do not possess the prerequisite skills.

## Do skills learned through PRT/NLP generalize across settings and people?

The ability of children with autism to generalize play skills based on this treatment method remains debatable.  It is still an open question whether the children who benefitted from Pivotal Response training in the above-mentioned studies already had (prior to PRT/NLP treatment) many of the skills needed to learn and generalize symbolic, complex and creative play.  We are still uncertain regarding whether it was the method of intervention or rather the children's readiness to generalize that made the difference, if indeed, these children did actually generalize play and social skills at all.

The claim that PRT/NLP skills will generalize across settings and people is more convincing when the consequence of using language is reinforcing.  To illustrate, if a child learns to ask for juice and receives juice every time he asks, the data suggest that this skill will generalize across settings.  Whether or not a less reinforcing request will generalize is still an open question.  One study[25] attempts to address this problem by gradually changing hidden reinforcing items in a bag to less preferred ones, without affecting the spontaneity of the child asking, "What's that?" referring to the hidden item in the bag.  Whether or not this question will be a permanent part of the child's asking repertoire down the road is unknown, although it is plausible that this skill may be maintained as long as the reward is unpredictable.   Nowhere is there any compelling evidence, however, that this question-asking skill will generalize more or less successfully if it were taught using an analog method (as long as the skill were generalized after being taught).

## What does the therapy actually look like?

PRT/NLP is described as the use of "loosely controlled environments [e.g. a playground] and that utilizes shared control [e.g. turn taking] and multiple exemplars [e.g. many toy materials]."[26] Techniques such as turn-taking opportunities, working on mastered skills and gaining the child's attention are used to set the child up for success. Parents are trained to use these techniques with their children to encourage language development and use. The three variables that structure the learning situation are described in the PRT/NLP manual as: 1) the child is given an instruction, question or spontaneous opportunity to respond; 2) the child responds, and 3) the child is given a consequence.[27] Although this sounds very similar to the traditional one-on-one behavioral treatment procedure, the natural consequence of the instruction or opportunity is of importance. To use their illustration: a child is cold while playing outside; the mother tells the child to put on a coat, and the child does. The natural consequence is that the child plays outside again, but this time he feels warm.[28] Natural consequences such as those illustrated above can be highly motivating and, therefore, useful when teaching and maintaining a skill as the reward is always present (in this case, warmth).

## Would I try it on my child?

If my child were recently diagnosed, I would not rely upon PRT/NLP to ameliorate her autism due to the lack of data reporting efficacy for young children who are not yet speaking. This is an example of a promising area of research that is leaving the laboratory too early and being incorporated prematurely by parents and educational systems prematurely. Because I wanted to provide my child with the most evidence-based treatment, PRT/NLP would not have been my choice. That said, in established, well-settled behavioral treatment programs, natural consequences that are reinforcing should be used whenever possible. This principle is a foundation in the PRT/NLP literature.

## What else do I think?

Most of these studies do not sufficiently rely upon standardized outcome measures.  The behavioral outcomes are generally measured by researchers who are part of the study as are the emotional and social outcomes (with the exception of the occasional study where they use the Vineland Adaptive Behavior Scales — a test which looks at a variety of behaviors). In addition, the social and language behaviors (the operationalization of the dependent measure) occasionally use researcher observation alone.  This is not an adequate or unbiased measure of treatment outcome and there is no indication within some of the studies about who is rating the observations. In addition, one study includes a measure of teacher reported social behaviors within the classroom.[29]  In my view, this is a biased measure of change because it is not clear how much information the teacher has about the study (as she was instrumental in choosing peers for the study).[30]

The authors of the PRT manual claim that it is designed for any child, including those who are nonverbal.  This conclusion is premature because subjects in all of the studies had baseline language abilities that were higher than those typically found in the population of young autistic children.  In contrast, Stahmer (1995) suggests that for individuals without sufficient language ability, the intervention might not be developmentally appropriate.[10]  In other words, if a child is not speaking yet, it is too soon for PRT.

This intervention approach emphasizes that the task must be child-led. The manual states that the child must be able to choose the topic of an activity and when to stop the activity. Concurrently, the authors state that disruptive behavior is not acceptable and parents must take control until the child is capable of non-disruptive behavior. It is not clear how this philosophy meshes with the child-led philosophy and how parents are to "take control" in this framework. It is likely that a child who has had no intervention at all, and subsequently has few skills, will be very resistant to initiating or remaining involved in an interaction.

Another issue of concern for the child-led approach is the lack of motivation when the material is difficult or intrinsically non-reinforcing. It is unlikely that a child will initiate learning difficult concepts, as he or she has no understanding of them and the concepts might not be relevant. In addition, when a child is in school, that child will be expected to participate in classroom learning, as do his peers. This will be an additional challenge unless the child has learned how to sit and learn material that is perhaps not intrinsically motivating. In addition, the application of this method in a mainstreamed classroom is problematic. The requirement that peers undergo extensive training in order to learn the strategies proposed by PRT/NLP is highly unrealistic.

Another problem with this approach is "where to begin." The authors recommend that instructions given to the child should be multi-cued instructions. Children with autism do not typically understand multi-cued instructions. Indeed, they need to be taught how to understand multi-cued instructions and there is no technique offered to guide parents in how to teach this to their children. Prior to using Pivotal Response Training, it can be argued that children need to be taught a variety of single instructions before they are expected to understand multi-cued instructions.

The last point I need to make regards efficiency. If we are required to wait for children with autism to initiate everything they need to learn, I am concerned that we will lose precious time that early intervention requires, and the future of these children may be compromised. In addition, it is extremely inefficient to find a direct, natural consequence for everything that the child must learn.

Another difficulty with this offshoot of behaviorism is that it smacks of the "parent as therapist" ideology of how autism should be addressed, wherein parents, as opposed to professionals, deliver most or all of the "treatment."[6,31,32] Laski et al. actually report on a parent-training as a positive outcome when they state:

> This study presented a promising new parent-training program designed to increase autistic children's Verbal Behavior. Post treatment increases in *parents' requests for vocalizations* from their autistic children were observed in the generalization settings. Additionally, *parents showed evidence* of generalizing these behaviors with the siblings of their autistic children. These generalization effects are encouraging in that they may provide additional support of the motivating qualities of natural language programs for both parent and child...[33] (emphasis added).

It goes without saying that it is not the parents with the neurological disorder, it's their child. The assumption that increased parent vocalization will cause increased child vocalization is not sufficiently supported by data. In addition, the expectation that the parents must be responsible for the therapeutic treatment of their child plays into the rationing of health care for children with autism, which governments will happily entertain if they receive academic justification for it.*

---

*The concept of parent as therapist is particularly offensive when one considers the fact that parents of children with autism also have to make a living like everyone, at the some time as being responsible for their autistic child's progress. I'd like to suggest that the free-wheeling 1950s "Leave it to Beaver" family unit is rare in 21st century modern society and would like to see any of these researchers be productive in their academic careers undertaking the role of therapist for their autistic children. Only in the field of autism are our children considered so unworthy that the responsibility of treatment falls on the family instead of on professionals in the field.

## What kind of study would I like to see the researchers do on Pivotal Response training and the Natural Learning Paradigm?

There may be a place for the use of PRT/NLP in the education of individuals with autism; however, exactly where and/or if it can be used effectively needs to be established. For individuals who have some language ability and are able to learn somewhat incidentally, i.e., they do not require mass trials of repetition in order to retain certain pieces of information, Pivotal Response behaviors may be a good method of prompting generalization of desired behaviors. Research to determine exactly who, and how much, this approach can help is desperately required. It also needs to be determined how effective this intervention is when compared to other treatments. I would like to see a between-within subject design utilizing a comprehensive protocol based on the PRT/NLP paradigm as compared to an intensive, well-settled behavioral treatment program. In addition, it is crucial that the PRT/NLP researchers use standardized language and IQ measures prior to and after the study to determine to what extent autism has been ameliorated using their protocol. The authors claim that one of the benefits of PRT is that the behavior will occur in natural environments; however, this has yet to be supported by high quality, long-term evidence. Clearly, a well designed, longitudinal study with large numbers needs to be conducted prior to recommending this method to anyone responsible for the treatment of children with autism.

## Who else recommends for or against Pivotal Response Training as a method for the treatment of autism?

The Developmental Behavioral Pediatrics On-line (a site closely connected with the American Academy of Pediatrics) has reviewed PRT and states: "Although each of the components of the Pivotal Response intervention model has been extensively tested, there are no randomized trials comparing PRT to any other intervention model.  The only published follow-up study was done retrospectively."[32,34]  Other than that, PRT/NLP has been protected from criticism as it falls under the general rubric of ABA which is a well-established discipline.

## So you're still on the horns of a dilemma?

I would recommend that prior to embarking on a program reliant solely on PRT/NLP, that you have your child in a well-settled behavioral treatment program and await more data which demonstrates that a comprehensive behavioral treatment program using PRT/NLP is more effective than a traditional behavioral treatment program.  That said, the incorporation of natural consequences when possible into a well-settled behavioral treatment program is certainly a powerful way to reinforce skills or positive behavior.

## What's the bottom line?

Based on the scientific research to date, there is not enough evidence that Pivotal Response Training/The Natural Learning Paradigm is globally effective in ameliorating the condition of autism.  There is some very preliminary evidence to suggest that this method can be used to target symbolic play skills in some individuals with autism who possess above average language abilities.  However, further studies with larger sample sizes and standardized testing are required to appropriately evaluate the method.

# Offshoots of Intensive Behavioral Therapies: Positive Behavioral Support

## What is Positive Behavioral Support?

Positive Behavioral Support (PBS) is behaviorism guided by philosophy. Practitioners of this method claim that it is a new field that has its roots in applied behavior analysis, the inclusion movement and person-centered values.[1] The philosophy promotes the inclusion of people with disabilities in mainstream society. By re-engineering the environment, it is claimed by PBS proponents that the individual's quality of life is enhanced and thereby, behavior problems can be minimized. What appears to differentiate PBS from other forms of behaviorism is the promotion of educational systems to take responsibility in the re-engineering of environment and the practice of PBS. Proponents claim that the elimination of problem behavior is not the direct focus of PBS, but rather, a fortunate by-product. They state: "the primary intervention strategy involves rearranging the environment to enhance life-style and improve quality of life rather than operating directly on reducing problem behavior per se."[2] They differentiate PBS from other forms of behaviorism by their "Life-span Perspective" and suggest that meaningful change may be slow and, in fact, may take decades.

Positive Behavioral Support is differentiated from traditional behaviorism by the emphasis on "ecological validity," which proponents define as the applicability of the science to real-life settings. In other words, their vision is for parents, teachers and job coaches, rather than professionals, to practice PBS. An additional component of the PBS philosophy is "stakeholder participation" which they define as a consumer-driven, rather than an expert-driven, applied science. In other words, the consumer is supposed to become an active participant in delivering the

PBS treatment.  The third concern of PBS practitioners is that the interventions be measured not by their "objective effectiveness" but rather by the impact on the person's quality of life (e.g., is the person happy and in an acceptable living arrangement).

## What evidence do the practitioners have that this really works?

Here is where Positive Behavioral Support becomes somewhat tricky to evaluate. Since PBS practitioners have themselves often come from the field of applied behavior analysis (ABA), some spending most of their academic career in this field, it is very difficult to separate much of the research they cite that has been done on ABA from the research that has been done on PBS specifically.[*] A comprehensive database search netted sixty-five (65) articles on Positive Behavioral Support (attempting to differentiate PBS from ABA).  Of these sixty-five articles, there were only six articles presenting experimental data of any kind on children with autism.  Of those six articles, one study concerned parent perceptions of an early intervention  program,[3] seven case studies were presented in four articles,[3,4,5,6,7,8] one single-subject case design demonstrated a decrease in disruptive behavior,[7] and one article reported on parent-professional collaboration.[8]  Aside from these articles, all other articles to which PBS lays claim actually flow from the field of ABA.  Another concern regards the time-line for progress; PBS proponents evaluate changes made along the life span. Understandably, it is very difficult to evaluate a treatment's value if its effect is observable only over decades.

---

[*]Proponents seem to have expropriated decades of research in applied behavior analysis as their own when they are demonstrating the efficacy of an intervention.[12]

## What does the therapy actually look like?

The difference between PBS and ABA is not in what you see, but rather, in the *design* of the interventions.  The process that the PBS practitioner goes through is much the same as that of a behavior analyst, although the terminology is different.  The PBS practitioner does a Functional Behavioral Assessment (FBA) to determine the function of the child's behavior and then designs an intervention to reduce or, ideally, prevent the behavior from occurring again.   However, the behavioral intervention that is chosen may or may not differ from that of a traditional behavior analyst, depending less upon what might actually be the ideal intervention, and more upon the PBS view of the *feasibility* of the intervention in the "real world."  In other words, the behavior to replace the problematic behavior must be:  "acceptable to caregivers; appropriate to the setting; within a person's skill set or easy to learn,"[9] and appears to be more concerned with philosophy rather than science-based measures of treatment outcomes.

## Would I try it on my child?

I have refused, and am vigilant, to protect my daughter from anyone with this treatment perspective whether they be an autism "professional" or a teacher.  In my view, PBS is a case of political correctness interfering with science.  I want to ensure that my child's treatment is not influenced by "resources" in the system at any one time (or lack thereof — most often the case).  Specifically, I do not desire that the educational system be responsible for her "support" because this rigid, calcified system has shown itself time and time again to be a receptacle for incompetence when it comes to children with autism.[10,11]  School districts often fund programs based upon the PBS philosophy because it is:  a) politically correct and in line with the prevailing educational philosophy for typically developing students, and b) is inexpensive, as untrained (or insufficiently trained) employees are expected to implement the interventions.

It is crucial that all the tools in the ABA toolbox are at the disposal of the professionals who design and implement my child's treatment program, and not only the ones that have been deemed as "acceptable" or "philosophically pure" according to the school district, but also the ones that may not have any relevance in my child's life or her autism treatment needs.

When philosophy, rather than data, influences decisions it is harmful. When my child was very young, prior to her being mainstreamed in school, she required an intensive one-on-one ABA treatment regime to reach the point where mainstreaming was desirable and possible. Without that work, her mere physical proximity to typically developing children would have been of no use. PBS might make everyone in the system feel as if they are good people; however, children with autism need to progress to the point where: 1) mainstreaming is actually of benefit to them, and 2) they are treated with dignity in a mainstream setting and not treated like the token disabled person whose disruptive nature is simply tolerated due to political correctness. This is all too often the case when philosophy, rather than science, guides decisions.

## What else do I think?

In my opinion, Positive Behavioral Support is a very dangerous field for children with autism. The reason this philosophy is dangerous (aside from the obvious which is research being subjugated by a form of religion – and I think PBS is a type of religion of political correctness), is that it denies children with autism access to proven, science-based treatment methods. Frankly, I find even the term Positive Behavioral Support offensive. The fact that it is "positive" behavior support carries a presumption that the PBS practitioner is different and apart from his "evil" ABA behaviorist counterpart. In fact, traditional behavior analysts have very stringent ethical guidelines that practitioners are required to follow in order to be certified.[12] All academic research done on human subjects must pass university ethics boards and any *clinical* treatment that may be considered ethically questionable cannot be conducted by reputable practitioners without judicial oversight. It is no longer the freewheeling 1950s where many ethically questionable activities can take place behind the walls of government institutions in the name of therapy. There are laws now in place which protect disabled people from direct harm.

I also find it interesting that PBS practitioners see no contradiction between inclusion and mainstreaming, and redesigning the environment to accommodate children with autism. To illustrate, if we do not teach children with autism to be able to cope with the general chaos of life, how are we going to have them go into a shopping mall and function properly? Asking the mall administration to turn off the music in the elevators prior to a child entering is not practical!

I live in a region where Positive Behavioral Support is used extensively by school districts and is wholeheartedly supported by government. This region happens to be an area where autism policy is functionally in the 1950s in terms of efficacy. Consequently, there is a large and steady exodus of parents out of the public school system into the private system, or home-schooling, due to this globally ineffective and harmful philosophy which masquerades as an applied behavioral science.

One final point on PBS: when one reads the literature from Positive Behavioral Support, autism appears to be an entirely different disability. These children seem to be very mild, and the behavior problems are all easy to control, as long as the environment is "re-engineered." Children with self-injurious behavior do not seem to be a challenge for this group. Perhaps children who participate in PBS studies are not classically autistic. My caveat regarding the type of children participating in PBS studies is also supported by Durand and Rost[13] who truthfully caution those reading the literature on PBS that there may be a selection bias in the subjects for the studies that they do conduct.

### What kind of study would I like PBS researchers to do?

I think that this group of researchers should abandon the anti-science, anti-intellectual discipline they have developed. They should return to the field of applied behavior analysis, compete with researchers in that field and have their PBS research properly scrutinized and evaluated by their ABA academic peers.

### Who else recommends for or against Positive Behavior Support as a method for the treatment of autism?

Mulick and Butter (2005)[14] provide a very useful, in-depth critical analysis of Positive Behavior Support that I highly recommend prior to even thinking about using this so-called autism treatment method. Mulick and Butter lay out the complete history of Positive Behavior Support and expose the pseudo-science of PBS in detail.

### So you're still on the horns of a dilemma?

If you are still not sure whether your child should be in a behavior management program based on Positive Behavior Support, I would encourage you to ask the purveyors of PBS how they intend to measure short-term outcomes. You need to make sure that these outcomes objectively measure the child's progress (measuring behavior and IQ) and not the approval rating or opinions of others about how the child is progressing.  In addition, it is crucial to ensure that the goals are short-term and substantive, rather than fuzzy, long-term quality-of-life goals which can be easily manipulated to appear rosy.

## What's the bottom line?

Based on the scientific research to date, there is no evidence to conclude that PBS is anything more than a philosophy rather than a science.  Consequently, there is no evidence to demonstrate that PBS ameliorates the condition of autism.

# Offshoots of Intensive Behavioral Therapies: Verbal Behavior

## What is Verbal Behavior?

In 1957, B.F. Skinner (the grandfather of behaviorism) published a book called *Verbal Behavior*.[1]   In this book, Skinner applied his ideas about learning to Verbal Behavior.  Specifically, Skinner defined various types of Verbal Behavior that humans exhibit. This typology improved behaviorist understanding of how different parts of language are developed and enabled them to teach the various functions of language and set up an environment to promote the use of these parts of language.  Sundberg and Partington (1998) take Skinner's ideas and apply them to teaching language to children with autism in a user-friendly format designed for the nonacademic audience. They define the various types of verbal behavior and provide a discussion of each language repertoire in their book, *Teaching Language to Children with Autism or Other Developmental Disorders*.  They describe these language repertoires as:  receptive (complying with or following directions); echoic (repeating what others have said); imitation (copying actions); tact (labelling); mand (asking); RFFC- Receptive by Function, Feature, and Class (identifying items based on their description); intraverbal (answering questions on a more conceptual level); textual (reading words), and written (scribing words that are heard).[2]

Put simply, Verbal Behavior Therapy is an attempt to utilize the principles of behaviorism to teach children with autism to communicate.  The concept of verbal behavior has existed for approximately fifty years; the primary impetus of verbal behavior is the application of the ideas of B.F. Skinner to children with autism.  Although Sundberg and Partington have been working on these ideas since approximately 1978, this area has become increasingly popular in the last ten years because ideas regarding how to teach language to children with autism are presented in a more accessible format than was previously available. In addition, there has always been a need to target language acquisition for children with autism as these children have significant language deficits.

## What evidence do the practitioners have that this really works?

Here's where the difficulty begins. Although the ideas of Skinner regarding verbal behavior are compelling and theoretically rich, the testing of these ideas has lagged far behind. Unfortunately, what little data does exist is not necessarily on children with autism.[3] A comprehensive literature search using all the major academic databases did not net even one study to provide evidence that a *comprehensive* Verbal Behavior program would significantly improve the language ability of children with autism, and/or facilitate more comprehensive or global improvement in their condition. However, Verbal Behavior researchers have done studies concentrating on evoking manding (asking)[4,5] and increasing vocal behavior.[6] This area will hopefully bear more fruit with additional studies.

## What does the therapy actually look like?

The teaching sessions are initially one-on-one (one therapist to one student) and they look very similar to traditional, well-settled behavioral treatment programs. Prior to working with the child to teach the various parts of language, there is 1) a language assessment using a Behavioral Language Assessment Form[7] that determines which skills the child has mastered and which skills need to be developed, and 2) an emphasis on making the therapeutic setting fun and reinforcing. The first skill they generally teach is Manding (which is teaching the child to request). Typically, the therapist has an item the child wants but needs help to acquire. This system can be used with children who cannot communicate vocally by using sign language or an augmentative communication system. Children are taught to request items they see and then items they cannot see. They are generally taught to mand using single words at first even when they are capable of using full sentences. Eventually, the child incorporates more words into the sentence and is able to mand without prompting or artificially setting up a reinforcing situation. In other words, the child requests because he truly desires or needs something. Over time, other parts of Verbal Behavior are taught.

From my reading of the verbal behavior material, there does not seem to be a consensus on how many hours per week a Verbal Behavior Therapy program should run. Data is taken throughout, generally using a data collection system designed by the pioneers of the application of Verbal Behavior, Sundberg and Partington.[7] For a user-friendly description of Verbal Behavior Therapy and samples of the data, the Mariposa School has created an easy to understand training manual.[8]

## Would I try it on my child?

Although I would not place my child in a program that worked solely using Verbal Behavior Therapy, if she were younger I would be open to applying the VB empirically supported areas to her program. I see very little difference in some of the techniques used in traditional IBT programs, although the terminology is different. At this point, my daughter already has amassed the skills that have empirical support from the Verbal Behavior literature the traditional way, in a best practices, outcome-based behavioral treatment program. Therefore, at this point those areas would no longer be appropriate for her based on her level of language development.

## What else do I think?

Practitioners in the area of Verbal Behavior do not appear to sufficiently address the issue of behaviors that interfere with learning.  Indeed, there are those who believe that autism is primarily a disorder preventable with Verbal Behavior Therapy.[9, 10]  Their thesis is that the various nonsocial (or anti-social) behaviors we see exhibited by people with autism are a result of the "core" deficit, which is a disorder of Verbal Behavior.  Drash and Tudor (2004) state: "Conceptualizing autism as a contingency-shaped disorder of Verbal Behavior may provide a new and potentially more effective paradigm for behavioral research and treatment in autism"[11]  Although this is an interesting proposition, it has not yet been supported by data; therefore, it is premature for parents to be told by those providing Verbal Behavior Therapy to end all other forms of behavioral treatment.  It would be much safer to incorporate those techniques which have some empirical support (albeit limited) such as the research done on the teaching mands for information.[5]  That said, based on the limited empirical support, it is important to track the child's progress with data to make sure that the child is aquiring more language.

## What kind of study would I like to see the researchers working on Verbal Behavior do?

This is an exciting, emerging area in which there is much work to be done.  Oak and Dickson (1989)[12] did a review of the literature and found very little empirical support.  Other researchers in this field are calling for more studies to be conducted.  I was particularly pleased to  find an article written by Carr and Firth (2005)[13] calling for additional empirical support.  These academics suggest (and I wholeheartedly agree) that there needs to be research done comparing the UCLA model (pioneered by Lovaas and colleagues) and the Verbal Behavioral model as there is no documented outcome from comprehensive Verbal Behavior programs. More research needs to be conducted on individual Verbal Behavior techniques in order for Skinner's theory of Verbal Behavior to be refined to reflect the empirical research done on this population of children.

## Who else recommends for or against Verbal Behavior as a method for the treatment of autism?

I could not find any organizations with an official stance on Verbal Behavior as it is classified under the umbrella of ABA, which is a science-based discipline. Therefore, it is for the consumer to rely on the community of academics in the field of applied behavior analysis to call for additional research, as did Carr and Firth (2005).

## So you're still on the horns of a dilemma?

If you would like to incorporate Verbal Behavior into your behavioral treatment program, make sure that you monitor the progress of the child, quantifying the gains using cold, hard data. In addition, the child should be assessed using psychometric testing on a yearly basis by a psychologist with no connection to the practitioners of Verbal Behavior. Moreover, it is important to monitor behavioral gains to see whether progress in Verbal Behavior is having a positive, neutral or negative effect on other behaviors indicative of autism. Monitoring behavior is crucial: if the child's behavioral gains begin to erode, it is important to recognize the behavioral backslide and take steps to reverse the trend.

## What's the bottom line?

Based on the scientific research to date, there is no data to suggest that a pure Verbal Behavior program will ameliorate the condition of autism; however, certain techniques used by practitioners promoting Verbal Behavior do have limited empirical support. In short, this field is still emerging.

# Offshoots of Intensive Behavioral Therapies: Fluency Training

## What is Fluency Training?

Fluency can be defined most simply as accuracy plus speed, or quality plus pace.[1]  Proponents of Fluency Training argue that the way traditional behaviorists measure whether a person has acquired a skill must take into account if the student provides the correct answer or not, *and* how long it takes the student to present the correct answer.  To illustrate, if a student is asked, "What's your name?" and it takes the student five minutes to answer, does the student actually have the skill?  The answer here is obviously "no."

Precision Teaching is the field that studies and applies fluency techniques to learning.  This field has influenced many areas of life, including educational systems (specifically in the areas of numeracy and literacy), competitive athletics, and organizational productivity.[2]  Precision teaching is not new.  In fact, many of us have been taught our multiplication tables using this very technique.  Those researchers and practitioners in the field of Precision Teaching have found that behavioral fluency is associated with positive learning outcomes.  Binder (1993) describes these general outcomes as "retention and maintenance of skills and knowledge; endurance or resistance to distraction; and application or transfer of training"[3]

Although the vast majority of research has been conducted on non-autistic students, this teaching method is now used by some on children with autism.  Some practitioners in the field of applied behavior analysis have incorporated fluency techniques in their comprehensive treatment programs for children with autism in areas where the skill lends itself to mastery through fast and frequent repetition. Other practitioners have abandoned most other tools in the ABA toolbox (including discrete trial training), and rely solely on fluency-based instruction.

## What evidence do the practitioners have that this really works?

The field of Precision Teaching is quite broad, laying claim to many peer-reviewed journal articles published on Fluency; however, data published on the use of Fluency for children with autism, specifically, is scarce. Five years ago there was almost no data on Fluency and autism. Since that time, approximately fifty papers and poster presentations have been made at ABA conferences; the proponents of Fluency have established a peer-reviewed journal, and they are also taking submissions from those collecting data on fluency instruction (primarily using a celeration chart – the chart used by these practitioners to measure Fluency). After a comprehensive literature search in many databases and through fugitive literature searches, I found eight articles providing data which measure the influence of Fluency-based instruction for specific skills on children with autism. Examples of skills taught using Fluency include improving speech intelligibility,[4] labelling pictures,[5] teaching visual pattern imitation,[6] reading comprehension,[7] joint attention,[8] prepositions,[9] and answering informational WH questions.[10]

Although this increased publication stream is a step forward for this emerging field as it applies to autism, almost all the articles were published in the recently established *Journal of Precision Teaching and Celeration*. In order to gain acceptance as a well-settled methodology for autism, these practitioners need to publish in well-established behavioral journals as well. It is particularly problematic that these practitioners have abandoned the well-established behavioral journals as the lion's share of the articles published on autism and

Fluency in the *Journal of Precision Teaching and Celeration* are written by the founder of the journal.

## What does the therapy actually look like?

The fundamentals of each skill are learned in a fast-paced way, with progress recorded on a celeration chart (a form of time-based measurement). The child is taught by practicing the skill rather than being told what to do (e.g., the use of flash cards would be common). The information would also be asked using what Fluency practitioners refer to as six multiple learning channels which are comprised of See-Write, Hear-Say, Free (recall) Write, See-Say, Free (recall) Say, Hear-Do. These channels constitute different ways to introduce and teach skills. Repetition through a varied number of learning channels is hypothesized to improve the learning and retention process and, thereby, achieve Fluency (once again, defined as accuracy and rate).

## Would I try it on my child?

Although I recognize that rate plus accuracy is important to truly master any skill, there is insufficient data demonstrating that a behavioral treatment program utilizing Fluency instruction *exclusively* (not taking advantage of the many different tools in the behavioral toolbox), will improve my child's abilities. I would have no problem, however, utilizing Fluency as a technique to teach a particular skill that has been well-established to benefit from role learning (such as memorizing multiplication tables or a vocabulary list); however, if my child were young, I would be very wary of replacing discrete trial training with Fluency-based instruction, as the former is a well-established technique used with autistic children, whereas the latter technique is still emergent as applied to children with autism. That said, I think there are some skills that lend themselves better to this teaching method than do others.

## What kind of study would I like to see the researchers working on Fluency do?

I would like to see the progress of children who have undergone Fluency-based instruction measured using nonfluency-based, standardized instruments. Specifically, IQ and language proficiency measures both pre and post treatment are necessary for these studies to track improvement. Because these practitioners use single-subject case designs exclusively, standardized measures are crucial to determine whether the children's gains are genuine. This is also the reason it is imperative for Fluency practitioners to publish their results in peer-reviewed journals of which they are not on the editorial boards. I am very optimistic regarding the potential of Fluency-based instruction to teach children with autism who have obtained a basic level of learning competence. However, prior to using a novel approach which may or may not produce the same positive outcomes, Fluency needs to be scrutinized more closely by those practitioners in the area of applied behavior analysis. In addition, I would like to see Fluency researchers create a between-subject design using their curriculum and comparing it to children in a best-practices, intensive, behavioral treatment program.

## Who else recommends for or against Fluency as a method for the treatment of autism?

This method has not yet gained much popularity as a comprehensive treatment for autism, although Fluency-based instruction is used in some programs as one technique in the ABA toolbox. Therefore, there is very little debate about Fluency; however, I expect that this may change as more parents choose to use Fluency-based instruction exclusively for their child's autism treatment program.

## So you're still on the horns of a dilemma?

If you would like to try Fluency-based instruction, I would recommend that you use a behavioral consultant who incorporates Fluency as one technique in a comprehensive treatment program, rather than use consultants who attempt to target *everything* through Fluency-based instruction.  In addition, I would have my child tested once a year, using a variety of psychometric and language assessment tests conducted by a psychologist with no emotional or financial investment in Fluency-based instruction.

## What's the bottom line?

Based on the scientific research to date, there is insufficient evidence to determine that an Intensive Behavioral Treatment program relying *solely* on the use of Fluency-based instruction will ameliorate the condition of autism, although there is limited evidence that points to the appropriate use of Fluency-based instruction for certain deficiences characteristic of autism.

## Endnotes for Intensive Behavioral Treatment

### Introduction

[1]Lieberman, D.A. 2nd Edition. 1993. *Learning, Behavior and Cognition.* Belmont, CA: Wadsworth Publishing.

[2]Behavior Analyst Certification Board. <http://www.bacb.com/pages/aboutBAs.html> (accessed Nov. 8, 2005).

[3]Matson, J. L., D.A. Benavidez, L.S. Compton, T. Paulawskyyj, and C. Baglio. 1996. "Behavioral Treatment of Autistic Persons: A Review of Research from 1980 to the Present." *Research in Developmental Disabilities.* No. 17, No. 6, p. 433-465.

[4]Freeman, S.K. 2003. *Science for Sale in the Autism Wars: Medically necessary autism treatment, the court battle for health insurance and why health technology academics are enemy number one.* Langley, BC: SKF Books, Inc.

### Home-based Treatment

[1]Metz, B., J.A. Mulick, and E.M. Butter. 2005. "Autism: A late 20th century fad magnet." In J.W. Jacobson, R.M. Foxx, and J.A. Mulick, eds., *Controversial Therapies for Developmental Disabilities: Fad, Fashion, and Science in Professional Practice*, NJ: Lawrence Erlbaum Associates, p. 237.

[2]Lovaas O.I. 1987. "Behavioral Treatment and Normal Educational and Intellectual Functioning in Young Autistic Children." *Journal of Consulting and Clinical Psychology,* Vol. 55, No. 1, pp. 3-9.

[3]Anderson, S.R., D.L. Avery, E.K. DiPietro, G.L. Edwards, and W.P. Christian. 1987. "Intensive Home-based Early Intervention With Autistic Children." *Education and Treatment of Children,* Vol., 10, Vol. 4, pp. 352-366.

[4]Birnbrauer, J.S., and D.J. Leach. 1993. "The Murdoch Early Intervention Program After 2 Years." *Behavior Change,* Vol. 10, No. 2, pp. 63-74.

[5]McEachin, J.J., T. Smith, and O.I. Lovaas. 1993. "Long-Term Outcome for Children With Autism Who Received Early Intensive Behavioral Treatment." *American Journal on Mental Retardation,* Vol., 97, No. 4, pp. 359-372.

[6]Smith, T., S. Eikeseth, M. Klevstrand, and O.I. Lovaas. 1997. "Intensive Behavioral Treatment for Preschoolers With Severe Mental Retardation and Pervasive Developmental Disorder ." *American Journal on Mental Retardation,* Vol. 102, No. 3, pp. 238-249.

[7]Eikeseth, S., T. Smith, E. Jahr, and S. Eldevik. 2002. "Intensive Behavioral Treatment at School for 4 to 7 Year-Old Children With Autism: A One-Year Comparison Controlled Study." *Behavior Modification,* Vol. 26, pp. 49-68.

[8]Howard, J.S., C.R. Sparkman, H.G. Cohen, G. Green, and H. Stanislaw. 2005. "A Comparison

of Intensive Behavior Analytic and Eclectic Treatments for Young Children With Autism." *Research in Developmental Disabilities,* Vol. 26, pp. 359-383.

[9]Sallows, G. O., and T.D. Graupner. 2005. "Intensive Behavioral Treatment for Children With Autism: Four-Year Outcome and Predictors." *American Journal on Mental Retardation,* 2005, Vol. 110, No. 6, pp. 417-438.

[10]Cohen, H., M. Amerine-Dickens, and T. Smith. 2006. "Early Intensive Behavioral Treatment: Replication of the UCLA Model in a Community Setting." *Journal of Developmental and Behavioral Pediatrics*, Vol. 27, No. 2S, pp. S145-55.

[11]Sheinkoph, S.J., and B, Siegel. 1998. "Home-based Behavioral Treatment of Young Children With Autism." *Journal of Autism and Developmental Disorders,* Vol. 28, No. 1, pp. 15-23.

[12]Smith, T. 1993. "Autism." In T.R. Giles ed., *Handbook of effective psychotherapy,* NY: Plenum, pp. 107-133.

[13]Smith, T., A. Groen, and J. Wynn. 2000. "Randomized Trial of Intensive Early Intervention for Children with Pervasive Developmental Disorder." *American Journal on Mental Retardation,* Vol. 105, pp. 269-285.

[14]Butter, E.M., J. Mulick, and B. Metz. 2006. "Eight Case Reports of Learning Recovery in Children with Pervasive Developmental Disorders After Early Intervention." Behavioral Interventions, Vol. 21, No. 4, pp. 227-243.

[14]Bibby, P., S. Eikeseth, N.T. Martin, O.C. Mudford, and D. Reeves. 2002. "Progress and Outcomes for Children With Autism Receiving Parent-Managed Intensive Interventions." *Research in Developmental Disabilities,* Vol. 23, pp. 81-104.

[15]Lovaas, O.I., (see n. 2 above), p. 3.

[16]Baer, D.M. 1993. "Commentaries on McEachin, Smith, and Lovaas: Quasi-Random Assignment Can Be As Convincing As Random Assignment." *American Journal of Mental Retardation*, Vol. 97, No. 4, p. 374.

[17]Sallows, G.O., T.D. Graupner, (see n. 9 above), p. 433.

[18]Guralnick, M., ed. 1999. *Clinical Practice Guideline: Report of the Recommendations. Autism/Pervasive Developmental Disorders, Assessment and Intervention for Young Children* (age 0-3 years). Albany, NY: New York State Department of Health, p. IV-15.

[19]Satcher, D. 1999. *Mental health: A report of the surgeon general.* U.S. Public Health Service. Bethesda, MD www.surgeongeneral.gov/library/mentalhealth/chapter3/sec6.html#autism (accessed Jan. 11, 2006).

[20]American Academy of Pediatrics. 2000. "Policy Statement: The Pediatrician's Role in the Diagnosis and Management of Autistic Spectrum Disorder in Children." *Pediatrics,* Vol. 107, pp. 1221-1226. www.aap.org/policy/re060018.html (accessed June 18, 2000).

[21]National Research Council. 2001. *Educating children with autism*, Committee on Educational Interventions for Children With Autism, Division of Behavioral and Social Sciences and Education, Washington, DC: National Academy Press. http://books.nap.edu/books/0309072697/html/index.html (accessed May 5, 2006).

[22]Volkmar, F., E.H. Cook, J. Pomeroy, G. Realmuto, and P. Tanguay. 1999. "Practice Parameters for the Assessment and Treatment of Children, Adolescents, and Adults With Autism and Other Pervasive Developmental Disorders." *Journal of the American Academy of Child and Adolescent Psychiatry,* Vol. 38 (sup), pp. 32S-54S.

[23]Lovaas, O.I. 2003. *Teaching individuals with developmental delays: basic intervention techniques.* Austin, TX: Pro-Ed, Inc., pp. 323-325.

[24]Maurice, C., G. Green, and S.C. Luce. 1996. *Behavioral intervention for young children with autism.* Austin, TX: Pro-Ed, Inc.

[25]Leaf, R., and J. McEachin. 1999. *A work in progress: Behavior management strategies and a curriculum for Intensive Behavioral Treatment of autism.* New York, NY: DRL Books, L.L.C.

[26]Cambridge Center for Behavioral Studies. http://store.ccbsstore.com/default.asp (accessed May 5, 2006).

## Centre-based Treatment

[1]McClannahan, L.E., MacDuff G.S., and Krantz, P.J. 2002. "Behavior Analysis and Intervention for Adults with Autism." *Behavior Modification*, Vol. 26, No. 1, pp. 9-27.

[2]Harris, S.L., and J.S. Handleman. 2000. "Age and IQ at Intake as Predictors of Placement for Young Children With Autism: A Four-to-Six-Year Follow-Up." *Journal of Autism Developmental Disorders*, Vol. 30, No. 2, p. 139.

[3]Strain, P.S., and L.K. Cordisco. 1994. "Chapter 5: The Creative Curriculum for Early Childhood." In S,L. Harris and J.S. Handleman, eds. *Preschool Education Programs for Children With Autism*. Austin, TX: Pro-Ed, Inc.

[4]Fenske, E.C., S. Zalenski, P.J. Krantz, and L.E. McClannahan. 1985. "Age at Intervention and Treatment Outcome for Autistic children in a Comprehensive Intervention Program." *Analysis and Intervention in Developmental Disabilities,* 1985, Vol. 5, pp. 49-58.

[5]Handleman, J.S., S.L. Harris, D. Celiberti, E. Lilleleht, and L. Tomchek. 1991. "Developmental Changes of Preschool Children with Autism and Normally Developing Peers." *The Transdisciplinary Journal,* Vol. 1, No. 2, pp. 137-143.

[6]Harris, S.L., J.S. Handleman, B. Kristoff, L. Bass, and R. Gordon. 1990. "Changes in Language Development Among Autistic and Peer Children in Segregated and Integrated Preschool Settings." *Journal of Autism and Developmental Disorders*, Vol. 20, No. 1, pp. 23-31.

[7]Harris, S.L., and J.S. Handleman. (see n. 2 above).

[8]Hoyson, M., B. Jamieson, and P.S. Strain. 1984. "Individualized Group Instruction of Normally Developing and Autistic-Like Children: The LEAP Curriculum Model." *Journal of the Division for Early Childhood*, Vol. 8, No. 2, pp. 157-172.

[9]Harris, S.L., J.S. Handleman, B. Kristoff, L. Bass, and R. Gordon, (see n. 6 above), p. 25.

[10]Harris, S.L., J.S. Handleman, B. Kristoff, L. Bass, and R. Gordon, (see n. 6 above), p. 24.

[11]Harris, S.L., and J.S. Handleman. 1994. "Chapter 5: The Douglass Developmental Disabilities Center." In S.L. Harris and J.S. Handleman, eds. *Preschool Education Programs for Children With Autism*. Austin, TX. Pro-Ed, Inc., p. 74.

[12]Hoyson, M., B. Jamieson, and P.S. Strain, (see n. 8 above), p. 159.

[13]Hoyson, M., B. Jamieson, and P.S. Strain, (see n. 8 above), p. 165.

[14]Harris, S.L., and J.S. Handleman, (see n. 11 above), p. 77.

[15]Hoyson, M., B. Jamieson, and P.S. Strain, (see note 8 above), p. 158.

[16]The Scientific Review of Mental Health Practice, www. srmhp.org/0101/autism.html (accessed Jan. 11, 2006).

[17]Association for Science in Autism treatment, www.asatonline.org/about_autism/autism_info04. html (accessed Feb. 21, 2006).

[18]Behavioral Analyst Certification Board, www.bacb.com/consum_frame.html (accessed Feb. 21, 2006).

## Offshoots:

### a) Pivotal Response Training

[1]Koegel, R.L., L. Schreibman, A. Good, L. Cerniglia, C. Murphy, and L.K. Koegel. 1989. *How To Teach Pivotal Behaviors to Children With Autism: A Training Manual*. Santa Barbara CA: University of California.

[2]Koegel, R.L., et al., (see n. 1 above).

[3]Bruinsma, Y., R.L. Koegel, and L.K. Koegel. 2004. "Joint Attention and Children With Autism: A review of the Literature." *Mental Retardation and Developmental Disabilities,* Vol.10, pp. 169-175.

[4]Koegel, R.L., S. Camarata, L.K. Koegel, A. Ben-Tall, and A.E. Smith. 1998. "Increasing Speech Intelligibility in Children with Autism." *Journal of Autism and Developmental Disorders,* Vol. 28, No. 3, pp. 241-251.

[5]Koegel, et al., (see n. 4 above), p. 246.

[6]Laski, K.E., M.H. Charlop, and L. Schreibman. 1988. "Training Parents to Use the Natural Language Pardigm to Increase Their Autistic Children's Speech." *Journal of Applied Behavior Analysis*, Vol. 21, No. 4, pp. 391-400.

[7]Koegel, R.L., L.K. Koegel, and A. Surratt. 1992. "Language Intervention and Disruptive Behavior in Preschool Children with Autism." *Journal of Autism and Developmental Disorders,* Vol. 22, No. 2, pp. 141-153.

[8]Pierce, K., and L. Schreibman. 1995. "Increasing Complex Social Behaviors in Children with Autism: Effects of Peer-Implemented Pivotal Response Training." *Journal of Applied Behavior Analysis,* Vol. 28, No. 3, pp. 285-295.

[9]Thorp, D.M., A.C. Stahmer, and L. Schreibman. 1995. "Effects of Sociodramatic Play Training on Children with Autism." *Journal of Autism and Developmental Disorders,* Vol. 25, No. 3, p. 265.

[10]Stahmer, A.C. 1995. "Teaching Symbolic Play Skills to Children with Autism Using Pivotal Response Training." *Journal of Autism and Developmental Disorders,* Vol. 25, No. 2, pp. 123-141.

[11]Pierce, K., and L. Schreibman. 1997. "Using Peer Trainers to Promote Social Behavior in Autism: Are They Effective at Enhancing Multiple Social Modalities?" *Focus on Autism and Other Developmental Disabilities,* Vol. 12, No. 4, pp. 207-218.

[12]Pierce, K., and L. Schreibman. 1997. "Multiple Peer Use of Pivotal Response Training to Increase Social Behaviors of Classmates with Autism: Results from Trained and Untrained Peers." *Journal of Applied Behavior Analysis,* Vol. 30, No. 1, pp. 157-160.

[13]Koegel, L.K., S.M. Camarata, M. Valdez-Menchaca, and R.L. Koegel. 1998. "Setting Generalization of Question-Asking by Children With Autism." *American Journal on Mental Retardation,* Vol. 102, No. 4, pp. 346-357.

[14]Koegel, R.L., Y. Shoshan, and E. McNerney. 1999. "Pivotal Response Intervention II: Preliminary Long-Term Outcome Data." *Journal of The Association for Persons with Severe Handicaps,* Vol. 24, No. 3, pp. 186-198.

[15]Koegel, L.K., C.M. Carter, and R.L. Koegel. 2003. " Teaching Children With Autism Self-Initiations as a Pivotal Response." *Topics in Language Disorders,* Vol. 23, No. 2, pp. 134-145.

[16]Koegel, R.L., G.A. Wener, L.A. Vismara, and L.K. Koegel. 2005. "The Effectiveness of Contextually Supported Play Date Interactions Between Children With Autism and Typically Developing Peers." *Research and Practice for Persons with Severe Disabilities,* Vol. 30, No. 2, pp. 93-102.

[17]Laski, K.E., M.H. Charlop, and L. Schreibman, (see n. 6 above), p. 394.

[18]Koegel, R.L., et al., (see n. 4 above), p. 246.

[19]Koegel, R.L., L.K. Koegel, and A. Surratt, (see n. 7 above), p. 150.

[20]Delprato, D.J. 2001. "Comparisons of Discrete-Trial and Normalized Behavioral Language Intervention for Young Children with Autism." *Journal of Autism and Developmental Disorders,* Vol. 31, No. 3, pp. 315-325.

[21]Koegel, R.L., L.K. Koegel, and A. Surratt, (see n. 7 above), p. 149.

[22]Koegel, R.L., et al., (see n. 4 above), p. 246.

[23]Stahmer, A.C., (see n. 10 above), p. 137.

[24]Stahmer, A.C., (see n. 10 above), p. 139.

[25]Koegel, L.K., et al., (see n. 13 above), p. 351.

[26]Pierce, K., and Schreibman, (see n. 11 above), p. 208.

[27]Koegel, R.L., et al., (see n. 1 above), p. 9.

[28]Koegel, R.L., et al., (see n. 1 above), p. 9.

[29]Pierce, K., and L. Schreibman, (see n. 8 above), p. 288.

[30]Pierce, K., and L. Schreibman, (see n. 8 above), p. 287.

[31]Schreibman, L., W.M. Kaneko, and R.L. Koegel. 1991. "Positive Affect of Parents of Autistic Children: A Comparison Across Two Teaching Techniques." *Association for Advancement of Behavior Therapy,* Vol. 22, No. 4, p. 488.

[32]Koegel, R.L., A. Bimbela, and L. Schreibman. 1996. "Collateral Effects of Parent Training on Family Interactions." *Journal of Autism and Developmental Disorders,* Vol. 26, No. 3, pp. 347-359.

[33]Laski, K.E., M.H. Charlop, and L. Schreibman, (see n. 6 above), pp. 398-399.

[34]Lisa Benaron. 2006. *Pivotal Response Intervention Model.* Pediatric Development and Behavior, www. dbpeds.org (accessed May, 5, 2006).

## b) Positive Behavioral Support

[1]Carr, E.G., et al. 2002. "Positive behavior support: Evolution of an applied science." *Journal of Positive Behavior Interventions,* Vol. 4, pp. 4-16, 20.

[2]Carr, E.G., et al., (see n. 1 above), p 7.

[3]Wehamn, T., and L. Gilkerson. 1999. "Parents of Young Children With Special Needs Speak Out: Perceptions of Early Intervention Services." *Infant-Toddler Intervention: The Transdisciplinary Journal,* Vol. 9, No. 2, pp. 137-167.

[4]Buschbacher, P.W., and L. Fox. 2003. "Understanding and Intervening With the Challenging Behavior of Young Children With Autism spectrum disorder." *Language, Speech and Hearing Services in Schools,* Vol. 34, No. 3, pp. 217-227.

[5]McCurdy, B.L., M.C. Mannella, and N. Eldridge. 2003. "Positive Behavior Support in Urban Schools: Can We Prevent the Escalation of Antisocial Behavior?" *Journal of Positive Behavior Interventions,* Vol. 5, No. 3, pp. 158-170.

[6]Lucyshyn, J.M., G. Dunlap, and R.W. Albin. 2002. *Families and Positive Behavior Support: Addressing problem behavior in family contexts.* Baltimore, MD: Paul H. Brookes Publishing, p. 465.

[7]Boettcher, M., R.L. Koegel, E.K. McNerney, and L.K. Koegel. 2003. "A Family-Centered Prevention Approach to PBS in a Time of Crisis." *Journal of Positive Behavior Interventions,* Vol. 5, No. 1, pp. 55-59.

[8]Marshall, J.K., and P. Mirenda. 2002. "Parent-Professional Collaboration for Positive Behavior Support in the Home." *Focus on Autism and Other Developmental Disabilities,* Vol. 17, No. 4, pp. 216-228.

[9]Fucilla, R. 2005. "Post-crisis Intervention for Individuals with Autism spectrum disorder." *Reclaiming Children and Youth,* Vol. 14, No. 1, pp. 44-51.

[10]Sallows, G.O., and T.D. Graupner. 2005. "Intensive Behavioral Treatment For children With Autism: Four-Year Outcome and Predictor." *American Journal on Mental Retardation,* Vol. 110, No. 6, pp. 417-438.

[11]Zane, T. 2005. Fads in special education: An overview. In J.W. Jacobson, R.M. Foxx, J.A. Mulick eds. *Controversial Therapies for Developmental Disabilities: Fad, Fashion, and Science in Professional Practice,* NJ: Lawrence Erlbaum Associates, p. 175.

[12]Behavior Analyst Certification Board, www.bacb.com/becom_frame.html (accessed June, 13, 2006).

[13]Durand, V. M., and N. Rost. 2005. "Does It Matter Who Participates In Our Studies?" *Journal of Positive Behavior Interventions,* Vol. 7, No. 3, pp. 186-188.

[14]Mulick, J.A., and E.M. Butter. 2005. Positive Behavior Support: A paternalistic utopian delusion. In J.W. Jacobson, R.M. Foxx, J.A. Mulick eds. *Controversial Therapies for Developmental Disabilities: Fad, Fashion, and Science in Professional Practice,* NJ: Lawrence Erlbaum Associates, p. 385.

## c) Verbal Behavior

[1]Skinner, B.I. 1957. *Verbal Behavior.* NY: Appleton-Century-Crofts.

[2]Sundberg, M.L., and J.W. Partington. 1998. *Teaching Language to Children with Autism or Other Developmental Disorders.* Danville, CA: Behavior Analysts, Inc., p. 298.

[3]Braam, S.J., and A.Poling. 1983. "Development of IntraVerbal Behavior in Mentally Retarded Individuals Through Transfer of Stimulus Control Procedures:  Classification of Verbal Responses." *Applied Research in Mental Retardation,* Vol. 4, pp. 279-302.

[4]Drash, P.W., L. R. High, and R.M. Tudor. 1999.  "Using Mand Training to Establish an Echoic Repertoire in Young Children with Autism." *The Analysis of Verbal Behavior*, Vol. 16, pp. 29-44.

[5]Sundberg, M.L., M. Loeb, L. Hale, and P. Eigenheer. 2002. "Contriving Establishing Operations to Teach Mands for Information." *The Analysis of Verbal Behavior,* Vol. 18, pp. 15-29.

[6]Miguel, C. F., J.E. Carr, and J. Michael.  2002. "The Effects of a Stimulus-Stimulus Pairing Procedure on the Vocal Behavior of Children Diagnosed with Autism." *The Analysis of Verbal Behavior,* Vol. 18, pp. 3-13.

[7]Behavior Analysts, Inc., www.behavioranalysts.com (accessed Dec. 28, 2006).

[8]The Mariposa School, http://www.MariposaSchool.org (accessed Dec. 28, 2006).

[9]Drash, P.W., and R.M. Tudor. 2000. "Is Autism a Preventable Disorder of Verbal Behavior?  A Response to Five Commentaries." *The Analysis of Verbal Behavior,* Vol. 20, pp. 55-62.

[10]Drash, P.W., and R.M. Tudor. 2004.  "An Analysis of Autism as a Contingency-Shaped Disorder of Verbal Behavior." *The Analysis of Verbal Behavior,* Vol. 20, pp. 5-23.

[11]Drash, P.W., and R.M. Tudor, (see n. 10 above), p. 5.

[12]Oah, S., and A.M. Dickinson. 1989. "A Review of Empirical Studies of Verbal Behavior." *The Analysis of Verbal Behavior,* Vol. 7, pp. 53-68.

[13]Carr, J.E., and A.M. Firth. 2005. "The Verbal Behavior Approach to Early and Intensive Behavioral Intervention for Autism: A Call for Additional Empirical Support." *Journal of Early and Intensive Behavioral Intervention,* Vol. 2, No. 1, pp.  18-27.

### d)  Fluency

[1]Binder, C. 1988. "Precision Teaching:  Measuring and Attaining Exemplary Academic Achievement." *Youth Policy,* Vol. 10, No. 7, pp. 12-15.

[2]The Fluency Project, http://www.Fluency.org (accessed Feb. 13, 2007).

[3]Binder, C.  1993. "Behavioral Fluency:  A New Paradigm." *Educational Technology*, pp. 8-14.

[4]Fabrizio, M.A., S. Pahl, and A. Moors. 2002.  " Improving Speech Intelligibility Through Precision Teaching." *Journal of Precision Teaching and Celeration*, Vol. 18, No. 1, pp. 25-27.

[5]Moors, A., and M.A. Fabrizio. 2002. "Using Tool Skill Rates to Predict Composite Skill Frequency Aims." *Journal of Precision Teaching and Celeration*, Vol. 18, No. 1, pp. 28-29.

[6]Fabrizio, M.A., and K. Schirmer. 2002. "Teaching Visual Pattern Imitation to a Child With Autism." *Journal of Precision Teaching and Celeration*, Vol. 18, No. 1, pp. 80-82.

[7]Fabrizio, M.A., K. Schirmer, and K. Ferris. 2002. "Tracking Curricular Progress With Precision." *Journal of Precision Teaching and Celeration*, Vol. 18, No. 2, pp. 78-79.

[8]Fabrizio, M.A., K. Schirmer, E. Vu, A. Diakite, and M. Yao. 2003. "Analog Analysis of Two Variables Related to the Joint Attention of a Toddler With Autism." *Journal of Precision Teaching and Celeration*, Vol. 19, No. 1, pp. 41-44.

[9]King, A., A.L. Moors, and M.A. Fabrizio. 2003. "Concurrently Teaching Multiple Verbal Operants Related to Preposition Use to a Child With Autism." *Journal of Precision Teaching and Celeration*, Vol. 19, No. 1, pp. 38-40.

[10]Zambolin, K., M.A. Fabrizio, and S. Isley. 2004. "Teaching a Child With Autism to Answer Informational Questions Using Precision Teaching." *Journal of Precision Teaching and Celeration*, Vol. 20, No. 1, pp. 22-25.

# Other School-based Therapies Section 1.2

▷ *TEACCH*

▷ *The Playschool (Colorado Health Sciences Center)*

▷ *Giant Steps*

▷ *Higashi/Daily Life Therapy*

▷ *The Walden Preschool*

# Other School-based Therapies: TEACCH

## What is TEACCH?

TEACCH (Treatment and Education of Autistic and Related Communication Handicapped Children) is a state run agency for individuals with autism and their families, and provides both a center-based and a community outreach program. Families can choose from a variety of treatment options to best meet their individual circumstances and needs. TEACCH views three levels of need which must be addressed: those of the child; those of the family, and those of the community.[1] The goal is to help foster independence and happiness for every child in the programs. In order to accomplish this, the TEACCH philosophy supports the individualization of programs not only for the child, but also for the family and community. In the center-based program, student to teacher ratios are not limited at the preschool age level; however, at the school-age level, ratios are limited to six children per one teacher. The curriculum emphasizes structured teaching and involves educational continuity across settings. To accomplish this, TEACCH proponents claim that the layout of the classroom and the way the environment is engineered help promote the child's independence. Classroom goals for each child include cognitive, fine motor, eye/hand integration, organizational skills, self-help skills, receptive and expressive language, and social interaction.

These programs are taught using structured teaching (i.e., clear, predictable, and rule-based), visual schedules (i.e., using pictures or lists to organize the child's day), environmental accommodation (i.e., organizing the classroom to minimize distraction) and a combination of other cognitive and behavioral approaches. To address problematic behaviors, the TEACCH model designs the environment and uses daily schedules to prevent problematic behaviors before they occur.

They also use functional analysis (analyzing a behavior with respect to its function) and, where necessary, the occasional time-out (removing the child from the situation).

The Home-Based component of TEACCH services uses programs which emphasize visual strengths, pre-academic or pre-vocational skills, structured teaching, a schedule and a communication system.  In the outcome study by Ozonoff and Cathcart (1998), the individualized curriculum was programmed to the child, based on the baseline scores (from a measure called the Psychoeducational Profile – Revised [PEP-R]), which indicated the child's strengths and weaknesses. The home program lasted ten weeks, wherein parents and two therapists met for an hour per week to work with the child.  While one therapist worked, parents and the other therapist observed and discussed techniques used.  Based on their observations, parents were instructed to work with their child for a half hour per day using the techniques taught by TEACCH staff.

## What evidence do the practitioners have that this really works?

There is little outcome data available to evaluate the efficacy of the center-based TEACCH program.  After combing through over fifty publications written on the TEACCH method, I could only find three peer-reviewed articles which provide outcome data on children who participated in a TEACCH program.[2,3,4]  The Lord and Schopler study (1989) reports  results for children who participated in the TEACCH program and found that despite the program, the children did not improve significantly based upon IQ scores.  In their original study, Lord and Schopler took seventy-one autistic children and compared them with seventy-one non-autistic, communicatively-handicapped children who also attended a TEACCH program.  Their findings regarding children with autism were that the IQ scores were stable despite treatment. They state: "...IQs at age 4 years were found to be highly correlated with performance IQ at age 10 years for both groups. Absolute difference scores and group means were also equivalent for both samples, with no difference in patterns of change or the relationship between performance IQ and language status..."[5] In other words, despite the TEACCH curriculum, according to Lord and Schopler's research, there was no significant gain in IQ scores for either group of children who participated in the TEACCH curriculum.

The next outcome study[6] presents data which addresses the TEACCH home-based program. The home-based study, conducted by Ozonoff and Cathcart (1998) divided the children in two groups. One group of eleven children received a home-based TEACCH program where parents were taught to work with their children. The other group of eleven children were not provided with any competing treatment. After four months of treatment, the children in the experimental group tested significantly better on fine motor and gross motor skills as well as nonverbal conceptual skills. Their overall skills, based on the Psychoeducational Profile – Revised (PEP-R), also improved over the control group.

It is important to appropriately evaluate the results of the Ozonoff and Cathcart (1998) study. Of note is that all the children in the study were in local day treatment programs in Utah, which, as the authors point out, is a state that relies heavily upon discrete trial training in their special educational programs. In addition, the home-based program relied on TEACCH methods, which included structured teaching administered by parents who were taught by the researchers. The results of their study actually tell us that for children with discrete trial training learning histories (i.e., intensive behavioral treatment), more intervention is better than less intervention; however, their study does not tell us that the

TEACCH intervention is responsible for the gains. The question remains whether the TEACCH home-based program, delivered by using parents (and their free labor) is as effective as the same number of hours in a home-based ABA program utilizing structured methods, such as discrete trial training, using IBT professionals.

Despite the critique above, this study does show much more in the way of positive results than the original TEACCH study; however, due to the weaknesses of the study, these results need to be taken with caution. One of the study's weaknesses is that the only measure used to define level of autism (the dependent variable) both at the pre-test and post-test is the Psychoeducational Profile – Revised (PEP-R). While the CARS was used pretreatment to determine autism, no mention of the CARS posttreatment results were made. The CARS scores were negatively correlated with change scores, which means that those children who had better CAR scores (indicating milder autism), fared better with the home-program than those children who were more severely affected. No individual CARS scores were made available at pre or post treatment, and only the average CARS scores for the group were available at pretreatment. Therefore, even if we accept the CARS scores as being a valid measure of autism, we have no information whether the child improved based on the treatment as measured by the CARS score.

In terms of the measure of the dependent variable (which is autism), the PEP-R is not sufficient when used on its own, because we do not have the amount of validity information that we have for other, more widely-used measures. It is essential that if the PEP-R is used, it should be in addition to other, more accepted measures which have proven validity.[*] The areas assessed by the PEP-R are imitation, perception, fine motor, gross motor, eye-hand integration, cognitive

---

[*]It is also problematic that both the CARS and the PEP-R are measures designed by one of the authors of the study.

performance and cognitive verbal skills.  I am not convinced that the variables of perception, fine motor, gross motor and eye-hand integration are important measures to gauge the degree of autism. The PEP-R does not measure behavior, which is a vital aspect of functioning that must not be ignored.  In addition to the PEP-R measure, these authors should have measured cognitive level by using tried and tested psychometric measurements to compare IQ scores pre and post experiment.

An additional issue is that the dependent variables (to measure autism) were measured by, "different testers, none of whom were blind to group assignment."[7] In fact, the PEP-R was administered to the experimental group by their graduate student therapist, while the control group was administered the PEP-R by the authors.  This introduces the possibility of experimenter bias in measuring the dependent variable and undermines our confidence in the results reported.

The final study which reports positive effects of the TEACCH program is Panerai et al., (2002).  This Italian study compared a group of eight children who participated in a residential TEACCH program set up at a hospital with a group of eight children who were integrated into the regular school system with a special education assistant where the staff did not use any techniques specific to teaching children with autism.  The children in the TEACCH program improved in many different areas relative to the control group (and these improvements were statistically significant). This finding is not surprising because the control group was not given any autism-specific treatment.  What is an unfortunate finding, though, is that after one year of treatment based on the Vineland Adaptive Behavioral Scales, there was no significant difference between the experimental and control groups when it came to receptive and expressive communication. In other words, a key deficit in children with autism — the ability to speak and comprehend the spoken word — was not improved with this therapy, even though the TEACCH program is designed specifically for children with autism. In addition, Table Eight of the Italian TEACCH study demonstrates that generically trained support teachers do no better than babysit children with autism when attempting to integrate them into an educational system.[8] Although this study is certainly valuable due to the comparison of TEACCH with an educational program with no autism-specific expertise, it does not shed light on the comparison between other effective treatments, such as those from the behavioral field, which is the main competitor treatment to TEACCH.

## What does the therapy actually look like?

Since TEACCH services are center-based , community based, and home-based, it is difficult to describe the services as a whole. The TEACCH classroom looks different than a typical classroom, with very few so-called "distractions" on the walls and on the boards. Children typically sit in a classroom cubicle so as not to be distracted by other activity in the classroom. Each child has a list of tasks that must be completed independently. Independent task completion is a high priority because the TEACCH philosophy is based on the foundation that the child will be placed in a vocation in which he will have to complete jobs independently. TEACCH emphasizes parental involvement and the training of parents as cotherapists. TEACCH outreach programs have not been described in sufficient detail to illustrate how the home and community programs look; however, they do speak of a number of treatment options which occur across many different settings, i.e., home, community, and workplace.

## What else do I think?

Given the philosophy of TEACCH, which involves the *accommodation* of strengths and weaknesses, rather than targeting weaknesses for intevention and elimination, children with autism who are involved in TEACCH programs may not be given opportunitites to overcome these deficits and function in a more typical way. Frankly, I do not understand how the TEACCH paradigm promotes integration of people with autism. It seems to me that this philosophy would tend to result in the segregation of autistic children because how can people with autism function in a mainstream setting without working on deficits with the goal of either eliminating or reducing the problems associated with those deficits? Proponents of TEACCH do not profess to eradicate autism; rather, their philosophy is the "goal of improved adaptation"[9] for children with autism. More recently, I was quite dismayed to come across an article by Jennett et al. (2003) in which autism was actually referred to as a "culture," rather than a neurological disorder — a widely recognized health problem. They state: "This contrasts with a primary value of the TEACCH approach of respecting the *culture of autism* (Mesibov and Shea, in press, emphasis added)."[10] It is most unfortunate when researchers define autism in this manner because if we magically transform autism into a culture, the argument absolves governments, insurance companies, and others of all responsibility to provide treatment to this most vulnerable group of children, for the fundamental reason that a culture is generally accepted, rather than targeted, for treatment as a pathology.

*The International Journal of Mental Health* highlighted the TEACCH program worldwide when one of the TEACCH proponents, Schopler, became a guest editor at the journal. Despite the fact that no less than two issues of this journal were devoted to TEACCH, not a single article reported compelling data on the efficacy of the treatment method.[11] What is impressive about the TEACCH Model is not so much its purported value in ameliorating autism, but rather its ability to proliferate worldwide, which is quite amazing given that this model is supported by so little data showing treatment efficacy. The TEACCH Model has been adopted by various systems in over twenty countries, including Belguim, Israel, Italy, Japan, Kuwait, Spain, Sweden, the United Kingdom, and even France, where many psychiatrists still approach autism in a misguided, outdated Freudian manner where the mother is blamed for causing the autism.  I would like to suggest that the reason behind the TEACCH proliferation is twofold: first, the TEACCH model is relatively easy and inexpensive for educational systems to adopt, and second, the TEACCH proponents are expert at integrating into existing systems (such as the educational system) in order to propagate the method.

It is also of some concern that the one measure for autism relied upon so heavily in TEACCH studies is the PEP-R.  Children could be taught how to perform well on the dependent measure, which may inflate the actual progress made as the dependent measure is so narrow (particularly in the areas of fine and gross motor skills).  In addition to this, behavior is not adequately tested and the two critically important dependent measures for individuals with autism, IQ and language, need to be more comprehensively tested pre and post study of the TEACCH method, and rely upon blind testers using widely accepted psychometric measures.

A problematic part of the one home-based TEACCH study[3] is its length.  The program was ten weeks of supervision (one hour per week).  After this period, parents (whose labor is free) became the ones solely in charge of programming and implementing the curriculum for a half hour per day.  Although this may be cost-effective for governments and educational systems, it is unlikely to be enough time to create meaningful change for children with autism.  The authors appear to be well aware of the resource problem, wherein Ozonoff and Cathcart (1998) state: "We hope these results will encourage teachers and other professionals to devise *cost-efficient means* of extending programing into the home"[12] (emphasis added).  I'm not sure when cost-effectiveness became the responsibility of researchers; however, it is a dangerous day when researchers trying to push a field forward are worried about government expenditures.

Finally, the TEACCH philosophy emphasizes the satisfaction and happiness of the parents who participated in the TEACCH study. More emphasis appears to be placed on parental satisfaction than on the effectiveness of autism treatment. Although, as a parent I am glad that they care about my happiness, I firmly believe that the progress of the child must remain the paramount concern of researchers and that the elements of each child's program must be motivated by that child's future and not a happiness rating for parents.

## Would I try it on my child?

At this point there are two reasons I would not enroll my child in a TEACCH program. First, the data is not sufficientaly strong to convince me that the TEACCH way is the best way. Second, call me fussy, but I want my child to be enrolled in a school or a treatment program that is going to squeeze out every last ounce of her potential and not "accomodate" her deficits. I want a program to actively target her deficits with the goal of eradicating or minimizing those deficits. In terms of happiness, I believe that my child's happiness is linked to her independence: and her independence and integration into society is dependent upon how capable an adult she will become. My happiness is directly linked to her reaching her fullest potential.

## What kind of study would I like to see the TEACCH people do?

The authors of TEACCH's outcome studies point out that there are problems with the study (they refer to it as "confounding variables") that prevent acceptance of their positive results as accurate.[13] I would like to see them rectify this issue by designing a study which includes the following elements, at minimum: an experimental and control group with at least twenty children per condition (per group). The control group (the group not receiving the treatment) would be children enrolled in regular special education in the United States (where there is strong federal legislation protecting children in the educational system).  Results of this study would at least determine whether a TEACCH classroom is superior to a standard special education classroom.  Next, it would be valuable to compare the TEACCH method against a classroom which relies heavily upon discrete trial training (a structured data-supported technique) and the various principles of applied behavior analysis as teaching techniques.  In addition, autism (the dependent variable) should be measured using many tests which are relevant to deficits common in autism (such as language, behavior, and IQ).  To achieve this, each child in the study should be given a full range of well-accepted tests which measure these three areas.  These tests should be administered by psychologists who are in no way related to the study. If the results from a study with the above elements demonstrate that children do indeed benefit significantly with a TEACCH program, then this could be considered a treatment option for some children.  However, more research on the TEACCH model is required before any conclusions can be made about its effectiveness.

## Who else recommends for or against TEACCH as a method for the treatment of autism?

In 1999, the New York State Department of Health issued a well done and very thorough report on clinical best practices for the treatment of autism in young children.  Data from the center-based TEACCH program was not reviewed because of its lack of rigorous study design; however, the home-based study was reviewed (included in the New York Report in the parent training section).  They concur that in the Ozonoff and Cathcart (1998) study (where children were simultaneously receiving treatment in the day), those children whose parents were trained (given eight to twelve sessions of home-based training) improved on the PEP-R outcome measure relative to the children whose parents did not receive training.[14]

## So you're still on the horns of a dilemma?

If you are still contemplating the merits of a TEACCH program, consider what The Association for Science in Autism treatment has to say.  This organization provides a rather lukewarm reception to TEACCH when it states:  "Research conducted by TEACCH and anecdotal reports suggest TEACCH shows promise [15,16] but *it is not objectively substantiated* as effective by independent researchers" (emphasis added).[17]  This is quite true.  Independent researchers should consider further investigation using well established research protocols.  Professionals considering TEACCH methods should consider that the TEACCH program lacks independent verification of its effectiveness, and should disclose this status to key decision makers influencing the child's intervention.

## What's the bottom line?

Based on the scientific research to date, there is not enough evidence to conclude that the TEACCH model is effective for the treatment of children with autism.

## Endnotes for TEACCH

[1]Lord, C., and E. Schopler. 1989. " The Role of Age at Assessment, Developmental Level and Test in the Stability of Intelligence Scores in Young Autistic Children." *Journal of Autism and Developmental Disorders,* Vol. 19, pp. 483-499.

[2.]Lord, C., and E. Schopler, (see n. 1 above).

[3]Ozonoff, S., and K. Cathcart. 1998. "Effectiveness of a Home Program Intervention For Young Children With Autism." *Journal of Autism and Developmental Disorders,* Vol. 28, No. 1, pp. 25-32.

[4]Panerai, S., L. Ferrante, and M. Zingale. 2002.  "Benefits of the Treatment and Education of Autistic and Communication Handicapped Children (TEACCH) Programme as Compared With a Non-specific Approach." *Journal of Intellectual Disability Research,* Vol. 46, No. 4, pp. 318-327.

[5]Lord, C. and E. Schopler. 1989. "Stability and assessment results of autistic and nonautistic language-impaired children from preschool years to early school age." *Journal of Child Psychology and Psychiatry*, Vol. 30, No. 4, pp. 575-90.

[6]Ozonoff, S., and K. Cathcart, (see n. 3 above).

[7]Ozonoff, S., and K. Cathcart, (see n. 3 above).

[8]Panerai, S., L. Ferrante, and M. Zingale, (see n. 4 above).

[9]Schopler, E., and G.B. Mesibov. 2000. "Cross-Cultural Priorities in Developing Autism Services." *International Journal of Mental Health,* Vol. 29, No. 1, pp. 3-21.

[10]Jennett, H.K., S.L. Harris, and G.B. Mesibov. 2003. "Commmitment to Philosophy, Teacher Efficacy and Burnout Among Teachers of Children With Autism." *Journal of Autism and Developmental Disorders,* Vol. 33, No. 6, pp. 583-593.

[11]Schopler, E., and G.B. Mesibov, (see n. 9 above).

[12]Ozonoff, S., and K. Cathcart, (see n. 3 above).

[13]Ozonoff, S., and K. Cathcart, (see n. 3 above), p. 30.

[14]Guralnick, M. ed. 1999. *Clinical Practice Guideline:  Report of the Recommendations. Autism/Pervasive Developmental Disorders, Assessment and Intervention for Young Children* (age 0-3 years).  Albany (NY): New York State Department of Health, pp. IV51-52.

[15]Lord, C. and E. Schopler, (see n. 5 above).

[16]Lord, C. and E. Schopler, 1994.  "TEACCH services for preschool children."  In S.L. Harris and J.S. Handleman, eds. *Preschool education programs for children with autism.*  Austin, TX: Pro-Ed. pp. 87-106.

[17]Association For Science in Autism treatment (ASAT), www.asatonline.org/about-autism-info14. html (accessed Nov. 21, 2005).

# Other School-based Therapies:  The Playschool

## What is The Playschool?

The Playschool is a preschool developed at the Colorado Health Sciences Center which offers a developmentally based curriculum focussing on the symbolic thought, communication and social/emotional development of the child with autism.  The major premise is that active learning in early childhood takes place through play.  The philosophical orientations which influenced the development of the Playschool curriculum is Mahler's Theory of Development of Interpersonal Relationships,* Piaget's theory of Cognitive Development, and Pragmatics Language Theory of Development.[1]  The instruction style at the Playschool is child-led (an orientation which has the child set the agenda for what he would like to do).  The curriculum includes language, affect (emotion), play and the development of social relationships.  This model focuses on communicative intent, non-verbal communication, child as integrator and organizer of his experience, child-led activities as a basis for communication, and the natural environment as the setting for development of language.[1]  These are all essentially "reactive language" strategies. The language part of the curriculum is based on a model termed INREAL (INclass REActive Language) where the speech and language pathologist (SLP) joins the child in the classroom as a teacher rather than pulling the child out into a resource room.[2]  In this setting, the SLP reacts to (rather than directs) the child to facilitate language acquisition.

---

*The importance of Mahler's Theory of Development of Interpersonal Relationships to the Playschool, is the attachment-separation-individuation process of interpersonal development. This process is hypothesized to take place at the earliest age and is seen to be important in autism by some because the theory describes both early separation experiences and the importance of social connectedness in ego development.

At the Playschool, an emphasis is placed on the development of positive emotions and a happy relationship between the child and the adult. The adult is required to initiate and maintain social experiences by joining the child's activities, and thereby turn them into social experiences.  In addition, learning is encouraged through the use of "planned physical space" which takes into account structure, routine, sensory stimuli and other engaging materials.  Specifically, distractions are minimized so that the child can concentrate on the activity at hand.  Through play, the child is encouraged to learn actively by the adult teaching developmentally appropriate skills.

The techniques used by this method to address problematic behaviors are either ignoring or redirecting inappropriate behavior.  In addition, attempts are made to increase the individual's repertoire of alternative, acceptable behaviors.  Existing behaviors are not targeted for decrease.  Occasionally, the child may be removed from the setting; however, it is not clear from the literature which situation or behavior calls for removal.  Behaviors that are considered maladaptive are handled based on the developmental or emotional meaning of the behavior.[3]  It is unclear exactly how injurious or destructive behaviors are handled other than the application of time-out or redirection procedures.

## What evidence do the practitioners have that this really works?

Although the Playschool model has been described often in the literature on early intervention, it was extremely difficult to find any research data on this method.  After a comprehensive database search, I netted four articles.[1,4,5,6*]  On closer inspection, it appears as if the children involved in the earlier studies were included in the 1991 study, which looks at outcome data for seventy-six children

---

*Rogers wrote many more articles on early intervention; however, in this section we included only those articles which were highly relevant to the Playschool model.

from 1981 to 1991, forty-nine of whom had autism. Because these children's data have been summarized by the 1991 article through reviewing their charts from 1981, I will discuss the study as presented in the 1991 article (the 1989 article reported on thirty-one of those forty-nine children with autism).

Rogers et al. report that children with autism made statistically significant gains on cognitive, language, fine and gross motor, and social and emotional measures after six to nine months of participation in the Playschool program. This study used a variety of tests including IQ, the Childhood Autism Rating Scale (CARS), the Early Intervention Developmental Profile and Preschool Profile (EIPPP) and a variety of language and communication scales. A large number of rating measures for one study is promising; unfortunately, the EIPPP was rated by the classroom teacher, who is an inappropriate person to be carrying out the assessment, given her interest in seeing improvement. Although the administrators of the CARS and Developmental Profile scales were not familiar with the expected outcome (hypothesis) of the study, we do not have that assurance in terms of those administering the IQ and Language tests. In addition, the testing was not sufficiently standardized, with many children completing a variety of IQ and language tests. The authors address the IQ standardization issue by creating a standardized score which takes the child's mental age and divides it by the chronological age. However, the lack of standardization is still not ideal as these circumstances open the door to possible influences (also called experimental confounds or bias) that may make the data meaningless.

Another problem with this between-within subject design is the comparison group. These researchers compare children with autism to children with a variety of behavioral and non-autistic developmental disorders. This may have been important for the researchers' purposes; however, it is irrelevant when it comes to determining the efficacy of one autism treatment protocol over another (which is important for our purpose).  Put simply, these studies lack an appropriate control group; therefore, the design is inadequate for examining outcome data. Rogers (1998) recognizes the lack of a control group as being problematic when she states:  "The two models [The Denver Playschool and LEAP] await the application of methodologies involving control groups of matched children, random assignment, blind raters, numerous outcome measures, and long-term follow-up before the effectiveness of the models can be evaluated according to the EST [Empirically Supported Treatments] criteria."[7]

In order to address the issue of an inadequate control group, the researchers use prediction analysis which is designed to take into account the concept that the children are improving based on the treatment and not simply due to maturation. Based on this analysis, they would have expected the children to develop only seven months of progress in a nineteen-month period.  However, the children with autism actually gained seventeen months of language in the nineteen-month period, at which point the gains stabilized but did not increase.  Although this is interesting and certainly suggests that this method is better than doing nothing, the important question remains whether the Playschool model is better than other treatment methods for children with autism.   In other words, could children with autism have actually surpassed their typically developing peers with early intensive intervention rather than lagged slightly behind, thereby, narrowing but never closing the gap?  The latter point is what Rogers et al. (1991) suggest.

An additional concern regards the individual progress of those children with autism in the study.  Since only the *average* (mean) scores of the group of children with autism were presented, we have no way to check whether some children gained significantly, relative to others who did not.  It would be interesting to see whether a subset of the children with milder autism improved at a greater rate than those more severely impacted.  For that, we would need each subject's pre and post scores which, unfortunately, were not presented in the 1991 or the 1987 Rogers et al. studies.

## What does the therapy actually look like?

The Playschool curriculum is delivered in a classroom setting, with six to twelve children, one teacher and two aides, although the Playschool Outreach Project took place in five special education classrooms in Colorado, in which there was at least one child with autism. No other information regarding the composition of these classrooms is provided in the literature on the Playschool method of autism intervention. While the articles discuss the general components of the curriculum that is taught, there is insufficient information on the specific content and I was unable to locate a published manual which lays out the treatment protocol in sufficient detail. It is known that some of the children were also provided with one-on-one psychotherapy sessions using play techniques. Although there is some variation, the Playschool is described as involving four and one-half (4 1/2) hours per day, twelve months per year.[8] In the Rogers et al. (1991) study, the average time spent by children at the Playschool was eighteen months.

## What else do I think?

Based on the information provided, it is difficult to determine exactly what the intervention at the Playschool looks like. The program is implemented in a classroom setting utilizing a structured environment and routine; however, it is unspecified as to how, precisely, this is accomplished. The researchers write, "the whole environment operated as an ego structure that regulates, mediates, selects, focuses, and organizes sensory stimulation for the children to maximize learning."[9] Unfortunately, it does not state how these goals are accomplished or how this environment maximizes learning. Equally unclear is the content of the curriculum. The basis for all teaching apparently was done through play; however, no more information than this is provided. It is not stated what the children learn through play, or what kinds of play tasks occur. The lack of clarity surrounding the procedures used makes it a difficult model to evaluate and replicate. In addition, reported results from the study are confusing and inconsistent due to the type of measures used and their lack of standardization. As a result, it is difficult to assess the significance of the observed changes. The intervention seems like a "hodgepodge" of approaches, some of which are conflicting, i.e., a child-led developmental approach combined with non-specific behavioral approaches. Finally, these researchers are sympathetic to the psychiatric approach to autism intervention which has *not* been demonstrated to be effective for children with autism. They state: "...there has been a strong tendency in the intervention field to eschew the 'psychiatric' approach. Unfortunately, this may have also led to relative neglect of sound treatment strategies for addressing the social, emotional, communicative, and ego deficiencies of children with Pervasive Developmental Disorders."[10] Unfortunately, these researchers do not present any data or evidence for the *sound* psychiatric treatment strategies to which they refer. In my view, that's a serious problem.

## Would I try it on my child?

Based on the data that has been collected from the Playschool autism intervention program, if my child were of preschool age, I would not put her into the Playschool preschool program. Although my personal philosophy would very much like to see a child-led approach be successful for autistic children, the studies published to date simply provide no evidence that this treatment program is effective for children with autism. Therefore, I would not have my child participate in the Playschool autism intervention program.

# What kind of study would I like to see the Colorado Health Sciences researchers do?

In order to be able to adequately assess the Colorado Health Sciences "Playschool" program as an effective intervention for children with autism, there needs to be improvements to the methodology used in their outcome studies. Although they published a study which describes how important it is to train teams to implement the program model,[1] there does not appear to be a strict treatment protocol that all practitioners must follow. Increasing the quality (or fidelity) of the treatment through a more explicit methodology, will increase the strength of the conclusions that can be made about the program based on evidence.

Currently, the available assessment of the Playschool program has insufficient controls to objectively make conclusions regarding its efficacy. What I would consider to be the essential components of future research done on the Playschool program would be: a randomly assigned control and experimental group; valid and reliable assessment measures; independently diagnosed subjects with autism; independent assessment of valid dependent measures; results based on standardized calculations, rather than a developmental rate, and an evaluation of the statistical and clinical significance of the results. It would be more valuable to have all of these components present in one outcome study, rather than several studies using only some of these important research requirements. To date, it is impossible to conclude that the Playschool program has beneficial effects for individuals with autism, because in the existing studies, the lack of control prevents the results from being attributed to the intervention alone. Additionally, further comparative research is required to assess whether the Playschool approach is as effective as current, evidence-based alternatives.

## Who else recommends for or against The Playschool as a method for the treatment of autism?

As compared to many other methods, there has been little attention paid to the Playschool program by parents or professionals, probably because this model has not been adopted on a broad basis.  Consequently, there are no reputable organizations taking a stand either way regarding the program.  That said, it is important to understand that the underlying philosophy of the Playschool  is treatment through play.  To see what many organizations have said about the lack of science  behind the role of "play" in the treatment of children with autism, please refer to the section in this book on the DIR "Floor-Time" model.

## So you're still on the horns of a dilemma?

I would like to leave you with a thought to ponder.  This treatment model has been around since 1981.  We are now twenty-five years on, and there has not been a single replication of this model using a between-subject design.  Rogers recommended that a controlled study be done on this treatment model back in 1998.  We are still waiting.  As your child has only one chance to have effective early intensive treatment, and the Denver Playschool model has not been measured against other intensive treatment methods with better outcome data, please understand that choosing this method — exclusively — will block more effective early intensive treatment options. Consequently, in my opinion, you would be engaging in experimentation with your child.

## What's the bottom line?

Based on the scientific research to date, there is not enough evidence to conclude that the Playschool autism intervention method is effective in substantively improving the condition of autism.

## Endnotes for Playschool

[1]Rogers, S., H.C. Lewis, and K. Reis. 1987. "An Effective Procedure for Training Early Special Education Teams." *Journal of the Division for Early Childhood,* Vol. 11, No. 2, pp. 180-188.

[2]Weiss, R. 1981. "INREAL intervention for language handicapped and bilingual children." *Journal of the Division of Early Childhood*, Vol. 4, pp. 40-51.

[3]Rogers, S., H.C. Lewis and K. Reis, (see n. 1 above), p. 82.

[4]Rogers, S., et al. 1986. "An approach for enhancing the symbolic, communicative, and interpersonal function of young children with autism or severe emotional handicaps." *Journal of the Division of Early Childhood*, Vol. 10, No. 2, pp. 135-45.

[5]Rogers, S.J. 1989. "An Effective Day Treatment Model for Young Children With Pervasive Developmental Disorders." *The American Academy of Child and Adolescent Psychiatry,* Vol. 28, No. 2, pp. 207-214.

[6]Rogers, S.J., and D.L. DiLalla. 1991. "A Comparative Study of the Effects of a Developmentally Based Instructional Model on Young Children with Autism and Young children with Other Disorders of Behavior and Development." *Topics in Early Childhood Special Education,* Vol. 11, No. 2, pp. 29-47.

[7]Rogers, S.J. 1998. "Empirically Supported Comprehensive Treatments for Young Children with Autism." *Journal of Clinical Child Psychology,* Vol. 27, No. 2, pp. 168-179.

[8]Rogers, S.J., H.C. Lewis and K. Reis, (see n. 1 above), p. 208.

[9]Rogers, S.J., H.C. Lewis, and K Reis, (see n. 1 above), p. 208.

[10]Rogers, S.J., H.C. Lewis, and K. Reis, (see n. 1 above), p. 213.

# Other School-based Therapies: Giant Steps

## What is Giant Steps?

The Giant Steps approach to autism intervention is based on a program developed in Montreal by Berringer in 1981. Subsequently, a Giant Steps school opened in St. Louis. The program develops Individual Education Plans (IEPs) for each child, which utilize a variety of therapies. The Giant Steps practitioners describe their mix of therapies as follows: The child receives, "speech therapy, occupational therapy, music therapy, play therapy/social communication, academic enrichment, acquired daily living skills, and a nutritional component."[1] The proponents of the Giant Steps-St. Louis model[*] describe it as an 'holistic' approach which uses multiple disciplines to address all the components that they determine to be relevant for the individual with autism. Kim and colleagues (1998), provide a sample of this cross-disciplinary programming, where, for example, if a child is working on letter recognition, the occupational therapist will expose the child to letters of different textures, the music therapist will introduce a musical exercise that uses letters, and the speech/language pathologist will engage the child in a language exercise that is related to teaching letters.

Another part of the Giant Steps autism intervention curriculum involves the use of what their therapists term "invitational equipment." Therapists encourage the student to use a particular piece of equipment by making it exciting. They explain these enticements, or invitations, as a way to allow the students to "reduce avoidance behaviors ... at their own rate," and to expose these students to "exploration of objects and activities in a nonthreatening way."[2] The third component of the Giant Steps program is to develop consistency between the

---

[*]We focus on the St. Louis program because the Montreal program has no publications based on the Montreal site.

school and home because this continuity is thought to maximize the child's progress. The Giant Steps therapists act as a liaison between both the school "shadow" (classroom aide) and the parents regarding specific behaviors or situations that arise. The philosophy of Giant Steps is to ultimately integrate the child into the neighborhood school. The classroom shadow provides information to the therapists at Giant Steps on how to adapt the child's program so it is consistent with the neighborhood school curriculum.

## What evidence do the practitioners have that this really works?

Unfortunately, there is no published research showing whether the Giant Steps program is actually effective or not for its participants. There is a detailed description of the program published in the *Focus on Autism and other Developmental Disabilities* (1998), but no systematically collected outcome data. In the article describing the Giant Steps — St. Louis program, the authors state: "The purpose of this article is to describe the Giant Steps — St. Louis program by presenting data collected during its first year of evaluation."[3] The description of the Giant Steps — St. Louis program is detailed; however, there is no meaningful data collected on whether the program is effective. The authors themselves state this to be the case as well: "However, the effectiveness of the program is yet to be proved. An evaluation examining child outcomes, family satisfaction and cost-effectiveness will provide additional information on the efficacy of this new program."[4] It is notable that the researchers formally admit that at this point they have no data regarding effectiveness. I first did a comprehensive database search in late 1998 and found only one descriptive article on this program. My latest database search was done in 2006 and there is still no additional data published on Giant Steps.*

*The database searches included Psychological Abstracts (PsycINFO), Medical Abstracts (MEDLINE), Educational Abstracts (ERIC) and the Cochrane Data-bases of Systematic Reviews (CDSR).

## What does the therapy actually look like?

Typically, a child will be in a Giant Steps program for half the day and in his neighborhood school for the remaining half. While at the Giant Steps program, the child may attend a general class for half an hour where the child works on a variety of typical school tasks such as spelling, punctuation or reviewing a schedule. The next three hours are spent participating in a variety of therapy sessions. These sessions typically include music therapy, several short sensory integration therapy sessions, an academic session and an occupational therapy/speech therapy session with another child and two therapists. Lunchtime and the afternoon may be spent with a shadow teacher or aide at the child's local school. While at school, the Giant Steps shadow adapts and modifies the curriculum where necessary and encourages peer interaction and friendships.

## What else do I think?

The abstract of the article on Giant Steps — St. Louis indicates that it will present, "data collected during its first year of evaluation."[5] As it turns out, this so-called data consists of quotes taken from the director of the program and from members of the board of directors from an interview with an unidentified individual. It also includes a single case study, which merely outlines the daily routine of one participant of the program. There is no information in the article regarding the efficacy of this treatment intervention for any individual with autism. In addition, this article was written seven years ago, yet no peer reviewed journal article presenting any data on the effectiveness of the program has been published since.

From the original article on the Giant Steps program, it is unclear how therapists teach academic deficits or address behavioral excesses. In addition, the article contains no information to indicate how or even *if* the therapists or aide evaluate the effects of the intervention, if any, on the child. There is mention in the article about which disciplines are employed (such as sensory integration and speech and language); however, there appears to be no explanation regarding *why* these disciplines are relevant and how they are applied. For example, the authors mention the use of a "nutritional component" to the IEP's; however, the only mention of an intervention for expanding a child's diet is "to expose the child to different food choices across school activities and at home."[6] The theories behind many of the anecdotal "interventions" chosen by Giant Steps appear quite weak and are unsupported by the data. Not only is there no evidence of the effectiveness of treatment outcome, there is no reason to believe that the treatment will be effective in ameliorating autism.

In short, I am unable to conclude that Giant Steps is a viable treatment option for individuals with autism because there is insufficient data to show that the curriculum is effective for children with autism. Individualized therapy is only as good as the method upon which it is based, and unfortunately, Giant Steps uses many therapies that are not scientifically substantiated such as music therapy, sensory integration therapy, speech therapy or play therapy. Despite this lack of evidence, Giant Steps relies heavily upon these therapies.

## Would I enroll my child in a Giant Steps program?

I would not enroll my child in a Giant Steps program because they have not shown *any* evidence that their school is effective. However, there are many aspects of their program that do appeal to me intuitively. For example, the fact that they try to prepare the child to integrate into his local school and target many different areas of deficit, such as peer interaction and classroom skills, is positive; however, good intentions are not sufficient. I would need to see a rigorous study that provides evidence of the effectiveness of the Giant Steps program before considering it for my child.

## What kind of study would I like to see the Giant Steps people do?

If the Giant Steps curriculum is to be considered a legitimate educational option for children with autism, I would need to see a study conducted which incorporates the following components: first, every child in the study would need to be diagnosed with autistic disorder or Pervasive Developmental Disorder Not Otherwise Specified (PDD-NOS). Next, there would need to be an experimental and a control group; the control group could be children with autism in the public school system and/or children using another well-settled type of therapy. In addition, I would like to see at least twenty children per experimental condition, each child tested on at least two widely-used, commonly-accepted autism measurements, before and after the Giant Steps intervention. Moreover, I would require that the researchers who administer the pre and post tests to the autistic children be uninformed as to which children are in the Giant Steps program and which are in the control group. Furthermore, the children in the control group would need to receive the same amount of one-on-one time as the children in the Giant Steps program. All the children in the public school setting would need to have a full-time aide trained in the other methods that were being compared.

Upon completion of the study, if the children enrolled in the Giant Steps program fare better than the children in the public school system, with full-time support, then we would know that the Giant Steps program is, indeed, superior to the public education system for children with autism. The next step would be for the Giant Steps practitioners to test their intervention model against the other research-oriented schools and home-based intensive intervention models designed for children of autism.

## Does anyone recommend for or against Giant Steps as a method for the treatment of autism?

Due to the lack of popularity of this type of school and the lack of publications generated by this group, there has not been much interest amongst the autism community. Therefore, researchers preparing clinical guidelines for the treatment of autism, such as the New York State Department of Health Report on Autism Treatment[7] have not included Giant Steps in their analyses. Although Giant Steps was not evaluated by the New York Report, various components that comprise the Giant Steps curriculum were. The New York Report evaluated music therapy, play therapy and sensory integration therapy and recommended against these therapies as treatments for autism.[7]

## So you're still on the horns of a dilemma?

If the lack of outcome data doesn't dissuade you from enrolling your child in a Giant Steps program, please understand that without augmenting your child's program with a well-settled treatment program, you may be completely wasting your child's valuable developmental window.

## What's the bottom line?

Based on the scientific research to date, there is no evidence that Giant Steps has an effective school-based curriculum which improves any of the symptoms of autism in children.

## Endnotes for Giant Steps

[1]Kim, S., L. Richardson, G. Yard, M. Cleveland and K. Keller. 1998. "Giant Steps – St. Louis: An Alternative Intervention Model for Children with Autism." *Focus on Autism and Other Developmental Disabilities,* Vol. 13, No. 2, pp. 101-107.

[2]Kim, S., L. Richardson, G. Yard, M. Cleveland and K. Keller, (see n. 1 above), p. 103.

[3]Kim, S., L. Richardson, G. Yard, M. Cleveland and K. Keller, (see n. 1 above), p. 101.

[4]Kim, S., L. Richardson, G. Yard, M. Cleveland and K. Keller, (see n. 1 above), p. 106.

[5]Kim, S., L. Richardson, G. Yard, M. Cleveland and K. Keller, (see n. 3 above), p. 101.

[6]Kim, S., L. Richardson, G. Yard, M. Cleveland and K. Keller, (see n. 2 above), p. 103.

[7]Guralnick, M., ed. 1999. *Clinical Practice Guideline: Report of the Recommendations. Autism/Pervasive Developmental Disorders, Assessment and Intervention for Young Children* (age 0-3 years). Albany (NY): New York State Department of Health, pp. IV-15 to 21, IV-14.

# Other School-based Therapies: Daily Life Therapy/The Higashi School

## What is Daily Life Therapy?

Daily Life Therapy (DLT) is an educational model which originated in Japan. It is based upon the method pioneered by Dr. Kiyo Kitahara.  The model is school-based and integrates students with autism and their typically developing peers.  Quill, et al. (1989) describe the following five principles which underline the therapy: 1) physical exercise; 2) an art-based curriculum (music, art and movement components); 3)  group instruction; 4) learning through imitation, and 5) highly structured routines.

The Daily Life Therapy model uses vigorous physical exercise to address stereotypic and undesirable behaviors.  Proponents of this approach believe that children with autism have high levels of beta-endorphins (a neurotransmitter that blocks pain and boosts the immune system), due to being in states of chronic hyper-arousal.  They claim that intense physical exercise results in the natural release of these beta-endorphins, which has a positive impact on behavior.[1]  A second component of DLT is a curriculum which is largely based on different art forms, which include the above-mentioned music, art and movement.  The rationale behind this curricular content is to develop the child's strengths, to give children the opportunity to express themselves and to develop self-esteem.[2]

Using the Daily Life Therapy model, learning is taught through gross-motor  and visual-motor imitation, and verbal  imitation.[3]  The Daily Life Therapy in Japan integrates autistic peers and uses peer models to facilitate imitation;  however, this component of the program is not available in the Daily Life Therapy school in Boston.  Consequently, the Boston Higashi School is a segregated setting.

## What evidence do the practitioners have that this really works?

Although we netted several articles which discuss the DLT method, there were only three articles devoted solely to this method and only one study with outcome data which is based on the Boston Higashi school.  There are currently no studies published on the Japanese DLT schools.  The Boston study[4] is an observational study with no pre and post measures taken on children in the study.  In addition, this study lacks a control group.  Without these measures or a control group, there is no way to conclude that the improvements purportedly made by the subjects were a result of the treatment.  An additional weakness of the study is that only six children participated and there were no IQ scores available for these children prior to attending the school. Furthermore, by the end of the observational study, only three of the original six children remained in the study.  Unfortunately, the significance of such a small number of children in the study becomes readily apparent when analyzing the results.  Data from the study demonstrate that one of the children's  appropriate responses actually *decreased* during intervention.  Because of the small sample size, we could mistakenly conclude that there was approximately a seventeen percent (16.67%) decrease in appropriate responses over the course of the therapy.   Also, while it appears that some improvement occurred in attending and with inappropriate responding amongst the children in the study, no significance values ("p value") are provided to determine the chances that these results did not, in fact, happen by chance.  Without these "significance" scores, it is difficult to conclude that meaningful changes occurred with these children via Daily Life Therapy.  In short, there are so many flaws in the design of this study, that I can make *no* conclusions whatsoever regarding the efficacy of Daily Life Therapy.

## What else do I think?

As mentioned above, the results of the study indicate that there was no improvement made in the participants' measure of "appropriate responding," and that one subject actually decreased in level of appropriate responses. Larkin and Gurry (1998) address the significance of this issue well in their discussion of DLT. In fact, they point out that while some progress was noted in behavioral issues, "the lack of progress in Appropriate Responses is very important."[5] They describe that the target students, "appeared not to learn to follow specific directions or to comprehend what the teacher was asking them to do."[6] While students may be behaving and attending more appropriately, it must be established what they are learning in regard to academics, language and communication skills. Larkin and Gurry (1998) describe the early curriculum as "nurturing," and they speculate that the reason for seeing no progress in appropriate responses may be that there are few demands placed on the youngest students. In other words, Larkin and Gurry suggest that due to a lack of emphasis on appropriate responses, there has been no progress in this area.

## What does the therapy actually look like?

Group instruction is provided in a classroom setting, with classroom sizes ranging from six to ten students. The student-to-teacher ratio is, on average, eight students to one teacher (8:1). The group of students is viewed as a whole and it is *group* achievement which is viewed as being paramount. Redirection is used exclusively to maintain the unity of the group.[7] Finally, independence is fostered through strict daily classroom routines in art, music and movement. The entire day is on a schedule and the beginning of each new activity is preceded by some type of routine, such as an imitation routine using physical exercise.

## Would I try it on my child?

Based on the research to date, very little can be concluded about the efficacy of Daily Life Therapy. The lack of data from the Japanese school forces parents to evaluate the therapy based solely on the single study of the Boston Higashi school in Massachusetts, which was established in 1987. I would not enroll my child in the Higashi school simply because the data is inconclusive. More research is required before it can be considered as a viable treatment option. However, some of the ideas of the Japanese Higashi curriculum such as: 1) physical exercise to decrease stereotypic behavior; 2) peer interaction; 3) imitation skills, and 4) a highly structured environment are compelling. Taken alone, there is some (although not comprehensive) evidence that the four elements in the Higashi curriculum listed above may be important for children with autism. Another reason I would not be inclined to put my child in this school is the lack of emphasis on teaching children with autism academic and functional skills. Although "attending" behavior and a decrease in inappropriate behavior are important, the reason for their importance is to have the child's deficiencies appropriately addressed, preventing anti-learning behaviors from blocking progress.

## What kind of study would I like to see the Higashi School do?

If the Higashi School is to be considered a legitimate educational option for children with autism, I would need to see strong data from a study which has, at minimum, a hypothesis stating that those children who participate in the Higashi School over the period of a year are expected to show a decrease in the symptoms associated with autism (based on commonly-accepted, rigorously-tested measures for autism). In addition, I would like to see a control group consisting of autistic children in the public school system, thereby creating a well-controlled study with at least twenty children per experimental condition in the study.

Furthermore, several widely-used, commonly-accepted autism measurements need to be administered to each child, before and after the treatment. Moreover, the researchers giving the autistic children the pre and post measure for autism must not know which children are in the Higashi School and which are in the control group (the children not enrolled in the Higashi school). Another important criterion for the study is that all the children in the experimental group should be enrolled in the *same* Higashi school.

Upon completion of the study, if the children in the Higashi School fair better than the children in the public school system, then we would know that the Higashi School is indeed a viable alternative to the public education system for children with autism. The next step would be for the Higashi School to test its intervention model against the other specialty school programs and home-based intensive behavioral intervention models designed for children of autism.

### Who else recommends for or against Daily Life Therapy as a method for the treatment of autism?

This innovative model gained popularity when it was introduced to the U.S. in 1987. The autism treatment model did not flourish in North America; therefore, the lack of interest did not motivate the international autism research community to further study this school. Consequently, we could not find clinical practice guidelines or other evaluations that address the efficacy of the Higashi School model.

### So you're still on the horns of a dilemma?

The Higashi model is not an option for most parents due to the small number of schools adopting this model; however, if you do live near one of the few sites that offer this program and would like to enroll your child, I would suggest that you consider the fact that due to the lack of data showing that this method is effective, you may want to augment your child's treatment with a well-settled treatment program so that your child will progress at least when *not* at school.

## What's the bottom line?

Based on the scientific research to date, there is insufficient evidence that Daily Life Therapy has an effective curriculum for decreasing the symptoms associated with the condition of autism in children.

## Endnotes for the Higashi School/Daily Life Therapy

[1]Quill, K., S. Gurry, and A. Larkin. 1989. "Daily Life Therapy: A Japanese Model for Educating Children With Autism." *Journal of Autism and Developmental Disorders,* Vol. 19, No. 4, pp. 625-635.

[2]Quill, K., S. Gurry, and A. Larkin, (see n. 1 above), p. 633.

[3]Quill, K., S. Gurry, and A. Larkin, (see n. 1 above), p. 631.

[4]Larkin, A.S., and S. Gurry. 1998. "Brief Report:  Progress Reported in Three Children With Autism Using Daily Life Therapy." *Journal of Autism and Developmental Disorders,* Vol. 28, No. 4, pp. 339-342.

[5]Larkin, A.S., and S. Gurry, (see n. 4 above), p. 341.

[6]Larkin, A.S., and S. Gurry, (see n. 4 above), p. 341.

[7]Quill, K., S. Gurry, and A. Larkin, (see n. 1 above).

# Other School-Based Therapies:  The Walden Preschool

## What is the Walden Preschool?

Originally established in 1985, the Walden Preschool offers a full-time classroom integrating children with autism into a group with their typically developing peers. The Walden Preschool is based on the Toddler Center Model, a day care for typical children.  The philosophy of the school is one of integration, with a focus on incidental teaching (unstructured and opportunistic) to facilitate language and social interaction. The curriculum is broken down according to first and second year goals. The goals within the first year are to facilitate the following objectives: social responsivity in the child towards teachers, materials and activities; verbal objectives such as choice-making and natural language consequences; play and daily living skills.[1] The second year format focuses on peer social interaction and kindergarten readiness.[2]  To achieve the above goals set out in the curriculum, teachers use incidental techniques (natural learning), an engineered setting (where the classroom is set up in a way that fosters learning particular skills) and child-preferred activities and materials (to entice the child to use certain materials). The environment is described as a "free-choice" classroom in which teachers must successfully "market" materials and activities to the children.[3] The student to teacher ratio is 3:1 (three children to one adult).

There are generally fifteen to eighteen children per class in this program, seven students with autism and eight to eleven typical peers. The instruction style is child-led with respect to learning, with the exception of some direct instruction to teach social interaction skills to both typically developing and autistic students. No student undergoes compliance training to avoid inadvertently decreasing spontaneous initiations between student and teacher. Behavior problems are addressed proactively by attempts at engineering the environment, the use of child-preferred activities and materials, limiting the classroom rules, minimizing "down time," and teaching replacement behaviors. The belief is that increasing "fun" decreases behavior problems.[4]  Once maladaptive behaviors occur, the authors explain that natural and logical consequences are used in response.  The Walden Preschool also claims to use only so-called "positive" behavior strategies, although they also describe the use of time-out procedures.  On rare occasions, a student may require an individualized behavior management procedure. However, they claim that behavior management procedures are generally avoided at the Walden Preschool.  Since the establishment of the original Walden Preschool and Toddler Programs, there have been some modifications to the model.  These will be discussed in the evidence section below.

## What evidence do the practitioners have that this really works?

There is currently no evidence that the original Walden Program is an effective intervention for children with autism. The only available information regarding outcomes of students at Walden are provided in book chapters[5,6] describing preschool programs for individuals with autism, rather than in peer-reviewed journal articles. The original data reports that the rate of verbalization for children with autism increased from four to thirteen percent (4 – 13%). Rates of peer interactions increased in six out of fourteen students with autism; however, it is unspecified how much increase was observed. Unfortunately, no trial-by-trial data is taken in the classroom. Assessments are based only on time samples on videotape. The nature and quality of language and interaction changes observed is unclear. It is unreported whether or not these changes are statistically significant, or if they could have been achieved simply by two years of maturation alone. Also, peer interaction changes were assessed using the indirect measure of how many times students with autism were approached by their typical peers. This assessment might not be a valid measure of gain in social interaction but, rather, merely measure the gains made by typical students in approaching their autistic counterparts.

More updated programs describe multiple zones (teaching stations) with a teacher in charge of each zone, rotating from zone to zone every fifteen minutes. The idea behind this setup is to increase opportunities for incidental teaching,[7] which is a significant component of the Walden philosophy. In addition, the newer rendition of the Walden School model provides one-on-one teaching pullout sessions in a different room. Although the original Walden model used incidental teaching exclusively, the Children's Toddler School (the CTS Program based in San Diego) incorporates discrete trial training (a highly structured behavioral teaching technique). This might be a much better model for the child, as it introduces discrete trial training into the CTS Program; however, this no longer qualifies as a partial replication of the original Walden program, but rather, a significant departure in philosophy and technique. In fact, the Stahmer et al.[8] model uses a large variety of techniques, including incidental teaching, pivotal response training, discrete trial training, structured teaching, and Floor-Time.[9]

The results of the Stahmer et al. study now reflect a melange of techniques, some of which have no evidence that they are, in any way, effective. For our purposes, the results of this quasi-experimental design are unfortunate because they might lead some parents to adopt a basketful of techniques, ninety-five percent of which may be ineffective. In my opinion, these researchers have done a disservice, as they have now further confused the question of efficacy in autism treatment. In addition, two children in the study received additional in-home therapy, and one of those children received ten hours of discrete trial training per week (which is highly effective). Unfortunately, the results of the study are all done by comparing the mean scores at entry with the mean scores at exit. Therefore, we have no idea whether a few children pulled up to the mean considerably, or whether all the children contributed almost equally to the scores. The statistics presented suggest that a few children were responsible for a higher post mean score.* Also, available publications give no indication whether the gains were due to discrete trial training, Floor-Time, pivotal response training, incidental teaching, or structured teaching. The researchers agree when they state: "Given that this program contains several elements (i.e., inclusive classroom, special skills training, parent training and support), it is not possible to determine which components were responsible or necessary for the children's progress."[10] The authors continue: "In all probability, the combination of these three elements contributed to the children's process."[11] This claim is one for which they have no support and which is not substantiated by science.

## What does the therapy actually look like?

The original Walden Preschool classroom operates out of Emory University, as part of the Emory Autism Resource Center. It is a full-time classroom which is attended year round. All students with autism must receive at least one independent diagnosis before admittance. Teaching occurs using incidental techniques, which are described by McGee, Daly and Jacobs[12] as follows: 1) the natural environment is arranged to attract the child; 2) the child then initiates the teaching experience; 3) the initiation by the child is treated as an opportunity to elaborate by the teacher; 4) the child's expected response is confirmed by the teacher, and 5) the access to the desired material or activity is granted contingent upon the desired response. Teachers are assigned to "zones" (teaching stations) within the classroom, based on activities, and are responsible for engagement and redirection of the students within that teaching station.

---

*The standard deviations are very large particularly when it comes to measuring communication - at intake M = 71.1, (s.d. 13.9) and at exit M = 79.3 (s.d. 17.1).

## Would I try it on my child?

Although my child is far beyond the preschool stage, I would have never put her into a program that uses the Walden Preschool model primarily because these researchers have not provided *any* reliable data whatsoever to show that incidental teaching actually works. In terms of their partial replication, they add everything but the "kitchen sink" to the Walden Preschool and this confounds the data. Simply put, I would not enroll my child in this program because I have no guarantee that most of the techniques used have any data supporting them. Unsupported eclecticism in autism treatment is highly problematic.

## What else do I think?

Inherent in the incidental approach (non-structured, opportunistic teaching) to teaching individuals with autism, is the requirement that the teaching experience be initiated by the child. One of the diagnostic criteria for autistic disorder is a severe deficit in social interaction, which includes social initiations. Despite the greatest effort by teachers, these "initiations" occur on a very infrequent basis, relative to typically developing children. This results in fewer learning experiences for the child afflicted with autism than that of the typical child. In addition to fewer opportunities, the child with autism often requires mass repetitions of information (or practice) in order for knowledge or skill development to occur.

The combination of fewer opportunities to learn and the requirement for greater exposure in order to learn, leads me to suggest that the incidental technique (where every opportunity must be anticipated and acted upon to maximize interaction) may not be intensive enough to maximize the child's development. This is particularly important during the early years of the child's life, when optimal potential for learning exists. While the chapter on the Walden Preschool method claims that research shows incidental teaching maximizes learning in this population, there is actually little peer-reviewed data on incidental learning on children with autism [13,14,15,16,17,18] and that which does exist, works only on very narrow, specific skills, with very few children, and does not control for prior learning histories, which may severely bias upward the purported effectiveness of the technique.  In short, although I applaud the preschool's attempt to include children with autism into a mainstream setting, successful inclusion takes much more work than simply putting the children together and watching the magic happen.

The preschool seems to recognize the need for one-on-one sessions for certain skills; however, these sessions in the original program[19] occur for only a short fifteen minutes at a time, no more than five times per day with an emphasis placed on the importance of learning as a group.

## What kind of study would I like to see the Walden people do?

In order to objectively assess the effectiveness of the Walden program for individuals with autism, it is necessary to have controlled research which determines whether their program is effective in producing significant change (that is not associated with maturation alone), in areas relevant to the diagnostic deficits and excesses associated with the disorder. Once significant change has been demonstrated, the efficacy of the program needs to be compared to the efficacy existing programs that are already effective.  I would need to see evidence that the learning which occurs in the Walden program is the same as, or better than, that which occurs in other treatment programs.  Specifically, instead of confounding the variables by using an eclectic approach, proponents of the Walden School should create an experiment where children are assigned to conditions in which incidental teaching, Floor-Time, pivotal response training, or structured teaching are used exclusively. Then the outcomes between conditions need to be compared.  Unfortunately, I doubt that researchers would be able to find enough parents to agree to have their children in this kind of study, since these methods *do not* represent state-of-the-art inclusion programs for children with autism despite what these researchers claim.[20]

## Who else recommends against the Walden Preschool Model as a method for the treatment of autism?

Although we could not find any reputable organizations that recommend for or against the Walden Preschool, many organizations have come out recommending against many components of the Walden Preschool model described by Stahmer et al. (2004).  For information on recommendations of each particular component in the latest incarnation of the Walden Model, I suggest that you go to the sections in the book which analyze the efficacy of  Floor-Time, Pivotal Response Training, TEACCH, and behavioral treatment.

## So you're still on the horns of a dilemma?

For parents evaluating autism treatment programs, the Walden School presents a difficult challenge, as eclecticism is generally thought of as being a good thing; however, it is crucial to recognize that in the world of autism treatment, there is a program around every corner supposedly offering "state-of-the-art" intervention techniques and it is often difficult to deconstruct baby-sitting from actual autism treatment.  It is important to remember, though, that every moment your child is not engaged in genuine science-based treatment, your child's valuable time is being wasted by perhaps well-meaning adults who may care deeply about children, but simply do not have data to support the treatment techniques they practice and endorse.  In other words, the road to hell is often paved with good intentions.

## What's the bottom line?

Based on the scientific research done to date, there is insufficient evidence to support the claim that either the original Walden Preschool or the updated Children's Toddler School has an effective curriculum for the treatment or education of children with autism.

# Endnotes for Walden Preschool

[1]McGee, G.G., T. Daly, and H.A. Jacobs. 1994. " The Walden Preschool." In S.L. Harris, and J.S. Handleman, eds., *Preschool Education Programs for Children With Autism.*   Austin, TX: Pro-Ed., pp. 127-162.

[2] McGee, G.G., T. Daly, and H.A. Jacobs, (see n. 1 above).

[3]McGee, G.G., T. Daly, and H.A. Jacobs, (see n. 1 above).

[4]McGee, G.G., T. Daly, and H.A. Jacobs, (see n. 1 above).

[5]McGee, G.G., T. Daly, and H.A. Jacobs, (see n. 1 above).

[6]McGee, G.G., Morrier, M. and Daly, T.  2000.  "The Walden Preschool."  In S.L. Harris and J.S. Handleman, eds., *Preschool Educational Programs for Children with Autism.* 2nd ed.  Austin, TX: Pro-Ed., pp. 157-190.

[7]Stahmer, A.C., and B. Ingersoll. 2004. "Inclusive Programming for Toddlers with Autism spectrum disorders:  Outcomes From the Children's Toddler School." *Journal of Positive Behavior Interventions,* Vol. 6, No. 2, pp. 67-82.

[8]Stahmer, A.C., and B. Ingersoll, (see n. 7 above).

[9]Stahmer, A.C., and B. Ingersoll, (see n. 7 above), p. 72.

[10]Stahmer, A.C., and B. Ingersoll, (see n. 7 above), p. 80.

[11]Stahmer, A.C., and B. Ingersoll, (see n. 7 above), p. 80.

[12] McGee, G.G., T. Daly, and H.A. Jacobs, (see n. 1 above).

[13]Farmer-Dougan, V. 1994. "Increasing Requests by Adults with Developmental Disabilities Using Incidental Teaching by Peers." *Journal of Applied Behavior Analysis,* Vol. 27, No. 3, pp.  533-544.

[14]Miranda-Linne, F., and L. Melin. 1992. "Acquisition, Generalization, and Spontaneous Use of Color Adjectives:  A Comparison of Incidental Teaching and Traditional Discrete-Trial Procedures for Children with Autism." *Research in Developmental Disabilities,* Vol. 13, No. 3, pp. 191-210.

[15]McGee, G.G., et al. 1992 " Promoting Reciprocal Interactions via Peer Incidental Teaching." *Journal of Applied Behavior Analysis,* Vol. 25, No. 1, pp. 117-126.

[16]Elliott, R.O. Jr., et al. 1991. "Analog Language Teaching Versus Natural Language Teaching: Generalization and Retention of Language learning for Adults with Autism and Mental Retardation." *Journal of Autism and Developmental Disorders,* Vol. 21, No. 4, pp. 433-447.

[17]McGee, G.G., et al. 1986. "An Extension of Incidental Teaching Procedures to Reading Instruction for Autistic Children." *Journal of Applied Behavior Analysis,* Vol. 19, No. 2, pp. 147-157.

[18]McGee, G.G., et al. 1985. "The Facilitative Effects of Incidental Teaching on Preposition Use by Autistic Children." *Journal of Applied Behavior Analysis,* Vol. 18, No. 1, pp. 17-31.

[19]McGee, G.G., T. Daly, and H.A. Jacob, (see n. 1 above).

[20]McGee, G.G., T. Daly, and H.A. Jacobs, (see n. 1 above), p. 80.

# Child-lead/Parent-facilitated Therapies

Section 1.3

▷ *Floor-Time (Greenspan/Developmental, Individual Difference, Relationship Model – DIR)*

▷ *Options Institute/Son-Rise Program*

▷ *Relationship Development Intervention (RDI)*

▷ *The Learning to Speak Program*

# Child-lead/Parent-facilitated Therapies: Floor-Time

## What is Floor-Time?

Floor-Time (also referred to as the Developmental, Individual Difference, Relationship Model – DIR) is rooted in a developmental approach to autism therapy. However, there are components of the psychodynamic (or Freudian) paradigm involved as well. This model is often referred to as the "Greenspan" method, named after the researcher who developed the treatment model. The philosophy of this approach is to turn everything the child does into a social interaction.[1] Greenspan et al. state: "...the earliest therapeutic goals are to mobilize shared attention, engagement, and intentional back-and-forth signaling. Interactive experiences enable the child to abstract a sense of self and form higher level cognitive and social capacities."[2] When interacting with the child, the parent is instructed to focus on the child's strengths, rather than weaknesses. The ratio is one adult to one child and the teaching style is child-led. As a result, parents are instructed to follow the child's lead and allow the child to guide which activity and interaction will occur. The curriculum follows a four-stage process, designed as follows; Floor-Time I, Attention, Engagement, and Intimacy; Floor-Time II, Two-way Communication; Floor-Time III, Feelings and Ideas; and Floor-Time IV, Logical Thinking. Each component addresses a different developmental issue to be targeted by parents interacting with the child on the floor. The curriculum emphasizes emotions and empathy. Behavior is addressed using a six-step procedure which includes: 1) Small steps; 2) Floor-Time; 3) Solve problems symbolically; 4) Empathize; 5) Create expectations and limits, and 6) The "Golden Rule" (more Floor-Time). This procedure is supposed to be followed for all problematic behaviors in autism, including sleeping, eating, discipline, toilet training, stubbornness and negativity, unusual fear, silly and anxious behavior, self-stimulation, repeating stories repetitively and swearing. Proponents of this method maintain that all behaviors must be accepted, insofar as the model's premise is that parental "acceptance" will teach the child to accept his or her own feelings and, subsequently, build a loving, interactive relationship with the parent.[3]

## What evidence do the practitioners have that this really works?

There is currently no clinically-validated evidence that the Floor-Time intervention is effective for individuals with autism. Currently, there is only anecdotal evidence from case studies which purport that children have benefited from this intervention: unfortunately, there are no controlled scientific studies testing the effectiveness of the Greenspan/DIR method. A comprehensive database search netted nine articles. Most of the articles were descriptive in nature, discussing the developmental perspective underpinning the Floor-Time intervention method. There were no outcome studies with controls that have produced data to support this method of autism therapy. The only difference between literature searches that I did ten years ago and today, is that now there have been case studies published. In fact, Greenspan and Wieder, retrospectively present 200 case studies of children who have undergone this therapy in a book they have published, as well as a report on these children in the *Journal of Developmental and Learning Disorders*.[4]   In addition, Wieder and the Greenspan did a follow-up study on sixteen children, ages twelve through seventeen. However, once again, their reliance on case studies is problematic due to the notorious lack of reliability of case studies, since there are no experimental controls. In their articles and books, proponents of the Greenspan/DIR method make many claims about what they call the "relationship based, affect cueing" approach (which refers to the way we process emotional information), but they offer absolutely no independent evidence that this approach is effective.

Proponents of the Greenspan/DIR approach are particularly critical of the treatment with the most scientific support at this time, and specifically name behavioral autism intervention as being responsible for more stereotyped and more repetitive behavior as the children grow.[5]  In other words, the Greenspan/DIR Model accuses intensive behavioral treatment of *creating* behaviors that are characteristic of autism.  These beliefs contradict existing research, which shows that behavioral approaches can lead to treatment gains in the child with autism.[*]

## What does the therapy actually look like?

Proponents of Greenspan's DIR method propose that parents engage in Floor-Time with their children for twenty to thirty minute periods of uninterrupted time, from six to ten times per day. During this time, the goal is to create social interaction between the parent and child, which can be accomplished if parents, "follow [their] child's lead and play at whatever captures [their] interest;" however, they add that it needs to be done in a way that, "encourages [their] child to interact with [them]."[6]  In order to practically apply this, it is advised that several tools be included to help facilitate the interaction. Parents are instructed in the Floor-Time method to use the "sensory interests" of the child, empathy, and vocal tone to interact with the child. They are also encouraged to adapt to the mood of the child, imitate the child and be "playfully obstructive." Proponents also state that children aim to please by nature, and as a result, if the

---

[*]It is not surprising that proponents of treatments without evidence supporting their efficacy would critique those treatments with overwhelming supporting data;  however these claims further confuse parents who need to know the state of the science  when it comes to autism treatment.  We could accurately characterize the rivalry between DIR and behavioral treatment as one of dueling philosophies.  Unfortunately for proponents of DIR, the field of behavioral treatment wins hands down when it comes to scientific support with data-based evidence produced from controlled studies.  For a review of the behavioral literature, please see the section on behavioral treatment.

child is having difficulties, it is often necessary to lower the expectations placed upon the child.

## What else do I think?

Practitioners of the Floor-Time method mention that, while it may be tempting to work on language skills, color recognition or other age appropriate behavior, they claim such an approach is ultimately not effective, in their view.[7]  Unfortunately, in the case of autism, age-appropriateness is difficult to gauge because these children vary so much.  However, if one waits until the child is ready (which is also difficult to define), the child may never be taught the skills which approach the level of his peers. There is much data in the literature on intensive behavioral treatment that contradicts the "wait and see" philosophy.  Proponents of Greenspan's DIR method also state that it is tempting to want to work on behaviors such as head-banging, throwing tantrums, repetitively opening and closing doors, but they urge that the primary goal of the treatment program is that the child must feel calm and focused.  Unfortunately, it may be critical to intervene and help a self-injurious child as waiting may endanger the child's health.  It could be a health concern if the child engages in self-injurious behaviors without adult intervention to end them.

In addition, the goals of the Floor-Time/DIR program are quite vague and assessed primarily through parental observation. Examples of questions the parent must ask when assessing the child are:  "Can the child calm himself or herself?"; Can the child be warm and loving?"; "Can the child engage in two-way gestural communication, express a lot of subtle emotion, and open and close many circles in a row?"; "Can the child engage in pretend play and or use words to convey intentions or wishes?"; "Can the child connect thoughts logically and hold a conversation for a sustained period of time?" Unfortunately, these are extremely subjective assessments. Parents will often have no point of reference to assess and evaluate information necessary to answer these types of questions. I likely would have answered these questions incorrectly regarding my child when she was young. Parents simply do not have the skill set required to accurately assess their child's behavior and language accurately. I would further note that a large number of professionals in the field of autism do not have these skills either.

Floor-Time/DIR practitioners claim that if parents are distracted or nervous, they will not be successful at helping the child tune in and stay calm, which is their prerequisite for success in the program. Also, parents are cautioned that their own feelings of depression, irritability or anger could well disrupt their child's treatment session. According to the Floor-Time/DIR philosophy, it is essential for parents to act like someone with whom the child would want to play. The above philosophy harkens back to the old Bettleheimian philosophy of blaming the parent if the child is not showing improvement as a result of intervention. Floor-Time/DIR proponents also include parental withdrawal as a factor which can contribute to autistic behavior. This view that parents are, *in any way*, the cause or contributors to autistic behavior simply cannot be countenanced as it is based purely on conjecture with *no* empirical support whatsoever. Greenspan et al. state: "Sally coped with her disappointment in her son by withdrawing from him emotionally... Sally slowly let her emotions thaw. As mother and son both opened up their range of communication, a chemistry evolved between them.[8] In my opinion, "mother withdrawal" is a convenient way of explaining away lack of progress when using the Floor-Time/DIR method (since if no progress is obvious, the blame can be laid at the ground of the internal emotional state of the mother — a very subjective measure). This disclaimer is a common red flag for ineffectual interventions. The "curriculum" (and I use the term loosely) emphasizes the child's strengths and focuses on "social" interactions; however, it is unclear how the skill deficits are overcome using the

Floor-Time/DIR method. Without intervention in these deficit areas, mainstreaming will be a goal that is simply unattainable for most of these children.

There are several flawed assumptions made by Floor-Time/DIR proponents, the most obvious is that by forcing the adult into a situation with the child, it becomes a social interaction.  This idea is particularly problematic with self-stimulatory and ritualistic behavior. The parent may become incorporated by the child as part of the self-stimulatory act or as part of some perseverative routine (such as a memorized play routine that must be followed precisely over and over again); however, this does not necessarily mean that the child is interacting with the parent in a social way.  Through incorporating the parent in a rigid routine, the child may avoid the parent's intrusion and continue to engage in behaviors that are intrinsically asocial or defined as antisocial based on societal norms. Greenspan et al., define adult interaction with an autistic child as interactive: "by drawing your child's motor behavior into interaction you are also making it purposeful rather than self-stimulatory.  Your child is now using his muscles to act or communicate intentionally."[9]  While attempting to make these types of interactions more social, it is quite possible that the adult may inadvertently reinforce harmful perseverative behaviors, thereby increasing their frequency. These perseverative behaviors may have no communicative intent for the child, whatsoever.  Nowhere in the DIR literature do I see these problems acknowledged and addressed.

## Would I try it on my child?

When my child was diagnosed many years ago, I chose this child-led method of treatment because I found the philosophy very compelling and the diagnosing psychiatrist offered this treatment.  Many of the ideas regarding child-development and fostering a sense of the social self were attractive since autism is characterized by social deficits.  Unfortunately, very quickly I learned that well-intentioned philosophy and effectiveness of treatment are completely unrelated. Although the child-led philosophy fit my personality well, I ultimately had to reject this method based on the fact that there was no data supporting its effectiveness; my child was wasting her time and I was wasting my money.

## What kind of study would I like to see Floor-Time/DIR practitioners do?

I would like to see DIR practitioners assess whether or not this particular intervention is effective for individuals with autism. As a result, a *controlled* study with relevant dependent measures such as DSM-IV diagnosis, autism rating scales and IQ testing is required. We would need pretests and post-tests for each child. Behavioral measures would be particularly important here, to assess whether or not the maladaptive behaviors increase or decrease in frequency as a result of this intervention. DIR needs to be compared with existing treatments, to assess whether its results can match the efficacy of other treatments. Unfortunately, this may be difficult to do; in order to create two groups of children who are randomly assigned, all parents must agree to have their child assigned to one or the other group in the study. As most parents have very strong views once they are introduced to the two methods, it is doubtful researchers could find a group of parents who would agree to random assignment. The ethics of random assignment in autism treatment studies are highly questionable, particularly in this case, if the DIR method is to be contrasted with an already well-settled method.

The research would also need to measure how the child's social interactions benefit from this approach. Can the child interact with peers and others in interactions that are meaningful to both, and in ways that the children will encounter in their natural environment and throughout their lives? A major challenge for these researchers will be in *objectively* defining and measuring dependent measures of *subjective* experience, such as emotion, empathy, quality of relationships and the child's acceptance of his or her own and others' emotions. It is understandable why DIR practitioners have no research to support their claims, considering that operationalizing a child's "sense of their own personhood"– the primary goal of this intervention – is near impossible to do in an accurate and reliable way. Unfortunately, until Floor-Time/DIR practitioners agree to offer their method for scientific scrutiny in the form of a controlled experiment, we will not know whether their technique has any value to offer the autism treatment community.

## Who else recommends for or against Floor-Time/DIR as a method for the treatment of autism?

The New York State Department of Health Report (1999) did a comprehensive literature review of the DIR method developed by Greenspan et al. They concluded the following: "...There is currently no adequate scientific evidence (based on controlled studies using generally accepted scientific methodology) that demonstrates the effectiveness of DIR-based interventions for young children with autism. Therefore, the use of these approaches cannot be recommended as a primary intervention method for young children with autism."[10] In addition, The Association for Science in Autism Treatment suggests that professionals need to disclose to those making treatment decisions for the child, the fact that there is no peer-review of this treatment method.[11] Further, Autism-Watch which is affiliated with "Quackwatch" considers this treatment method "Unsettled or Investigational."[12]

## So you're still on the horns of a dilemma?

If you choose this method for your child, you need to understand that the method is purely experimental. I urge you to have your child assessed using traditional psychometric measures by an independent, licensed psychologist prior to treatment and visit the psychologist yearly to gauge whether there is any objective improvement in your child's condition. Understand, however, that you will not know how far your child may have progressed with treatments which are more scientifically substantiated than the Floor-Time/DIR method, as you will have spent valuable time on an unsettled treatment when your child is young and most ready for developmental progress.

## What's the bottom line?

Based on the scientific research to date, there is not enough evidence to conclude that DIR is an effective treatment for children with autism.

## Endnotes for Floor-Time

[1] Greenspan, S.I. 1992. *Infancy and early childhood: The practice of clinical assessment and intervention with emotional and developmental challenges,* Madison, CT: International Universities Press.

[2]Greenspan, S.I., and S. Wieder. 19991. "A functional developmental approach to autism spectrum disorders." *Journal of the Association for Persons with Severe Handicaps*, Vol. 24, No. 3, p. 152.

[3] Greenspan, S.I., S. Wieder, and R. Simons. 1998. *The child with special needs: Encouraging intellectual and emotional growth.* Reading, MA, US: Addison-Wesley/Addison Wesley Longman, Inc.

[4]Greenspan, S.I., and S. Wieder. 1997. "Developmental patterns and outcomes in infants and children with disorders in relating and communicating: A chart Review of 200 cases of children with autistic spectrum diagnoses." *Journal of Developmental and Learning Disorders*, Vol. 1, No. 1, pp. 87-141.

[5]Greenspan, S.I., (see n. 1 above).

[6]Greenspan et al., (see n. 3 above), p. 124.

[7]Greenspan et al., (see n. 3 above), p. 419.

[8]Greenspan et al., (see n. 3 above), p. 364.

[9]Greenspan et al., (see n. 3 above), p. 364.

[10]Guralnick, M. ed. 1999. Clinical practice guideline: Report of the Recommendations. Autism/Pervasive Developmental Disorders, Assessment and Intervention for Young Children (age 0-3 years), Albany (NY): New York State Department of Health, p. IV-58.

[11]The Association for Science in Autism treatment. www,asatonline.org/about_autism/autism_info10.html, (accessed Apr. 18, 2005).

[12]Autism-Watch, www.autism-watch.org, (accessed Apr. 18, 2005).

# Child-lead/Parent-facilitated Therapies: Options Institute/Son-Rise Program

## What is Options?

The Son-Rise program, run at the Options institute in Massachusetts, is designed for individuals with a variety of diagnoses, including Autism and Pervasive Developmental Disorder. The program is home-based and, notably, is implemented by parents and their staff of volunteers. The philosophy of the program is total acceptance of the child (including all behaviors). According to the institute, there is no behavior that is inappropriate; therefore, adults are encouraged to accept all behaviors and try to understand them in the context of the child's world.[1] In order to convey the message of total acceptance and a non-judgmental attitude towards the child, adults are instructed to engage in whichever behavior their child chooses.[2] The ratio of intervention is 1:1 (one adult to one child), and the teaching style is child-led (where the adult follows the child's interest and does not dictate the structure or the content of the interaction). The program philosophy maintains that the child is the best person to guide what learning should occur. No predetermined tasks are taught; what the program attempts to do, instead, is encourage participation and motivation.[3]

## What evidence do the practitioners have that this really works?

There is currently no data to suggest that this intervention is effective. After doing a comprehensive literature search, we netted only two published articles, neither of which presented any outcome data. One article studies family stress among those parents who chose the Son-Rise method for their child and the other described the Son-Rise program itself. In short, there is no data concerning efficacy. The Kaufmans, who are the main proponents of this approach, claim their child recovered from autism via the Options method. They have written about their own experience, and a made-for-television movie was made about their story.  Other than these sources, the institute relies upon the anecdotal reporting of parents who have completed the program. Unfortunately, these reports represent an unspecified number of people, with no objective method of assessment. In addition, the subjective parental reporting has taken place after considerable financial cost on the part of parents which biases the parents' observations because they are heavily invested (emotionally and financially) in the outcome.

When contacted by this author, the institute reported that they have not produced any "statistics" because they have been too busy helping as many children as possible. They reported that the lack of data was due to the time and money that research would involve.[4] While I was informed that they have, "seen radical, if not miraculous results from this approach," their brochure does go on to caution that, "doing a Son-Rise program is no guarantee of any results."[5]

## What does the therapy actually look like?

The Options Institute offers a series of Son-Rise programs from Start-up to "Maximum Impact."  These are available at various teaching centers, including Massachusetts, Illinois, Northern California and Rotterdam.  The program runs from four to five days and offers training to parents on how to understand and teach their children. The approach emphasizes parental involvement. The focus is on parental acceptance of the child and their child's special needs, and on developing a relationship or bond between parent and child. The cost of the intervention varies with the amount of courses and consultation the parent seeks from the institute's staff. The courses range from $1500 – $2000 (USD). Information provided by the Options Institute indicates that parents can spend anywhere from a few hundred dollars to $13,000 USD.  Hours of intervention are unspecified; however, the Institute recommends as many hours as possible. One-to-one intervention at the Institute takes place in a separate room, free from distractions.  The techniques used do not include the use of any physical prompting or guiding of the child. The parent is instructed to take on a non-judgmental attitude and imitate whatever the child does. Apart from this, it is relatively unclear exactly what techniques are employed.

## What else do I think?

The philosophy and the practice of the Son-Rise programs seem somewhat contradictory. While the philosophy emphasizes the acceptance of all behaviors and the rejection of imposing adult priorities upon children, the program proceeds to spend the maximal number of hours possible intervening to teach socialization skills and other new behaviors.[6]  Additionally, Son-Rise literature states that no predetermined tasks are taught; rather, the child is allowed to create the child's own learning situations.[7]  At the same time, the intensive Son-Rise Program teaches parents and others how to determine baselines, observe behaviors and chart progress.[8]  The catalogue also states that parents are taught, "proven educational tools," to facilitate the growth of the child.[9]  This would appear to indicate that recording behavioral change is emphasized, which seems to contradict the philosophy of the program. This is an important point because the Institute contrasts itself with behavioral and Lovaasian interventions (Intensive Behavioral Treatment) by claiming that the Options Institute accepts the children rather than trying to modify them or judge some behaviors as better than others.[10]  If this were true, then what would be the purpose of charting behavioral change?

As is discussed in Section Two, the emphasis on *objective* assessment of progress is stressed within the field of research on treatment outcomes. Without the criterion of objectivity, individuals who have a stake in observing positive results might give biased reports.  This is particularly important with parental reporting, as there is no one with a greater investment in a child than the parents. For researchers who are examining outcomes of interventions for childhood disorders, independent assessment is particularly significant.  It is not difficult to understand that for parents who are desperate for help and respite from the daily challenges of having a child with autism, merely having a professional with whom to consult would likely improve their state of mind. The Options approach seems to emphasize changing the perspective of the parents on their child's disorder. They focus on having the parents view the diagnosis as a gift or special challenge, one that should not be negative, but rather an opportunity. It is likely that helping parents accept the diagnosis of their child and remove their own sense of grief has an effect on how the parent views the child. As a result, it may *seem* as though the child is improving, merely because the parents are feeling better. While this may seem to be a helpful experience for parents, it can also be viewed as inadvertently exploiting their desperation and need for help. Most importantly, the Options philosophy prevents the child from receiving intervention that is effective in helping to achieve important skills which will lead to greater independence.

Finally, the Options website, brochure information and e-mail correspondence received from the Institute, all make a point of contrasting their approach with  Lovaas' intensive behavioral treatment protocol, or other behavioral methodologies. They emphasize the many ways in which their methods are in opposition to the methods employed by Lovaas and applied behavior analysis, despite the efficacy indicated by the large amounts of behavioral research. The catalogue[11] also discourages the use of contradictory interventions, as they can result in confusion for the child. This may steer parents away from interventions that have been proven more effective, toward the Son-Rise program that has not been proven effective. What I find disturbing is the amount of marketing hype that accompanies the information regarding Options (particularly the glossy brochures and video tapes attempting to sell the parent on the method).

## Would I try it on my child?

I would not try this method on my child because proponents of Son-Rise offer no scientific evidence whatsoever that their method works. Although the philosophy of total acceptance may be instinctively appealing to loving parents who are desperate to have their child or toddler protected from the cruel outside world, there is no appeal to me (as a loving parent) in a treatment that may be completely ineffective, and indirectly harmful by replacing my child's chance at receiving evidence-based treatment.

## What kind of study would I like to see the Options proponents do?

First, I would like to see them acknowledge that this population of children deserves the kind of best possible outcome from treatments that only controlled and unbiased research can offer. Next, I would like to see some validation of the claims that are being made. Controlled outcome data on the progress being made by children exposed to this intervention is desperately needed. The Institute should explicitly clarify the methods they are using, so that others can replicate and evaluate the approach. If they are unable to produce outcome data themselves, there may be others willing to do so. However, in order to do this, they need to provide detailed information regarding their procedures.

## Who else recommends for or against Options as a method for the treatment of autism?

One organization that recommends against the "Son-Rise" method is Quackwatch. This organization is on the lookout for treatments with insufficient or no science behind them and has listed the Options method on its dubious treatments roster.[12]

## So you're still on the horns of a dilemma?

In the final analysis, you are in charge of which treatment you use with your child. However, be forewarned that there are no peer-reviewed journal articles reporting data on the effectiveness of Son-Rise/Options. Therefore, if you use this method on your child, you are simply experimenting. Unfortunately, this scientifically unsubstantiated method may be indirectly harmful because it is wasting your child's valuable time when he or she could be receiving treatment that is beneficial and scientifically substantiated.

## What's the bottom line?

Based on the scientific research to date, there is no evidence to conclude that the Son-Rise/Options method is an effective treatment for children with autism.

## Endnotes for Son-Rise/Options Institute

[1]Kaufman, N., and S.L. Kaufman. undated. *The "HEART" of What We Teach*. The Son-Rise Program at The Option Institute. [Catalogue], p. 7.

[2]C. Egan, personal communication, April 14, 2000).

[3]Kaufman, N., and S.L. Kaufman, (see n. 1 above), p. 6.

[4]C. Egan, (see n. 2 above).

[5]Kaufman, N., and S.L. Kaufman, (see n. 1 above), p. 5.

[6]Kaufman, N., and S.L. Kaufman, (see n. 1 above).

[7]Kaufman, N., and S.L. Kaufman, (see n. 1 above), p. 5.

[8]Kaufman, N., and S.L. Kaufman, (see n. 1 above), p. 15.

[9]Kaufman, N., and S.L. Kaufman, (see n. 1 above), p. 15.

[10]Kaufman, N., and S.L. Kaufman, (see n. 9 above), p. 15.

[11]Kaufman, N., and S.L. Kaufman, (see n. 1 above), p. 19.

[12]Kaufman, N., and S.L. Kaufman, (see n. 1 above).

# Child-lead/Parent-facilitated Therapies: Relationship Development Intervention (RDI)

## What is Relationship, Development Intervention Therapy?

Proponents of Relationship, Development Intervention (RDI) characterize autism as a disorder in which the afflicted persons are not purportedly interested in connecting emotionally with other people.[1] This approach attempts to teach people with autism to value interpersonal relationships by enjoying shared experiences, as opposed to interacting simply to attain a preferred object or goal. The pioneer of this method, Dr. Steven Gutstein, describes the approach as "teaching emotional intelligence" rather than teaching children to "fake" conformity by memorizing social scripts.[2] The goal is to teach people with autism to value relationships and thereby increase their quality of life. Proponents of RDI make it clear that this is not a cure for autism, although they suggest that RDI Therapy will establish neural pathways in the area of the brain that regulates emotion and motivation.[3]

## What evidence do the practitioners have that this really works?

Although there are several books authored by Gutstein and Sheely, at this point there is only one peer-reviewed journal article that presents data on the efficacy of RDI.[4] The article has been accepted for publication by *The Journal of Autism and Developmental Disorders*.[*] The one study was a retrospective between-subject

---

[*]*The Journal of Developmental and Behavioral Pediatrics* has published abstract reporting results of an RDI study that looks almost identical to the study that is to be published in the *Journal of Autism and Developmental Disorders*; however, that study is not presented with the abstract.

design with seventeen children having autism spectrum disorder in the treatment group and fourteen children in the control group.  Most of the children in the control group received an unspecified type of behavioral intervention.  The other two children participated in weekly social skills groups. Gutstein reports that the group of children who received RDI Therapy scored better on the Autism Diagnostic Observation Schedule (ADOS) and were more likely to move from special education to regular education classes than the control group.

Although these results sound promising, there were several serious flaws in the study.  The author points to the following limitations: first, the children were a small sample and high functioning without significant cognitive impairment.[5]  In addition, this was a retrospective study and there was neither random assignment nor subject matching.  Aside from the author's critique, there are two other issues that indicate the two groups were different from the outset of the study (prior to the treatment).  The children in the RDI group were: 1) one year younger, and 2) had higher IQs than the control group (an additional twelve points on average).  Finally, and arguably the most substantive flaw in the study, is that there were more children with an Asperger's Syndrome (AS) diagnosis in the RDI group than in the control group.  Unfortunately, the considerable difference between groups at the outset of the study makes a between-subject comparison misleading.

In terms of the pre and post scores for the RDI group of children, it is difficult to discern the actual improvement of each child as individual scores for each child were not presented.[*]  It is difficult to establish whether all the children in the RDI group benefitted, or rather, whether the twenty-nine children with Asperger's Syndrome benefitted tremendously (which raised the mean scores

---

[*]The pre-mean results are compared to the post-mean results rather than a within-subject analysis being conducted to compare each child's pre and post treatment scores.

for the entire RDI group significantly). If, indeed, these result are accurate, then it is crucial that the profile of the children who improve be defined explicitly; unfortunately, in the promotional literature, RDI Therapy is claimed to be of benefit for all people on the autism spectrum.[6] Based on the data presented, however, there is no evidence supporting this claim.

## What does the therapy actually look like?

This is a parent-directed therapy. Parents learn the technique through video-tapes, consultants and books, and then parents conduct approximately nine (9) hours a week of therapy (according to the study and the promotional literature). That said, the promotional literature also describes RDI as a lifestyle that is incorporated into the family.

The program teaches six areas of Relationship Intelligence in which children with autism spectrum disorders are claimed to be deficit. These areas are discussed in some length in Gutstein et al. (2002) where the authors make a case for teaching social competence to adults with Asperger's Syndrome (AS). They argue that therapy can help develop experience-sharing relationships and, thereby, improve the quality of life for people with AS. During RDI Therapy, foundation skills are taught through simple shared interaction. These skills are then built upon with adults guiding the child until such time as the child is competent enough to be moved to peer interaction. Initially, these interactions would take place in distraction-free environments and gradually move to more typical settings. The technique is implemented from the earliest age through turn taking and social games (e.g., peek-a-boo) as a conduit to facilitate the interaction. Gutstein has written several books which describe these interactive cognitive exercises and activities in some depth.[7,8]

## What else do I think?

This is a relatively new therapy which may or may not bear fruit. I find the concept of teaching people afflicted with Asperger's Syndrome to increase their relationship intelligence compelling. I have concerns with the promotional website that claims that RDI will work for all people afflicted with autism spectrum disorder, even those who are severely autistic, non-verbal, and cognitively impaired. The website claims that even non-verbal children will benefit because RDI "dramatically increases children's motivation to communicate and to use meaningful reciprocal language."[9] In addition, RDI is said to "be helpful with a number of problems like 'stimming'..."[10] However, the peer-reviewed article does not present sufficient data which supports these claims. My major concern is that a parent will implement an RDI program with a severely afflicted child, hoping to get the results reported on the website (in the form of testimonials) and thereby, not look at best practices for autism treatment and waste that child's valuable time.

## Would I try it on my child?

There is insufficient data on RDI for me to experiment with this treatment on my child; however, as this is a relatively new treatment, I am very interested in reading and evaluating future studies. Although I am very skeptical about RDI Therapy being effective on young children with autism, or children with autism who are pre-verbal, I am somewhat more hopeful that RDI will be effective for persons with Asperger's Syndrome and, perhaps, people with very high functioning autism. However, until I see some firm evidence to this effect, I would not experiment with my child.

## What kind of study would I like to see proponents of RDI do?

I would like to first see RDI Therapy tested on adolescents and adults with Asperger's Syndome prior to tests conducted on individuals with autism. The study design should be a double-blind (where neither the experimenter, the child or his parents know who is receiving the treatment), between-subject design using random assignment to conditions. Although the RDI researchers do not like IQ testing as a measure for progress, it is still important that they incorporate several of these measures into their studies. Specifically, cognitive measures need to be used in addition to the Autism Diagnostic Observation Schedule, ADOS (which measures play, social interaction, and communication) to offer a preliminary evaluation of the RDI program.

## Who else recommends for or against RDI Therapy as a method for the treatment of autism?

RDI has only recently been introduced into the world of autism treatment as a new alternative. Therefore, there has not been much written that either supports or refutes the method.

## So you're still on the horns of a dilemma?

Since there is insufficient data supporting this method, it is important to understand that using this method on a child essentially amounts to experimentation. That said, as long as effective treatment is being provided to the child and RDI does not interfere with the provision of the primary treatment, the biggest gamble is spending money on a treatment that may not be effective. As the RDI is taught to parents and then administered by the parents to the child, there is a limit to the cost; however, it is important to take into account the energy drain on the parent for a treatment that is not yet shown to be effective.

## What's the bottom line?

Based on the scientific research to date, there is not enough evidence that RDI is an effective treatment for decreasing the symptoms associated with autism.

## Endnotes RDI Therapy

[1]Gutstein, S. E. 2004. "The Effectiveness of Relationship Development Intervention in Remediating Core Deficits of Autism-Spectrum Children. *Journal of Developmental & Behavioral Pediatrics,* Vol. 25, No. 5, p. 375.

[2]Gutstein, S.E., (see n. 1 above), p. 30.

[3]Gutstein, S.E., (see n. 1 above), p. 30.

[4]Gutstein, S., and R. Sheely. 2002. *Relationship Development Intervention Activities for Young Children.* London: Jessica Kingsley Publications.

[5]Gutstein, S., and R. Sheely, (see n. 4 above), p. 9.

[6]Gustein, S., and R. Sheely. *Introductory Guide for Parents, Going to the Heart of Autism, Asperger's Syndrome & Pervasive Development Disorder,* www.rdiconnect.com (accessed Oct. 25, 2005).

[7]Gutstein, S., and R. Sheely. 2002a. *Relationship Development Intervention with Young Children, Social and Emotional Development Activities for Asperger Syndrome, Autism, PDD and NLD.* London: Jessica Kingsley Publishers.

[8]Gutstein, S.E., and R.K. Sheely. 2002b. *Relationship Development Intervention with Older Children, Adolescents and Adults: Social and Emotional Development Activities for Asperger Syndrome, Autism, PDD and NLD.* London: Jessica Kingsley Publishers.

[9]Gutstein, S., and R. Sheely, (see n. 6 above).

[10]Gutstein, S., and R. Sheely, (see n. 6 above).

# Child-lead/Parent-facilitated Therapies: The Learning to Speak Program

## What is the Learning to Speak Program?

Learning to Speak is a program designed for parents to teach their language-delayed children to speak. The method was designed for children considered intellectually normal with speech delays not associated with mental retardation.[1] It is important to note that this program was not designed for children with autism specifically, and is recommended only for children with autism who are not intellectually impaired. The Learning to Speak manual (1984) was designed for individuals who have a minimum mental age of 12 months. Parents are advised that they may need professional help if their children's delays exceed 10 months.[2] According to Zelazo (1984), the Learning to Speak Program is based on the developmental foundations of language and some principles from the field of behaviorism.[3] The curriculum is progressive: first sounds and words are taught; then two-word combinations are introduced; and finally, complex sentences are taught. In order to accomplish these goals, the manual suggests using the techniques of non-verbal imitation, verbal imitation, contingent rewards and prompts.

The program begins with assessment of the level of language of each child. Formal language instruction occurs at the level on which the child is assessed. Skills are then generalized to other settings. Parents are urged to use contingencies (rewards), events outside of the sessions (such as bathtub time, getting dressed), and props (such as toys or three-dimensional objects) to encourage language. The ratio is one child per teacher (who is generally the parent) and the instruction style is a combination of child-led and adult-led.

The Learning to Speak manual also offers suggestions on how to overcome non-compliant or resistant behavior in order to enable learning to occur. Resistant behaviors are addressed by removing all rewards for those behaviors, while simultaneously rewarding alternative, more desirable behaviors. The two specific behavior reduction strategies mentioned in the manual are extinction (ignoring or removing attention from a behavior), and time-out (removing the child from the stimulating activity or by removing the stimulating activity from the child).

## What evidence do the practitioners have that this really works?

There is currently no evidence that this is an effective intervention for individuals with autism. After doing a database search (psychinfo, medline, eric, and Cochrane Collection) on the Learning to Speak program and research conducted by Zelazo (the developer of the method), we found over ten journal articles. However, most of the articles were theoretical in nature. After excluding the descriptive articles devoid of data testing the method, we netted only one peer-reviewed study. Although this one peer-reviewed article does provide a description of data,[4] according to Zelazo[5] the data described has not been peer-reviewed. Despite the lack of peer-review for the data, it is important to mention that Zelazo did report improvement among children with autism (although the forty-four children in the study proportedly were diagnosed with "developmental delays of unknown etiology [cause]"[6] and not autism). Zelazo reports statistically significant improvement on many verbal measures and compliance behaviors, which is not surprising considering that part of his method borrows from basic behavioral principles.

## What does the therapy actually look like?

The recommended intensity of this program is twelve minutes per day, five days per week until the various levels have been completed. To provide the child with the feeling of success, the session begins and ends each day with the practice of mastered material; the middle of the session focuses on new material. When the child provides a correct response, he or she receives both tangible rewards (e.g., food) and social rewards (e.g., verbal praise). To teach the child the correct response, the adult uses imitation and shapes verbal approximations (e.g., the sound "cu" will be shaped into the word "cup"). Early stages of therapy include both nonverbal and verbal imitation where the adult shapes the child's sounds into single words. Once sixty single words have been acquired, these words are first paired into two word sentences and then eventually into complex sentences.

## What else do I think?

There is currently no peer-reviewed research to support this intervention for children with autism. It is also not clear that the authors actually intended this intervention to be used for individuals with autism. It appears as though the method was designed for a different group of children and then applied to children with autism, despite the lack of data for the method on this population of children. In addition, the Zelazo Method uses a very low level of treatment intensity (only twelve minutes per day). Based on what we know about autism and the difficult nature of the condition, particularly when it comes to language, twelve minutes daily would appear to be far too low to meet the serious needs of the individual afflicted with autism. Presumably, this is why Zelazo et al. (1984), recommend a minimum mental age of twelve months and professional guidance for individuals with delays greater than ten months. These recommendations in effect work to exclude most untreated individuals with autism, whose delays would generally exceed those mentioned by the authors. This would also include children without mental retardation who receive low scores on IQ tests due to one of the hallmarks of autism amongst young children, which is *noncompliance*. In other words, if the child does not cooperate during the testing, his score will be deceptively low and he will be excluded from the population Zelazo recommends for the therapy. Additionally, authors do not make it clear how to structure the learning situation. For compliant children, it is recommended that they sit in a chair; however, for noncompliant children, parents are instructed to follow the child's lead and accept unstructured learning situations. The authors do not address how the noncompliant child will learn from this method.

Other areas of potential confusion for parents using the Zelazo Method regard problematic behavior and prompting. The authors recommend the use of prompts to facilitate success for their children; however, they do not discuss the systematic fading of prompts towards independence. In addition, the behavioral strategies of extinction and time-out are mentioned, but parents are not told how to select a strategy based on the function of the behavior for the child. If a behavior does not serve the purpose of gaining attention for the child, then ignoring the behavior will not likely be successful. Moreover, if a child is acting out as a form of escape from a situation or task, the use of time-out will actually reward the child for misbehaving. In short, the entire field of behaviorism is much more complex than the way it is presented in the Learning to Speak program.

The Learning to Speak program manual discusses many effective learning strategies (e.g., shaping, prompting, behavioral intervention, compliance training and the use of imitation to facilitate language acquisition); however, there is nowhere near enough information provided in order for these strategies to be applied effectively. It is unrealistic to expect parents to implement this program based on the limited information in the manual. In addition, the manual oversimplifies language development and teaching for individuals who have particular delays in these areas.   Finally, it is interesting that in this method, it is only parents with minimal training who are expected to be competent speech therapists for their children.  This is the perfect type of therapy that governments and health insurance companies can endorse because it costs them very little money, as parents are free labor.  In fact, proponents of this method consider parents ideal therapists because they are with their children much during the infant and toddler years.  Zelazo states in his 1997 article, "These factors, along with a more exclusive reliance on *parents as therapists*, render Learning to Speak an extremely efficient intervention program in both time and financial cost to the taxpayer, although it is intensive for parents initially"[7] (emphasis added). It is my view that researchers doing pure research should not be concerned with government policy or taxpayer money; their main priority should be research that moves the autism treatment field forward in terms of efficacy and successful outcomes for the children.   Another troubling part of this research is the funding source.  According to Zelazo, the Office of Special Education looked at preliminary data prior to funding this research project to the tune of $750,000.[8*]  That kind of interference in science is a red flag in my case.

## Would I try it on my child?

I would not try the Learning to Speak Method on my child simply because there is no independent data which provides evidence for the efficacy of this method for autism.  If the method were scientifically substantiated (and not directly supported by the Office of Special Education), requiring only twelve minutes a day to make a significant difference in the life of a child with autism, it might be worth trying.  However, the concept that such a low level of treatment intensity,

---

*Although it is not clear from the article, it appears as if the Office of Special Education that funded this research is a U.S. agency.  Their research was funded from the Office of Special Education (No. G00760379) and the Tufts-New England Medical Center Hospital.

and a vaguely defined method would be able to generate positive outcomes with autistic children who have such serious developmental and language disorders, seems far too good to be true, and consequently, difficult to believe without more serious evidence.

## What kind of study would I like to see Zelazo and Colleagues do?

The language program described in this manual requires the same evaluation as any treatment option. There needs to be controlled research evaluating the effects of this program. These researchers need to use standardized, widely accepted diagnostic protocols to define all the children in his study and the method would require implementation by highly skilled practitioners for the same amount of time daily (rather than using parents as therapists), in order to increase the consistency and skill in the delivery of the therapy. The study would have to randomly assign children to experimental and control groups or at least match the children in each condition with the control group receiving generic speech and language therapy for the same amount of time per day. Most important, all direct ties to government special needs stakeholders must be severed prior to embarking on any research which tests the efficacy of this treatment method.

## Who else recommends for or against the Learning to Speak program?

This is a rather obscure treatment method which targets language therapy. Consequently, there is little written by others in the autism field regarding this treatment for children with autism. In addition, there is no debate in the field about the efficacy of this treatment, partially because it has been developed in Canada and is not widely supported by state governments in the United States. As governments come to rely on this method more for children with autism, there may be a debate opened up about the lack of evidence regarding the efficacy of the Learning to Speak program. However, up to this point, we know of only one government that has attempted to provide this training to parents of children with autism– the Government of Newfoundland/Labrador, Canada.

## What's the bottom line?

There is no evidence suggesting that this is an effective intervention for individuals with autism. In fact, there is no evidence to suggest that this intervention was even designed for use on individuals with autism.

## Endnotes for the Learning to Speak Program

[1] Zelazo, P. R. 1984.  *Learning to Speak:  A Manual for Parents.*  Hillsdale, NJ: Lawrence Erlbaum Associates, Inc.

[2] Zelazo, P. R., (see n. 1 above).

[3] Zelazo, P. R. 1997. "Infant-Toddler Information Processing Treatment of Children with Pervasive Developmental Disorder  and Autism: Part II. *Infants and Young Children,* Vol. 10, No. 2, p. 4.

[4] Zelazo, P. R., (see n. 3 above).

[5] Zelazo, P. R., (see n. 3 above), p. 11.

[6] Zelazo, P. R., (see n. 3 above), p. 7.

[7] Zelazo, P. R., (see n. 3 above), p. 6.

[8] Zelazo, P. R., (see n. 3 above), p. 8.

# Biomedical Therapies    Section 1.4

▷ *Diet/Nutrition Therapy (Gluten and Casein-free Diet)*

▷ *Chelation Therapy*

▷ *Intravenous Immunoglobulin Therapy*

▷ *Secretin*

▷ *Vitamin B6 and Magnesium*

# Biomedical Therapies: Diet/Nutrition Therapy

## What is Diet/Nutrition Therapy?

The use of diet or nutrition therapies to treat autism takes many forms, each with a unique explanation about how certain types of foods are negatively purported to affect a child with autism. While all of the interventions have been grouped in the same section, an explanation of each of the underlying theories will be provided separately.

*Gluten and Casein-free Diets*

The first and most popular diet intervention involves the elimination or reduction of gluten or casein, or both in the diet of an autistic person. The belief in this dietary intervention is based primarily on the age at which the disorder is discovered. Researchers hypothesize that there is a relationship between the onset of autism and significant dietary changes, believed to involve food derived peptides (which are proteins).[1] As a result, researchers in these studies have categorized individuals with autism into three subgroups; types A, B1 and B2. Type A is comprised of children who developed autism late (late onset infantile autism or childhood onset PDD). This group is given a gluten-free and casein-(milk products) reduced diet, due to the retrospective observation that when their gluten intake increased, the autism appeared to be caused (for 90 percent of these children).[2] The next group of children is categorized as Type B1 because their autism was observed as early onset with later regression. They were given gluten and casein-free diets, as were those children categorized as Type B2, early onset infantile autism, without worsening symptoms. Researchers in this field believe that the early onset was due to the fact that only milk was being consumed at this stage and must therefore be the cause of the onset of autism.[3]

### Candida Diet

Another offshoot of Nutrition therapy is the Candida diet, which is thought to be an effective treatment for autism by its proponents. It is hypothesized that *Candida albicans* (yeast) can become overabundant and deprive the body of nutrition by interfering with digestion.[4] In turn, this is said to interfere with neurotransmission in the brain. Some believe that this can lead to several disabilities, of which autism is included.

### Ketogenic Diet

Another diet that is claimed to originate from the treatment of epilepsy and cancer is the Ketogenic Diet.[5] Proponents of the diet, as it applies to autism, hypothesize that the Ketogenic Diet helps metabolize glucose in children with autism and, thereby, lessens the symptoms of autism.

### Nutritional Therapy

Another popular treatment for autism is the use of vitamins and minerals to treat what are considered, by proponents, to be nutritional imbalances. These researchers claim that by balancing the body's chemistry, the symptoms of people with autism will decrease.[6] Proponents test children for over eighty nutritional deficiencies (examples of the chemicals that these researchers claim to have found to be "out of balance" are copper, zinc, lead, cadmium and sodium). Then they give the children additives to purportedly create balance in the body chemistry.[*]

---

[*]The most popular deficiency diets are those that recommend Vitamin B6 and magnesium. Due to the popularity of Vitamin Therapy, a separate section has been devoted to the analysis of that treatment.

# What evidence do the practitioners have that this really works?

Our database searches netted dozens of articles discussing various types of nutritional diet therapies intended for the treatment of autism. Once we rejected the reviews, commentaries and testimonials due to their lack of controlled data, we were left with very few peer-reviewed journal articles that supported the efficacy of Diet/Nutrition Therapy.

### Gluten and Casein-free Diets

Our search netted eight articles[*] which collected behavioral data on the effectiveness of Gluten and Casein-free Diets for autism. Once we excluded a survey article[12] and an article documenting referral of nutritional therapies,[13] we were left with six articles on this approach to autism intervention.[1,2,14,15,16,17] This research is affiliated with two groups, one at the Department of Pediatric Research at the University of Oslo, Norway (the Reichelt Knivsberg group) and the other at the Department of Paediatrics of the University of Rome.[14]

Specifically, only one of these studies has a control group,[17] which leaves opportunities for many confounding variables (other uncontrolled influences) to explain results or changes. An additional problem with a lack of control group when the studies are conducted over months or years is that there is no control over maturation effects (improvements that may naturally occur as children age). The gains that were made due to maturation alone (or the fact that many of these children were in specialized educational environments and perhaps improving) were not taken into account in these studies; yet these gains may have

---

[*]There were five additional articles found in our Gluten and Casein search; however, these were excluded because they simply measured increased peptide levels without testing the diet and without using any traditional measures for autism.[7,8,9,10,11]

been responsible for the observed improvement. (Please see Section Two for an explanation on the weaknesses of within-subject designs).  The Knivsberg et al. (2002) study does have a control group, which is a major improvement over the other five studies on Gluten and Casein-free Diets.

An additional weakness of this group of studies is that the measures of the dependent variables of autism are flawed.  The reported results on behavior change were done by parents in several of the studies,[1,2,16] (For a discussion regarding the dangers of relying on parental reporting, please see Section Two).  In addition, in the Lucarellie et al. (1995) study, it was not specified who administered the measures.  Furthermore, all these researchers use tests that have questionable validity when it comes to autism.  The Diagnosis of Psychotic Behavior in Children (DIPAB) was developed in 1975 for psychosis, not autism.[18]  Our knowledge of autism has increased significantly in the last thirty years and we are now able to differentiate between autism and psychosis. With that increased knowledge, there are also independently validated measures that should have been used instead.  Additional outdated and non-autism specific measures that have been used in this research is a non-verbal cognitive test developed forty-seven years ago (the C-Raven test – Raven, 1958), the Illinois Test of Psycholinguistic Abilities developed thirty-seven years ago,[19] and a Norwegian Autism Observation Scale designed twenty-four years ago.[20]  An additional measure of questionable validity is the Behavior Evaluation Scale (BSE) that has not been independently validated using already agreed upon, validated autism scales.

Yet another problem with all the studies is that only one of them[16] was single blind.  None of the other studies had sufficient controls against experimenter bias. The 2002 study conducted by Knivsberg et al. was a significant improvement on all the studies which have preceded this study; however, the 2002 study suffers from several flaws. Although information on autistic traits was collected (often with outmoded testing) and individual reports were written on each child's level of functioning, there was no objective behavioral measure (e.g. amount of self-stimulatory behavior per day per child) that could be compared pre-and post treatment. In addition, parents were heavily involved in the study and knew to which experimental group their child was assigned. The project leader, however, did not. In short, although this study was the best published so far for this method of autism intervention, the flaws in the study make it premature to accept it as evidence that supports the effectiveness of the Gluten and Casein-free Diet.

### Candida Diet

In terms of evidence for the efficacy of the Candida Diet, we only found one study[4] and that study only presents case histories which are completely uncontrolled. In addition, in the two case studies described by Adams and Conn (1997), both of the children were involved in educational treatment concurrently. This further confuses (confounds) the results of this retrospective study. Moreover, parental reporting was relied upon heavily in these two case histories. Finally, improvement was not objectively measured.

### Nutritional Deficiency Diet

We found only one peer-reviewed journal article on Nutrition Therapy (excluding all the articles written about Vitamin B6 and Magnesium). The researcher, Isaacson (1996), concludes that after supplementing the children with a variety of vitamin and mineral supplements, there was "significant general improvement in all symptoms."[21] There are several methodological problems with this study. First, the chemical imbalances that were identified were determined using hair analysis, which can be a controversial procedure, particularly when done by a commercial laboratory.[22] Second, the relationship between autism and chemical imbalance has not yet been established. Finally, the conclusion that children

173

improved is based on one follow-up visit in a retrospective study.  There are no criteria laid out for how the improvement was measured, and the improvement is examined retrospectively.  This opens the results up to recall bias, which in this case is doubly problematic because the recall is being made by parents who are not unbiased even in the best of scenarios.

*Ketogenic Diet*

We netted only one peer-reviewed journal article on the Ketogenic Diet. Evangeliou et al. (2003) did a within-subject design which included thirty children with autism.  A number of children stopped the diet prior to completion of the study (40 percent) which left eighteen out of the original thirty children remaining in the study.  The researchers found that two of the children significantly improved, eight patients improved less significantly and there was minor improvement for an additional eight patients (these improvements were measured with the Childhood Autism Rating Scale, CARS).  The researchers report significant improvement with two children (a twelve point change in the CARS) to the extent that these children were able to attend a mainstream school. (Yet, it was not specified if there was an in-class aide or if the children were functioning in class independently).

Although this study reported promising results and did have some impressive controls (e.g., the children were administered the diet in a hospital throughout the study, and the psychiatrist who evaluated the children did not know which children were in the study and which were not), there are several limitations to the study.  The CARS is one screening device for autism; however, more psychometric testing needs to be done with those children to be able to measure meaningful change.  In addition, observational data which measures the relative decrease of stereotypy and other self-stimulatory behaviors characteristic to children with autism must be collected.  Furthermore, we must consider that those who worked in the hospital were not blind to the treatment. They knew which children were on the diet and could have influenced the outcome of the study (see Section Two on self-fulfilling prophecy). Another critique of the study is that 40 percent of the children in the study withdrew prior to study completion. Although we still have pre-and post measurements of those children who remained, the large attrition rate does not inspire confidence, particularly when the authors claim that all children benefitted from the study.

An additional unexplained finding is that the children's improvement was maintained long after they discontinued the diet. This could be due to a long-term effect of the diet; however, an alternate explanation is that there is a confounding variable completely unrelated to the diet, which is responsible for the improvement. That said, these findings are sufficiently robust with a small subset of the children in the study that they invite replication by other researchers with no relationship to this research group.

## What does the therapy actually look like?

### Gluten/Casein-free Diet

The gluten/casein-free diet attempts to eliminate all products which contain gluten (such as most breads, cakes and other carbohydrates which contain wheat) and all products which contain casein (such as milk and cheese). The diet is generally carried out for a year and monitored. Once parents are convinced that the diet is working, they end up keeping the child on the diet permanently. Parents generally control the diet in consultation with a nutritionist and, sometimes, a medical doctor.

### The Candida Diet

The Candida diet follows a complex seven stage procedure developed by MacFarland (1992). The body is said to be detoxified by eliminating a large variety of foods (such as milk products, corn products, sugars) from the diet. Gradually, foods are then reintroduced.  It is unclear from the article as to how reintroducing certain foods balances the yeast; however, the concept is that as a result of the therapy, the body's yeast level is supposed to come into balance.

### *The Ketogenic Diet*

The Ketogenic Diet was adapted for children to make sure that thirty percent of the child's daily intake comes from medium-chain triglyceride oil (found in foods such as coconut oil).  The rest of the child's food must be balanced as follows:  30 percent cream, 11 percent fat, 19 percent carbohydrates and 10 percent protein.[5] This modified diet, the John Radcliffe diet, was adapted due to its purported ease of management.  The researchers do not go into detail about how long the children should remain on the diet; however, children in the study were on the diet for four weeks and then diet-free for two weeks, over a six month period.

## What else do I think?

Many parents are attracted to diet/nutrition interventions because it is a non-medicinal approach that appears to be relatively easy to follow.  People often gravitate to this type of intervention due to the observation that their child with autism either has strong food preferences, food aversions, or gastrointestinal discomfort or distress.  I suspect that some of the anecdotal results may be a product of a small subset of children who may have allergies which make them miserable.  Once they feel better, perhaps some of their behaviors improve simply because they are not suffering.  This finding, however, has no effect on autism intrinsically; rather, it may be that children with autism are often under-served by mainstream medicine because they don't have the verbal ability to complain about feeling physical discomfort whether due to allergy or illness.

The question about the relationship between autism and nutrition remains.  We simply do not know whether a relationship exists. What we do know is that it is very important to take the uncontrolled, anecdotal reporting of this relationship skeptically. Only the true experimental design can begin to shed light on whether or not there is a relationship between diet/nutrition and autism.  Unfortunately, to date none of the research conducted utilizes a true experimental design with adequate controls and an accepted measurement of the dependent variable, autism. To illustrate this lack of accepted measure for autism, whether we are measuring chemicals in hair analysis or peptides* in urine (which are heavily used in many of these studies), these tests do not measure the degree of autism.  Only widely accepted behavioral and psychometric measures that have been validated to test autism should be used to determine the degree of autism before the diet and the degree of autism during and after the nutritional intervention.

## Would I try it on my child?

I would not try Diet/Nutrition Therapy on my child until some better data is produced to convince me that there is any truth to the idea that diet can ameliorate the symptoms of autism.  That said, if I were worried that my child were allergic to any food source, I would go to a mainstream allergist and have her tested.  I would not expect the elimination of an allergin to improve her autism; rather, I'd expect the elimination of the allergin to eliminate the allergic reaction (which has not been shown to have any relationship to autism).

---

*This area is concerned with a particular class of opioid peptides (which are a type of amino acid).  The opioid peptides that are associated with milk – casomorphin, and gluten – gluten exorphin, are hypothesized to be the culprits in reference to autism.

## What kind of study would I like to see proponents of Nutrition Therapies do?

At this point, none of the nutrition therapies have established a relationship between nutrition and autism.  Prior to conducting any research on treatment, the gluten/casein-free diet researchers must first firmly establish a causal relationship between peptide levels and autism.  Specifically, they need to demonstrate a direct relationship between the excess of opioid peptides (amino acids that have the effect similar to opiates in the brain) and behaviors characteristic of autism.  Either the opioid peptide – autism relationship needs to be established, or the researchers should only use behavior scales to measure the degree of autism prior to and after the diet.

If and when researchers can *demonstrate* these relationships, then they need to study whether there is a particular subset of people with autism who may hypothetically benefit from this type of intervention.  In other words, the research question should be whether there is a particular subset of the autistic population of children who have components of their diet which are causing their autistic characteristics? If so, then, and only then, is there justification for investigation into treatment.  Well-controlled research into the efficacy of diet  intervention for individuals with autism should not use measures that are biomedical; rather, measures used for autism must be standard behavioral measures because autism is a behavioral diagnosis.  Until such time as we have a firm biomedical indicator which can measure degree of autism, an indicator which, at this point, still eludes us, nutritional studies cannot reasonably make any claims of autism improvement based on biomedical measures.

There are two studies that I would like to see independently replicated.  The first study is the Knivsberg et al. 2002 study.  They need to use updated, internationally accepted measures for autism and a double-blind design where children are either being fed the Gluten/Casein-free diet, or another diet that is accepted as healthy. As mentioned before, double-blind means that neither the researchers nor the parents can know which children are assigned to which group (experimental or control). The second study that needs to be *independently* replicated is the Ketogenic Diet as the results of a subset of those children who remained in the study appear robust. First, proponents of the Ketogenic Diet need to determine the way in which Ketone bodies[*] affect the brain, and more specifically, autism, which is a disorder of the brain. Without an independent replication either supporting or refuting these findings, the Ketogenic Diet could turn into the next fad where children with autism are subjected to yet another treatment without sufficient evidence. In addition, proponents of the Candida Theory need to first firmly establish the relationship between an overgrowth of yeast and autism.

## Who else recommends against Diet /Nutrition Therapy as a method for the treatment of autism?

There is a long line of organizations recommending against Diet/Nutrition Therapies as a treatment for autism. According to the New York State Department of Health Report on Best Practices for Autism, "The use of special diets that eliminate milk-products, gluten products, or other specific foods from the diet is not recommended for the treatment of autism in children."[23]  In addition, Quackwatch (a health-related watchdog organization) considers Dietary Supplements a "Doubtful or Discredited Treatment."[24] Another organization that considers the science  behind gluten and casein-free diets as methodologically weak is the Association for Science  in Autism  Treatment  (ASAT).[25]  The American Academy of Child and Adolescent Psychiatry in their practice

---

[*]Ketone bodies are the three chemicals that are a by-product of the process by which fat is broken down in the body.

parameters of assessment and treatment also recommend against these diets.[26] In a technical report on autism, the American Academy of Pediatrics states: "The presence of allergies or food intolerance in children often stimulates families to explore unconventional diets... Another recent investigation failed to document a higher prevalence of hypersensitivity to common food allergens in children with ASD, compared with controls."[27]

## So you're still on the horns of a dilemma?

It might interest the reader to know that these theories have been around for many years.  The first accounts suggesting that diet could influence autism date back to 1981.[28]  Twenty-five years have passed and there is still no independent scientific support for the various theories on diet and nutrition.  Therefore, it might be a good idea to wait until this research is done and published in peer-reviewed journals; otherwise, you are essentially engaging in pure experimentation with your child.

## What's the bottom line?

Based on the scientific research to date, there is not enough evidence that Diet/Nutrition Therapies of any kind are an effective treatment for improving the symptoms associated with autism.

## Endnotes for Diet /Nutrition Therapies

[1]Reichelt, K.L., H. Scott, A.M. Knivsberg, F. Nyberg, and V. Brandtl. 1990. "Childhood Autism: A Group of Hyperpeptidergic Disorders. Possible Etiology and Tentative Treatment." *Beta-Casomorphins and Related Peptides*. Uppsala: Fyrris Tryck, pp. 163-173.

[2]Reichelt, K.L., A.M. Knivsberg, G. Lind, and M. Nodland. 1991. "Probable Etiology and Possible Treatment of Childhood Autism." *Brain Dysfunction,* Vol. 4, No. 6, pp. 308-319.

[3]Reichelt, K.L., H. Scott, A.M. Knivsberg, F. Nyberg, and V. Brandtl, (see n. 1 above).

[4]Adams, L., S. Conn. 1997. "Nutrition and Its Relationship to Autism." *Focus on Autism and other Developmental Disabilities,* Vol. 12, No. 1, pp. 3-58.

[5]Evangeliou, A., J. Vlachonikolis, H. Mihailidou, M. Spilioti, A. Skarpalezou, N. Makaronas, et al. 2003. "Application of a Ketogenic Diet in Children With Autistic Behavior: Pilot Study." *Journal of Child Neurology,* Vol. 18, No. 2, pp. 113-118.

[6]Isaacson, R.H., M. M. Moran, A. Hall, B.J. Harman, M.S.W. Prehosovich and M. A. Prehosovich. 1996. "Autism: A Retrospective Outcome Study of Nutrient Therapy." *Journal of Applied Nutrition,* Vol. 48, No. 4, pp. 110-118.

[7]Reichelt, K.L., H.K. Hamberfer, and G. Saelid. 1981. "Biologically Active Peptide Containing Fractions in Schizophrenia and Childhood Autism." *Advances in Biochemical Psychopharmacology,* Vol. 28, pp. 627-643.

[8]Israngkun, P.P., H.A.L. Newman, S.T. Patel, V.A. Duruibe, and A. Abuissa. 1986. "Potential Biochemical Markes for Infantile Autism." *Neurochemical Pathology*, Vol. 5, pp. 51-70.

[9]Reichelt, K.L., G. Saelid, T. Lindback, et al. 1986. "Childhood Autism: A Complex Disorder." *Biological Psychiatry,* Vol. 21, pp. 1279-1290.

[10]Shattock, P., A. Kennedy, R. Rosell, and T. Berney. 1990. "Role of Neuropeptides in Autism and Their Relationships With Classical Neurotransmitters." *Brain Dysfunction,* Vol. 3, pp. 328-345.

[11]Reichelt, K.L., A.M. Knivsberg, M. Nodland, and G. Lind. 1994. "Nature and Consequences of Hyperpeptiduria and Bovine Casomorphins Found in Autistic Syndromes." *Developmental Brain Dysfunction,* Vol. 7, pp. 71-85.

[12]Cornish, E. 2002. "Gluten and Casein Free Diets in Autism: A Study of the Effects on Food Choice and Nutrition." *Journal of Human Nutritional Dietetics.* Vol. 15, No. 4, pp. 261-269.

[13]Bowers, L. 2002. "An Audit of Referrals of Children With Autistic Spectrum Disorder to the Dietetic Service." *Journal of Human Nutritional Dietetics*, Vol. 15, pp. 141-144.

[14]Lucarelli, S., T. Frediani, A.M. Zingoni, F. Ferruzzi, O. Giardini, F. Quintieri, et al. 1995. "Food Allergy and Infantile Autism." *Panminerva-Medica,* Vol. 37, No. 3, pp. 137-141.

[15]Knivsberg, A.M., K. Wiig, G. Lind, M. Nodland, et al. 1990. "Dietary Intervention in Autistic Syndromes." *Brain Dysfunction,* Vol. 3, Nos. 5-6, pp. 315-327.

[16]Knivsberg, A.M., K.L. Reichelt, M. Nodland, and T. Hoien. 1995. "Autistic Syndromes and Diet : A Follow-up Study." *Scandinavian Journal of Educational Research,* Vol. 39, No. 3, pp. 223-236.

[17]Knivsberg, A.M., K.L. Reichelt, T. Hoien and M. Nodland. "A Randomised, Controlled Study of Dietary Intervention in Autistic Syndromes." 2002. *Nutritional Neuroscience,* Vol. 5, No. 4, pp. 251-261.

[18]Knivsberg, A.M., K.L. Reichelt, M. Nodland, and T. Hoien, (see n. 16 above), p. 225.

[19]Kirk, S.A., J.J. McCarthy, and W.D. Kirk. 1961. *Illinois test of psycholinguistic abilities (ITPA).* Urbana: University of Illinois Press.

[20]Tafjord, M. 1982. *Obsevasjon av fornutsetnninger for lek og aktivitet, Observasjonsskjema.* [Observation of prerequisites for play and activity: Observation schedule], Oslo: Statens Spesiallaererhogskole.

[21]Isaacson, R.H., et al., (see n. 6 above), p. 112.

[22]Barrett, S. 1985."Commercial Hair Analysis, Science or Scam?" *Journal of the American Medical Association,* Vol. 254, No. 8, pp. 1041-1045.

[23]Guralnick, M. Ed. 1999. *Clinical Practice Guideline: Report of the Recommendations. Autism/Pervasive Developmental Disorders, Assessment and Intervention for Young Children* (age 0-3 years). Albany (NY): New York State Department of Health, p. IV-104.

[24]Quackwatch, http://www.autism-watch.org, (accessed Apr. 18, 2005).

[25]Association for Science in Autism Treatment (ASAT), http://www.asatonline.org/resources/library/informed_choice.html, (accessed May 10, 2005).

[26]The American Academy of Child and Adolescent Psychiatry in Their Practice, http://www.aacap.org/AACAPsearch/SearchResults.cfm, (accessed Feb. 21, 2006).

[27]Committee on Children with Disabilities. Technical Report. 2001. "The Pediatrician's Role in the Diagnosis and Management of Autistic Spectrum Disorder in Children." *Pediatrics,* Vol. 107, No. 5, p. e85, www.aacap.org/clinical/parameters/summaries/autism.htm, (accessed Feb. 21, 2006).

# Biomedical Therapies: Chelation Therapy

## What is Chelation Therapy?

Chelation Therapy is the process by which harmful metal toxins are extracted from the body. Chelating agents (two types of amino acids) are injected into the child to bind to these metal ions and remove them from the body. This therapy is used on individuals with autism, based on the belief that autistic behaviors are a result of chronic metal toxicity in the child. It is thought that if the chelating agents can remove the offending toxins from the body, the symptoms of autism will improve. It is further hypothesized that the metals are introduced into the body from the environment through air, water, ingested orally or absorbed through the hands. In addition, the toxin of thermerisol (given through childhood vaccinations until recently) has been added to this list of contributing toxins.

## What evidence do the practitioners have that this really works?

Currently, there is no scientific data published in peer-reviewed journals to suggest that Chelation Therapy is an effective treatment for individuals with autism. Our database searches found no articles with outcome data regarding the effectiveness of chelation in improving the symptoms of autism. To date, there is only anecdotal support in the form of parental reports. (Please see Section Two for a discussion on the dangers of anecdotal parental reporting in autism treatment studies). Included in anecdotal evidence is a book by Hallaway and Strauts (1995), who provide a parental report about the treatment of Hallaway's twin boys using Chelation Therapy.

It is important to note that screening children for lead poisoning (not autism) is well accepted in mainstream medicine and lead toxicity is a legitimate health problem that is treatable using chelation. The American Academy of Child and Adolescent Psychiatry, adopted guidelines for lead screening and treatment in 1995, using blood tests. If a child shows elevated levels of lead in his or her blood, the mainstream medical profession typically recommends treatment using a form of chelation that differs from the chelation used on autistic children (calcium EDTA versus disodium EDTA). However, at this point, the hypotheses that metal toxicity *causes* autism, and that chelation will cure or successfully treat autism, have not been sufficiently tested and there is no evidence to support the claims. Consumers are confused about chelation being an accepted practice for children who have ingested "true" heavy metals that cannot be flushed out of the body any other way.

There are many correlational studies that have determined the symptoms of lead poisoning in animals and humans. There are also many reports of lead poisoning and an increased number of persons affected with a variety of symptoms. It appears that the symptoms are extremely varied and diverse, affecting people in different ways. At this point, it is unclear whether lead poisoning, or *any* heavy metal poisoning, plays any role in the cause of autism. Although it is beyond the scope of this book, the reader should know that chelation is being praised by its practitioners as being a cure for everything from clogged arteries to sexual disfunction.

## What does the therapy actually look like?

Chelation Therapy for the treatment of autism involves either oral or intravenous agents (depending on the chelating agent used), to remove harmful toxins from the bloodstream. The intravenous dosage takes anywhere from ten minutes to over three hours to administer, depending on the agent required.[1] When chelation is used to treat a variety of ailments other than its traditional use (lead poisoning), it is often done over a much longer period of time. Side effects vary with the type of agent used. They can include convulsions, severe constipation, bowel paralysis, acute toxicity, kidney failure and allergic reactions. In addition, there have been deaths associated with chelation and over fifteen state medical licensing boards have taken action against practitioners of Chelation Therapy.[2]

## What else do I think?

Lead poisoning is an important environmental issue which does have far reaching effects on human and animal health. It might be possible that occasionally a child with autism might have been exposed to lead; however, the symptoms would be typical of lead poisoning, not autism. To date, there is no experimental evidence which examines the issue of lead poisoning in individuals diagnosed as having autism and the purported therapeutic effects of treating these individuals with Chelation Therapy. Although the question regarding the relationship between thermerisol (mercury) in vaccines and autism has not been definitively answered, the theory that chelation can extract thermerisol and repair possible damage to the brain, has no supporting evidence. Proponents of Chelation Therapy suggest that autism is a result of heavy metal poisoning; however, they have no evidence to support this assertion. The diagnosis of autism is based on a variety of behavioral characteristics, and as of 2006, there is still no commonly-accepted, biological marker associated with autism. In other words, we can't do things like find a tumor, count blood cells or measure lead levels to determine whether the child has autism. After Chelation Therapy, we still can't use a biological marker to see if there has been significant improvement in the child's degree of autism. Proponents of chelation use hair analysis,[*] which is not yet accepted by the

---

[*]Although hair analysis is typically used to determine drug abuse (in the field of toxicology), it is not widely accepted that heavy metal poisoning can be determined through hair analysis. For an in-depth discussion on the shaky ground of hair analysis, Quackwatch has done a wonderful job of exposing the weaknesses of commercial hair analysis.[3]

mainstream medical community for this application.  Arguably, these commercial labs also have an economic incentive to be in the hair analysis business.

## Would I try it on my child?

My child does not suffer from the majority of symptoms that are well accepted as being caused by lead poisoning; however, if she did, I would have her tested by a reputable physician — for lead poisoning, not autism. In addition I would not allow the diagnosis to be done with hair sampling from a commercial laboratory because they have an economic incentive to find toxicity.  More research needs to be done before a relationship between heavy metal toxicity and autism is established, particularly as the risks of chelating a child with autism are kidney failure and death.  In short, I would never put my child at risk with a treatment that has no peer-reviewed evidence about its efficacy and has a very poor safety record.

## What kind of study would I like to see the chelation practitioners do?

Prior to any study on chelation for autism, proponents of this method need to find a more reliable way to measure toxicity than *commercial* hair analysis alone. Once there is evidence that some children with autism have high levels of heavy metals in their blood, then a study could be done only with those children who have elevated levels of the toxin in question.  Every child with autism who is a candidate for chelation due to excessive levels of metal toxicity would then need to receive a diagnosis of autism by an *independent* registered psychologist who would also measure each child in the study using autism rating scales, IQ and objective behavioral tests or measures (taking great care to avoid any parental reporting in the study design).  Each child would need to be randomly assigned to an experimental and control group, without experimenter knowledge regarding which children are in which group. After the treatment or placebo (given to the group not receiving the treatment), each child would need to have the same battery of tests performed by the psychologist prior to the study. For confidence in the results, I would suggest a study should include twenty children per group, for a total of forty children in the proposed study. If the results were to show that, for example, cognitively impaired children's IQ rise significantly with Chelation Therapy, that would show us that the hair sampling technique effectively identifies children who have heavy metal poisoning and that the heavy metals do indeed affect cognitive ability of children afflicted with autism. That, in itself, would not test the "chelation treats autism" hypothesis. However, if there is a significant difference between objective behavioral measures and scales rating severity of autism before and after the treatment, that would tell us that chelation does have an effect on the degree of autism within this group of children. A study such as this would be able to teach us much about the relationship between autism and chelation. Unfortunately, I think that this kind of study would be potentially harmful considering the lethal effects of Chelation Therapy on some children. This is a serious ethical obstacle to any future chelation study.

## Who else recommends for or against chelation as a method for the treatment of autism?

There are several medical associations and a few consumer groups that warn against Chelation Therapy in general, and a few refer to autism chelation treatments specifically. The American Academy of Pediatrics states:

> ...there is no evidence that Chelation Therapy will improve developmental function when given to treat mercury toxicosis. Moreover, chelating agents can have significant toxicity (e.g. hepatoxicity) and precipitate allergic reaction.[182] Chelation Therapy is therefore not recommended for the purpose of improving neuro-developmental function in children with ASD.[4]

In addition, the National Council Against Health Fraud recommends against Chelation Therapy. They state: "The National Council Against Health Fraud believes the Chelation Therapy is unethical and should be banned and that Chelation Therapy of autistic children should be considered child abuse."[5]

An additional resource established to debunk scientific quackery is Quackwatch. They have an entire website devoted to the issue of chelation, for a variety of medical conditions. Particularly interesting on their website are documents surrounding several court cases which were launched either due to the death of an individual after chelation, or the suspension of professional licenses from a variety of chelation practitioners.

## So you're still on the horns of a dilemma?

Before you decide whether or not to put your child through chelation, I would strongly suggest that you read the guidelines of the American College of Preventative Medicine Practice Policy Statement, which describes the conditions under which a child may be at risk for heavy metal poisoning and, if so, which proper steps to take.[6] If your child does not meet the at-risk criteria, please understand that in chelating your child, you are engaging in high-risk experimentation that, in isolated cases, can result in death.

## What's the bottom line?

Based on the scientific research to date, there is no evidence that Chelation Therapy is an effective treatment for decreasing the symptoms of autism in children.

# Endnotes for Chelation Therapy

[1]Hallaway, N., and Strauts, Z. 1995. *Turning lead into gold*: *How heavy metal poisoning can affect your child and how to prevent and treat it*. Vancouver, BC: New Star Books Ltd.

[2]Quackwatch, www.quackwatch.org/01QuackeryRelatedTopics/hair.html, (accessed Feb. 16, 2006).

[3]Quackwatch, (see n. 2 above).

[4]Committee on Children With Disabilities. 2001. "Technical Report: The Pediatrician's Role in the Diagnosis and Management of Autistic Spectrum Disorder in Children." *Pediatrics,* Vol. 107, No. 5, p. e85, www.pediatrics.aappublications.org/cgi/content/full/107/5/e85, (accessed Feb. 13, 2006).

[5]The National Council Against Health Fraud. undated. NCAHF, Policy Statement on Chelation, www.ncahf.org, (accessed Aug. 9, 2005).

[6]Lane, W. G. 2001. "Screening for elevated blood lead levels in children." *American Journal of Preventive Medicine*, Vol. 20, No. 1, p. 78-82, www.acpm.org/pol_practice.htm#several, (accessed Feb. 16, 2006).

# Biomedical Therapies: Intravenous Immunoglobulin

## What is Intravenous Immunoglobulin Therapy?

Intravenous Immunoglobulin (IVIG), a form of blood/plasma, is used as a therapy for autoimmune disorders and is actually considered medically necessary for dozens of conditions. It is paid for by insurance companies such as Aetna. The theory posited by proponents of IVIG therapy, is that there is a relationship between autism and autoimmune disorders. Some researchers have suggested that autism *is* an immune-related disorder, and have treated autism using IVIG to address the autoimmune phenomenon that they claim to observe in individuals with autism.[1] Although there are some differences in the way that IVIG is administered, typically the treatment itself involves the administration of IVIG every four weeks for at least six months.

## What evidence do the practitioners have that this really works?

Our database search netted three articles which present data on IVIG therapy.[1,2,3] None of these studies used control groups or random assignment and two of the three studies measured the dependent variable, autism, in a problematic manner. The results of the first preliminary study indicated that behavioral, speech and cognitive improvements were observed in ten autistic individuals who were treated with a six month course of IVIG.[1] Unfortunately, the dependent variable, autism, was operationalized in an unstructured and extremely subjective way. Various behavioral therapists, speech therapists and psychiatrists involved in the child's life reported changes, and these reports were subsequently converted into an arbitrary rating scale using numbers one through four (1-4) to indicate degree of improvement. In addition, no "p-values" were reported to indicate whether or not the changes in this rating scale were statistically significant.

Despite the researchers' conclusion that children with autism improved, the insufficient rating scales prevent us from making any meaningful conclusions based on the results of this study.  The potential for bias in the dependent measure is high, and the lack of control prevents changes observed from being attributed to the intervention.  An additional flaw in this study design is that some of these children were in behavioral and speech/language therapy programs at the time.  Without controlling the variable of "other therapies" by utilizing a control group, one cannot attribute, with confidence, any results to the IVIG therapy.  To his credit, an IVIG researcher named Gupta, states that: "a controlled double-blind, placebo-controlled multicenter study is being planned."[4]  We very much look forward to that study.

The second IVIG study was conducted on ten children with autism (Pliopys, 1998).  It also did not go into sufficient detail to tell us how the dependent variable, autism, was measured prior to the study.  This is not a small point.  If we cannot properly measure the degree of a child's autism at the beginning of a study, we will assuredly not be able to accurately measure the degree of autism after the treatment has been applied in the study.  Pliopys reported no improvement in nine out of the ten subjects; however, one child appeared to improve dramatically.  Unfortunately, due to the lack of rigor in the pre and post measures of autism, we have no idea whether the improvement actually occurred and, if it did, whether the improvement can be attributed to the IVIG treatment.   This is unfortunate because if there is a subset of children who do benefit, it would be beneficial to know which subset of children may be candidates for this therapy.  The last study we found in our search, the DelGiudice-Asch et al. (1999) study, gave IVIG Therapy to five children with autism and found no improvement among the children.  The difference in this study from the two earlier studies is that these researchers  measured the dependent variable, autism, utilizing four different psychometric and autism scales.  Their ability to objectively measure improvement in post treatment makes this the strongest of the three studies.

## What does the therapy actually look like?

IVIG treatment is a two hour intravenous administration of a course of immunoglobulin, a protein antibody found within the bloodstream which binds to antigens (substances which create an immune response, i.e., an allergic reaction, in the body) and subsequently deactivates them. Maintenance doses are given every four to six weeks; however, at treatment outset, they may have to be administered at higher rates. The cost of this procedure is approximately $100 U.S. per gram, including procedural costs (approximately $3000 USD per treatment). Subjects are first prescribed a course of Benadryl to combat possible side effects, which include dizziness, nausea, abnormally rapid beating of the heart, headache, fever and muscle pain.

## What else do I think?

It is quite difficult for consumers to differentiate between IVIG as an experimental procedure or an accepted best practice treatment, because it is used so commonly for a variety of disorders.  This treatment operates under the assumption that autism somehow involves possible infectious agents and or immune deficiencies.[1] Yet, importantly, all the possible explanations for how and why IVIG may be effective for individuals with autism are, at this point, unproven. If indeed autism may be an immune-related disorder for some individuals, we need firm evidence establishing this to be the case.  IVIG is postulated to work by either suppressing particular antibodies or by easing brain inflammation; however, these researchers have insufficient evidence to claim that autism is caused by particular antibodies or brain inflammation.  As autism cannot yet be diagnosed and measured by looking at a physiological marker (e.g., a blood test), the auto-immune theory of autism remains as a theory, still to be supported by data.

### Would I try it on my child?

If researchers could make the link between auto-immune disorders and autism, and show that IVIG does indeed *ameliorate* the condition of autism, I would be very interested in providing this therapy for my child.  However, until the research is done, I would not subject my child or my wallet to this treatment.

### What kind of study would I like to see the researchers studying the effects of Intravenous Immunoglobulin do?

I would like to see a randomly assigned, double-blind, placebo-controlled crossover study, with subjects receiving IVIG treatment. The dependent measures used to evaluate the effectiveness of the intervention should be well-validated and measure IQ or cognitive functioning, language and behavior. These measures should be assessed by raters who do not know the purpose of the study.   In addition, an analysis of severity, frequency and longevity of side effects should also be done. Finally, the results should be reported using statistical levels of significance, so we know the results are likely not due to chance.

### Who else recommends against Immunoglobulin therapy as a method for the treatment of autism?

There are several associations that warn against IVIG treatment for autism.  The New York State Department of Health has the following to say about the therapy: "It is strongly recommended that intravenous immune globulin therapy not be used as a  treatment for autism in children because of the substantial risks and lack of proven benefit associated with this intervention."[5]  In addition, the policy statement of the American Academy of Pediatrics reads: "Unproven therapies also may be based on pathophysiology and limited research, but they lack accepted standards of proven effectiveness (e.g., the use of immunoglobulins in the treatment of autism)."[6] In May, 2005, this policy was reaffirmed. Furthermore, Dr. Marie Bristol-Powers of the National Institute of Child Health and Human Development states: "Treatment studies do not support the clinical use of IVIG, which would support a immunological factor in autism."[7]

## So you're still on the horns of a dilemma?

You might want to read Hyman et al. (2000),[8] in which they speak about the lure of complimentary and alternative medicare. Keep in mind that if IVIG is eventually found to be effective, there will be controlled studies available to demonstrate its efficacy. Before this happens, please understand that you are engaging in pure experimentation with your child if you employ IVIG treatment in the effort to ameliorate autism.

## What's the bottom line?

Based on the scientific research to date, there is not enough evidence that the use of Intravenous Immunoglobulin (IVIG) is an effective treatment for decreasing the symptoms associated with autism.

# Endnotes for Immunoglobulin therapy

[1]Gupta, S., S. Aggarwal, and C. Heads. 1996. "Dysreglated Immune System in Children With Autism: Beneficial Effects of Intravenous Immune Globulin on Autistic Characteristics." *Journal of Autism Developmental Disorders,* Vol. 26, pp. 439-452.

[2]Piloplys, A.V. 1999. ""Response to Letter by dr. Gupta Concerning The Treatment of Autistic children With Intravenous Immunoglobulin." *Journal of Child Neurology,* Vol. 14, No. 3, pp. 203-205.

[3]DelGuidice-Asch, G., L. Simon, J. Schmeidler, C. Cunningham-Rundles, and E. Hollander. 1999. "Brief Report: A Pilot Open Clinical Trial of Intravenous Immunoglobulin in Childhood Autism." *Journal of Autism and Developmental Disorders,* Vol. 29, No. 2, pp. 157-160.

[4]Gupta, S., S. Aggarwal, and C. Heads, (see n. 1 above), p. 451.

[5]Guralnick, M., ed. 1999. *Clinical practice guideline: Report of the Recommendations. Autism/Pervasive Developmental Disorders, Assessment and Intervention for Young Children* (age 0-3 years). Albany (NY): New York State Department of Health, p. IV-91.

[6]Committee on Children with Disabilities. 2001. "Technical Report: the Pediatricians Role in the Diagnosis and Management of Autistic Spectrum Disorder in Children." *Pediatrics*, Vol. 107, No. 5, p. e85, http:pediatrics.aapublications.org/cgi/content/full/105/5/e85, (accessed Feb. 16, 2006).

[7]Bristol-Powers, M. 2001. "The Etiology of Autism and NICHD Research." *National Institute of Child Health & Human Development,* Washington, DC: National Academy of Sciences.

[8]Hyman, S.L., and S.E. Levy. 2000. " Autistic Spectrum Disorders: When Traditional Medicine is Not Enough." *Contemporary Pediatrics,* Vol. 10, p. 101.

# Biomedical Therapies: Secretin

## What is Secretin Therapy?

Proponents of Secretin Therapy believe that the use of secretin (a gastrointestinal peptide which is a kind of hormone), for individuals with autism, results in an improvement of autistic behavior. Some researchers believe that there may be a link between the brain and gastrointestinal functioning in autistic children. Specifically, these researchers hypothesize that gastrointestinal difficulties found in people with autism contribute to the cause of autism, and that by forcing the pancreas to greatly increase the production of fluild, there is significant improvement in the symptoms of people suffering with autism.[1]

## What evidence do the practitioners have that this really works?

Two literature searches, one in 2000 and one in 2006, were conducted. The 2000 literature search uncovered four articles, two of which were between-subject, double-blind, placebo designs. The first study included twenty-five children and the second study used sixty children. Neither of those studies reported any improvement in the symptoms associated with autism. One of these designs was done in two stages; the first stage was designed to identify children who seemed to be the most likely candidates to improve using secretin. These children were given secretin injections, and using the CARS measure, parents reported any improvement that might have occurred. Those children who were seen to benefit, were assigned to the double-blind, placebo, crossover study.* This procedure

---

*In this study design, one group initially receives the treatment and the other receives the non-treatment. In the next stage, the groups are switched so that the original group receiving the treatment then receives the non-treatment, and the non-treatment group then receives the treatment. Neither the researchers nor the patients (nor their parents) know when each group is receiving the treatment.

was an attempt on the part of the researchers to create an experiment where if indeed secretin is an effective treatment for autism, they would be most likely to find that result. Although I believe that parental reporting is very unreliable, I respect the fact that these researchers attempted to create conditions where secretin may have been most likely to have a positive effect. Despite this design, no meaningful results were reported.[2,3] The other articles were simply case studies.[1,4]

Another comprehensive literature search in 2006 found much more research had been conducted on secretin. This search netted twenty articles that present data on the effects of secretin treatment. Of these 20 articles, five showed that secretin had an effect on the subjects' autism and fifteen articles demonstrated no effect. The question is, what differentiates the five studies that report results from the fifteen that do not? Of the five positive studies, only two are randomized, double-blind, placebo controlled trials.[5,6*] The third study is a non-randomized study with no placebo condition[7] and the fourth study is an uncontrolled trial in which the researchers rely on weekly parental reporting to assess improvements, using a questionnaire designed to measure symptoms.[8] The final study[1] in this group was a case study reporting on three children. The study that deserves attention is the Kern et al. (2002) study, as their experiment was well designed, utilizing controls, employing different measures for autism and differentiating groups of children into those with gastrointestinal distress and those without. Their study is notable because for the dependent variable, autism, they used the

---

*The Jun et al. 2000 study is published by Tzu Chi Medical Journal which is a journal published by the Buddist Compassion Relief Tzu Chi Foundation founded in 1989. This article was not found in the mainstream journals, i.e., Medline, Cochrane Collection, and is not available through regular channels. A request to purchase this article through the journal received no reply. Therefore, we could not review the journal. Although the journal claims it uses a peer-review process, because 99 percent of the scientific data bases do not list the journal as one of the thousands of journals in existance, it is questionable whether the findings reported by the article are scientifically sound.

Aberrant Behavior Checklist (ABC), parts of the MacArthur Communicative Development Inventory (CDI) and a Global Assessment scoring as well.  In addition, the researchers used a GI assessment rating (it should be noted, however, that the CDI and the GI ratings relied on parental reporting).  They found statistically significant and meaningful differences between the two groups, primarily in the Irritability, Agitation and Crying ratings.[*]

In contrast, of the fifteen studies that found no effect for secretin, thirteen were randomized, double-blind, placebo-controlled studies and of those, six included a cross-over design, clearly a much more rigorous design than most of the studies which reported results.  Of note is that of the fifteen studies, five studies[9,10,11,12,13] used porcine secretin rather than synthetic secretin to control the potentially differing effects of these two types of secretin.  Porcine secretin was used to address criticism about the lack of results to the synthetic rather than the natural hormone (referred to as biologic or porcine).  In fact, Unis et al. (2000), used both types of secretin in an effort to find out if there is a difference.  They found none.  Finally, the company sponsoring the research, Repligen, reported that at the beginning of this year their clinical trials did not find any benefit for the children in the study.[14]

## What does the therapy actually look like?

Different researchers used various techniques to measure gastrointestinal distress prior to treatment using Secretin.  In the Horvath et al. (1998) study, secretin was given during an upper gastrointestinal endoscopy (while inserting a small scope in the upper GI tract) for each patient. The patients were put under a general

---

[*]The "Irritability, Agitation and Crying" ratings were significant ($p < .05$). Although these researchers also report other findings as significant, their p values are too high for me to agree regarding statistical significance ($p < .08$ and $p < .10$).

anesthetic, and biopsies of the esophagus, stomach and duodenum were taken. In addition, pancreatic and intestinal digestive enzymes were measured.  Before the biopsies were taken, secretin was injected in order to stimulate the secretion of pancreatic juice (to make the pancreas secrete enzymes). In other studies, patients received an intravenous dose of secretin on a one time basis or over two or three visits.  In Horvath et al. (1998), the gastric juices were collected and analyzed, and the tissues from the esophagus, stomach and duodenum were examined under a microscope.  A sample of juice from the pancreas was taken before the secretin was given, and three additional samples were taken during the ten minute period that followed.  All three patients received a follow-up dose three to eight months later.  Although the studies differed somewhat, most of them used a single dose of secretin.  In contrast, Sponheim et al (2002), used a controlled design where each child was given three doses of secretin over three months.  They also found that secretin has no effect on the disorder of autism.

## What else do I think?

In the articles that reported any meaningful results, the children were all suffering from chronic diarrhea.  The diarrhea could be responsible for interfering with learning and possibly exacerbating autistic behavior.  One can reasonably expect that diarrhea may work to foster a poor disposition in the sufferer.  If indeed the diarrhea abates and the digestive system improves, this could help the overall behavior of the child to improve.  It is understandable how this observation inadvertently lead a researcher or parent to conclude that secretin has improved the symptoms of autism in a child.  However, it is possible that the autism may not have improved at all; rather, the symptoms of gastrointestinal distress may have disappeared or been ameliorated, which would lessen the degree of irritability, improve concentration and the general well-being in many children, but not (importantly) children with autism exclusively.

An additional significant complication within this area of research is that it is unclear to what extent children may have been involved in other treatment programs. One child had reportedly undergone high-dose steroid therapy and intravenous immunoglobulin treatment, without any reported effect. Another child had been placed on an elimination diet specifically to treat the diarrhea, which also had no effect. The researchers provide no timeline for these interventions, making the need for a control group all the more important in some of these studies.

## Would I try it on my child?

My child does not suffer from chronic gastrointestinal distress. However, if she did, I would make sure that we visited a reputable gastrointestinal specialist to attempt to treat the GI tract and not blame her behavior on autism, but rather, on the fact that she was suffering. It has been my observation over the last fourteen years that children with autism are often underserved by the medical community because it is so difficult to differentiate behaviors with a non-physiological source from those caused by an underlying medical condition that may be successfully treated, for the simple reason that the autism frequently blocks communication between the child and the doctor.

## What kind of study would I like to see the researchers looking at secretin do?

After all the research done regarding the relationship between autism and secretin, this question appears to have had considerable research funding already spent in this research area. I would be interested, though, to see whether secretin is a potential treatment for gastrointestinal distress in general, not simply for children with autism. If indeed secretin is a treatment for certain GI conditions, then everyone suffering may benefit, including children with autism; however, this research would be unrelated to autism specifically.

## Who else recommends against secretin as a method for the treatment of autism?

The New York State Department of Health Report was the first out of the gate in 1999 when they stated: "The use of hormone therapies (such as ACTH or secretin) is not recommended as a treatment for autism in young children, until such methods have been shown to be effective and safe for use in this age."[15] Since then there have been a few others who have also recommended against the use of secretin as a treatment for autism. Quackwatch (2005)[16] has recommended against secretin, as has the American Academy of Child and Adolescent Psychiatry (2002).[17] The Committee on Children with Disabilities of the American Academy of Pediatrics, also recommends against the use of secretin for autism treatment. They state: "This and more recent studies have failed to demonstrate any scientific evidence to justify the use of secretin infusion to treat children with ASD."[18]

## So you're still on the horns of a dilemma?

I recommend that you read Sturmey (2005),[19] who does an in-depth review of the literature on secretin and concludes that secretin is ineffective. Based on the literature to this point, the use of secretin to treat autism can be regarded as completely experimental.

## What's the bottom line?

Based on the scientific research to date, there is not enough evidence that Secretin is an effective treatment for improving the symptoms of autism in children.

## Endnotes for Secretin

[1]Horvath, K., G. Stefanatos, K.N. Sokolski, R. Wachtel, L. Nabors, and J.T. Tildon. 1998. "Improved Social and Language Skills After Secretin Adminstration in Patients With Autistic Spectrum Disorders." *Journal of the Association for Academic Minority Physicians,* Vol. 9, No. 1, pp. 9-15.

[2]Chez, M.G., and C.P. Buchanan. 2000. "Reply to B. Rimland's 'Comments on Secretin and Autism: A Two-Part Clinical Investigation'." *Journal of Autism and Developmental Disorders,* Vol. 30, No. 2, pp. 87-94.

[3]Sandler, A.D., K.A. Sutton, J. DeWeese, M.A. Girardi, V. Sheppard and J.W. Bodfish. 1999. "Lack of Benefit of a Single Dose of Synthetic Hyman Secretin in the Treatment of Autism and Pervasive Developmental Disorder." [see comments] *New England Journal of Medicine,* Vol. 341, No. 24, pp. 1801-1806.

[4]Richman, D.M., R.M. Reese and D. Daniels. 1999. "Use of Evidence-based Practice as a Method for Evaluating the Effects of Secretin on a Child with Autism." *Focus on Autism and Other Developmental Disabilities,* Vol. 14, No. 4, pp. 204-211.

[5]Jun, S.S., P_.C.H. Kao and Y.C. Lee. 2000. "Double Blind Crossover Study of Secretin/Secrepan Treatment for Children With Autistic Symptoms." *Tzu Chi Medical Journal,* Vol. 12, No. 3, pp. 173-181.

[6]Kern, J.K., S. Van Miller, P.A. Evans and M.H. Trivedi. 2002. "Efficacy of Porcine Secretin in Children With Autism and Pervasive Developmental Disorder." *Journal of Autism and Developmental Disorders,* Vol. 32, No. 3, pp. 153-160.

[7]Robinson, T.W. 2001. "Homeopathic Secretin in Autism: A Clinical Pilot Study." *The British Homeopathic Journal,* Vol. 90, No. 2, pp. 86-91.

[8]Lonsdale, D. 2000. "A Clinical Study of Secretin in Autism and Pervasive Developmental Delay." *Journal of Nutritional Environmental Medicine*, Vol. 10, No. 4, pp. 271-280.

[9]Corbett, B., K. Khan, D. Czapansky-Beilman, N. Brady, P. Dropik, D.Z. Goldman, et al. 2001. "A Double-blind, Placebo-controlled Crossover Study Investigating the Effect of Porcine Secretin in Children With Autism." *Clinical Pediatrics,* Vol. 40, No. 6, pp. 327-331.

[10]Unis, A.S., J.A. Munson, S.J. Rogers, E. Goldson, J. Osterling, R. Gabriels, et al. 2002. " A Randomized Double-blind, Placebo-controlled Trial of Porcine Versus Synthetic Secretin for Reducing Symptoms of Autism." *Journal of the American Academy of Child & Adolescent Psychiatry,* Vol. 41, No. 11, pp. 1315-1321.

[11]Owley, T., W. McMahon, E.H. Cook, T. Laulhere, M. South, L.Z. Mays, et al. 2001. "Multisite, Double-blind, Placebo-controlled Trial of Porcine Secretin in Autism." *Journal of the American Academy of Child & Adolescent Psychiatry,* Vol. 40, No. 11, pp. 1293-1299.

[12]Roberts, W., L. Weaver, J. Brian, S. Bryson, S. Emelianova, A.M. Griffiths, et al. 2001. "Repeated Doses of Porcine Secretin in the Treatment of Autism: A Randomized, Placebo-controlled Trial." *Pediatrics,* Vol. 107, No. 5, p. E71.

[13]Honomichl, R.DE., B.L. Goodlin-Jones, M.M. Burnham, R.L. Hanse and T.F. Anders. 2002. "Secretin and Sleep in Children With Autism." *Child Psychiatry and Human Development,* Vol. 33, No. 2, pp. 107-123.

[14]Autism: Secretin Therapy Found Unsuccessful. *Pediatric Alert* 01600184, 2004, Vol. 29, No. 2, pp. 8-9.

[15]Guralnick, M., ed.  1999.  *Clinical practice guideline:  Report of the Recommendations. Autism/Pervasive Developmental Disorders, Assessment and Intervention for Young Children* (age 0-3 years).  Albany (NY): New York State Department of Health, p. IV-87.

[16]Quackwatch, http://www.quackwatch.org/01quackeryrelatedtopics/autism.html, (accessed Oct. 5, 2005).

[17]American Academy of Child and Adolescent Psychiatry, Policy Statement, 2005, http://www. aacap.org/publications/policy/ps39.htm#top, (accessed Aug. 8, 2005).

[18]Technical Report. 2001. "The Pediatrician's role in the Diagnosis and Management of Autistic Spectrum Disorder in Children." *Pediatrics*, Vol. 107, No. 5, pp. 1-18.

[19]Sturmey, P. 2005. "Secretin is an Ineffective Treatment for Pervasive Developmental Disabilities: A Review of 15 Double-blind Randomized Controlled Trials." *Research of Developmental Disabilities*, Vol. 26, No. 1, pp. 87-97.

# Biomedical Therapies: Vitamin B6 and Magnesium

## What is Vitamin B6-Magnesium Therapy?

Proponents of Vitamin B6-Magnesium Therapy have reported that the urine of people with autism has higher than average levels of a particular type of acid called homovanillic acid (HVA), produced when dopamine is metabolized.[1] This finding has lead these researchers to suggest that people with autism metabolize dopamine differently than those without autism.[2] In other words, dopamine (which is a neurotransmitter) is hypothesized to be used differently within the bodies of autistic people than those without autism. These researchers administered pyridoxine (vitamin B6) to those who had higher than normal levels of HVA and noticed that their autistic subjects experienced a decrease in the level of HVA in their urine. Their biochemical measures attempt to determine the amount of dopamine and homovanillic acid in the urine.

These researchers also employ electrophysiological measures (using electrodes) to argue that children with autism have abnormal response times to sound and light.[*] Vitamin B6 and Magnesium Therapy is hypothesized to alter the child's perception of sound and light in the brain.[3] Specifically, these researchers expect that the Vitamin B6 and Magnesium Therapy should decrease the amount of dopamine used up by the body (metabolized), and correct abnormalities in the child's response times to sound and light.[**] The researchers recommend a large dosage of both B6 and magnesium for an indefinite period of time. Although they are not explicit in the relationship between this treatment and behaviors

---

[*]Abnormal response times to sound and light has been conceptualized in this literature by the term "average cortical evoked responses."

[**]Whether the abnormalities in the child's responses have been corrected or not are measured by cortical evoked responses.

associated with autism, these researchers predict that behaviors characteristic of autism will decrease. As autism is measured largely on behavior, if Vitamin B6 - Magnesium Therapy is effective, we should expect to see behaviors associated with autism diminish as a result of this treatment.

## What evidence do the practitioners have that this really works?

We did a comprehensive database search and found much written about vitamin B6 and magnesium as a treatment for autism. There were over thirty articles either presenting data, reviewing data or debating the merits of the treatment. When we filtered out the commentary from the research articles, we netted twenty studies. Once we excluded the case studies,[4,5] the Parent Survey[6] and the subjective behavioral reporting,[7] we were left with sixteen studies to review on Vitamin B6 - Magnesium Therapy. Of the studies which report positive results, fourteen were done by two groups of researchers: Barthelemy, Martineau and LeLord, and Rimland. These researchers use physiological pre-and post treatment measures. As interesting as this may be, prior to accepting the notion that any physiological changes are actually indicators that the treatment is effective, these researchers must first demonstrate how these physiological changes (such as response time to sound and light) are in any way relevant to autism. Although over a quarter of the studies were double-blind, random assignment,[*] and placebo controlled (with additional studies designed as crossover studies where the groups alternated receiving either the treatment or the placebo), they all share a design shortcoming. The operationalization of their measure of the dependent variable, autism, is problematic. These studies all measure autism using behavioral scales

---

[*]Nye et al. (2005) rejected all the studies due to the lack of rigor in their design in terms of inadequate concealment of randomization and more than a twenty percent attrition rate of subjects. Despite these critiques, we decided to look at the studies because they did have some form of randomization procedure.

that are *not* widely accepted by researchers in the field of autism. Instead, they use measures that they have designed themselves or that were designed in the hospital doing the research, rather than measures that have been designed and tested independently (e.g., the Autism Behavioral Checklist, ABC, the Childhood Autism Rating Scale, CARS, the Autism Diagnostic Interview - Revised, ADI-R, the Autism Diagnostic Observation Schedule, ADOS). The Behavior Summarized Evaluation Scale (BSE) was developed by Barthelemy (1981) and used in Martineau et al. (1985), Martineau et al. (1986) and Martineau et al. (1988). A modified BSE scale, called the Echelle Bretonneau III was used by Jonas et al. (1984). The Bretonneau II was used by Barthemelemy et al. (1983), Lelord et al. (1981) and Barthelemy et al. (1980). In addition, a Target Symptoms Checklist was developed by Rimland (1978) but not independently tested for validity. In 1986 and 1997, Barthelemy et al. attempted to validate the BSE Scale. In 1997 they added nine additional items to the scale and compared their scale with Rimland's E2 scale, rather than other well-established scales in the field of autism assessment. In short, the scales used by proponents of Vitamin B6 and Magnesium Therapy need to be independently validated using well-excepted autism scales, rather than relying on each others' unvalidated scales or validating their own scales with other unvalidated scales.

Unfortunately, these measures for autism lack the validity and reliability that other measures have gained as a result of repeated use and evaluation by a much wider group of researchers. In terms of the biochemical and physiological measures (e.g., the average cortical evoked response), there is no data to suggest either biochemical measures or electrophysiological measures increase or decrease the symptoms associated with autism. In other words, increases or decreases in these measures have no scientifically-established relationship to the typical symptoms of autism which are, at this point, behaviorally-defined as we do not have any other way to measure autism.

In contrast, the two studies that found no results[8,9] did use widely recognized measures.  Tolbert (1993) used the Ritvo-Freeman Real Life Rating Scale for Autism, validated by Freeman et al. (1986). Findling et al. (1997) used a variety of accepted measures including the Childhood Autism Rating Scale (CARS), the Clinical Global Impression Scale (CGI), the Children's Psychiatric Rating Scale (CPRS), the NIMH Global Obsessive Compulsive Scale (OCS), and additional Parent and Teachers Rating Scales (the PRS and TRS) to measure autism (the dependent variable in the research).[*]  It is important to use widely-recognized, standardized measures in all autism research because these measures have been tested for accuracy in measuring autism by many diverse researchers throughout many years of research.  Findling et al. need to be commended in their attempt to use a large variety of measures, affording every opportunity to capture any treatment effect, even if only a small or targeted one.

Although it can be seen as a positive step to see researchers innovate and attempt to measure autism in a better way, it is crucial that any newer, more accurate scales have significant overlap with the older less precise measures, to make sure that the newer scale is indeed measuring autism more accurately.  The measures used in the studies that report positive results do not give us that assurance due to their lack of rigorous testing and their apparent choice *not* to use well-established measures.

The second issue associated with several of the studies in the Vitamin B6-Magnesium literature is that those who rated the autistic subjects after the study were not blind to all conditions of the treatment[3,4,10,11] or the details about who

---

[*]These measures were a combination of accepted autism scales (the Childhood Autism Rating Scale (CARS), developed and validated by Schopler et al. 1980 and Dilalla et al. 1994), or widely-accepted measures from the field of child psychiatry and psychology (the Clinical Global Impression Scale (CGI) National Institute of Mental Health, 1985; the Children's Psychiatric Rating Scale (CPRS) (Campbell et al. 1985); NIMH Global Obsessive Compulsive Scale developed by Insel et al. (1983).

completed the behavioral measures were not clear.[12]  In other words, in many of these studies, the researchers were not blind to the fact that these autistic individuals were given vitamin B6 and magnesium.  Put simply, the problem of non-blind raters introduces bias in the evaluation portion of the experiment.  A third problem with three of the studies has to do with lack of a control group.[4,13,14]  In addition, of the fourteen articles, five studies did not give autistic people in the control group a placebo.  Therefore, those who were responsible for the care of the person with autism knew that he or she was either in the control or treatment group.  That is a problem for objective research to move forward, insofar as the care giver's behavior towards the autistic subject may have reflected that knowledge and unduly influenced the outcome.

Another critique of over one-third of the studies is that the researchers did not report significance levels (i.e., did the results happen by chance?).  We do not know whether the behavioral results of  vitamin therapy are meaningful if the researchers involved do not report the significant levels (p-values).  Without the p-values, we do not know whether these results may have happened randomly or due to the treatment.  Four of the studies[4,13,15,16] report changes without a p value.  Lelord et al. (1981) report that "none of the trends associated with B6 responsiveness is statistically significant"[17] for the first phase of the study.  In the second phase, children are presented as improved or not improved (using aggregate statistics with p-values); however, we are given little other information in terms of how meaningful these improvements are.[*]  Finally, although the urine samples are used to measure the amount of vitamins secreted by the children, these measures do not in themselves measure the degree of autism, and therefore, cannot be used to measure an improvement in the symptoms of autism.

---

[*]Figure 1 does not clarify which questions show statistically significant improvement and which do not.  In addition, there is no table representing a comparison between pre-test, placebo, and post test scores with p values.  It is up to the reader to attempt to extrapolate the raw data from the figure.

## What does the therapy actually look like?

The administration of the vitamin B6 and magnesium can be in pill or liquid form.  Although there are variations, according to the proponents of this therapy, the vitamin should be given to the person twice per day.  In the studies that were conducted, children typically received thirty mg/kg of vitamin B6 and ten to fifteen mg/kg of magnesium lactate per day.

## What else do I think?

Based on science, there are many questions left unanswered with this treatment method .  We still have no idea whether vitamin B6 and magnesium, in fact, benefits people with autism.  If there is a population of people with autism who may benefit, then we need to find out which persons afflicted with autism are the best candidates for this treatment.  We also need to know the effect of megadoses of vitamin B6 and magnesium over a prolonged period.  In addition, will those individuals who may benefit from the treatment need to increase the dose due to satiation and will that be problematic, considering how high the dose is at the beginning of the treatment?   Prior to asking these questions, though, is the major question regarding whether Vitamin B6-Magnesium Therapy is indeed effective.  It is not possible to conclude, based on the given data, that vitamin B6-magnesium has *any* effect on autism and its associated behaviors.  Mixed results are found in the literature; therefore, additional well-controlled and well operationalized research is required to evaluate the effectiveness of vitamin B6-magnesium treatment.  In addition, more research is essential regarding the short and long term side effects before this treatment can be endorsed by the scientific community and (most importantly) used by parents.

## Would I try it on my child?

I would not try this therapy on my child for several reasons. First, my child does not tolerate strange tasting liquids and does not like to swallow pills. So, before I have a daily battle on my hands, I need to know that this is scientifically substantiated. Second, let's say I can manage to teach her to like her daily dose (hidden in ice-cream), how can I trust my observation as to whether this treatment is working? I may want the treatment to work so desperately that I may see progress that, in fact, may not be there, or I may be so cynical that I do not see the benefits that are actually taking place. Third, I am somewhat concerned about any possible side effects of high doses of magnesium, about which my daughter may or may not complain.

## What kind of study would I like to see the vitamin B6 and magnesium proponents do?

I would like the proponents of Vitamin B6 and Magnesium Therapy to replicate the study done by Findling et al. (1997), utilizing the more mainstream measurements of the dependent variable (autism) in his study and include various forms of IQ testing as well. In addition, the pre-and post psychometric measures must be administered by psychologists who are completely unaware that the children to be evaluated are in a study. Furthermore, I would like to see a well-documented, rigorous, random assignment procedure *with no one invested in the study who is knowledgeable as to which condition the child is assigned*. If the parents are to administer the pill, they must not know the experimental condition of their child, and they must not be given the responsibility of taking data of any kind. Finally, the researchers must publish their new results in a peer reviewed journal and share their experimental procedure in sufficient detail so the scientific community can properly attempt to replicate these findings.

## Who else recommends against Vitamin Therapy as a method for the treatment of autism?

There are several groups which recommend against Vitamin B6-Magnesium Therapy for autism.  The New York Report has the following to say about vitamin therapy: "Administering high does of vitamin B6 (pyridoxine) and magnesium is not recommended as an intervention for autism in young children ... Administering high doses of any type of vitamin or trace mineral is not recommended as a treatment for autism in young children."[18]  In addition, the Association for Science in Autism Treatment (ASAT) states, "A number of scientific reviewers have concluded that many of those treatments have proved ineffective or harmful.  The research that appears to support several other treatments is methodologically weak, and still others have yet to be evaluated carefully.  These include ... vitamin megadoses."[19]  In addition, the American Academy of Child and Adolescent Psychiatry also recommends against vitamins[20] and the American Academy of Pediatricians says the following about vitamins: "[Studies] have been criticized for their methodological shortcomings and failure to address the issue of safety of use."[21]

## So you're still on the horns of a dilemma?

Considering that research on Vitamin B6 and Magnesium Therapy has been available since 1968, and there has not been even one independent replication of these studies a good thirty-eight years later, you might want to consider waiting until an independent replication of this research is published; otherwise, you are engaging in pure experimentation.

## What's the bottom line?

Based on the scientific research to date, there is insufficient evidence to validate Vitamin B6-Magnesium Therapy as an effective treatment for improving the symptoms of autism.

## Endnotes for Vitamin B6 and Magnesium Therapy

[1]Martineau, J., C. Bathelemy, B. Garreau, and G. Lelord. 1985. "Vitamin B6, Magnesium and Combined B6-MG: Therapeutic Effects in Childhood Autism." *Society of Biological Psychiatry,* Vol. 20, No. 5, pp. 467-478.

[2]Barthelemy, C., B. Garreau, I. Ledet, D. Ernoug, J.P. Muh, and G. Lelord. 1981. "Behavioral and Biological Effects of Oral Magnesium, Vitamin B6 and Combined Magnesium - Vitamin B6 Administration in Autistic Children." *Magnesium-Bulletin,* Vol. 2, pp. 150-153.

[3]Martineau, J., C. Barthelemy, C. Cheliakine, and G. Lelord. 1988. "Brief Report: An Open Middle-term Study of Combined Vitamin B6-Magnesium in a Subgroup of Autistic children Selected on Their Sensitivity to This Treatment." *Journal of Autism and Developmental Disorders,* Vol.18, No. 3, pp. 435-447.

[4]Martineau, J., C. Barthelemy, and G. Lelord. 1986. Long-term Effects of Combined Vitamin B6-Magnesium Administration in an Autistic Child." *Society of Biological Psychiatry,* Vol. 21, No. 5-6, pp. 511-518.

[5]Clark, J.H. 1993. "Symptomatic Vitamin A and D Deficiencies in an Eight-year-old With Autism... Intake Consisting of Only French Fried Potatoes and Water for Several Years." *Journal of Parenteral and Enteral Nutrition,* Vol. 17, No. 3, pp. 284-286.

[6]Rimland, B. 1988. "Controversies in the Treatment of Autistic Children: Vitamin and Drug Therapy." *Journal of Child Neurology*, Vol. 3, pp. S68-72.

[7]Moreno, H. 1992. "Clinical Heterogeneity of the Autistic Syndrome: A Study of 60 Families." *Investigacion Clinice*, Vol. 33, No. 1, pp. 13-31.

[8]Tolbert, L., T. Haigler, M.M. Waits, and T. Dennis. 1993. "Brief Report: Lack of Response in an Autistic Population to a Low Dose Clinical Trial of Pyridoxine Plus Magnesium." *Journal of Autism and Development Disorders,* Vol. 23, No. 1, pp. 193-199.

[9]Findling, R.L., K. Maxwell, L. Scotese-Wojtila, J. Huan, T. Yamashita, and M. Wiznitzer. 1997. "High-dose Pyridozine and Magnesium Administration in Children With Autistic Disorder: An Absence of Salutary Effects in a Double-blind, Placebo-controlled Study." *Journal of Autism and Developmental Disorders,* Vol. 27, No. 4, pp. 467-478.

[10]Rimland, B., E. Callaway, and P. Dreyfus. 1978. "The Effect of High Doses of Vitamin B6 on Autistic Children: A Double-blind Crossover Study." *American Journal of Psychiatry,* Vol. 135, No. 4, pp. 472-475.

[11]Lelord, G., J.P. Muh, C. Barthelemy, J. Martineau, B. Garreau, and E. Callaway. 1981. "Effects of Pyridoxine and Magnesium on Autistic Symptoms -- Initial Observations." *Journal of Autism and Developmental Disorders,* Vol. 11, No. 2, pp. 219-230.
\
[12]Menage, P., G. Thibault, C. Barthelemy, and G. Lelord. 1992. "CD4 = CD45RA +T Lymphocyte Deficiency in Autistic Children: Effect of a Pyridoxine-Magnesium Treatment." *Brain Dysfunction,* Vol. 5, No. 5-6, pp. 326-333.

[13]Martineau, J., C. Barthelemy, S. Rux, and B. Gareau. 1989. "Electrophysiological Effects of Fenfluramine or Combined Vitamin B6 and Magnesium on Children With Autistic Behaviour." *Developmental Medicine and Child Neurology,* Vol. 31, No. 6, pp. 721-727.

[14]Rimland, B. 1974. "An Orthomolecular Study of Psychotic Children." *Child Behavior Research,* Vol 3, No. 4, pp. 371-377.

[15]Jonas, C. T. Etienne, C. Barthelemy, and J. Jouve. 1984. "Clinical and Biochemical Value of Magnesium + Vitamin B6 Combination in the Treatment of Residual Autism in Adults." *Thérapie,* Vol 39, No. 6, pp. 661-669.

[16]Lelord, G., E. Callaway, J.P. Muh, J.C. Arlot, D. Sauvage, B. Garreau, et al. 1978. "Modifications in Urinary Homovanillic Acid After Ingestion of Vitamin B6; Functional Study in Autistic children (author's translation)." *Revue Neurologique (Paris),* Vol. 134, No. 12, pp. 797-801.

[17] Lelord, G., et al., (see n. 11 above).

[18]Guralnick, M. ed. 1999. *Clinical Practice Guideline: Report of the Recommendations. Autism/Pervasive Developmental Disorders, Assessment and Intervention for Young Children* (age 0-3 years). Albany(NY): New York State Department of Health, p. IV-99.

[19]Association for Science in Autism treatment (ASAT). www.asatonline.org/resources/library/informed_choice.html, (accessed Aug. 25, 2006).

[20]Szymanski, L, B.H. King. 1999. "American Academy of Child and Adolescent Psychiatry Working Group on Quality Issues: Practice Parameters for the Assessment and Treatment of Children, Adolescents and Adults with Mental Retardation and Comorbid Mental Disorders." *Journal of the American Academy of Child and Adolescent Psychiatry*, Vol. 38, p. 30.

[21]Committee on Children With Disabilities. 2001. "Technical Report: The Pediatricians Role in the Diagnosis and Management of Autism spectrum disorders in Children." *Pediatrics*, Vol. 107, p. 13.

# Speech and Language Therapies Section 1.5

▷ *Fast ForWord Program*

▷ *The Hanen Method*

▷ *Lindamood-Bell Learning Processes*

▷ *The SCERTS Model*

# Speech and Language Therapies: Fast ForWord

## What is Fast ForWord?

Fast ForWord is a computer training program designed to improve children's understanding of speech and language. The proponents of this method work on various parts of language "by modifying speech acoustically to create an expanded form of the successive speech components."[1] According to the Fast ForWord developers, there are seven exercises which make up the Fast ForWord program. Each exercise is said to adapt to natural speech and attempts to address: 1) auditory processing (the ability to differentiate sounds, words, and relevant language from noise); 2) phonological analysis (where the function and similarities of the sounds are targeted), and 3) language skills.

## What evidence do the practitioners have that this really works?

At this point, there is one study that has been conducted to test the Fast ForWord computer program, part of which included children with autism and Pervasive Developmental Disorder not otherwise specified (PDD-NOS); however, this study was not published in a peer reviewed journal.[2] It is also unfortunate that the principal investigator, Tallal, did not improve the study to be of sufficient quality for peer review as this researcher is no stranger to the peer review process, with over twenty peer-reviewed journal articles to her name, published on the subject of language.

A positive characteristic of the study is that it includes twenty-nine participants with autism or PDD-NOS. This is a large number of participants in the field of autism research (two or three subjects seems to be the norm in most research projects conducted on children with autism). In addition, the results appear promising.  The researchers presented results that are highly significant on each of the outcome tests.  They note that fifteen of the twenty-nine children with PDD improved significantly.[*]

Unfortunately, there are several weaknesses associated with this research.  The study was conducted by eighty-four professionals working at thirty-five different sites across North America.  It is a design flaw to have so many professionals involved in one study at so many different locations.  Despite the fact that the computer is collecting the data (so inter-observer reliability is not a problem), I would be nervous about the lack of standardization.  We do not know what else occurs with the child during the sessions.  Were professionals at some sites helping the child one-on-one, whereas at other sites might have been letting the child complete the program independently?  Were some of the children receiving standard speech and language therapy concurrently or were they all receiving no other language therapy aside from this program?  In addition, it is not clear whether these children were involved in other therapies at the same time or before.  We need these points clarified in the article which presents the promising data.

Another flaw in the study design was that each clinician decided which pre- and post language tests should be used on their client. Lack of standardization in testing is an important concern.  All children should have had the same tests used for the pre-and post testing.  We would then be able to compare the results of all the children in the study and control the tendency for clinicians to recommend a particular test because it is thought that the child's gain could be measured better using one test over another.  In short, whatever is done with one child, needs to be done with every child.  If the researchers thought that some

---

[*]The actual data demonstrated these children improved by one or more standard deviations on every tested measure (which is a meaningful result).

children do better with one test over another, then both tests must be given to each child. For research purposes, my preference is that researchers administer a range of tests to each child. An additional weakness in their 1997 study is that the clinician who administered the test might profit from the service provided. This study was done at thirty-five sites where Fast ForWord is being offered for a price; unfortunately, it is essential that the experimenter have no vested interest in the outcome of the study. In other words, the outcome of the study should have no bearing on whether or not a clinician is going to have data which may encourage parents to have their children use the Fast ForWord computer program. In terms of experimenter effects in general, the clinician who knows that the child is going to be in a study, *should not assess that child in that study*. Under such circumstances, bias could occur. Put simply, a researcher with no profit motive should be conducting the pre and post tests.

Another weakness of the study is the absence of a control group. This is problematic because researchers using a within-subject design cannot control for other variables which may contribute to the improvements observed. In addition, without a control group, if the researchers who test the children prior to and after the study know that these children are in the study, then they also know that these children are receiving the treatment. A single-blind test could easily avoid this problem, where the clinicians doing the pre and post testing would know nothing about the study and would not know that some children have received this treatment, whereas others did not.

Another flaw of note in the 1997 study is that the Society of Neuroscience Reprint Series is not peer-reviewed, but rather a journal supported by the Scientific Learning Corporation, which is the company that provides the Fast ForWord computer program. In addition, the research supports this corporation. Unfortunately, the presentation of the results in the Society for Neuroscience is unwittingly deceptive to the untrained observer as the results of the study are presented in a very compelling way and have an aura of legitimacy. If these researchers were to test the results of the Fast ForWord program in a manner that could be peer reviewed, this would help parents of children with autism tremendously.

## What does the therapy actually look like?

Children start the Fast ForWord program either in a clinic or in their homes. In both settings, the sessions are one hundred minutes per day, five days per week, for a minimum of four weeks. The initial four weeks are approximately $2,450 USD within the clinic and $2,050 USD when done within the home.[*] Both the clinic and home programs require additional costs for pre-testing and consultation, as well as additional weeks, if recommended. The home programs also have optional computer rental for US $219.95 per month.

The Fast ForWord computer programs use computer-generated speech, which has been digitally modified.[3] The developers of Fast Forword hypothesize that the problem for many individuals with language learning difficulties is the speed of processing, rather than the speech itself.[4] As a result, the Fast Forword program dramatically slows down and expands parts of language in order to make auditory discrimination easier.[5] The content of the program includes sound exercises, and more complex word exercises. Each of these exercises is comprised of five levels of difficulty, with one being low complexity and speed, and five being comparable to natural speech.[6] These programs are presented in a game format, and include rewards in the form of onscreen animation and token economy systems.

---

[*]These prices are approximate and may have increased due to inflation from the time they were originally quoted.

At any given level, the individual is maintained at a minimum of eighty percent accuracy to ensure success, and the Scientific Learning Corporation provides ongoing performance evaluation.[7]

## What else do I think?

The use of Fast ForWord for individuals with autism assumes pre-existing skills which many children with autism may not possess (including language comprehension). Therefore, in order for a child with autism to use this computerized treatment program, the child must have a minimal level of language comprehension, which means that we must logically use other methods to first bring the child to the level where he or she could take advantage of this computer-based therapy. An additional difficulty for children with autism is the amount of focus required to use the computer program. The autistic child must be able to pay attention and focus for quite a long time, as this method requires one hundred minutes per day for twenty to sixty days. This attention span may be difficult for some children with autism to achieve.

## Would I try it on my child?

I would love to try this method on my child. She has the attention span and enough language comprehension to be a candidate. There is no down side for her because I do not see this as a risky treatment and the theory targeting various areas of language has *strong* intuitive appeal. However, until I can see more evidence that Fast ForWord is effective, i.e., via a peer-reviewed study with better controls, I'm going to wait to absorb the inconvenience of taking my child to a practitioner who offers this therapy, to possibly waste her time during a summer holiday and spend the large sum that this method requires. The principal researcher of the Fast ForWord system is quite honest when she discusses the fact that the Fast ForWord program is based on three assertions that are still highly debatable.

In fact, she states: "Fast ForWord could be a big step Backward."[8] That said, this company is quite prolific in terms of developing new products.

## What kind of study would I like to see the Fast ForWord researchers do?

I would like to see a study using a randomly-assigned experimental and control group with experimenters who are blind about which condition the child is assigned. In addition, they need to use consistent, commonly-accepted pre-and post measures administered to each child in the study, and there needs to be a central site administering the treatment and the placebo. If these practitioners want to do a within-subject design with no control group, we would need to see guarantees that the children were not receiving any other additional therapy concurrently. In addition, the children would need to be tested at many different points, prior to, during and after the completion of the study. Furthermore, the researcher needs to ensure that all the children in the study received an independent diagnosis of autism or PDD-NOS. Moreover, it would be prudent for these children to have a battery of generally-accepted psychometric tests administered to discern whether the therapy has any effect on IQ. Finally, it would be advantageous to have the children tested long after the treatment has been provided to determine whether or not the gains are maintained.

If the results do show that children in the treatment group significantly improve their language skills relative to the control group, then I would be very interested in having my child try this therapeutic language program. I truly do hope that this computer training program is tested independently as these are researchers who have created a system that, if effective, could be easily adopted by educational systems and Speech and Language Pathologists.

## Who else recommends for or against Fast ForWord as a method for the treatment of autism?

At this time, there are no reputable sources recommending for or against Fast ForWord for children with autism.

## So you're still on the horns of a dilemma?

I would recommend reading Tallal's article in the American Speech-Language-Hearing Association, where she frankly speaks about the experimental nature of the Fast ForWord program,[8] in order to put this research initiative in its proper context.

## What's the bottom line?

Based on the scientific research to date, there is insufficient evidence that the Fast ForWord method of autism intervention is an effective treatment for improving the language impairment in autism. We eagerly await more data.

## Endnotes for Fast ForWord

[1]Tallal, P. et al. 1997. *Rapid Training-Drive Improvement in Language Ability in Autistic and Other PDD Children*. Berkley (CA): Scientific Learning Corporation: Society for Neuroscience, Vol. 23, p. 490.

[2]Tallal, P., and M. Merzenich.  1997.  *Fast forword Training For Children With Language-Learning Problems: Results from a National Field Study by 35 Independent Facilities*. Rutgers University, University of CA at San Francisco (CA): American Speech-Language-Hearing Association, Boston, MA.

[3]Bolton, S. 1998. "Auditory Processing and Fast ForWord." *Curriculum/Technology Quarterly.* Vol. 7, No. 2, pp. 2-4.

[4]Tallal, P. et al., (see n. 1 above).

[5]Bolton, S., (see n. 3 above).

[6]Bolton, S., (see n. 3 above).

[7]Bolton, S., (see n. 3 above).

[8]Tallal, P., and M. L. Rice. 1997. " Evaluating New Training Programs for Language Impairment." *American Speech-Language-Hearing Association,* Vol. 39. No. 3, pp. 12-13.

# Speech and Language Therapies: The Hanen Method

## What is the Hanen Method?

The Hanen Method was developed by the Hanen Centre, a Canadian, non-profit organization established in 1975 that develops programs to help train professionals and parents in early language intervention. In 1992, they published their original manual called "It Takes Two to Talk"[1] and in 1999, they published a manual entitled, "More Than Words."[2] These two manuals outline the Hanen method for teaching children with autism to communicate. The program takes a social-interactionist perspective on autism treatment, and emphasizes learning communication in everyday activities. To accomplish this, practitioners use emotion (affect), predictability, structure and visual aides. The child leads his or her own communication development, while the parent acts as a facilitator of interaction.

In order to promote language development, parents are instructed to follow the '4 I's'. These are: 1) "Include the child's interests," which involves joining in on whatever the child is doing, with the purpose of teaching joint attention; 2) "Imitate what the child does," which is done to capture the child's attention and show the children that they have an effect on other people; 3) "Intrude," insist on joining the child, and 4) "Interpret," which involves rephrasing what the child is trying to say with the purpose of modeling so the child can imitate.[3] In addition to these guidelines, parents are told to play "People Games" in which they employ four techniques that go by the acronym "R.O.C.K." These techniques include: R - Repeat what you do and say with the purpose of showing the child how to communicate; O - Offer the child the opportunity to take a turn by pausing at the same place in the games; C - Cue the child to take a turn, first using "explicit signals" and then turning to natural signals, and K - Keep it fun! Keep it going!  This is accomplished by the parent being very animated so the child will want to stay involved.[4]  The program the Hanen Centre espouses applies the 4 "I's" and the "R.O.C.K." guidelines to routines, songs, books and toys in order to facilitate learning in individuals with autism.

## What evidence do the practitioners have that this really works?

To date, there is no evidence to suggest that this method is effective. The Hanen Centre was contacted and they indicated that they had no research to offer on the efficacy of this intervention for autism.  In addition, a comprehensive database search netted no evidence whatsoever regarding the efficacy of the Hanen method on children with autism.  Several studies were conducted on children with language delays; unfortunately, these children had a variety of developmental delays, none were identified as having a firm diagnosis of autism.[5,6,7]

## What does the therapy actually look like?

Typically, the Hanen program involves hiring a speech and language pathologist (SLP) to teach a *group of parents* who all share the cost of the twelve to thirteen week course.[*]  The course is two and one half hours per week and involves an orientation, an assessment of parent-child interaction, eight training sessions, three video feedback sessions, and a report by the Speech and Language Pathologist (SLP).  The report by the SLP appears to be the only system for objectively evaluating treatment effects.  This is problematic as the SLP has a

---

[*]When we first started researching this book, this was the primary offering for parents.  Since that time, the Hanen Centre has become more prolific in disseminating their methods and offers a variety of different training modules, and additional books and videos.

vested interest in the program's success.  In addition, there appears to be no standardization among the  practitioners who evaluate the progress using this method as each SLP measures progress according to her own criteria and assessment measures.  Also problematic is that there is no system of data collection to evaluate how the child responds when the parents implement the program.

## What else do I think?

Hanen provides a couple of disclaimers which are of great interest. One specifies that the Hanen program, "Is not designed to replace other treatments."[8] Specifically, the website states that the Hanen program is not designed to replace Applied Behavior Analysis (ABA) for individuals with autism.  If ABA is being used, they encourage the Hanen approach to be integrated within the home. Unfortunately, these programs may not be entirely complimentary because the Hanen method: 1) encourages a child-led approach in the natural environment, and 2) encourages parental involvement in the child's preferences, including self-stimulatory behavior. These two components are in opposition to an ABA approach, which initially uses a direct instruction approach to learning.  Here teaching occurs with the therapists breaking tasks down into small components and teaching directly to the child, *prior* to the tasks being generalized to the natural environment. ABA also targets self-stimulatory behaviors for elimination or replacement because these behaviors are seen to interfere with the child's ability to learn.  However, some of the components of the Hanen method are strikingly similar to ABA programs, including the use of positive feedback for appropriate behavior, as well as the use of prompting and prompt fading. Hanen also encourages repetition and routine, which are generally-accepted components of many ABA programs.

A second disclaimer that the Hanen website includes relates to their teaching approach.  As one of the 4 "I's," the Hanen method encourages that the parent imitate what the child does. This is done in order to show the child that he or she has an effect on others. The Hanen website then includes the statement that, "not all ASD kids will imitate on their own," and that "for these kids a more structured approach is recommended."[8]  Although this statement acknowledges that the Hanen method may not be appropriate for some children with ASD, it may inadvertently give parents of children with autism the impression that the Hanen method is effective for a considerable number of children on the autism spectrum.  Unfortunately, many children with autism are not going to respond to the child-led, unstructured approach, which is the very reason that this intervention is being sought by parents – that it is child-led. To say that not all of these children are able to imitate is a significant understatement.  The majority of children with autism are unable to imitate without being taught to do so, which is one of the reasons that they have not been able to learn language from the natural environment.

In addition, the concept that the teaching of turn-taking and "people games" is sufficient to address the complex deficits and detrimental maladaptive behaviors characteristic of autism, is highly misleading.  A more accurate statement would be that perhaps some of the children can acquire routines using this method as long as they already have imitation and attending skills, and can be disengaged from self-stimulatory and self-injurious behaviors in order to participate in social interaction.  However, this excludes the vast majority of the autistic population prior to effective intervention and does not address the issue that learning opportunities occur infrequently in the natural environment, are often academic in nature (e.g., writing, math, etc.) and/or are cognitively overwhelming for the child.

## Would I try it on my child?

I would not try this therapy on my child, either alone or in combination with another treatment method (as recommended by the Hanen Centre) due to the complete lack of evidence provided by proponents of this method as it applies to children afflicted with autism. Not only is there no evidence regarding the effectiveness of this method, the philosophy of the method is not compelling where children with autism are concerned. Unfortunately, despite the lack of evidence for the Hanen method in the area of autistic disorder, this child-led method appears to be the method of choice amongst Speech and Language Pathologists in Canada. Fortunately, for parents in the United States, the Hanen method has not gained wide acceptance thus far. Therefore, it is somewhat easier to find a Speech and Language Pathologist who does not use the Hanen method for children with autism in the U.S. as compared to Canada.

## What kind of study would I like to see the practitioners of the Hanen Method do?

I would like to see the Hanen Centre produce some outcome data on the efficacy of their treatment approach, specifically for children with autism. It would be encouraging to see a study using a control group and several reliable and valid outcome measures which gauge the improvements in language, taking maturation effects over time into account. In addition, outcome measures should address a comprehensive examination of the skill deficits and behavioral excesses of this population. An independent clinician would make the diagnosis of autism and would administer base-line and post-treatment measures. Furthermore, a Speech and Language Pathologist with no interest in the outcome of the study should administer *standardized* language tests. If an initial experiment indicates that the Hanen method is worthwhile for this population, its treatment effects should be compared with other interventions that have proven efficacy in autism treatment.

A comparative study would establish which treatment programs offer the child the best possible outcome. This will allow parents to make informed choices based on the state of the science.

## Who else recommends for or against the Hanen Method for the treatment of autism?

Due to the lack of popularity of the Hanen Method in the United States, much attention has not been paid to it (in contrast to Canada, where, as mentioned before, this method is widely used by Speech and Language Pathologists to treat autism). Consequently, neither Quackwatch, nor any federal or state governmental agencies have conducted comprehensive reviews of the Hanen Method in their clinical practice guideline evaluations.

## So you're still on the horns of a dilemma?

If you are interested in using the Hanen method despite the lack of data supporting this method, I suggest that you have your child evaluated by a clinical psychologist with no vested interest in the Hanen Method, and then use a Speech and Language Pathologist on a short term basis to provide the treatment. I would then return to the same psychologist and have the child tested again to determine whether or not the child has benefitted from the additional use of the Hanen Method. It would be most unfortunate to waste your child's time using the Hanen Method exclusively when there are other methods with better evidence regarding efficacy for autism treatment.

## What's the bottom line?

Based on the scientific research to date, there is no evidence that the Hanen Method is an effective method for improving the language impairment associated with autism.

# Endnotes for the Hanen Therapy

[1]Manolson, A. 1992. *It Takes Two to Talk.* Toronto, ON:  A Hanen Centre Publication.

[2]Sussman, F. 2002. *More Than Words: The Hanen Program for Parents of Children With Autism spectrum disorder.* Toronto, ON: The Hanen Centre, www.hanen.org, (accessed Feb. 21, 2006).

[3]Sussman, F., (see n. 2 above).

[4]Sussman, F., (see n. 2 above).

[5]Girolametto, L.E. 1988. "Improving The Social Conversation Skills of Developmentally Delayed Children:  An Intervention Study." *Journal of Speech and Hearing Disorders,* Vol. 53, pp. 156-167.

[6]Tannock, R., L.E. Girolametto, and L. Siegel. 1992. "The Interactive Model of Language Intervention: Evaluation of its Effectiveness for Pre-School-Aged Children with Developmental Delay." *American Journal of Mental Retardation*, Vol. 97, No. 2, pp. 145-160.

[7]Girolametto, L., P.S. Pearce, and E. Weitzman. 1996. "The Effects of Focused Stimulation for Promoting Vocabulary in Young Children With Delays:  A Pilot Study." *Journal of Children's Communication Development*, Vol. 17, No. 2, pp. 39-49.

[8]The Hanen Centre, www.hanen.org, (accessed Feb. 21, 2006).

# Speech and Language Therapies: Lindamood-Bell Learning Processes

## What is the Lindamood-Bell Learning Processes?

According to the Lindamood-Bell Corporation, Lindamood-Bell Centers of Learning are designed to offer programs that develop the "sensory-cognitive" processes, which proponents state are the basis for learning academic skills such as, "reading, spelling, math, visual-motor skills, language comprehension, and critical thinking."[1] The centers offer clinical, school and workshop programs addressing the many academic skill deficits seen in learners of all ages. There are several different curricula and materials designed and sold by Lindamood-Bell and their publishing company, Gander Educational Products. The particular curriculum is determined for each child based on initial assessments.

## What evidence do the practitioners have that this really works?

There is currently no evidence that the Lindmood-Bell learning processes are an effective intervention for individuals with autism. Lindamood-Bell do have over a dozen peer-reviewed journal articles on different learning disabilities such as dyslexia, spanning from 1991 to 2002. The latest comprehensive database search in 2006 found no peer-reviewed studies on the efficacy of this method for children with autism. The Research and Development Department at Lindamood-Bell were contacted by us in the past for information regarding outcome data on the use of their products for individuals with autism. They shared plans to collect data on their method; unfortunately, the design they described does not meet the minimum standards of rigor for scientific inquiry. According to Lindamood-Bell, there will be no experimental design; rather, they will select a handful of students, in an unspecified manner, and present pre-and post Lindamood-Bell results.

The information provided to me indicates that there will not be a sufficiently large number of students to perform group statistics and there will be no independent diagnosis of autism required for the children in the prospective research at Lindamood-Bell. Finally, the case studies will be reported in their own brochure information — they will not be published within a peer-reviewed journal.

## What does the therapy actually look like?

The particular Lindamood-Bell programs which are used for individuals with autism are unspecified. The practitioners give each client a battery of tests to assess where the problems lie and then determine the program which best serves the needs of the client. The programs are available to students in either a clinical or school setting. Costs for the programs vary, depending on the individual assessment of the student. They have over forty centers which offer one-to-one instruction with trained personnel, throughout the United States and one practitioner in the United Kingdom.

## Would I try it on my child?

I would very much like to try this curriculum on my child; however, I would first require some evidence that these curricula are effective for children with autism before investing time and money on the method. I would be very interested in understanding which prerequisite skills are necessary, prior to purchasing the materials. I would also like to see some evidence that children with autism benefit as long as they have the prerequisite skills. This is one of those unfortunate situations where there may be some very valuable materials here for autism; however, without any rigorous testing of these materials on children with Autistic Spectrum Disorder, we will never know with certainty whether what they have to offer is valuable for children with autism.

## What else do I think?

Despite the current lack of peer-reviewed supportive research on Lindamood-Bell products and services for individuals with autism, informational material regarding international conferences on the topic claim to have research-driven programs for developing language and literacy.  However, nowhere is it specified where the available research on these products can be found as it relates specifically to children with autism specifically.  Several speakers report case studies with individuals "on the autistic spectrum."  Unfortunately, case studies are an inappropriate assessment of any given treatment modality because there is no control over confusing (confounding) variables which may be responsible for the changes observed. Also, the autistic spectrum is a diverse and varied one. It ranges from individuals diagnosed with Rett's syndrome and severe autism, to individuals who are diagnosed with Asperger's syndrome. There is a great deal of both "inter" and "intra" diagnostic variability in autism spectrum disorders and, as a result, there is great diversity in the number and severity of skill deficits. Moreover, the kinds of programs offered by Lindamood-Bell have prerequisite skills that might only be attained by a small portion of individuals with an autistic spectrum disorder.  This is not an insignificant point insofar as it is the overall value of the method for this group of children.

Informational material provided by Lindamood-Bell indicates that they approach autism as a "Language Processing Spectrum Disorder." While language is an important skill deficit for this population, there are other skill deficits and behavioral excesses that do not pertain to language processing but which also form diagnostic criteria for the disorder.  These other skill deficits and excesses are not addressed through the kinds of academic programs provided in the Lindamood-Bell system.

## What kind of study would I like to see the Lindamood-Bell practitioners do?

I would like to see them conduct research which can stand up to the scrutiny of peer review, rather than work that is published solely in marketing materials. Also, clarification is required on exactly who, if anyone, can benefit from these programs. Specifically, what kinds of language prerequisites are required in order to successfully learn the skills being targeted? We do not know. Additionally, how useful and generalizable are the skills being acquired? Once again, we do not know. The child is being assessed with pre-and post tests, so what exactly is being assessed? Does the child acquire a skill or learn material? Does the learning acquired through a Lindamood-Bell program generalize to other settings, tasks and materials? We similarly do not know these things either, which are holes that need to be filled.

## Who else recommends for or against Lindamood-Bell as a method for the treatment of autism?

The Lindamood-Bell system is not widely used by parents of children with autism. Therefore, there has been little scrutiny among those in the autism community and no official statements from reputable organizations regarding the state of the science with Lindamood-Bell materials.

## So you're still on the horns of a dilemma?

Despite the lack of data supporting this method for children with autism, if you are still interested in using the method, I suggest that you have your child evaluated by a clinical psychologist with no vested interest in the Lindamood-Bell Learning Process and then use one of their consultants so that you are sure that the treatment fidelity is high. I would then go back to the same psychologist and have the child retested to determine whether or not the child has benefitted in any way from this learning system.  It is important to follow your child's progress using generally accepted tests rather than measures created, or supplied by, the practitioner who is providing the treatment.

## What's the bottom line?

Based on the scientific research to date, there is no evidence that the Lindamood-Bell Learning Processes are an effective treatment for improving the language impairment that is characteristic of autism.

## Endnotes for Lindamood-Bell

[1]Lindamood-Bell Learning Processes (n.d.). San Luis Obispo, CA. p. 1.

# Speech and Language Therapies: The SCERTS Model

## What is the SCERTS Model?

The SCERTS Model is an approach that concentrates on improving the communication and social ability of children with autism. SCERTS (which stands for Social Communication Emotional Regulation, and Transactional Support[1]) concentrates on enhancing the child's joint attention skills, in order to improve his ability to communicate with others. In addition, this model targets the child's ability to use symbols and thereby improve communication, play and creative language. Further, emotional regulation is taught to improve the child's self-regulation, ability to find emotional support in others and be able to handle overwhelming sensations that practitioners refer to as dysregulation. The SCERTS Model also concentrates the child's ability to use a variety of educational, interpersonal, family and professional supports. The goals are taught in a developmental sequence, in different settings and, often, in a natural and inclusive environment (such as a school). This method could be categorized as one that is based upon a developmental perspective.

## What evidence do the practitioners have that this really works?

There is no data supporting the SCERTS Model. Proponents claim that this model has been developed based on over twenty years of research and that it is "consistent with recommended tenets of 'evidence-based' practice";[2] however, the articles that they use to support the model are mostly theoretical. In short, there is a conspicuous lack of well-designed studies (evidence) supporting this philosophy. Other than the publications from the developers of the SCERTS Model, the areas of "empirical" support for the SCERTS Model come out of the Positive Behavioral Support literature (which is long on philosophy and short on data), the Floor-Time literature (which also suffers from a lack of data) and the Hanen literature (which is not empirically supported either). Please see the various sections in the book for more detail on each of the areas which are relied upon by the SCERTS Model. Proponents claim that their model is consistent with the recommended practices for autism treatment; however, until the SCERTS Model is independently tested, its claim of empirical support is highly questionable.

## What does the therapy actually look like?

The SCERTS model uses one-on-one instruction for children who need more support, or group instruction for those who need less support. The intervention takes place in the school classroom and uses a structured special education teaching approach, utilizing a variety of prompting methods when necessary. Proponents claim that they take advantage of the children's strengths to target their weaknesses (e.g., using visual rather than auditory teaching). To the untrained eye, at times the model in the classroom looks like traditional structured special education teaching. When SCERTS is used in a segregated setting, there is typically a special educational teacher and a number of school aides are assigned to several children. There is also a play component where the children are encouraged to engage in pretend play. An additional facet of the program incorporates opportunities for the children to use different types of apparatus typically found in Sensory Integration Therapy, e.g., special swings. Another facet of the curriculum addresses the ability of children to regulate their emotions by giving them the tools to feel better, e.g., to ask for help if they are having difficulty. Teachers and aides will also soothe a child by applying physical pressure techniques based on the literature on Sensory Integration Therapy. The curriculum also includes teaching children to calm others if they see that a peer is upset.  There is an integrated component of the program which helps typical peers learn to relate to children with autism spectrum disorder.

The curriculum is adapted or modified to emphasize visual strategies in the form of pictures with which to communicate, i.e., through the use of the Picture Exchange Communication System (PECS), and encourages the child to read books about emotions.  Parents are looked upon as collaborators and included in the educational process by incorporating the PECS icons in the home. Practitioners of the SCERTS Model also provide emotional support for parents For an in-depth demonstration of the SCERTS Model, developers of the model have produced three videos illustrating their model for children needing varied amounts of support.  The first video is an introduction and overview of the model and the other video-tapes show the SCERTS model on children who initially need considerable support and then, subsequently, less support.

## Would I try it on my child?

While most of the concepts in the SCERTS Model seem appealing (particularly the part where the school system is actually supposed to be cooperative and listen to parents), if my child were starting out with little language and poor attention skills, I would not utilize this method.  The SCERTS Model does incorporate visual strategies, which are important for many children with autism spectrum disorder (including the PECS system).  However, I would want my child to graduate quickly from PECS to text and verbalization because it is preferable to communicate in the world verbally (if possible).  I did not see proponents of the SCERTS Model present sufficient strategies in their literature to curb various self-stimulatory and anti-learning behaviors characteristic of autism that blocks attention.  I would be concerned that my daughter would not make enough progress due to the interference of problematic behaviors.  In addition, although play, communication and creative language sound like wonderful goals, until there is evidence that these goals have been met using this method, I would not have my child enrolled in the SCERTS educational program.

## What else do I think?

Much of the SCERTS Model is concerned with: 1) how adults and schools systems make decisions about children with autism spectrum disorder, and 2) the support that families and professionals require to be successful, rather than about the efficacy of the model for autism intervention. Quite troubling is that the SCERTS Model has all the appearance of being a method designed to rehabilitate existing, inadequate schools systems so they can adapt to coping with autistic children in the school, rather than offer the most effective treatment possible for autism spectrum disorder. It was in 1982 when one of the developers of the SCERTS Model first started discussing the role of the Speech and Language Pathologist in the assessment and intervention of children with autism.[3] It is over twenty-four years later, and although proponents of SCERTS have written much about this topic and developed a model, they still have not tested their model independently. In short, an independent test on the SCERTS Model is long overdue.

## What kind of study would I like to see the SCERTS practitioners do?

Due to their claim that the SCERTS Model addresses what practitioners define as the "core" challenges of children with autism,[4] it is time for the SCERTS Model to test their protocol against the main competitor which is, at this point, Intensive Behavioral Treatment. To do this, I'd like to see a between-subject design utilizing a variety of autism measures including IQ tests, and Speech and Language measures.  Proponents of SCERTS disagree with utilizing IQ and post-intervention placement measures.  They state: "These measures may not be ecologically valid because they do not measure changes within natural environments, do not address the core 'deficits' in ASD, and are particularly problematic for infants and young children."[5]  The discounting of these measures results in a lack of objective testing; therefore, along with their goals of measuring improvement in communication, motivation, social competence and generalization of skills, SCERTS researchers would be well advised to use the widely accepted measures from autism research as well (which includes cognitive testing and behavioral measurement).

## Who else recommends for or against SCERTS as a method for the treatment of autism?

Although the SCERTS Model has not been recommended specifically by any reputable clinical practice guidelines, the New York State Department of Health Report has recommended against the DIR method, upon which SCERTS claims to be partially based.  For more detail on the lack of scientific support for the other models upon which the SCERTS Model rests, please read the sections in this book on the Hanen Method and Positive Behavioral Support.

## So you're still on the horns of a dilemma?

Despite the lack of data on the SCERTS Model, if you still would like to essentially experiment with your child by placing him in a school system that adopts this model, I would encourage you to have an independent, licenced psychologist take baseline data prior to beginning the SCERTS program, and then have the child retested at regular intervals (e.g., yearly) to ensure that some progress is actually being made. If there is no objectively-measured progress within one year, it would be wise to choose an alternative, well-settled autism treatment for your child.

## What's the bottom line?

Based on the scientific research to date, there is no evidence that the SCERTS Model is an effective treatment to ameliorate the symptoms associated with autism.

# Endnotes for the SCERTS Model

[1]Prizant, B.M., A. Wetherby, E. Rubin, and A.C. Laurent. 2003. "The SCERTS Model: A Transactional, Family-Centered Approach to Enhancing Communication and Socioemotional Abilites of Children With Autism spectrum disorder." *Infants and Young Children*, Vol. 16, No. 4, pp. 296-316.

[2]Prizant, B.M., A. Wetherby, E. Rubin, and A.C. Laurent, (see n. 1 above), p. 298.

[3]Prizant, B.M. 1982. "Speech-Language Pathologists and Autistic Children: What is Our Role? Part 1. Assessment and Intervention Considerations. Part II. Working With Parents and Professionals." *American Speech and Hearing Association Journal,* Vol. 24, pp. 463-468, 531-537.

[4]Prizant, B.M., A. Wetherby, E. Rubin, and A.C. Laurent, (see n. 1 above), p. 313.

[5]Prizant, B.M., A. Wetherby, E. Rubin, and A.C. Laurent, (see n. 1 above), p. 313.

# Miscellaneous Therapies Section 1.6

▷ *Art Therapy*

▷ *Auditory Integration Training*

▷ *Craniosacral Therapy*

▷ *Dolphin Assisted Therapy*

▷ *Exercise Therapy*

▷ *Facilitated Communication Training*

▷ *Holding Therapy*

▷ *Music Therapy*

▷ *Pet-facilitated Therapy*

▷ *Sensory Integration Therapy*

▷ *Vision Therapy*

# Miscellaneous Therapies: Art Therapy

## What is Art Therapy?

Art Therapy is based on the philosophy that through the artistic process, we can reach a person with autism. Although there does not seem to be a singular philosophy which drives Art Therapy as applied to children with autism, there is a Freudian overtone from this work which assumes that people with autism require their ego to be developed, and that Art Therapy can accomplish this goal.[1] In addition, Art Therapy is believed to help children with autism organize their sensory world (i.e., help process the incoming information from their five senses).[2] Furthermore, Bentivegna et al. (1983) provide a case study about a child who attended psychotherapy and art therapy concurrently. The child is described as able to communicate with the outside world through his artwork. There does not appear to be a uniform Art Therapy protocol that is embraced by practitioners; rather, there is a variety of philosophies which promote the use of art to "reach" the child with autism.

## What evidence do the practitioners have that this really works?

Despite a thorough search through many data bases, I did not net any peer-reviewed journal articles reporting data on the efficacy of Art Therapy for persons with autism. The eight articles found tend to analyze communication through the artwork and compare an autistic person's artwork to the typical population; however, none of these articles even attempt to show how Art Therapy actually ameliorates the condition of autism. One article[3] chronicles the attempted use of art as a way to integrate children with autism with their non-disabled peers. These researchers found that art was a good medium to increase the social behavior of the non-disabled peers toward the children with autism. However, there was nothing inherent in Art Therapy that improved the condition of autism.

## What does the therapy actually look like?

Although there does not seem to be one distinctive protocol utilized to work with children with autism using Art Therapy, materials and activities which promote creativity[4] are introduced to the child. Art Therapy, as described by Buck et al. (1984), appears to be client-led, having the person with autism independently explore the art materials that are presented.

## What else do I think?

Some forms of Art Therapy have much in common with Sensory Integration Therapy, because the child experiences the materials in a sensory manner. In addition, there seems to be a undercurrent of Freudian or Bettleheimian philosophy in Art Therapy, yet there is no data supporting either Freud's or Bettleheim's philosophy when it comes to autism. In fact, Bettleheim's philosophy regarding the supposed cause of autism (the refrigerator mother hypothesis — "cold, uncaring mother") has been thoroughly discredited.

## Would I try it on my child?

No I would not. I would be more than willing to have my child take art lessons as a form of productive leisure or as a hobby, if she enjoyed art. However, I have seen absolutely nothing in the scientific literature to indicate that Art Therapy even deserves the word "Therapy" attached to it.

## What kind of study would I like to see the Art Therapy practitioners do?

Prior to rigorously testing Art Therapy, there needs to be a defined treatment protocol developed. Once the independent variable of Art Therapy is defined objectively and operationalized so that it can be tested, only then is the supposed treatment protocol worthy of the term "therapy." However, not only is there no well-defined protocol for Art Therapy, but there isn't even a theory that hypothesizes *why* Art Therapy should work for children with autism. Clearly, this is a fundamental prerequisite for testing this method.

## Who else recommends for or against Art Therapy as a method for the treatment of autism?

Art Therapy has been ignored, for the most part, by those writing clinical practice guidelines, as this therapy is not considered dangerous nor is it prohibitively expensive: therefore, parents have nowhere to go to check on the efficacy of Art Therapy.

## So you're still on the horns of a dilemma?

Due to the complete absence of any data on the effectiveness of Art Therapy, I would caution against the use of this so-called treatment, *especially* if it is to the exclusion of validated autism treatment. Art Therapy has not been demonstrated to be harmful; however, I would expect no results other than perhaps an enjoyable leisure time activity for your child. I would stress again that Art Therapy cannot be characterized as therapy for autism.

## What's the bottom line?

Based on the scientific research to date, there is no evidence to conclude that Art Therapy is an effective treatment for improving the symptoms characteristic of autism.

## Endnotes for Art Therapy

[1]Scanlon, Kathleen. 1993. "Art Therapy with Autistic Children." *Pratt Institute Creative Arts Therapy Review*, Vol. 14,  p. 37.

[2]Scanlon, K., (see n. 1 above).

[3]Schleien, S., T. Mustonen, and J. E Rynders. 1995.  "Participation of children with autism and non-disabled peers in a cooperatively structured community art program." *Journal of Autism and Developmental Disorders*, Vol. 24, No. 4, pp. 397-413.

[4]Bentivegna, S., L. Schwartz, and D. Deschner. 1983.  "The use of art with an autistic child in residential care." *American Journal of Art Therapy*, Vol. 22, pp. 51-56.

# Miscellaneous Therapies: Auditory Integration Training

## What is Auditory Integration Training?

Auditory Integration Training (AIT) was developed by Dr. Guy Berard in the 1960s and was popularized in the United States by Dr. Alfred Tomatis, as a treatment for many cognitive or behavior problems, including autism. Berard suggests that autism is due, in part, to distortions in hearing, which create avoidance behaviors in individuals with autism, particularly as a reaction to extremely acute sounds.[1] Auditory Integration Training was developed to lessen autistic behaviors by "re-educating" the hearing system. Auditory re-education is believed to take place through mechanical massage of the different parts of the ear (ossicles, eardrum and cochlea) and, thereby, correct auditory distortions. There is no clear data on how exactly Auditory Integration Training works in the ear, but several explanations are available in the literature.

## What evidence do the practitioners have that this really works?

Our database research found many published and unpublished articles on Auditory Integration Training (AIT). Most of those articles were either only opinion pieces, reviews, or commentary. There were twenty-eight studies in which researchers actually collected data on the AIT intervention; however, most were either unpublished, presented at conferences, or published in non-peer reviewed journals, pamphlets or short books. Not surprisingly, most of the studies which were unpublished or published in non-peer-reviewed newsletters or reports found that AIT was of benefit (please see page Section Two for a discussion on the importance of peer review). There were in total, nine peer-reviewed studies which presented data. Of these nine, three were case studies[2,3,4] which lack scientific rigor, and two were open pilot studies (the researchers were not blind to experimental procedures) with no control groups or appropriate within-subject design procedures.[5,6] There are four peer-reviewed studies on AIT which randomly assign subjects to either experimental or control groups (where those in the control group received a placebo treatment that closely mimicked the treatment procedure). Two of the studies reported results which they attributed to AIT.[7,8] In contrast, two of the studies reported either no effect of AIT on autism[9] or reported effects which could not be attributed to AIT.[10]

These four studies merit closer examination. In the first study where researchers reported positive results for AIT,[11] seventeen autistic children and adolescents participated. Each subject had a diagnosis of autism from an independent agency. The researchers matched pairs of subjects in terms of the subject's age, sex, hearing sensitivity and possible ear infections, and then randomly assigned subjects from the matched pair to the control or experimental condition (which is a good idea as seventeen subjects is not a large number and matching pairs helps ensure that the two groups are similar); however, the one variable that researchers did not use to match children in the study was degree of autism (using objective behavioral and IQ measures). Unfortunately, degree of autism is the most important variable that should have been used for matching.

There were several major flaws in the study. First, the researchers over-relied upon parental reporting, using the Aberrant Behavior Checklist (ABC), the Hearing Sensitivity Questionnaire (HSQ) and the Fisher's Auditory Problems Checklist (FAPC). An additional problem with the study is that only the ABC research instrument was used to measure improvement in the children's behaviors. Ideally, several autism measures should have been used to ensure that the reported results are accurate. Furthermore, the researchers did not succeed in creating two groups that were similar. Their strongest measure for autism, the Aberrant Behavior

Checklist (ABC), demonstrated that the groups were significantly different at the outset of the study.  Although they attempted to deal with this problem by using statistical procedures (they subtract the pretest score from the three month score to measure the change only), this completely undermines the belief that random assignment and matching did, in this case, create two groups which were similar at the beginning of the first study.  In other words,  this major flaw calls into question all the results of these researchers' studies.  After attempting to account for the basic flaw of the two research groups of children being initially different, these researchers did find a difference in the groups after the treatment based on the ABC scores and in four of the sub-scales in the ABC. However, due to initial difference between groups, I consider these results unreliable to arrive at any conclusions about how well AIT works to treat autism.

The second study[12] showed major improvements in the experimental design over the initial study.[13]  Eighty children participated in the study and were randomly assigned to the study groups.  It is notable that eighty children in autism-related research is an impressive number of subjects for one study.  Noteworthy also is that all children in the experiment were diagnosed from an independent agency.  The study tested the children prior to and after the treatment, by using a variety of psychometric measures: the Autism Behavior Checklist (ABC); the Developmental Behavior Checklist (DBC) in a teacher and parent version; parts of the Peabody Picture Vocabulary Test(PPVT), and the Leiter International Performance Scale (LIPS).  The study followed the children for twelve months after the completion of the study.  The use of a number of tests to rate variables which are indicators of autism, administered by teachers and psychologists, is a significant improvement over prior studies testing AIT.  In this study, an independent psychologist tested the children using the ABC, LIPS, and PPVT measures and trained the child to go through a specialized hearing test (an audiometric assessment).  In addition, there were tests to demonstrate that different researchers, taking the same data, recorded the same results (please see Section Two for a discussion on inter-observer reliability).

Bettison's results show that the groups were indeed similar prior to treatment, which is important because a study needs to compare one group to another. (This improvement is in contrast to the study conducted by Rimland (1994), in which the groups were different prior to treatment). This finding gives me a high degree of confidence that as long as there are no other serious flaws in the study, we can take the results of the Bettison study seriously.

What did Bettison find?  Well, her results are quite interesting.  She found that the children improved in *both* the experimental and the control group.  When comparing the experimental and control group after the treatment, there was no significant difference between each group of children on most measures (specifically the Autism Behavior Checklist (ABC), the Developmental Behavior Checklist (DBC), and the IQ tests).  In other words, both sets of autistic children improved — even the children who did not receive the auditory integration training but, instead, listened to unmodified music.  Put simply, the Auditory Integration Training itself had *no* effect on degree of autism.  Many of the improvements of both groups are statistically significant, which is somewhat perplexing.  Mudford et al. (2005) suggest that this may be an experimental artifact.  Specially, they suggest that the improved scores may be the result of administering the same questionnaires multiple times (each child would have been evaluated with the questionnaire ten times — five times by the parent and five times by the teacher on five different occasions).  The results of particular interest are the improvement of both groups on two cognitive tests (the PPVT and the LIPS).  Unfortunately, despite the statistical significance, the standard deviation of the results is very large (which increases the possibility that results could have happened by chance alone).  In addition, the behavior test administered by the teacher (the DBC) provided an interesting result. The control group had a statistically significant, but weak, change. Of note is that when the teacher and the parents fill out the exact same questionnaire (the DBC), the improvements the parents see are much greater than what the teacher records, which further exemplifies my profound mistrust of parental reporting.* Keep in mind that the teachers and parents are observing the same children. Bettison also makes the same observation, that parental reporting is inflated due to parental high hopes for their children.

Aside from the hypothesized questionnaire effect, there are other possibilities about why both groups improved. First, there may be another influence *present* at the same time as the experiment but not *a result* of the experiment. What causes this confounding influence may not be clear; however, the fact that the study compares two groups, allows us to make sure this unintended influence does not fool us into thinking that the Auditory Integration Training actually has an effect. Another explanation for the improvement of both groups is that there may be no effect other than maturation effects, paired with the effect of the various educational or other treatment programs in which the children are enrolled. In short, based on the results of the best designed study on AIT, there is insufficient evidence to conclude that auditory integration training is an effective treatment for children with autism.

Another question that arises from this research is the premise upon which this therapy is based: AIT practitioners assume that auditory distortions do exist in the first place.[14] This belief has not yet been verified due to the obstacle of audiometrically testing individuals with autism.[15]

---

*The teacher scores for the experimental group were 42.93 before, and 40.33 after the experiment. The teacher scores for the control group were 44.85 before, and 38.30 after the experiment; Parent scores for the experimental group were 64.80 before, and 52.88 after the experiment. Parent scores for the control group were 63.13 before, and 47.20 after the experiment.

There is also evidence to support the hypothesis that AIT is *not* an effective treatment for autism.  Zollweg et al.[16] used a double-blind experimental design and found that the behavior of *both* the treatment and control groups improved slightly (based on the Aberrant Behavior Checklist [ABC]) which once again, as in the Bettison study, suggests that AIT was not responsible for the improvement. By far the best design study in this literature is Mudford et al. (2000).[17]  These researchers measure autism using behavioral rating scales, direct observation and psychometric measures in a crossover design (i.e., the children in the experiment experience both the experimental and control conditions) where the children were randomly assigned in terms of base-line measures.  They found no results and conclude that "no children could be identified as benefiting from auditory integration training to a clinically or educationally significant degree."[18]

## What does the therapy actually look like?

Auditory Integration Training involves the electronic processing of music which has been modulated and filtered through headphones. The music typically contains tracks with a fast tempo and wide frequency.[19]  There are two types of auditory integration training offered, the Berard method and the Tomatis method. These two methods differ in the underlying theory, amount of treatment and in type of sounds used.  The Berard method was developed to address the supposed auditory perception problems which result in autism.  The Tomatis method was developed to address the purported disruption in the mother-child bond which he believes occurs in utero due to the mother's use of harsh and cold tones.  As a result, Berard targets hypersensitivity to sound whereas Tomatis targets listening and comprehension.  To address the hypersensitive perception to certain sounds, the Berard approach attempts to filter out frequencies to which the individual is thought to be overly sensitive. These frequencies are selected based on hearing tests done with special audio equipment prior to AIT.[20]  In order to accomplish change in listening and comprehension, the Tomatis approach consists of three phases that 1) filter out low frequency sounds, leaving only high frequency sounds which are said to "energize" the brain, as well as recreate sounds from within the womb; 2) recreate sounds from after birth, and 3) have the individual read aloud.

The Berard and Tomatis approaches also differ with respect to frequency and duration of training. While the Berard method recommends no more than ten hours of AIT, administered over ten days in two, half hour sessions per day, the Tomatis approach recommends much higher levels of AIT. There are two options for intensity and duration in the Tomatis method. For individuals with autism, it is recommended that they receive 150-200 hours of AIT over six to twelve months. There is also a short course that can be administered which involves two and one-half to three hours per day for ten to twelve days.

## What else do I think?

The reported presence of side effects is an important issue in the use of AIT. Research is required to examine whether or not this training method creates any side effects. Monville[21] noted tantrums and aggression in ten percent of children, while Link[22] reported that one third of the children may have experienced seizures, and that there was an increase in negative behavior and perseveration. In addition to this, Link[23] reports the possibility of AIT inducing seizures in individuals diagnosed with Landau-Kleffner syndrome.

Auditory Integration Training (AIT) is a method of treatment for individuals with autism which is used often, despite the distinct lack of supportive research. It is of great financial cost to parents and there may be the possibility of negative side effects. The abundance of anecdotal evidence on AIT, particularly the book, *Sound of a Miracle: A Child's Triumph over Autism,*[24] which purports AIT as a cure for autism, has made AIT popular, despite the distinct lack of methodologically sound data.

## Would I try it on my child?

At this point I would not try AIT on my child. There is not enough good science behind this treatment and I am somewhat concerned about the reported side effects of aggression, tantrums, and seizures. In addition, the cost of using an unproven treatment in time and money is a further factor in my decision not to have my daughter undergo this treatment. When my daughter was first diagnosed fourteen years ago, I did research AIT as a serious option because she seemed to have very sensitive hearing and would be a candidate for this method. However, once I researched the amount and quality of scientific evidence for this method, I decided to wait for more evidence. Now I'm still waiting; however, now there have been a few well done studies which strongly support the contention that AIT does not ameliorate the symptoms associated with autism.

## What kind of study would I like to see the Auditory Integration Training practitioners do?

I would like to see the Mudford et al.[25] design replicated by Rimland and Edelson (two proponents of AIT) utilizing the same measures for the dependent variable of autism that Mudford et al. (2000) used. In addition, this replication would need to have psychologists with no relationship to AIT administer the various measures used. If the results of the 2000 study were replicated, then parents would know with more certainty that AIT is not an effective treatment for autism.

## Who else recommends for or against Auditory Integration Training as a method for the treatment of autism?

There are many professionals and organizations recommending against AIT. In a 1998 policy statement authored by the American Academy of Pediatrics, they state that: "Although two investigations indicated AIT may help some children with autism, as yet there are no good controlled studies to support its use. ... Until further information is available, the use of these treatments [AIT] does not appear warranted at this time, except within research protocols."[26] In addition, the New York Department of Health issued a report on best practices for the treatment of children with autism. Regarding Auditory Integration Training, they have this to say: "The one study that met criteria for evidence about efficacy found no differences in children receiving auditory integration training and children listening to unmodified music. Because of the lack of demonstrated efficacy and the expense of the intervention, it is recommended that auditory integration training not be used as an intervention for young children with autism."[27] Further, the Association For Science in Autism treatment (ASAT) states: "Professionals considering AIT should portray the method as experimental and should disclose this status to key decision makers influencing the child's intervention."[28]

## So you're still on the horns of a dilemma?

If you are still wondering whether you should try Auditory Integration Training, I suggest you read the Mudford article[29] which critically reviews this treatment in comprehensive detail. It is important to recognize that AIT, at this point, is entirely experimental and that the scientific evidence is growing to support the view that AIT is an ineffective treatment for autism.

## What's the bottom line?

Based on the scientific research to date, there is not enough evidence to conclude that Auditory Integration Training is an effective treatment for autism

## Endnotes for Auditory Integration Training

[1] Berard, G. 1993. *Hearing Equals Behavior*. New Canaan, CT: Keats.

[2] Link, H.M. 1997. "Auditory Integration Training (AIT): Sound therapy? Case Studies of Three Boys With Autism Who Received AIT." *British Journal of Learning Disabilities*. Vol. 25, pp. 106-110.

[3] Madell, J.R., and D.E. Rose. 1994. "Auditory Integration Training." *Face to Face, American Speech-Language-Hearing Association*, pp. 14-18.

[4] Brown, M.M. 1999. "Auditory Integration Training and Autism: Two Case Studies." *British Journal of Occupational Therapy*, Vol. 62, No. 1, pp. 13-18.

[5] Gillberg, C., M. Johansson, S. Steffenburg, and O. Berlin. 1997. "Auditory Integration Training in Children With Autism. Brief Report of an Open Pilot Study." *Autism*, Vol. 1, No. 1, pp. 97-100.

[6] Rimland, B., and S.M. Edelson. 1994. "The Effects of Auditory Integration Training on Autism." *American Journal of Speech Pathology*, Vol. 5, pp. 16-23.

[7] Rimland, B., and S.M. Edelson. 1995. "A Pilot Study of Auditory Integration Training in Autism." *Journal of Autism and Developmental Disorders*, Vol. 25, No. 1, pp. 61-70.

[8] Bettison, S. 1996. "The Long-Term Effects of Auditory Training on Children With Autism." *Journal of Autism and Developmental Disorders*, Vol. 26, No. 3, pp. 361-374.

[9] Mudford, O.C. et al. 2000. "Auditory Integration Training for Children With Aut ism: No Behavioral Benefits Detected." *American Journal on Mental Retardation*, Vol. 105, No. 2, pp. 118-129.

[10] Zollweg, W. 1997. "The Efficacy of Auditory Integration Training: A Double Blind Study." *American Journal of Audiology*, Vol. 6, No. 3, pp. 39-47

[11] Rimland, B., and S.M. Edelson. 1995. "Brief Report: A Pilot Study of Auditory Integration Training in Autism." *Journal of Autism and developmental Disorders*, Vol. 25, No. 1, pp. 62-69.

[12] Bettison, S., (see n. 8 above).

[13] Rimland, B., S.M. Edelson, (see n. 11 above).

[14] Link, H.M., (see n. 2 above).

[15] Link, H.M., (see n. 2 above).

[16] Zollweg, W., (see n. 10 above).

[17] Mudford, O.C. et al., (see n. 9 above).

[18] Mudford, O.C. et al., (see n. 9 above).

[19]Link, H.M., (see n. 2 above).

[20]Link, H.M., (see n. 2 above).

[21]Monville, D., and N. Nelson. 1994. *Parental Perceptions of Change Following AIT for Autism.* Presented to the American speech-Language-Hearing Conference, New Orleans.

[22]Link, H.M. (see n. 2 above).

[23]Link, H.M. (see n. 2 above).

[24]Stehli, A. 1991. *The Sound of a Miracle: A Child's Triumph Over Autism.*  New York: Doubleday.

[25]Mudford, O.C. et al., (see n. 9 above).

[26]Committee on Children with Disabilities. 1998. "Auditory Integration Training and Facilitated Communication for autism." *Pediatrics*, Vol. 102, No. 2, p. 433.

[27]Guralnick, M. ed. 1999. *Clinical Practice Guideline: Report of the Recommendations. Autism/Pervasive Developmental Disorder s, Assessment and Intervention for Young Children* (age 0-3 years).  Albany (NY): New York State Department of Health, p. IV-63.

[28]Association for Science in Autism treatment (ASAT), www.asatonline.org/about_autism/autism_ info08.html, (accessed Aug. 19, 2005).

[29]Mudford, O.C. et al., (see n. 9 above).

# Miscellaneous Therapies: Craniosacral Therapy

## What is Craniosacral Therapy?

Craniosacral Therapy is a technique whereby the practitioner softly touches and manipulates the head of a person with autism. According to those who practice Craniosacral Therapy, the manipulation of the head is done to release restrictions in the Craniosacral system (CSS). The theory behind this therapy is that the patient benefits because the treatment creates changes to the central nervous system. The philosophy that accompanies the practice of Craniosacral Therapy emphasizes natural alternative medicine rather than traditional western medicine. Specifically, there is a belief that so-called "energy cysts" develop in areas of prior physical trauma and/or emotional shock.[1] In addition, cells and organs are thought to have a consciousness and practitioners have the patient communicate with the brain using imagery and dialogue.[2] Explanations as to why Craniosacral Therapy is thought to be effective for individuals with autism are not well developed. The therapy does make claims that it can be used for treatment as well as prevention of autism.[3]

## What evidence do the practitioners have that this really works?

Our extensive database searches found *no* peer-reviewed journal articles on Craniosacral Therapy reporting outcome information on this treatment for autism. The only facts available regarding the effects of this type of therapy are case histories reported by Upledger who pioneered the use of this treatment. Based on material generated by the Upledger Institute, it is reported that the use of Craniosacral Therapy on infants acts in a preventative way for many childhood disorders, including autism. However, there are no peer-reviewed studies as of yet to support these claims. Despite the lack of peer-review, Craniosacral Therapy has generated much non-peer reviewed literature in the form of promotional and teaching materials (over one hundred monographs, newspaper articles, newsletter entries, a dozen books, and ten videotapes).

There has been one non-peer reviewed study examining the differences between autistic individuals before and after the therapy. The researchers compared blood, specific physical characteristics and did a hair mineral analysis of individuals with autism to typically developing individuals. When they found unspecified abnormalities, they then used Craniosacral Therapy to treat and thereby correct these supposed differences amongst the autistic subjects. The authors studied twenty-five out of fifty-one individuals enrolled in the Genessee Intermediate School District Center for Autism. The most obvious flaw in this research is that these researchers do not establish the relevance of the physical, blood and hair mineral abnormalities as they specifically relate to autism. It has not yet been determined that these abnormalities are characteristic, of or relevant to, autism. Specifically, these researchers do not assess whether these symptoms are related to the various deficits and excesses which characterize autism and are used to make the behavioral diagnosis of autism. In other words, did the lessening of these purported abnormalities indeed improve the degree of functioning, the behaviors, or the communication skills in the autistic individual? The researchers do not address this central question. In formal terms, the dependent variable of autism is not operationalized properly (please see Section Two for a discussion on the operationalization of the dependent variable).

## What does the therapy actually look like?

Craniosacral Therapy addresses the craniosacral system in the human body, including the membranes and fluid surrounding the spinal cord, brain, and the skull, face and mouth bones, down to the tailbone.[4] In Craniosacral Therapy the practitioner uses a light touch (defined as 5 grams of pressure or less), around the area defined as the "Craniosacral system."

## What else do I think?

There is no peer-reviewed, published data regarding how well (or if) Craniosacral Therapy works and there is too little information regarding what is actually supposed to happen as a result of this therapy. Data that does exist in the literature with regards to Craniosacral Therapy and individuals with autism does not include an evaluation of its use as a treatment for autism. It has only been used as an intervention for certain physical symptoms, which are neither necessarily a result of autism nor are symptoms that contribute to the diagnosis of autism. This therapy does not address the serious language, social and play deficits, or the behavioral excesses, such as self-stimulation, rigidities and ritualistic behaviors often characteristic of autism.

## Would I try it on my child?

I would not try this on my child because I have not seen any evidence that this therapy could be effective in ameliorating the symptoms of autism. This is a great example of a therapy backed only by theory, but no evidence whatsoever, being offered up to parents (at a considerable cost per hour) as a purportedly legitimate intervention.

## What kind of study would I like to see the practitioners of Craniosacral Therapy do?

There needs to be further research into the theory underlying the use of Craniosacral Therapy for individuals with autism. Specifically, researchers need to use a controlled design to assess whether Craniosacral Therapy is effective in the reduction of the various well defined and generally-accepted symptoms characteristic of autism.  There needs to be double-blind, pre-and post testing using commonly-accepted tests for autism and the researchers must not know which children are in the experimental and control groups.  In addition, before I am convinced that Craniosacral Therapy works as a treatment for autism, I need to see a well-designed study with outcome data published in an academic, peer-reviewed journal and replicated, before recommending Craniosacral Therapy.

## Who else recommends against Craniosacral Therapy as a method for the treatment of autism?

There have not been any organizations or groups who have recommended against this therapy for children with autism because Craniosacral Therapy is not a commonly-used treatment for autism; however, when this therapy is used on individuals with other conditions and diseases, Quackwatch recommends against this treatment.[5]

## So you're still on the horns of a dilemma?

If you are still thinking of this therapy to lessen the degree of autism in your child, I would suggest that you visit any reputable neurosurgeon to have him share his medical opinion regarding the effectiveness of Craniosacral Therapy.

## What's the bottom line?

Based on the scientific research to date, there is no scientific evidence that Craniosacral Therapy is an effective therapy for autism.

## Endnotes for Craniosacral Therapy

[1]1999. For Continuing Education, Continuing Care.  Palm Beach Gardens, FL:  The Upledger Institute, Inc., p. 4.

[2](see n. 1 above), p. 6.

[3](see n. 1 above), p. 5.

[4](see n. 1 above), p. 2.

[5]Barrett, S. "Craniosacral Therapy."  http://www.quackwatch.org/01Quackery Related Topics/cranial.html, (accessed Feb. 13, 2006).

# Miscellaneous Therapies: Dolphin-assisted Therapy

## What is Dolphin-assisted Therapy?

Dolphin-assisted Therapy (DAT) is the practice of having persons with special needs swim with dolphins. Practitioners of this therapy have differing opinions on how the therapy method helps, whom it helps and what effects can be expected from this therapy. We originally found two sources of information on this intervention, one from "Dolphin Reef" in Eilat Israel,[1] and the other from "Island Dolphin Care" based in Florida.[2] Our latest search netted several different DAT programs, including one in Crimea in the Ukraine.[3]

The concept of using dolphins as a treatment for autism came from the observation of a diver in Israel, who observed that when people came to see the dolphins, they often expressed many emotions (including happiness, excitement and tears of joy). This led the diver to believe that human exposure to dolphins may be a therapeutic, emotional process for some people.

The practitioners in Dolphin Reef (Israel) claim that Dolphin-assisted Therapy addresses some of the cognitive and emotional needs of the child. The cognitive issues are addressed on the diving platform, where the child watches the dolphins swim in the water, then feeds the dolphins and adjusts to the diving gear. Some hand signals are often taught to the autistic person to communicate with the dolphins. Then, when the child is ready and willing, he or she is moved into the water with the dolphins. In the water, the child learns to interact with the dolphin. The dolphin's non-judgmental attitude toward the individual with special needs is theorized to be extremely helpful in having the individual "accept himself or herself." Practitioners believe that learning to socially interact with dolphins will then generalize to improvement in social interaction with people.

The practitioners of Dolphin-assisted Therapy in Florida do not make the same claims about the effects of this therapy as do the Israeli practitioners. The Floridians propose that some changes may be seen in the child after therapy; however, these changes are attributed to the child's purported increase in self-esteem, confidence and motivation,[2] as opposed to any healing effect of dolphins. In fact, the Island Dolphin Care website states that, while some believe in these healing properties, there is very little scientific evidence to support these beliefs.[1] In addition to this, they state clearly that there may be little or no improvement for children with behavioral problems, extreme fears or those who are moderately or severely autistic or disabled.   In addition to time in the water with the dolphins, the Island Dolphin Care site creates a psycho-educational program for the child, using behavioral and educational techniques in a classroom setting.

## What evidence do the practitioners have that this really works?

There is no evidence that Dolphin-assisted Therapy is an effective intervention for autism. Our comprehensive database searches found four articles on DAT, but only one Belgian article that attempts to measure the efficacy of Dolphin-assisted Therapy.  This study evaluated whether Dolphin-assisted Therapy enhanced the learning of autistic children, specifically measuring attention and motivation.  Unfortunately, the study's flaws were so great that the researchers themselves could not make any conclusions about whether dolphins had a therapeutic effect on children with autism.[4]  Therefore, there are no published studies with reliable outcome data to evaluate the effectiveness of Dolphin-assisted Therapy for children with autism.  In marked contrast, there is no shortage of non-peer reviewed information on DAT.  In one television broadcast on dolphin therapy (funded by the Government of Canada) entitled, "The Body, Inside Stories," the audience is taken to Eilat, Israel, where a section of the Red Sea is cordoned off to house several dolphins. The film proceeds to claim that the treatment is very effective, not only for individuals with autism, but also for those with other disorders. The documentary follows the treatment of a group of adolescents and adults with autism who are brought down to Dolphin Reef for DAT.  The claim is made that individuals with autism can hear the sounds of dolphins, that typically developing persons are unable to hear.  These dolphin "voices" are hypothesized to draw autistic people out of their isolated world. Despite the observation that some individuals with autism seem to have more sensitivity to sound, there is no research to suggest that individuals with autism have the ability to hear dolphin sounds that others cannot hear.  In addition, the film provides anecdotes of people who claim to have directly benefitted from the intervention  (please refer to Section Two for a discussion of the use and abuse of anecdotal information).  The claim of the Israeli proponents of Dolphin-assisted Therapy is that the autistic individuals were more "relaxed" after the intervention.  In addition, dolphin therapy is claimed to be worthwhile because 1) it will provide more contact with others, and 2) individuals with autism will be happier, use more language and need less medication.  There was no evidence presented in the broadcast regarding these kinds of supposed gains, nor is there any peer-reviewed, published literature which supports the notion that meaningful outcomes result from Dolphin-assisted Therapy.

## What does the therapy actually look like?

In Eilat, Dolphin-assisted Therapy involves three, four day sessions, of an unspecified duration.  At *Island Dolphin Care* in Florida, therapy generally is conducted from one to three weeks.  It costs approximately $2,000 USD per week, which includes five dolphin sessions and four classroom sessions. In both these centers, the autistic person wearing a life jacket, is placed in the water. The therapist helps the child become comfortable with the water and the dolphin. With the help of the therapist, the child interacts with the dolphin and is given rides on top of the dolphin as it swims around the pool.

## What else do I think?

This type of "intervention" can be extremely appealing to parents who are desperate for an effective intervention for their child. Most tempting about this intervention is that it presents itself as a "quick-fix" option which sounds pleasant and enjoyable for both the family and the affected child.

It is likely that many of the reported positive changes seen in the child after Dolphin-assisted Therapy from *Island Dolphin Care,* may be attributable to educational and behavioral techniques used on the child and shown to the parents, rather than any healing properties of dolphins. Put simply, a dolphin ride may be a very reinforcing experience to a child. To their credit, the *Island Dolphin Care* website repeatedly denies that there are any miracle cures or healing that occurs through the use of Dolphin-assisted Therapy. They emphasize that it is not a medical treatment, and that no medical cures or changes in diagnoses have been observed or should be expected from Dolphin-assisted Therapy.

Based on the fact that there is no evidence whatsoever to support this type of therapy, I cannot seriously consider Dolphin-assisted Therapy as a "therapy" at all for individuals afflicted with autism. While this may be a great vacation spot for families who have members with special needs, it should not be confused with valid treatment for this serious disorder.

## Would I try it on my child?

I would not enroll my child in this therapy with the expectation of any progress. If I thought my child would enjoy swimming with dolphins and I had the extra cash for a holiday in sunny Israel or Florida, I would love to give her the experience. However, I would not dignify the experience by using the term therapy or treatment and, again, I would have no expectations for any measurable improvement in her autism.

## What kind of study would I like to see Dolphin Therapy researchers do?

If the practitioners of this method make therapeutic claims regarding Dolphin-Assisted Therapy, then I would expect to see research which meets the minimal scientific criteria for well designed studies. In addition, I would like to see the *Island Dolphin Care* practitioners provide rigorous research supporting the notion that their psycho-educational programming is worthwhile for families of individuals with autism. It is possible that they are using standard, well-established teaching techniques for children with autism. However, it is not made clear from their promotional materials whether or not their educational techniques are innovative and untested or based upon well-established educational standards.

## Who else recommends against Dolphin Assisted Therapy as a method for the treatment of autism?

None of the professional or academic associations which evaluate treatment claims have studied the claims made for Dolphin-assisted Therapy. I believe this lack of interest is because this type of intervention is simply not taken seriously by scientists in the field of autism research or treatment. Moreover, no one sees it as a dangerous intervention, and therefore, it has been largely ignored. A treatment that is quite expensive, but unproven, is not generally of concern to the scientific community, unless it is actually harmful to the child.  It may, however, be of concern to the community of parents (to which I belong) who have to shell out large sums of money to have their child participate in unproven treatments.

## So you're still on the horns of a dilemma?

Our literature search did not produce even a single, peer-reviewed article with reliable data on this kind of therapy.  Therefore, based on the information we've provided in this section, it is up to the reader to decide whether experimenting with Dolphin-assisted Therapy is worth the money and time.

## What's the bottom line?

Based on the scientific research to date, there is no evidence that Dolphin-assisted Therapy is an effective treatment for individuals with autism.

## Endnotes for Dolphin-assisted Therapy

[1]Dolphin Reef, www.dolphinreef.co.il, (accessed Feb. 16, 2006).

[2]Island Dolphin Care, www.dolphinsplus.com/dolphin-therapy.htm, (accessed Feb. 16, 2006).

[3]Dolphin-assisted Therapy, www.dolphinassistedtherapy.com, (accessed Feb. 16, 2006).

[4]Servais, V. 1999. Some comments on context embodiment in zootherapy: The case of the autidolfijn project. *Anthrozoos*, Vol. 12, pp. 5-15.

# Miscellaneous Therapies:  Exercise Therapy

## What is Exercise Therapy?

The use of exercise as an intervention for individuals with autism is based on the theory that the physiological effects of exercise decrease some of the symptoms of autism.  Those who recommend this intervention believe that through exercise, the body creates certain chemicals that help reduce self-stimulatory and rigid behavior amongst people with autism. They hypothesize that physiological changes in the brain caused by strenuous physical activity can help individuals with autism. The result of these chemical changes, they maintain, is that stereotypic or repetitive behavior decreases.  Based on an area of research that looks at the effect of physical exercise on motivation, attention, aggression and other emotions, these researchers believe that  exercise is an effective intervention which can target many of these areas in people with autism.[1]

## What evidence do the practitioners have that this really works?

Our database searches netted forty-one entries on exercise and autism.[*]  Of those, nine peer-reviewed studies on exercise indicate initial improvement. All of these studies demonstrate positive results, specifically reporting decreases in stereotypic or repetitive behaviors in subjects who underwent exercise therapy. The following statistical significance scores (p values)[**] were reported for three of

---

[*]There are many more articles which discuss the effects of exercise on individuals with various types of developmental delays; however, these studies did not address autism specifically.

[**]In Rosenthal-Malek and Mitchell (1997), after exercise, the adolescent subjects exhibited less self-stimulatory behaviors ($p$ less than or equal to .01 and .001), got higher scores on academic tests ($p < .05$), and completed more of their workshop tasks ($p < .01$).[2]  In Elliott et al. (1994), the problematic behaviors of the autistic adults meaningfully decreased after the vigorous exercise condition ($p < .001$).[3]  In Watters and Watters (1980), self-stimulatory behaviors decreased after physical exercise as well ($p = .05$).[4]

the studies. In Rosenthal-Malek and Mitchell (1997), after exercise the adolescent subjects exhibited less self-stimulatory behaviors, got higher scores on academic tests, and completed more of their workshop tasks.[2]  In Elliott et al. (1994), the problematic behaviors of the autistic adults meaningfully decreased after the vigorous exercise condition.[3]  In Watters and Watters (1980), self-stimulatory behaviors decreased after physical exercise, as well.[4] Levinson and Reid (1993), found that rigorous exercise (jogging) did decrease stereotypic behavior but that the effect of exercise was not apparent one and one-half hours after exercise. No effects were found for mild exercise (walking).[5] Allison et al. (1991) found that exercise (jogging)  and medication in combination, significantly decreased aggression, better than exercise or medication alone in a single subject case design (SSCD) involving an adult autistic male subject.[6] Using a SSCD, Celiberti et al. (1997) found that exercise did have the effect of decreasing physical self-stimulatory behavior. Of note is that the researchers report sustained behavioral changes more than forty minutes after jogging.[7] Kern et al. (1984, 1982), also report similar results from vigorous exercise (jogging).  They found that it decreased stereotypic behaviors and increased task-oriented behavior amongst children with autism.[8,9] Powers et al. (1992) reported similar results using roller skating, rather than jogging, as the form of exercise.[10]

On the whole, these studies were designed and executed quite well.  Some studies have observers who did not know which subject was in the experimental or control conditions.  This "blind" procedure limited any bias that could come from those researchers recording the results.  In addition, as mentioned above, three of the studies used statistical significance scores (p values). The p values in these studies indicate statistically significant levels of improvement in common negative autism behaviors, due to physical exercise. Celiberti et al. (1997) report clinically significant results of exercise as well[7] (please see Section Two for a discussion regarding significance).

A few of these studies measured behavior in a competent manner. They recorded a comprehensive list of self-stimulatory behaviors of the children in the study. The self-stimulatory behaviors were recorded for a short period of time on a schedule (e.g., for five minutes of every fifteen minute interval before the exercise and then after the exercise). This objective measure is extremely helpful to determine the true outcome of the therapy.

Most of the research on exercise employs Single Subject Research Designs where a base-line is measured, and then the treatment is given and withdrawn, given and withdrawn. In the case where the behavior is easy to observe and measure, an SSRD is appropriate (please see Section Two for a discussion on SSRD).

Collectively, the numbers of subjects in this area of the literature is very small (thirty-six persons with autism over a thirty-year period). In addition, most of the studies were conducted in the early 1990s. The largest study used seven subjects in a design where each person experienced *both* conditions repeatedly. This study was designed to compare subjects with themselves in *both* the control and experimental conditions. The results would give us more confidence if the number of children in the studies was much higher and the research more current.

## What does the therapy actually look like?

In every study, subjects participated in some kind of physical activity. In most of the studies, the children or adolescents jogged anywhere from eight to twenty minutes per exercise session. In other studies, the subjects used a treadmill moving four miles per hour or exercised using rollerskates. It is important to keep in mind that the physical activity described was used for research purposes only and was not necessarily chosen because it was the best form of exercise.

## What else do I think?

The theory underlying exercise therapy for individuals with autism intuitively makes sense. We know the benefits of cardiovascular exercise for everyone. For individuals with autism, exercise may also serve to decrease many of the stereotypic deficits and excesses associated with autism.  In other words, the well-documented physiological changes associated with exercise for the population at large may also have the effect of decreasing observed stereotypic behaviors in individuals with autism.[11]

Exercise therapy appears to address the inherent differences between the amount of energy expended by some children with autism and their typically developing peers.  Typical children seem to spend hours a day engaged in nonstop action, while many autistic children are either not active, or they spend hours engaging in activities which may not be as physically strenuous.  Engaging the child in appropriate cardiovascular activity seems to temporarily replace inappropriate behavior, while maintaining or increasing the amount of energy the child expends.

Although exercise seems to have an effect, it is important to remember that the effects of physical exercise on self-stimulatory behaviors seem to be short term only.  For benefits to be maintained, the autistic person may need to exercise directly before the academic routine.  In addition, no studies have been done to date on the satiation effects of exercise, and the consequences that satiation might have on levels of stereotypic or repetitive behavior.  In other words, as the child becomes more fit, do levels of exercise have to be continually increased to get the same effect or can levels of physical exercise remain the same or decrease, yet still benefit the child by maintaining the decreases in stereotypic behavior? There is insufficient research at present to answer that question.  I am also concerned that the amount of research done on exercise has actually decreased.

There is still much we do not know about how or why exercise decreases stereotypic and aggressive behavior for individuals with autism. Based on the amount of research conducted and the results of that research, we are not in a good position to decide whether it is worth spending therapeutic time on exercise.

## Would I try it on my child?

This is a difficult question for me to answer. I think the data is clear that vigorous activity does have a suppressing effect on self-stimulatory behavior. I also know that exercise will not harm my daughter in any way. In fact, it may increase her health and physical well-being. That said, my child's self-stimulatory behavior has diminished considerably over the years; therefore, I do not see her as a good candidate for this type of therapy. If, however, the stereotypic behavior were interfering with her learning, I might have her engage in exercise, and schedule the therapy immediately before she had to sit down and concentrate. I would, however, take very good data (objective measures) to make sure that her stereotypic behaviors did indeed diminish after exercise, since it would be a waste of time if we did not see meaningful results. The biggest hurdle to this kind of therapy is that it takes time and does not seem to be long-lasting (although more research needs to be conducted on the long term effects). At this point, based on what little we do know about this method, it makes little sense to do the therapy with the child on a regular basis unless the therapy helps the child focus on an activity which immediately *follows* the Exercise Therapy. Hopefully, with additional research into Exercise Therapy, we will be able to know how to use the therapy to get the best results in the least amount of time.

## What kind of study would I like to see Exercise Therapy researchers do?

As I've suggested earlier, more research into this therapy is required, using much larger sample sizes.  I would like to see the study by Rosenthal-Malek and Mitchell (1997), in which they measured self-stimulatory behavior rates, academic performance and work completion, replicated using a Between-Within Subject Design with a larger number of children, and done over a longer period of time.  These researchers could then better determine the level and frequency of exercise necessary.  We would be in a much better position to use this therapy with people afflicted with autism.

In addition, an increased understanding into the use of exercise to control stereotypic behaviors may answer the question of why exercise lowers levels of stereotypic behavior.   We need to know the physiology behind the effect of a decrease in self-stimulatory behavior; what is the body chemistry associated with Exercise Therapy that is behind the behavioral effects we observe.  An understanding of this may lead to an understanding of the cause of stereotypic behavior in people with autism, and may help researchers understand the cause of autism and develop effective drugs to treat the disorder.

## Who else recommends for or against Exercise Therapy as a method for the treatment of autism?

For the most part, this area has been ignored by most practitioners and researchers. There is no money to be made on this kind of research (in the short term), the research does not demonstrate the effects to be long lasting and there is no danger to exercise; therefore, neither much concern nor much interest has been voiced about exercise therapy from either the community of autism researchers or parents of children with autism.

## So you're still on the horns of a dilemma?

If you would like to incorporate exercise into your child's life because you think it may be healthy for him, that's fine. However, if you are incorporating exercise because you think it will be therapeutic for autism, then I would have a behaviorist set up a program and monitor whether, indeed, the moderate exercise is having an effect on your child's behavior. Without setting up an objective way to measure whether exercise is helping, you may end up doing something that may not actually be bearing any fruit and may actually be wasting your child's therapeutic time, when another more valuable therapy could be administered to better effect.

## What's the bottom line?

Based on the scientific research to date, there is some evidence that exercise therapy is effective for *temporarily* decreasing stereotypic behavior in people with autism; however, there is no evidence to show that Exercise Therapy has any long term effect in ameliorating the symptoms associated with autism.

## Endnotes for Exercise Therapy

[1]Kern, L. et al. 1982. "The effects of Physical Exercise on Self-Stimulation and Appropriate Responding in Autistic Children." *Journal of Autism and Developmental Disorders,* Vol. 12, No. 4, pp. 399-419.

[2]Rosenthal, M.A., and M. Stella. 1997. "Brief Report: The Effects of Exercise on the Self-Stimulatory Behaviors and Positive Responding of Adolescents With Autism." *Journal of Autism and Developmental Disorders,* Vol. 7, No. 2, pp. 193-202.

[3]Elliott, R.O. et al. 1994. "Vigorous, Aerobic Exercise Versus General Motor Training Activities: Effects on Maladaptive and Stereotypic Behaviors of Adults With Both Autism and Mental Retardation." *Journal of Autism and developmental Disorders*, Vol. 24, No. 5, pp. 565-576.

[4]Watters, R.G., and W.E. Watters. 1980. "Decreasing Self-Stimulatory Behavior With Physical Exercise in a Group of autistic Boys." *Journal of Autism and Developmental Disorders,* Vol. 10, No. 4, pp. 379-387.

[5]Levinson, L.J., and G. Reid. 1993. "The Effects of Exercise Intensity on the Stereotypic Behaviors of Individuals With Autism." Adapted. *Physical Activity Quarterly*, Vol. 10, No. 3, pp. 255-268.

[6]Allison, D.B., V.C. Basile, and R.B. MacDonald. 1991. "Brief Report: Comparative Effects of Antecedent Exercise and Lorazepam n the Aggressive Behavior of an Autistic Man." *Journal of Autism and Developmental Disorders*, Vol. 21, No. 1, pp. 89-95.

[7]Celiberti, D.A. et al. 1997. "The Differential and Temporal Effects of Antecedent Exercise on the Self-Stimulatory Behavior of a Child With Autism." *Research in Developmental Disabilities*, Vol. 18, No. 2, pp. 139-150.

[8]Kern, L, et al. 1984. "The Influence of Vigorous Versus Mild Exercise on Autistic Stereotyped Behaviors." *Journal of Autism and Developmental Disorders*, Vol. 14, No. 1, pp. 57-67.

[9]Kern, L. et al., (see n. 8 above).

[10]Powers, S., S. Thibadeau, and K. Rose. 1992. "Antecedent Exercise and its Effects on Self-Stimulation." *Behavioral Residential Treatment,* Vol. 7, No. 1, pp. 15-22.

[11]Quill, K., S. Gurry, and A. Larkin. 1989. "Daily Life therapy: A Japanese Model for Educating Children With Autism." *Journal of Autism and Developmental Disorders,* Vol. 19, No. 4, pp. 625-635.

# Miscellaneous Therapies:  Facilitated Communication Training

## What is Facilitated Communication?

Facilitated Communication (FC) is a technique which uses physical prompting to help individuals with developmental disabilities (including autism) communicate. The woman who first developed FC, Rosemary Crossley, designed this method for people who had little or no control of their muscles and, therefore, could not communicate.  Helpers (termed "facilitators") physically help a person use a keyboard or letter board by holding their arm, forearm or wrist in a specific way above a communication board.  The hand-over-hand or physical prompting is then supposed to be faded gradually, leaving the person to communicate by him or herself; however, many people using FC are never able to communicate independently and need the services of a facilitator permanently.  Those who use FC claim that people with many disabilities (including autism) may have advanced literary skills, along with well-developed cognitive skills.  In other words, they believe that people with autism are smart and able to communicate at a high level.[1]  In order to bring out their higher level thoughts and ideas, people who use FC believe that these disabled people need someone to help them communicate. Although independent typing is seen as an eventual goal to work towards, many do continue to require the help of the facilitator and are never able to have the facilitation eliminated.  It is important to understand that the claims made by those who developed FC, were originally made about individuals who did not have good muscle control (people suffering from neuromotor disabilities such as cerebral palsy).  The method and its claims were later applied to persons with autism.

## What evidence do the practitioners have that this really works?

Our literature search uncovered over fifty articles on Facilitated Communication. This is one of the most controversial treatments in the field of autism. After excluding the literature reviews, theoretical pieces, commentary and replies to editors (there were over two dozen!), there are thirty[*] articles which presented data on Facilitated Communication, showing that FC is not an effective treatment for autism. All of these articles are published in peer-reviewed journals and some of these articles (which we will speak about later) are very well done, following the rules of the scientific method. However, in scientific terms, the theory of Facilitated Communication has been falsified by no less than thirty different studies. There are a number of articles which present data to show that FC is purportedly effective; however, most of this data is *not* presented in peer-reviewed journals, but rather, in unpublished papers,[31] books,[32,33,34] internet sites,[35,36] and letters to the editor.[37] In addition, there is a personal account or narrative written ostensibly by a person with autism who independently types but who claims to have learned these typing skills through Facilitated Communication.[38] The data are presented through case studies, surveys, or qualitative studies which suffer from a lack of experimental controls and often do not refer to autism specifically or exclusively.[39,40,41,42,43,44,45] After separating these types of papers from those which actually do attempt to use science to test whether Facilitated Communication works, there are only seven peer-reviewed journal articles that present data to support the use of FC.[46,47,48,49,50,51,52] After evaluating these articles,

---

[*2]Bebko et al., 1996; [3]Beck et al. 1996; [4]Bomba et al. 1996; [5]Burgess et al. 1998; [6]Duchan, 1999; [7]Eberlin et al. 1993; [8]Edelson et al. 1998; [9]Cabay, 1994; [10]Hirshoren et al. 1995; [11]Kerrin et al. 1998; [12]Kezuka, 1997; [13]Montee et al. 1995; [14]Moore et al. 1993a; [15]Moore et al. 1993b; [16]Myles et al. 1996a; [17]Myles et al. 1996b; [18]Myles et al. 1994; [19]Oswald, 1994; [20]Perry et al. 1993; [21]Perry et al. 1998; [22]Regal et al. 1994; [23]Simon et al. 1994; [24]Simpson et al. 1995; [25]Smith et al. 1993; [26]Smith et al. 1994; [27]Szempruch et al. 1993; [28]Vazquez, 1994; [29]Vazquez, 1995; [30]Wheeler et al. 1993.

I am quite confident in concluding that there is insufficient evidence to support the use of FC for individuals afflicted with autism. Although there are several studies which report positive results, there is much more compelling evidence that FC is not effective. In science, the burden is on researchers to demonstrate a causal relationship. Each of the following studies attempts to do this, yet all have limitations.

Olney (2001), reports positive results in a within-subject designed study with nine subjects (six of whom have an autism spectrum disorder), sixty-six percent of whom could type independently. This study reports that the subjects did better when facilitated by a facilitator in the "blind" condition, compared to the unfacilitated condition. There are a few flaws in this study, the major one being that commercially available computer games were used in the blind conditions. We do not know how familiar either the subjects or the facilitators were with these computer games. The study was done between 1997 and 2001, and published in 2001, and the vast majority of those computer games were introduced to the market in the late 1980s. That is problematic because the facilitator may also have been familiar with the sequencing (and answers) of some of the games. As well, the subjects (most of whom could type independently) may also have memorized some of the answers and used the facilitator as a prompt to score higher than when typing independently. Another flaw in the study is that from the first to the last facilitated session, nine months elapsed. During this time, the facilitators and the subjects could have gained experience elsewhere with the computer games. These researchers would have been well-advised to simply use the card stimulus technique utilized by those demonstrating that FC is not effective, as in this way, the experimenter (who cannot be in any way invested in the outcome of the study) has full control of the unknown stimulus (which in this case could be a word on an index card).

In a single-subject case design, Olgetree et al. (1993), found that a child received a score of zero out of eight responses in a matching game that was intended to validate FC. The play condition of the study did not successfully validate FC either. The researchers made positive conclusions regarding FC, even though they report, "it is these authors' opinion that there is not sufficient evidence to suggest that L.B. [the child] used FC independently in either play context."[53] In yet another single-subject case design, Weiss et al. (1996), tested a thirteen-year-old boy with autism to attempt to validate FC. Although this study is one of the strongest in the literature providing evidence that FC is effective with some people, it also suffers from control issues. First, the experimenter reads the story out loud and types the story into the word processor in view of the child. Then the experimenter facilitates for the child. The child does respond correctly to some questions, and inaccurately to others; however, the experimenter knows the story, so any accurate response could be attributed to the experimenter. In the third phase, the facilitator is supposedly uninformed; however, we have no description of how that is assured. That said, this study is the strongest case study in the literature, but so far has not been replicated (although over ten years have elapsed since the original study was done).

Another study done by Sheehan et al. (1996), had three persons with autism and mental retardation use FC in an attempt to validate the method. They claim that all three subjects did communicate novel information to a naive facilitator. This study also has a few shortcomings. First, the naive facilitator was in the room with the experimenter who presented the original information: "During this period, the naive facilitator who had presented the stimuli to the facilitated speaker offered encouragement, redirection, feedback and asked clarifying questions of the speaker."[54] This kind of cueing is a variable which could confound the entire experiment. Second, one of the subjects could type independently, but at a lower level of literacy. They describe him as taking the facilitator's hand for more complex thoughts. One explanation for the difference regarding information this subject knows, but refuses to type independently, could be a compliance issue, rather than a knowledge issue (particularly with information to which he responds verbally). Third, the amount of unknown information was extremely low for all subjects (average of one unknown piece of information communicated per session over three sessions). The one subject who communicated an average of twelve pieces of information per session had more independent communicative ability than the others; therefore, he may have indeed been communicating with the help of prompting, which should be faded. Either way, this is not strong evidence for FC. Even if we take at face value that some true communication occurred (which appears doubtful), in the best-case scenario, one small piece of information every six minutes is inefficient. In the worst-case scenario, one piece of novel information per session (which may be an hour in length) is highly inefficient. Another study often touted as lending support for FC is Vazquez (1994); however, in her 1995 study, she clearly states: "These results are consistent with the vast majority of the controlled validation studies to date indicating that typed messages attributed to nonspeaking persons with autism originate solely from the facilitator..."[55]

The largest study done on FC, that reports success with FC, is Cardinal et al. (1996). This study also suffers from several serious flaws, three of which need to be highlighted. First, in one study which shows success with FC, only seventeen of the forty-three people in the study were autistic. Other diagnoses include Cerebral Palsy, Mental Retardation, Down Syndrome and other developmental disabilities. Unfortunately, participants' results were not reported based on diagnosis. Therefore, it is impossible to know which group of people benefitted from FC. Theoretically, other disabled persons, particularly those with physical disabilities such as Cerebral Palsy, could benefit from the use of FC since they have severe muscle control difficulties and may be unable to type independently.

The participation in the study of children without autism may account for any success reported from this study, (although it is outside the scope of this book to make any conclusions regarding the effectiveness of FC for individuals with other disabilities).  Second, the task given to the subjects in this study was to type one simple word, flashed to them out of a possible one hundred words.  These one hundred words are all very basic.  In my opinion, typing a single word out of a list of one hundred simple words does not demonstrate intelligence or high level communicative abilities.  Moreover, the authors of the study which showed success using FC, mention that the subjects received higher scores *without* a facilitator after they had been taught with the facilitator than when they first were scored without a facilitator.  In other words, after learning the words, the subjects' scores actually improved.  Even the authors observed that the subjects learned through facilitation and were able to type some correct answers independently.  If this observation by the authors of this study is correct, then why is facilitation necessary at all?  Why don't the facilitators just teach the students with autism how to type simple words that the students already know on a keyboard (such as the words used in the study)?

The ability to type could be taught using words already known by autistic students, using a variety of prompts from obtrusive (such as a full physical prompt), to unobtrusive (such as a nonphysical modeling prompt) to an eventual fade out of all prompts.  In this way, everyone can be sure that the autistic person is indeed communicating thoughts at his/her level of communicative ability, with no possibility of facilitator influence.  Without requiring full prompt fading, it can be convincingly argued that the autistic person will never be able to communicate on his or her own.

Over two dozen well-executed studies show that once the influence of the facilitator is properly controlled in first rate research (using a variety of techniques), people employing FC show that they are not able to communicate significantly better with this method than if they were simply typing on their own. The best studies use three conditions: facilitated; non-facilitated, and distractor (as illustrated in Wheeler et al. 1993). In the facilitated condition, the autistic person is shown a picture on a card but the facilitator is not. Then the subject is asked to identify the picture, through the use of FC. The non-facilitated condition uses the same procedure, except the autistic person has to type the answer independently. In the distractor condition, both the subject and facilitator receive their own cards, which are the same for half of the time and different for the other half of the time. This experimental design is very effective in demonstrating that the facilitator is doing the communicating, not the autistic person. The study design is elegant because it uses easy stimuli, gives the autistic person an opportunity to show his cognitive and independent typing skills, and catches the facilitator in the act of doing the communicating, instead of the autistic person.

In conclusion, the vast majority of the studies in the literature on Facilitated Communication clearly show that FC is ineffective in experimental trials where the facilitator did not know the question asked to the person with autism, and therefore, could not help the person answer correctly . In other words, the success seen in FC is a direct result of the facilitator guiding the autistic person.

## What does the therapy actually look like?

The person with autism sits in a chair at a desk and the facilitator takes his or her arm and helps reach towards the keyboard, often above the area where the person is to type. The autistic person is then asked a question or shown a card, and is guided by the facilitator. Generally using one finger, the autistic person types the answer.

# What else do I think?

The fact that the vast majority of controlled studies find no results supporting Facilitated Communication, does not seem to trouble supporters of FC.  They criticize the studies in two ways.  First, they see the experiments as being too "over-controlling."[56]  Put simply, they think that there is too much pressure on the autistic person to perform and as a result, the subject does not cooperate.  I believe that the first criticism is unfounded as in many of the studies reviewed, the children knew their facilitators prior to the study.[3,4,16,22,23,24,26]  Also, in many of these studies the setting for the experiment was comfortable and relaxed in the child's regular school setting.  To avoid possible anxiety, one experiment was conducted in the child's home.[3]  The second criticism has to do with what the FC supporters call "one-place-in-time experiments."  Here they claim that the FC users need more practice than the testing condition allows.  I do not accept the second criticism as valid because in five of the studies reviewed, the children had a reasonable amount of experience with FC before the data was collected (e.g., Vazquez 1994 – one year; Bomba et al. 1996 – ten weeks of daily individualized instruction;  Beck et al. 1996 – six months to two years;  Eberlin et al. 1993 – twenty hours of FC training, and Simon et al. 1994 – five to thirteen months experience).

Many FC researchers believe that it is inappropriate to use quantitative scientific methods to test Facilitated Communication.  They prefer qualitative methods because they believe that the environment will affect the outcome of the study.  Unfortunately, qualitative methods are very unreliable when trying to test whether a technique is scientifically valid.  The responsibility lies with the professionals who recommend a particular method to come up with an objective way to test the effectiveness of their intervention method.  To this point, the Facilitated Communication researchers have not suggested a way to test FC objectively.

This rejection of the scientific method (with all of its tools of empiricism) is a red flag. Most of the studies that found no results when testing FC did try to create a scientific study in an environment where the autistic students would feel comfortable and able to do their best. In my opinion, the fact that not one of their relatively well-designed studies found FC useful is a significant finding and one upon which we can reasonably base conclusions.

I cannot recommend the use of Facilitated Communication for individuals with autism, due to the overwhelming evidence that the facilitator is influencing the answers that are being attributed to the autistic person. In addition, it is important to realize that communication problems in people with autism generally have more to do with the actual understanding and use of language, not a physical inability to communicate. As a result, FC does not address the underlying communication deficits facing individuals with autism. Before typing a clear, coherent sentence, most children with autism first need to be taught to use and comprehend language. One of the criticisms leveled against those who do not believe the claims made by FC practitioners is the assumption that if one cannot communicate, then one must be mentally retarded.[57] I do not share this belief; autism is characterized by a profound difficulty to communicate. In other words, a very bright child with autism may have no ability to communicate (until taught). That does not mean that he or she additionally has a diagnosis of mental retardation.

Unfortunately, many negative consequences have resulted from the inappropriate use of FC on children and youth with autism. False reports of physical and sexual abuse have surfaced, due to the influence of the facilitator on the message ostensibly typed by the autistic person. These very serious accusations have caused much harm for families and caretakers. Unfounded allegations of abuse (over sixty legal cases)[58] are yet another example of what can happen when parents of children with autism put too much faith in the "professionals" without critically evaluating what these professionals are offering.  Once again, this is why we parents must let science be our guide.

## Would I try it on my child?

Absolutely not.  My autistic child does not need to be guided on a typewriter to type.  In fact, she touch types by herself.  I was pleased when we taught her to type independently as this is another means for her to express herself.  I should mention that her communication and cognitive skills are completely in-sync with her ability to point to and answer questions on an IQ test.  Although she is marginally more articulate in writing or typing than speaking, her communication skills are not significantly more complex when she types.   When my daughter was very young and did not know how to communicate at all, I did not try FC with her for two reasons:  1)  there is no science behind the method and much evidence showing that it is ineffective; 2) it did not make sense to me that an autistic child who does not understand language, could suddenly learn how to communicate through a keyboard as long as a facilitator was present, but not when she was on her own, and 3) when too much power is given to the "professionals" who have "special" powers to communicate with the child, the parent is inadvertently putting the child at risk, as happened many times in the history of FC. As parents, we are desperate; remember, the road to hell was paved with good intentions.  There are many uninformed people who regularly attribute high level language skills to nonverbal children with autism.  It is extremely unlikely that without having been taught high-level skills, the child could have learned these skills on his or her own.  Autism is a condition characterized by difficulty in communication.  My child has learned many of the skills she needs to communicate and uses those skills regularly; however, she acquired these skills through a lot of hard work on her part.  I have also met many nonverbal children who use either a picture communication system or a computer to type independently with great effect. However, all these children worked hard to learn enough language to communicate.

## What kind of study would I like to see the FC people do?

At this point, there is enough evidence for us to know that FC is *not* effective for children with autism. Therefore, it is highly unlikely that the FC people could design a study using rigorous science and get positive results. Reputable scientists have been studying this method for over ten years and have not yet found evidence that the technique works. In short, I would encourage the FC practitioners to change their focus from facilitated communication to teaching independent communication for children with autism through a keyboard or similar device. No one would think twice about a teacher using hand-over-hand prompts to teach a child any skill, as long as the prompts are faded in a timely fashion, with the understanding that without independence, the child does not truly possess the skill.

For those children with both autism and severe gross or fine motor difficulty (which is not a primary characteristic of autism), the facilitator must be mechanical in nature (a mechanical rest). Edelson et al. (1998) introduced such a mechanism and found that with a mechanical hand-support device that did not include any human facilitation, six autistic individuals who had extensive experience with Facilitated Communication, were not able to communicate in any meaningful way. Clearly in this case, the gross and fine motor issues were not the reason that the autistic subjects could not communicate independently. In short, there should be no human influence in Facilitated Communication, because it has been shown by Burgess et al. (1998) how even the most conscientious facilitator can inadvertently lead the child by engaging in what they term "automatic writing" (also observed amongst those in a hypnotic state, or those using an Ouija Board).[59] Kezuka (1997) also observed the same phenomenon. An additional reason to make sure that the child is independently communicating through an augmentative device (if needed) is because it has been shown[60] that educators and therapists working with children with autism using Facilitated Communication do not have sufficient understanding of scientific validity. They also have little faith in the scientific method[61] and believe that these children are much more capable than their behavior and other measures indicate.[62]

## Who else recommends against Facilitated Communication as a method for the treatment of autism?

What's very interesting about the FC controversy is that there is an unprecedented number of reputable autism researchers who have jumped into the controversy and have either done studies which disprove the method or have written commentary repudiating the method. As well, there is a long line of reputable organizations which recommend against FC. In 1993, the American Academy of Child and Adolescent Psychiatry developed a policy statement also endorsed by the American Academy of Pediatrics, regarding Facilitated Communication. They state: "Studies have repeatedly demonstrated that FC is not a scientifically valid technique for individuals with autism or mental retardation. In particular, information obtained via [FC] should not be used to confirm or deny allegations of abuse or to make diagnostic or treatment decisions."[63] Their position was updated in 1997. In 1998, the American Academy of Pediatrics released this policy statement: "In the case of FC, there are good scientific data showing it to be ineffective. Moreover, as noted before, the potential for harm does exist, particularly if unsubstantiated allegations of abuse occur using FC."[64] The American Speech-Language-Hearing Association also recommends against Facilitated Communication. They state: "... experiment investigations have not only failed to validate facilitated communication, they have also repeatedly unwittingly authored messages for communicators. Authorship issues continue to be a major concern of qualitative as well as experimental research."[65] In addition, in 1999, the New York State Department of Health issued an excellent report on best practices for the treatment of autism in young children. Regarding Facilitated Communication, they state: "Because of the lack of evidence for efficacy and possible serious *harm* of using facilitated communication, it is strongly recommended that facilitated communication not be used as an intervention method in young children with autism"[66] [emphasis added]. Since then, the Association for Science in Autism Treatment (ASAT) has joined against FC. They state: "Accumulated peer-reviewed, empirically-based research studies have not supported the effectiveness of facilitated communication. Equally important, the research has substantiated the potential for great harm."[67] Quackwatch also has much to say about FC. They state: "... many scientific studies have demonstrated that the procedure is not valid because the outcome is actually determined by the facilitator."[68]

## So you're still on the horns of a dilemma?

If you are still thinking about this form of intervention for your child, I strongly urge you to read Jacobson et al. (2005), which devotes an entire chapter to this unsubstantiated treatment and presents the entire history of Facilitated Communication. This article will give you further background which you may need to make an informed choice. Remember, it was through this method that false allegations were made by facilitators that parents were abusing their children. These children were actually taken away from their families until the courts got involved and protected the families from false allegations! Due to the horrendous history involving Facilitated Communication and the courts, there are many articles written on the harm of relying on Facilitated Communication as a form of accurate communication from children with autism.[69,70,71,72,73,74,75]

I strongly suggest that prior to adopting FC as a communication device for your child, that you read the seven articles pertaining to FC and the history of false allegations of abuse.

## What's the bottom line?

Based on the scientific research to date, there is no evidence that Facilitated Communication is an effective treatment for individuals with autism. It also carries risk for parents or guardians of the child with autism.

# Endnotes for Facilitated Communication

[1]Borthwick, C., and R. Crossley. 1999. "Language and Retardation." *Psycoloquy,* Vol. 10, p. 38.

[2]Bebko, J.M., A. Perry, and S. Bryson. 1996. "Multiple Method Validation Study of Facilitated Communication: II. Individual Differences and Subgroup Results." *Journal of Autism and Developmental Disorders,* Vol. 26, No. 1, pp. 19-43.

[3]Beck, A.R., C.M. Pirovano. "Facilitated Communicators' Performance on a Task of Receptive Language." *Journal of Autism and Developmental Disorders,* 1996, 26(5), pp. 497-513.

[4]Bomba, C., L. O'Donnell, C. Markowitz, and D.L. Homes. 1996. "Evaluating the Impact of Facilitated Communication on the Communicative Competence of Fourteen Students with Autism." *Journal of Autism and Developmental Disorders,* Vol. 26, No. 1, pp. 43-59.

[5]Burgess, C.A., I. Kirsch, H. Shane, K.L. Niederauer, S.M. Graham and A. Bacon. 1998. "Facilitated Communication As An Ideomotor Response." *American Psychological Society,* 1998, Vol. 9, No. 1, pp. 71-74.

[6]Duchan, J.F. 1999. "Views of Facilitated Communication. What's the point?" *Language, Speech and Hearing Services in Schools,* Vol. 30, pp. 401-407.

[7]Eberlin, M., G. McConnachie, S. Ibel and L. Volpe. 1993. "Facilitated Communication: A Failure to Replicate the Phenomenon." *Journal of Autism and Developmental Disorders,* Vol. 23, No. 3, pp. 507-529.

[8]Edelson, S.M., B. Rimland, C.L. Berger, and D. Billings. 1998. "Evaluation of a Mechanical Hand Support for Facilitated Communication." *Journal of Autism and Developmental Disorders,* Vol. 28, No. 2, pp. 153-157.

[9]Cabay, M. 1994. "Brief Report: A Controlled Evaluation of Facilitated Communication Using Open-ended and Fill-in Questions." *Journal of Autism and Developmental Disorders,* Vol. 24, No. 4, pp. 517-527.

[10]Hirshorn, A., and J. Gregory. 1995. "Further Negative Findings on Facilitated Communications." *Psychology in the Schools,* Vol. 32, No. 2, pp. 109-113.

[11]Kerrin, R.G., J.Y. Murdock, W.R. Sharpton, and N. Jones. 1998. "Who's Doing the Pointing? Investigating Facilitated Communication in a Classroom Setting with Students with Autism." *Focus on Autism and Other Developmental Disabilities,* Vol. 13, No. 2, pp. 73-79.

[12]Kezuka, E. 1997. "The Role of Touch in Facilitated Communication." *Journal of Autism and Developmental Disorders,* Vol. 27, No. 5, pp. 571-593.

[13]Montee, B.B., and R.G. Miltenberger. 1995. "An Experimental Analysis of Facilitated Communication." *Journal of Applied Behavior Analysis*, Vol. 28, No. 2, p. 189.

[14]Moore, S., B. Donavan, and A. Hudson. 1993. "Brief Report: Facilitator-Suggested Conversational Evaluation of Facilitated Communication." *Journal of Autism and Developmental Disorders,* Vol. 23, No. 3, pp. 541-553.

[15]Moore, S., B. Donavan, A. Hudson, J. Dykstra, and J. Lawrence. 1993. "Brief Report: Evaluation of Eight Case Studies of Facilitated Communication." *Journal of Autism and Developmental Disorders,* Vol. 23, No. 3, pp. 531-538.

[16]Myles, B.S, and R.L. Simpson. 1996. *Impact of Facilitated Communication Combined with Direct Instruction on Academic Performance of Individuals with Autism.* Vol. 11, No. 1, http://web13.epnet.com/citation.asp?tb=1&_ug+sid+7AC27503%2 (accessed Sept. 21, 2005).

[17]Myles, B.S., R.L. Simpson, and S.M. Smith. 1996. "Collateral Behavioral and Social Effects of Using Facilitated Communication with Individuals with Autism." *Focus on Autism and Other Developmental Disabilities,* Vol. 11, No. 1, pp. 163-169, 190.

[18]Myles, B.S., and R.L. Simpson. 1994. "Facilitated Communication with Children Diagnosed as Autistic in Public School Settings." *Psychiatry in the Schools*, Vol. 31, pp. 208-221.

[19]Oswald, D.P. 1994. "Facilitator Influence in Facilitated Communication." *Journal of Behavioral Education,* Vol. 4, No. 2, pp. 191-200.

[20]Perry, A., S. Bryson, and J. Bebko. 1993. "Multiple Method Validation Study of Facilitated Communication: Preliminary Group Results." *Journal of Developmental Disabilities,* Vol. 2, No. 2, pp. 1-19.

[21]Perry, A., S. Bryson, and J. Bebko. 1998. "Brief Report: Degree of Facilitator Influence in Facilitated Communication as a Function of Facilitator Characteristics, Attitudes and Beliefs." *Journal of Autism and Developmental Disorders,* Vol. 28, No. 1, pp. 87-90.

[22]Regal, R.A., J.E. Rooney, and T. Wandas. 1994. "Facilitated Communication: An Experimental Evaluation." *Journal of Autism and Developmental Disorders*, Vol. 24, No. 3, pp. 345-354.

[23]Simon, E.W., D.M. Toll, and P.M. Whitehair. 1994. "A Naturalistic Approach to the Validation of Facilitated Communication." *Journal of Autism and Developmental Disorders,* Vol 24, No. 5, pp. 647-657.

[24]Simpson, R.L., and B. S. Myles. 1995. "Effectiveness of Facilitated Communication With Children and Youth With Autism." *The Journal of Special Education,* Vol. 28, No. 4, pp. 424-439.

[25]Smith, M.D., and R.G. Belcher. 1993. "Brief Report: Facilitated Communication with Adults with Autism." *Journal of Autism and Developmental Disorders,* Vol. 23, No. 1, pp. 175-183.

[26]Smith, M.D., P.J. Haas, and R.G. Belcher. 1994. "Facilitated Communication: The Effects of Facilitator Knowledge and Level of Assistance on Output." *Journal of Autism and Developmental Disorders,* Vol. 24, No. 3, pp. 357-367.

[27]Szempruch, J., and J.W. Jacobson. 1993. "Evaluating Facilitated Communications of People With Developmental Disabilities." *Research in Developmental Disabilities,* Vol. 14, pp. 253-264.

[28]Vázquez, C.A. 1994. "Brief Report: A Multitask Controlled Evaluation of Facilitated Communication." *Journal of Autism and Developmental Disorders*, Vol. 24, No. 3, pp. 369-379.

[29]Vásquez, C.A. 1995. "Failure to Confirm the Word-Retrieval Problem Hypothesis in Facilitated Communication." *Journal of Autism and Developmental Disorders,* Vol. 25, No. 6, pp. 597-610.

[30]Wheeler, D.L., J.W. Jacobson, R.A. Paglieri, and A.A. Schwartz. 1993. "An Experimental Assessment of Facilitated Communication." *Mental Retardation,* Vol. 11, No. 1, pp. 49-60.

[31]Crossley, R. 1988. Unexpected communication attainments by persons diagnosed as autistic and intellectually impaired. Unpublished paper presented at International Society for Augmentative and Alternative Communication, Los Angeles, CA.

[32]Crossley, R., and A. MacDonald. 1984. *Annie's Coming Out.* NY: Viking Penguin.

[33]Biklen, D. and D.N. Cardinal. 1997. *Contested Words, Contested Science: Unraveling the Facilitated Communication Controversy.* New York, NY: Teachers College Press.

[34]Olney, M. 1997. A Controlled study of facilitated communication using computer games. In D. Biklen and D.N. Cardinal, eds., *Contested words, contested science: Unraveling the facilitated communication controversy.* New York, NY: Teachers College Press.

[35]Borthwick, C., and R. Crossley, (see n. 1 above).

[36]Olney, M. 2001. "Evidence of literacy in individuals labeled with mental retardation." *Disability Studies Quarterly,* Vol. 21, No. 2, pp. 1-12.

[37]Calculator, S.N., K. Singer. 1992. "Preliminary Validation of Facilitated Communication." *Topics in Language Disorders,* Vol. 12, No. 1, pp. 9-16.

[38]Rubin, S., D. Biklen, C. Kasa-Hendrickson, P. Kluth, D.N. Cardinal, and A. Broderick. 2001. "Independence, Participation, and the Meaning of Intellectual Ability." *Disability & Society,* Vol. 16, No. 3, pp. 415-429.

[39]Niemi. J., and E. Kärnä-Lin. 2002. "Grammar and Lexicon in Facilitated Communication: A Linguistic Authorship Analysis of a Finnish Case." *Mental Retardation,* Vol. 40, No. 5, pp. 347-357.

[40]Broderick, A.A., and C. Kasa-Hendrickson. 2001. "Say Just One Word at First: The Emergence of Reliable Speech in a Student Labeled with Autism." *Journal of the Association for Persons with Severe Handicaps,* Vol. 26, No. 1, pp. 13-24.

[41]Schubert, A. 1997. "I Want To Talk Like Everyone: On the Use of Multiple Means of Communication." *Mental Retardation,* Vol. 35, No. 5, pp. 347-354.

[42]Crossley, R., and J. R. Gurney. 1992. "Getting the words Out; Case Studies in Facilitated Communication Training." *Topics in Language Disorders,* Vol. 12, No. 4, pp. 29-45.

[43]Biklen, D., M.W. Morton, D. Gold, C. Berrigan, and S. Swaminathan. "Facilitated Communication: Implication for Individuals with Autism." *Topics in Language Disorders,* Vol. 12, No. 4, pp. 1-28.

[44]Biklen, D., and A. Schubert. 1991. "New words:  The Communication of Students with Autism." *Remedial and Special Education*, Vol. 12, No. 6, pp.  46-57.

[45]Biklen, D. 1990. "Communication Unbound: Autism and Praxis." *Harvard Educational Review,* Vol. 60, pp.  291-314.

[46]Broderick, A.A., and C. Kasa-Hendrickson, (see n. 40 above).

[47]Cardinal, D.M., D. Hanson, and J. Wakeham. 1996. "Investigation of Authorship in Facilitated Communication." *Mental Retardation,* Vol. 34, pp.  231-242.

[48]Ogletree, B.T., and A. Hamtil. 1993. "Facilitated Communication:  Illustration of a Naturalistic Validation Method." *Focus on Autistic Behavior*, Vol. 8, No. 4, pp.  1-10.

[49]Olney, M., (see n. 36 above).

[50]Sheehan, C.M., and R.T. Matuozzi. 1996. "Investigation of the Validity of Facilitated Communication Through the Disclosure of Unknown Information." *Mental Retardation*, Vol. 34, No. 2, pp.  94-107.

[51]Vazquez, C.A., (see n. 28 above).

[52]Weiss, M.J., S.H. Wagner, and M.L. Bauman. 1996. "A Validated Case Study of Facilitated Communication." *Mental Retardation,* Vol. 34, No. 4, pp.  220-230.

[53]Olgetree, B.T., and A. Hamtil, (see n. 48 above), p. 7.

[54]Sheehan, C.M., and R.T. Matuozzi, (see n. 50 above), p. 99.

[55] Vazquez, C.A., (see n. 29 above), p. 608.

[56]Cardinal, D.M., D. Hanson, and J. Wakeham, (see n. 47 above), p. 239.

[57]Borthwick, C., and R. Crossley, (see n. 1 above).

[58]Margolin, K.N. 1994. "How Shall Facilitated Communication Be Judged?  Facilitated Communication and the Legal System."  In: Shane, H.C. ed., *Facilitated Communication. The Clinical and Social Phenomenon*, San Diego, CA: Singular Press, pp. 227-258.

[59]Burgess, C.A., I. Kirsch, H. Shane, K.L. Niederauer, S.M. Graham and A. Bacon,  (see n. 5 above), p. 71.

[60]Kezuka, E., (see n. 12 above).

[61]Dillon, K.M., J.E. Fenlason, and D.J. Vogel. 1994. "Belief In and Use of a Questionable Technique, Facilitated Communication, For Children With Autism." *Psychological Reports,* Vol. 75, pp.  459-464.

[62]Dillon, K.M., J.E. Fenlason, and D.J. Vogel, (see n. 61 above), p. 459.

[63]American Academy of Child and Adolescent Psychiatry, http://www.aacap.org/publications/policy/ps30.htm#TOP, (accessed May 5, 2006).

[64]Committee on Children With Disabilities. 1998. "Auditory Integration Training and Facilitated Communication for Autism." *Pediatrics,* Vol. 102, No. 2, pp. 431-433.∎

[65]Technical Report. 1994. *Facilitated Communication, American Speech-Language-Hearing Association* Vol. III-113, p. 12. http://www.asha.org (accessed Oct. 3, 2005).

[66]Guralnick, M., ed. 1999. Clinical Practice Guideline: Report of the Recommendations. Autism/Pervasive Developmental Disorders, Assessment and Intervention for Young Children (age 0-3 years). Albany, NY: New York State Department of Health, p. IV-65.

[67]Association for Science in Autism Treatment (ASAT), http://www.asatonline.org/about_autism/autism_info09.html, (accessed Oct. 3, 2005).

[68]Quackwatch, www.autism-watch.org/rx/fc.shtml (accessed Oct. 3, 2005).

[69]Howlin, P. 1994. "Facilitated Communication: A Response by Child Protection." *Child Abuse & Neglect,* Vol. 18, No. 6, pp. 529-530.

[70]Howlin, P., and D.P.H. Jones. 1996. "An Assessment Approach to Abuse Allegations Made Through Facilitated Communication." *Child Abuse & Neglect: The International Journal,* Vol. 20, No. 2, pp. 103-110.

[71]Jones, D.P. 1994. " Autism, Facilitated Communication and Allegations of Child Abuse and Neglect." *Child Abuse and Neglect,* Vol. 18, pp. 491-493.

[72]Myers, J.E.B. 1994. "The Tendency of the Legal System to Distort Scientific and Clinical Innovations: Facilitated Communication as a Case Study." *Child Abuse & Neglect*, Vol. 18, No. 6, pp. 505-513.

[73]Siegel, B. 1995. "Assessing Allegations of Sexual Molestation Made Through Facilitated Communication." *Journal of Autism and Developmental Disorders,* Vol. 25, No. 3, pp. 319-326.

[74]Bligh, S., and P. Kupperman. 1993. "Brief Report: Facilitated Communication Evaluation Procedure Accepted in a Court Case." *Journal of Autism and Developmental Disorders*, Vol. 23, No. 3, pp. 553-557.

[75]Starr E. 1994. "Facilitated Communication: A Response by Child Protection." *Child Abuse and Neglect,* Vol. 18, No. 6, pp. 515-527.

# Miscellaneous Therapies:  Holding Therapy

## What is Holding Therapy?

Holding Therapy is a technique developed by Martha Welch, a New York psychiatrist.  This form of therapy requires that the mother hold her autistic child close to her body, in an attempt to address the belief that the individual with autism has a need to attach and bond to his or her mother.[1]  This therapy is based on the theory that the root cause of autism is the withdrawal of human contact, due to the disturbed attachment which has supposedly occurred in the child's early social environment.[2]  Building upon this idea, the goal of Holding Therapy, is to "repair" the mother-child attachment.  This is seen as key, by holding therapists, in the treatment of autism.[3]  The time that the mother holds the child is designed to stimulate attachment and bonding between mother and child.

## What evidence do the practitioners have that this really works?

There is currently no scientific evidence that Holding Therapy is an effective treatment for individuals with autism. A comprehensive literature search netted eighteen articles which mentioned Holding Therapy and autism. The best articles describe case studies.[4]  Of those articles, only two studies had any data and one of those is a 1985 controlled study done by Rohmann et al. (written in German). In this study, although researchers randomly assigned children to experimental and control groups, the outcome was entirely based on parental reporting, which is highly problematic.  In Holding Therapy, the parent is heavily involved in administering the actual therapy; therefore, under no circumstances should the parent take data. (Please see Section Two on "self-fulfilling prophecy" for further discussion on parental reporting). Additional *anecdotal* reporting comes primarily from Welch, the founder of Holding Therapy.  Currently, there are no objective, well-executed, controlled tests of Holding Therapy.  In addition, it is unclear what, if any, other interventions are being implemented concurrently with these children.  It is also not clear how long these children undergo Holding Therapy. There are many unanswered questions about how the "cure" is measured or determined.  We are not given information about :1) which tests are being used to measure progress; 2) the significance of the changes being observed, and 3) whether these children even have an independent diagnosis of autism.  Finally, only the successes of Holding Therapy are reported, which leads to biased results. If only the successes are reported (through anecdotal evidence only), the consumer is mislead to believe that this intervention is highly successful.  Theoretically, there could be large numbers of unreported children with autism from this group who have not benefited from the intervention.

## What does the therapy actually look like?

The holding therapists recommend that holding be done at least once a day, for at least one hour per session. It is carried out with the child and mother sitting face-to-face. This position is reportedly used to maximize the awareness of both mother and child to one another.[5] The child's arms and legs are wrapped around the mother. According to Welch, there are three phases which mother and child experience: 1) confrontation; 2) rejection, and 3) resolution.  In the confrontation phase, both mother and child come to feel anger regarding the relationships they have in their lives. The rejection phase occurs when the child physically or emotionally resists the holding. During this phase, the mother must physically restrain the child while verbally communicating to the child about her feelings.  A desperate struggle reportedly takes place,[6] which is then followed by the resolution phase.  At this stage, the child stops resisting and mother and child are physically and emotionally "molded."[7] Welch describes the third stage as including, "tender intimacy with intense eye contact, exploratory touching ... and gentle conversation."[8]

## What else do I think?

It is widely accepted by researchers today that autism is a neurological disorder. In addition, autism is understood by most reputable researchers and clinicians in the field as completely unrelated to any allegedly disrupted bonding process between mother and child. Given that it is widely rejected that autism is the result of a disrupted mother-child bond, I have no reason to believe that Holding Therapy is effective for children with autism. This argument once again places the responsibility for the child's disorder directly on the shoulders of the mother. The origins of this theory are in observations long ago that there is little in the way of what can be considered 'normal' interaction between these children and their mothers. However, it is now widely held that, due to the nature of the disorder, parents had been trained by the child to interact less as a result of constant rejection or indifference from the child, not the parent. In other words, parents do not cause autism; rather, parents react to the autism. This is the nature of the disorder and completely unrelated to good or negligent parenting. Holding Therapy is one of the few treatments which continues to rely on the widely discredited view that the mother is somehow responsible for her child's autism.

An additional problem with Holding Therapy concerns the researchers' explanations as to why the therapy may be unsuccessful. When Holding Therapy fails, it is once again blamed on the mother's inability to bond with her child. This fail-safe explanation (also called a circular argument or tautology) should be a red flag for parents who are evaluating interventions for their children. Any treatment that cannot fail, even theoretically, can be said to fail the test of what scientists call "falsifiability" (see Section Two for a discussion on falsifiability). Proponents of this method claim that the therapist plays an integral role in assessing Holding Therapy, because only they are able to interpret the messages being sent between mother and child.[9] They alone claim to be able to determine how the mother's inabilities frustrate the child and subsequently cause the child to withdraw. This is the second red flag. If a legitimate researcher cannot measure an effect (even perhaps indirectly), it may as well not exist. In other words, for data collection purposes, observational objectivity is crucial.

## Would I try it on my child?

I would not try this therapy on my child for two reasons: first, as you have probably surmised, my reasoning has to do with science. At this point, there is no science supporting the method. The second reason for my rejection of this therapy is its entire premise. I find the notion that children with autism suffer with the affliction because they have not sufficiently bonded to their parents during early social environment to be seriously flawed. In my opinion, the observed lack of attachment and purported lack of bonding occurs due to a neurological dysfunction and not due to some activity the mother did or failed to do. Quite frankly, I'm quite tired of hearing about how autism is somehow due to lack of bonding between mother and child. This theory harkens back to echoes of Bruno Bettelheim's "refrigerator mother" theory of autism, which plagued parents for decades before it was discredited in the 1950s. I would never try a therapy on my child that is so unfounded, and across the board, anti-mother. The harsh reality is that mothers of children with autism actually deserve a medal, not constant criticism from so-called experts about their supposed maternal inadequacy.

## What kind of study would I like to see the Holding Therapy Practitioners do?

Given the highly questionable theoretical basis for Holding Therapy (the "refrigerator mother" theory), it is doubtful that any successful results would be generated using rigorous science.  However, given that there are still a small number of practitioners using Holding Therapy as an intervention, despite the lack of data, I believe that it needs to be systematically evaluated, according to generally agreed upon scientific principles which motivate good research. Specifically, I would like to see the Holding Therapy practitioners conduct a study that complies with the various criteria for well-designed scientific studies.[10] Only after conducting a rigorous study which produces successful outcomes could we ever consider Holding Therapy a legitimate treatment option for children with autism.  In the absence of any scientifically verifiable results, I would not consider this a legitimate therapy for autism.

## Who else recommends against Holding Therapy as a method for the treatment of autism?

Holding Therapy was in vogue in the 1980s but has fallen out of favor with most members of the autism treatment community.  The Association For Science  in Autism treatment considers Holding Therapy to be in the group of treatments that have yet to be evaluated carefully.[11]  In addition, Quackwatch has characterized Holding Therapy accurately, in my view, based on theories which come from the field of psychoanalysis and have no effective evidence to date.[12] Finally, the National Council Against Health Fraud does not endorse Holding Therapy for children with attachment disorders.[13]

## So you're still on the horns of a dilemma?

If the lack of science isn't enough to dissuade you from considering Holding Therapy, you may be interested to know that in February 2005, the state of Utah ordered practitioners of Holding Therapy to end the practice because it has been alleged to constitute a form of abuse.[14]

## What's the bottom line?

Based on the scientific research to date, there is *no* evidence that Holding Therapy is an effective treatment for individuals with autism.

# Endnotes for Holding Therapy

[1]Welch, M.G. 1989. "Toward Prevention of Developmental Disorders." *Pre and Peri Natal Psychology Journal,* Vol. 3, No. 4, pp. 319-328.

[2]Welch, M.G., (see n. 1 above), p. 321.

[3]Welch, M.G., (see n. 2 above), p. 321.

[4]Stades-Veth, J. 1988. "Autism/Broken Symbiosis: Persistent Avoidance of Eye Contact with the Mother. Causes, Consequences, Prevention and Cure of Autistiform Behavior in Babies through Mother-Child Holding." ERIC ED294344, pp. 33.

[5]Welch, M.G. 1988. *Holding Time.* NY: Fireside, p. 25.

[6]Welch, M.G., (see n. 5 above).

[7]Welch, M.G., (see n. 5 above), p. 47.

[8]Welch, M.G., (see n. 5 above).

[9]Welch, M.G. 1983. "Appendix I: Autism Through Mother-Child Holding Therapy." In Tinbergen, E.A. and N., *Autistic children – New hope for a cure*. London: George Allen & Unwin, pp. 323-335.

[10]The Consolidated Standard of Reporting Trials (CONSORT), www.consort-statement.org/downloads/download.htm, (accessed Feb. 13, 2006).

[11]Association For Science in Autism Treatment, www.asatonline.org/resources/library/informed_choice.html, (accessed May 10, 2006).

[12]Quackwatch, www.quackwatch.org/01quackeryrelated topics/autism.html, (accessed May 10, 2006).

[13]The National Council Against Health Fraud, www.ncahf.org, (accessed Aug. 9, 2006).

[14]Consumer Health Digest No. 05-07, www.ncaf.org/digest05/05-07.html, (accessed Feb. 8, 2006).

# Miscellaneous Therapies:  Music Therapy

## What is Music Therapy?

It is difficult to precisely identify what comprises music therapy, given the extreme variability amongst the approaches outlined by the many studies examined here.  The underlying theories behind music as a therapeutic approach for individuals with autism are numerous.  In fact, the goals of Music Therapy programs are so varied that Kaplan et al. (2005) actually quantified the different studies in relation to their goals.  They found that 41 percent of the interventions focus on language and communication, followed closely by 39 percent which concentrate on behavior and psychosocial goals.  In addition, Whipple (2004) did a meta-analysis on studies which report on Music Therapy for children with autism, in an attempt to discern whether Music Therapy, in its various forms, is effective.

Some investigators propose that there is a relationship between music and behavior or attention.[1,2,3,4]  Others propose that music can produce increased engagement,[5,6] communication,[7,8] and develop relationships.[9]  Still others claim that music can enhance memory, learning and cognition,[10] or serve as an effective contingent reinforcer.[11]  Another group of researchers study the impact of music as a relaxant for people with autism.[12,13,14]  And finally, one researcher examined whether or not individuals with autism have a developmental difference which gives them preference for music over visual stimuli.[15]

Music is presented in various styles and tempos, and the teacher to student ratio varies from one-on-one to group sessions.  The only consistent factor across all studies was that the subjects were exposed to music, in one form or another.

# What evidence do the practitioners have that this really works?

Our comprehensive literature search took us to over half a dozen databases, in which we found over fifty articles relating to autism and Music Therapy. Once we weeded out for studies that only present *data* on Music Therapy with autistic subjects, we found twenty-one studies, only fourteen of which were peer-reviewed. The rest (seven) were either unpublished Master of Arts theses and Ph.D. dissertations, or presentations at conferences which have not been subjected to peer-review, and therefore, are of very limited value (and not discussed here). Of the fourteen peer-reviewed journal articles, we've divided them into successful versus unsuccessful studies.

*"Successful" studies*

There were eleven studies categorized as "successful" based on the results of their research and of those studies, two were removed due to lack of scientific rigor.[14,15] The remaining nine studies involved a total of twenty-seven individuals with autism. Although these studies reported improvements in various areas, most of the improvements related to music (which makes sense, because many children with autism find music reinforcing). The non-music categories did not create the same results.[16] In addition, parents reported better results than the professionals. To illustrate, in Edgerton (1994) there were eleven children with autism who took part in the study. This study did not use a standardized communication instrument; rather, the researchers created their own instrument for the study (the Checklist of Communicative Responses/Acts Score Sheet [CRASS]). This is problematic in itself, as the CRASS has not been extensively tested for validity and reliability (see a discussion in Section Two on the importance of validity). In addition, in terms of the Behavior Change Survey results, those evaluating the children all knew that the children had undergone the treatment.

Predictably, the parents observed the greatest behavior change, which was negligible, followed by the teachers' observation. These observations are compared to the Speech Therapists who reported no change whatsoever.[17*] Therefore, although the authors report success, their results actually paint a very different picture. Another study with one child reported results of increased sociability and pretend play; an alternative explanation for this increased sociability and pretend play could have been that the mother was actively engaging in the child's perseverative play (plucking out fluff from the bedspread) and ritualized play sequences (defined as a set of behaviors using a toy or doll done exactly the same way, repetitively), which is not technically pretend play (pretend play can be defined as including original play sequences created by the child with some variation for each play session).

Another interesting study which reports data from ten children with autism is Buday (1995). This research tested whether music could help children with autism learn targeted signs and words. This well done study found that children learned to vocalize and sign fourteen target words better when those words were put to music rather than when the words were read out loud while the music was playing. The author, quite rightly, cautions the consumer about these results to note that these children learned the words in an experimental setting. The children were not tested to see whether they use these words to communicate outside of the setting, and these words came from rhyming phrases which may have enhanced their ability for memorization when set to music. Other non-rhyming words may not have the same effect. In addition, learning a sign or word may bear no relationship to understanding the word or how and when to use it. This area requires additional research to discern whether, indeed, music has any true

---

*The parents observation was negligible (mean = 4.8), followed by the teachers at (mean = 4.7). The Speech Therapists reported no change whatsoever (mean = 4.2) [even a score of mean = 5 would indicate only a slight change].[17]

value in speeding up meaningful sign or word acquisition among children with autism. Note: memorization may be enhanced using this technique; however, more research needs to be done prior to recommending the use of music to aid in the acquisition of meaningful language comprehension and use.

Another study in the Music Therapy field uses social stories set to music or read to the child regarding a behavior that needs to be eliminated.[4] The researchers found that singing or reading the social story resulted in a decrease in those behaviors, more so than in the control condition where no social story was used. However, only one of the four children in the study responded better when the social story was sung rather than when it was read. The study results support the use of social stories rather than the use of music with social stories.

Finally, one study worth mentioning[7] used music as a positive reinforcement to increase spontaneous speech among children with autism. Although the Music Therapy field embraces this study, it is actually a study that belongs in the behaviorist field (the field of applied behavior analysis) because the study tests music as a reinforcer rather than making conclusions on any potentially therapeutic property inherent in music.

*"Unsuccessful Studies"*

There were three studies which found no strong evidence regarding the effective use of Music Therapy for children with autism. Hairston (1991) found that mentally retarded, non-autistic subjects made more gains than mentally retarded, autistic subjects and that no gains made by autistic subjects were statistically significant. Burleson (1989) found that children with autism or schizophrenia were more successful on a task when background music was played. Their finding, however, did not reach statistical significance.[*] Despite this weak finding, more

---

[*]$p < .062$.

research could be conducted on the effect of music in focussing autistic children when they are engaged in a repetitive task. This begs the question, however, as to why would we want autistic children engaging in repetitive tasks in the first place (unless there were a vocational component to be taught). The last study, Thaut (1987), tested the preferences of autistic children for visual versus musical stimulus, and found that there was no statistically significant difference in terms of preference. There was no therapeutic component to this study.

## What does the therapy actually look like?

Part of the difficulty in evaluating Music Therapy in the treatment of autism stems from the different procedures and approaches the many examiners have used. Not only is the independent variable diverse across the studies, but so too is the dependent variable. Music Therapy has been hypothesized to have a variety of effects on different aspects of the autistic population. In general, studies evaluated here include the effects of Music Therapy on development, stimuli preferences, task performance, memory and learning, social interaction and behavior. In addition, the way in which Music Therapy is presented to the participant varies. In the studies mentioned above, the therapeutic process included musical improvisation, varied beats, varied rhythms, Musical Interaction Therapy and Creative Music Therapy. Adding to the inconsistencies are the subject to therapist ratios with which the music therapy is presented. For some, it is one-on-one therapy, while for others it occurs in group or classroom settings.

## What else do I think?

The mechanism by which Music Therapy is thought to affect individuals with autism is unknown, so far. For many, the observation that many individuals with autism enjoy music may create the impression that they are somehow learning or benefiting from it. While many children with autism do enjoy listening to and playing music, there is insufficient evidence to conclude that the population of individuals with autism at large enjoys music.

Given the diversity of the supporting theories behind music as a therapeutic process for individuals with autism and the lack of supporting data for the various theories, it is difficult to conclude that any of them is therapeutic. Theories include everything from music as a contingent reinforcement, to music as a method for identifying traumatic attachment events in the individual's past and to help them to develop insight into their own personalities. While there may be no apparent negative side effects to Music Therapy, which may account for its popularity, there appear to be no consistent positive effects either. There are dangers to using approaches which have not been proven effective, because they may prevent the use of effective approaches. In addition, there is always the danger of inadvertently reinforcing undesirable or maladaptive behaviors when using therapies that do not have established, systematic procedures which have been proven effective and are standardized. In other words, music may be reinforcing to many people with autism and may inadvertently reinforce the wrong things. It is important to recognize this property as music therapists, due to bad timing, may unwittingly reinforce problematic behaviors through their use of music.

## Would I try it on my child?

My child is very musical. She is one of those people with autism who is very musically talented and loves everything to do with music. In fact, most of her life is spent either playing music (she plays six instruments – three quite well) and writing or composing musical scores. Would I categorize what she does as

Music Therapy? Most emphatically, *NO*. Has music made her life fuller and happier? *YES*, without a doubt. For children with autism who enjoy music, it is clear that music can enhance their life similar to the enrichment typically-developing children receive with music. The difference is that music may be an important conduit for an autistic person to join a peer group, as music is often played in groups. In addition, if the autistic person is talented, there may be vocational opportunities in the world of music for that person. In addition, music is a very good leisure skill; however, what I have described is *not* therapy. Based on the research to date, Music Therapy will not ameliorate autism; therefore, I would not pay for music therapists to work with my child. I have, however, spent considerable sums of money to give my child lessons for various instruments, because music enriches her life immeasurably.

## What kind of study would I like to see the Music Therapists do?

In order to appropriately and accurately evaluate the effects of Music Therapy on individuals with autism, there needs to be a standardized and well-operationalized independent variable. In other words, music therapists need to develop a therapy protocol (the specifics of how the treatment is operationalized); then, that protocol needs to be tested. This is the first step to understanding the effects of Music Therapy and enabling the research to be replicated. A therapeutic protocol may also give us insight into the mechanism by which Music Therapy is effective if indeed any therapeutic gains are observed. Experimental designs including control groups, random assignment, significant subject sizes and results that include statistical levels of significance are overdue in this area. There is much work that needs to be done before Music Therapy can be justified as a treatment option for individuals with autism.

## Who else recommends for or against Music Therapy as a method for the treatment of autism?

The most well-known clinical practice guidelines which recommend against the use of Music Therapy is the New York State Department of Health clinical practice guidelines for autism treatment. The guidelines state: "Because of the lack of demonstrated efficacy, music therapy cannot be recommended as an intervention method for young children with autism."[18] As Music Therapy has not been reported to be dangerous for children, professional organizations have, for the most part, ignored this therapy. In addition, since Music Therapy is so poorly defined, many parents have put their autistic children into lessons and group classes and have redefined these classes as being somehow therapeutic, because their children are engaged in and look forward to the class.

## So you're still on the horns of a dilemma?

If you are still considering Music Therapy for your child, it is important to keep in mind that this therapy has no data to support any claims that the method improves the symptoms of autism. If music brings joy to your child and gives him skills that your child can use to be part of a group and/or spend hours of leisure time productively, then by all means give him or her musical opportunities. I would suggest that we remove the word "therapy" from the term "Music Therapy," and then have the child who enjoys music, enjoy as much of it as possible, from all that the broad field of music has to offer.

## What's the bottom line?

Based on the scientific research to date, there is not enough evidence to demonstrate that Music Therapy is an effective treatment for improving the symptoms associated with autism.

## Endnotes for Music Therapy

[1]Durand, V.M., and E. Mapstone. 1998. "Influence of 'Mood-Inducing' Music on Challenging Behavior." *American Journal on Mental Retardation* , Vol. 102, No. 4, pp. 367-378.

[2]Burleson, S.J., D.B. Center, and H. Reeves. 1989. "The Effect of Background Music on Task Performance in Psychotic Children." *Journal of Music Therapy,* Vol. 26, No. 4, pp. 198-205.

[3]Kostka, M.J. 1993. "A Comparison of Selected Behaviors of a Student With Autism in Special Education and Regular Music Classes." *Music Therapy Perspectives,* Vol. 11, pp. 57-60.

[4]Brownell, M.D. 2002. "Musically Adapted Social Stories to Modify Behaviors in Students With Autism: Four Case Studies." *Journal of Music Therapy,* Vol. 39, No. 2, pp. 117-144.

[5]Wimpory, D.C., P. Chadwick, and S. Nash. 1995. "Musical Interaction Therapy for Children With Autism: An Evaluative Case Study With Two-Year Follow-Up. Brief Report." *Journal of Autism and Developmental Disorders,* Vol. 25, No. 5, pp. 541-553.

[6]Wimpory, D.C., and S. Nash. 1999. "Musical Interaction Therapy: Therapeutic Play for Children With Autism." *Child Language Teaching & Therapy,* Vol. 15, No. 1, pp. 17-28.

[7]Watson, D. 1979. "Music as Reinforcement in Increasing Spontaneous Speech Among Autistic Children." *Missouri Journal of Research in Music Education,* Vol. 4, pp. 8-20.

[8]Edgerton, C.L. 1994. "The Effect of Improvisational Music Therapy on the Communicative Behaviors of Autistic Children." *Journal of Music Therapy,* Vol. 31, No. 1, pp. 31-62.

[9]Toolan, P.G., and S.Y. Coleman. 1994. "Music Therapy, A Description of Process: Engagement and Avoidance in Five People With Learning Disabilities." *Journal of Intellectual Disability Research,* Vol. 38, No. 4, pp. 433-444.

[10]Buday, E.M. 1995. "The Effects of Signed and Spoken Words Taught With Music on Sign and Speech Imitation by Children With Autism." *Journal of Music Therapy,* Vol. 32, No. 3, pp. 189-202.

[11]Hairston, M.P. 1990. "Analyses of Responses of Mentally Retarded Autistic and Mentally Retarded Nonautistic children to Art Therapy and Music Therapy." *Journal of Music Therapy,* Vol. 27, No. 3, pp. 137-150.

[12]Orr, T.J., B.S. Myles, and J.K. Carlson. 1998. "The Impact of Thythmic Entrainment on a Person With Autism." *Focus on Autism and Other Developmental Disabilities,* Vol. 13, No. 3, pp. 163-166.

[13]Wigram, T. 1995. "A Model of Assessment and Differential Diagnosis of Handicap in Children Through the Medium of Music Therapy." In T. Wigram, B. Saperston, and P.A. Langhorne, *Handbook of Art and Science of Music Therapy.* England: Harwood Academic Publishers, pp. 181-193.

[14]Barber, C.F. 1999. "The Use of Music and Colour Therapy as a Behaviour Modifier." *British Journal of Nursing,* Vol. 8, No. 7, pp. 443-448.

[15]Thaut, M.H. 1987. "Visual Versus Auditory (Musical) Stimulus Preferences in Autistic Children: A Pilot Study." *Journal of Autism and Developmental Disorders,* Vol. 17, No. 3, pp. 425-431.

[16]Parteli, L. 1995. "Aesthetic Listening Contributions of Dance/Movement Therapy to the Psychic Understanding of Motor Stereotypes and Distortions in Autism and Psychosis in Childhood and Adolescents." *Special Issue: European Consortium for Arts Therapy Education (ECATE). The Arts in Psychotherapy,* Vol. 22, No. 3, pp. 241-247.

[17]Edgerton, C.L., (see n. 8 above), p. 47.

[18]Guralnick, M., ed. 1999. Clinical Practice Guideline: Report of the Recommendations. Autism/Pervasive Developmental Disorders, Assessment and Intervention for Young Children (age 0-3 years). Albany, NY: New York State Department of Health, p. IV-15 to 21, IV-24.

# Miscellaneous Therapies:  Pet-facilitated Therapy

## What is Pet-facilitated Therapy?

Those who practice Pet-facilitated Therapy (also called Animal-Assisted Therapy) claim that in the same way that peer-mediated therapy helps a child with autism improve their social behavior, so can the use of pets to change the social behavior of children with autism.  Pet facilitators usually use dogs as the pet of choice and argue that because dogs are socially demanding (licking, barking and tending to follow a child), their inherent sociability can be harnessed to increase social interaction for children with autism.

## What evidence do the practitioners have that this really works?

Our comprehensive data search netted three peer-reviewed journal articles (and a number of Master of Science degree theses and presentations at conferences on this topic, which have been excluded).  Only two of the peer-reviewed articles[1,2] present data on an increase in the sociability of children with autism through Pet-facilitated Therapy.

The two articles which provide data support the contention that Pet-facilitated Therapy is responsible for systematically changing the social behavior of the children in the study.  One study included twelve children with autism between five and ten years of age.  Over several sessions, the therapist established contact between the child and dog, and taught the child various games and activities appropriate for dog play.  Next, the therapist engaged in turn-taking with the child.  The researchers measured the amount of social interaction and social isolation that the child exhibited, and found that the introduction of the dog increased the rate of social interaction with the adult and dog. Even after the dog was withdrawn, the rate of social interaction with an adult improved over the base-line, although that result diminished somewhat over time. The study design was a within-subject design where base-line measures were taken, treatment followed, and posttreatment measures were subsequently recorded for that child.

Although the study design was acceptable, there is some question about whether the pet is responsible for increased sociability. To their credit, the researchers state: "But it was not the dog alone that created the change ... The therapist's orchestration of the child-dog and then child-therapist contact was critical."[3] They also refer to prior research in the behavioral literature which demonstrates the strength of the adult-led, active role in therapy. In addition, they acknowledge an increase in the social isolation of the child after the study was completed.

The second study was a very well controlled, within-subjects, repeated-measures design in which each child experienced each experimental condition weekly. The children played with a ball, a stuffed-dog, or a live dog each week, over a fifteen-week period, and found significant differences between children in the three experimental conditions. The child's behavior was significantly different in the live-dog condition as compared to the other two conditions. Of note is that the hand-flapping (a form of self-stimulatory behavior) increased significantly in the live-dog condition. In addition, when the live dog was present, the children paid significantly less attention to the therapist than in the other two conditions. Based on these results, the authors attribute tentative support for Pet-facilitated Therapy, although they make it clear that this was research and not therapy. In other words, they did not attempt to change the behavior of the children in the study, but rather, wanted to see if the dog alone would elicit the change in sociability.[4]

The researchers' interpretation of the results of this study warrant some further discussion.  If we assume that the data was taken accurately and that the results did indeed occur, the next question is whether their discussion of these results has merit and whether these results of increase in hand-flapping indicate a result which is meaningful for the child.  The observation regarding the increase in hand-flapping may have been due to the excitement of the presence of a dog, rather than increased sociability (which is the goal of the study).  There are many other ways to elicit hand-flapping in children with autism, e.g., fast-forwarding a videotape may create the same excitement. Hand-flapping may simply tell us that the children were excited at the novelty of a dog.  Whether the excitement of the dog would be satiated over time is an open question.  Unfortunately, self-stimulatory behaviors such as hand-flapping can disrupt therapy and, thereby, may need to be controlled in order for the child to focus attention to the task at hand.

The second notable result is that the children responded less to the therapist when the dog was present, presumably because the dog is more exciting than the therapist.  This finding may support the contention that a child is less primed for therapy because of the distraction of a dog.  What is unclear, though, is whether excitement is considered pro-social behavior.  Excitement over a dog may have no relationship whatsoever to the prospect of excitement around people, which is the hope of the Pet-facilitated therapy folks.  They essentially hope to use the dog as the transitional object toward a relationship with people.  We define dogs as social animals; children with autism may be reacting to dogs on a whole different level that may or not be social.  Put simply, children with autism may find dogs inherently reinforcing due to other doglike properties that may have nothing to do with canine sociability, such as the way dogs breathe after a run.

## What does the therapy actually look like?

The therapist teaches the child to engage in the care and handling of domestic animals within a classroom. Often the children are taught to take responsibility for the daily care routines of the pets.

## What else do I think?

I am very skeptical of the term "therapy" in this case. The fact that animals are used does not define the activity as therapy. When we use toys or food, we do not say that the therapy is toy-assisted or food-assisted; rather, the therapy may be successful based on already, scientifically substantiated techniques. In this case, it appears as though the animals may become reinforcing to the children, not only because they are different and perhaps exciting, but also because they have predictable routines which may be intrinsically reinforcing to children with autism. The concept of a reinforcer has been heavily studied in the field of behaviorism and may provide a better explanation for the findings than the concept of a therapeutic pet. I have no issue with using dogs as reinforcers for a child. My sense of unease comes from actually calling this a therapy, and I have nightmares about parents going out to buy a dog because they think that their child's autism will be ameliorated in so doing.

## Would I try it on my child?

My child has a dog. In fact, she's had a very well-trained dog for the last ten years and has a good relationship with her dog. That said, do I think that the dog has improved her ability to socially interact with other people and would I purchase the dog with this expectation? Of course not. One thing that I've noticed (a purely anecdotal observation) is that having a dog makes people more likely to approach us and ask her questions about her dog. In that respect, the dog indirectly provides her with social opportunities. In addition, I would use the dog as a reinforcer if I thought that would help her learning. In my daughter's case, though, I doubt that the dog is sufficiently reinforcing for her so that it can be used as a reinforcer. In short, the dog does not ameliorate her autism; however, the dog makes her happy and has enriched her life a great deal.

## What kind of study would I like to see the Pet-facilitated Therapists do?

This group of researchers should either look into the literature on reinforcement, and publish more explicitly based on that literature (if indeed the researchers agree that it is the reinforcing nature of the pets that is creating improvement) or they need to design an experiment whereby the use of an animal is done with people who do not understand the principles of behaviorism. This would separate the variables of reinforcement from the variable of "pet." If the introduction of a pet to children with autism by individuals who make no demands on the child in a child-led environment, created an increase in social interaction relative to children in the same situation without a dog, then an argument could be made that the dog created the social interaction, rather than the adult. The variables of "pet" and "therapist" must to be isolated.

## Who else recommends for or against Pet-facilitated Therapists as a method for the treatment of autism?

There has been little written that recommends Pet-facilitated Therapy for children with autism. As this is not a dangerous therapy (and perhaps because many people think that every kid should have a dog), this purported therapy has been all but ignored by Quackwatch, the Association for Science in Autism treatment (ASAT) and every other reputable clinical guidelines, such as the

New York State Department of Health Clinical Practice Guidelines on autism. The sole organization that has taken interest in this area is the Washington State University College of Veterinary Medicine's People-Pet Partnership (PPP) program.  They conduct research aimed at understanding the Human Animal Bond, which includes the bond between animals and children with autism.[5] They approach this topic from an animal perspective rather than from the field of autism research.  Although they do not recommend Pet-facilitated Therapy for children with autism, this is a research interest of theirs.

## So you're still on the horns of a dilemma?

If you are a dog lover and you are willing to spend the money for a specially trained dog, there is no downside risk to owning an obedient, loving dog. However, I suggest that you go into this endeavour with realistic expectations about the therapeutic value of the dog.  The experience may be great for your child; however, do not expect therapeutic results.

## What's the bottom line?

Based on the scientific research to date, there is insufficient evidence to conclude that Pet-facilitated Therapy is an effective treatment for improving the symptoms associated with autism.

## Endnotes for Pet-facilitated Therapy

[1]Martin, F., and J. Farnum. 2002. "Animal - Assisted Therapy For Children With P.D.D." *Western Journal of Nursing Research,* Vol. 24, No. 6, pp. 657-670.

[2]Redefer, L.A., and J.F. Goodman. 1989. "Brief Report: Pet-facilitated Therapy With Autistic Children." *Journal of Autism and Developmental Disorders,* Vol. 19, No. 3, pp. 461-467.

[3]Redefer, L.A., and J.F. Goodman, (see n. 2 above).

[4]Martin, F., and J. Farnum, (see n. 1 above).

[5]Washington State University College of Veterinary Medicine's People-Pet Partnership (PPP) program, www.vetmed.wsu.edu/depts-pppp (accessed Feb. 21, 2006).

# Miscellaneous Therapies: Sensory Integration Therapy

## What is Sensory Integration?

According to professionals who practice Sensory Integration Therapy (SIT), people who suffer from autism have difficulty in processing sensory information from their environment. I am certain that many of us have likely noticed that our children seem to be sensitive (to an unusual degree) to certain sensory information, such as sound, touch or taste. These practitioners define sensory information as information we see, hear, feel, taste and smell. They also consider sensory information to include the way we see ourselves and our body "in space" and in relation to objects and people. A clumsy person with autism would be defined by proponents of SIT as having sensory issues. Those who use Sensory Integration Therapy as a treatment for autism, describe this technique as a method to organize the information a person receives so that the person can better utilize. In their words, Sensory Integration is defined as, "The organization of sensory input for use, [which is to perceive] ...the body or the world, or an adaptive response, or a learning process, or the development of some neutral function ..."[1] Simply put, according to proponents of this intervention method, autism is a form of sensory dysfunction.

The woman who developed this form of therapy is Ayers. She hypothesizes that SIT helps a person with autism interact with the environment by coordinating the central nervous system.[2] Ayers claims that in some individuals with autism, there is a disorder in brain functioning which makes the integration of sensory stimuli difficult.[3] In order to treat this sensory-specific brain dysfunction, those who practice SIT are of the view that treatment must first identify the person's neurological needs, and then stimulate the person in accordance with those needs, to help him or her adapt to this stimulus. In her own words, Ayers sees the process as "sensory stimulation and adaptive responses to it according to the child's neurological needs."[4] Proponents of SIT believe that for individuals with autism, learning about the environment and how to act within the sensory world has somehow been disrupted and must be repaired to address the disorder. These SIT practitioners claim that the sensory approach improves the ability of children with autism to integrate sensory information.[5] Specifically, Sensory Integration therapists believe that the brain has not yet developed the ability to integrate environmental stimuli. To overcome this problem, therapists adapt the environment to meet the needs of the individual's nervous system.  Once the environment is adapted to enable the integration of sensation, proponents of this intervention method believe that the brain will then be able to reorganize itself.[6]  Ayers describes the therapy as follows: "The central idea of this therapy is to provide and control sensory input, especially the input from the vestibular system, muscles and joints, and skin in such a way that the child spontaneously forms the adaptive responses that integrate those sensations."[7]

## What evidence do the practitioners have that this really works?

Our comprehensive literature search found over fifty articles and books on Sensory Integration Therapy from 1968 through to 2006.  There were additional articles attempting to test whether children with autism have sensory sensitivity, but these were excluded because they did not discuss Sensory Integration as a treatment for autism.  Of those fifty articles, only eleven reported data on SIT as a treatment for children with autism, including three case studies.   There were a few studies done on children with other diagnoses; however, as these children did not suffer from autism, these articles were not included.   Although it is a positive step that research is being conducted on this method, most of the studies were conducted from 1977 to 1992, with three studies published in 1999, one of which is a case study.[8]  The most recent data reported on SIT was seven years ago (1999), yet there has been much heated debate in the literature regarding the quality of these studies.[9,10,11]

All of these SIT studies are plagued by serious flaws. First, only one of the studies on SIT uses a control group (a fundamental flaw in my view) and when researchers use a Single-Subject Case Design (SSCD), it is not designed with sufficient controls. Without sufficient controls, either in a SSCD or a between-subject design (one with a control group), the results of the study can be attributed to any number of factors that may have nothing to do with the treatment. In other words, there may be many other variables at play, independent of the Sensory Integration Therapy (which is the independent variable), that may influence results of the study. The lack of experimental controls questions the results found by all the SIT studies, but particularly those of Cook[12] and Ayers.[13] Both of these studies were long-term SSCD studies (Cook's study was done over two years and Ayers' was one year in duration). There was no control for maturation effects (children develop as they get older) which may have produced improvements in subjects merely through aging, as opposed to any connection to the intervention. In addition, any finding noted by many of the researchers may have been the result of other variables occurring at the same time as the therapy. For example, Ray, et al. (1988),[14] designed a case study in which a child learned thirteen new words over a one month period through the use of a swing. We have no way of knowing whether the swinging motion created these gains, or rather, the positive reinforcement of using the swing paired with the attention of the person teaching the words created enough motivation for the child to attend and, therefore, learn the new words. Put differently, any observed progress of the child cannot be confidently attributed to SIT because other variables may have confounded the results of the various studies.

Unfortunately, the way these SIT studies measure sensory integrative dysfunction (the dependent variable), before and after the therapy, is also problematic. In all of the studies, with the exception of Ayers,[15] sensory integrative dysfunction (the dependent variable) is being measured either through researcher observation, parental reporting, or both.  I know some of you may be thinking, "What's wrong with researcher observation?"  While observation is an important tool in measuring the effectiveness of a treatment, it is very important that the observer be independent of the research, quantifying the observed behavior based upon generally accepted scientific principles of research.  This is crucial, particularly when there is no control group.  If there were an experimental and control group, then researchers associated with each study could make research observations using pre-and post measures as long as they did not know who was assigned to which group in the experiment.  Each of these studies violates this procedure because none have a "blind" observer.  Parental reporting is also suspect (see the discussion in Section Two) because it is susceptible to bias.   While the Ayers article uses parental reporting in addition to other measures, these other measures are also problematic.

Lack of standardization of "before and after" measures for autism and sensory dysfunction plague this research. The study conducted by Ayers et al.,[16] uses a variety of measures to test the sensory dysfunction of the child.  Some subjects were measured on motor proficiency and vocabulary, while others were measured on language or auditory comprehension.  Subjects were also measured using the Ornitz scale, which measures reaction to sensory input.  These measures need to be standardized for each child and several commonly-accepted measures for autism, not just sensory dysfunction, are required.  An example of lack of standardization is in the Case-Smith[17] study, in which five children undergo therapy.  Improvements noted include the finding that four children demonstrated "decreased frequency of nonengaged behavior and that three children increased their frequency of 'goal-directed' play."[18]  This finding tells us nothing about whether autism was ameliorated with SIT.  There are many other possible explanations for this observation that may be independent of Sensory Integration Therapy but, rather, may be an effect of the child learning a new repertoire of play skills based on one-on-one repetitive teaching.  In Short, Sensory Integration needs to be separated from teaching to see whether it is effective.  Case-Smith, et al.,[19] dismiss standardized measures as inappropriate due to noncompliance. Noncompliance is a challenge for many researchers in the field of autism and is not a legitimate justification for a lack of objective measures.  Several standardized measures could be used in addition to the three measures used by Ayers, such as a variety of autism rating scales, psychometric testing and measures of adaptive functioning.

An additional flaw in this subfield is the operationalization of autism. It is essential to examine how the dependent variable, autism, is actually being measured.  In the case of the Ayres article, reaction to sensory input is measured. Unfortunately, reaction to sensory input does not even begin to measure autism. Psychometric and language tests are wholly ignored in the SIT literature, as well as a measure of excesses in behaviors common among children with autism. In a study done by Grandin,[20] she reports a decrease in tense and aggressive feelings in herself when using the "squeeze machine," which she designed for personal use.  Although this is interesting, the question remains as to whether the squeeze machine effectively treats (resolves) behavior deficiences or provides any improvements in intellectual or adaptive functioning (if we accept the findings that the squeeze machine does in general calm people with autism).  Edelson et al. (1999)[21] attempted to test this hypothesis on twelve children with autism by randomly assigning subjects to either an experimental or control group. Although the groups were randomly assigned, the *pretreatment* mean scores for the behavioral measure were appreciably different between groups (which means that there is no utility to doing a between-subject analysis as the groups were different at the outset), and there were not enough data points for withdrawing and introducing the treatment to allow a within-subject design analysis (as is common in SSCDs). Although one could argue that the Edelson et al.[22] study operationalized autism in a meaningful way, i.e., behaviorally (although they used a parent rating scale which is less reliable than a professional rating scale), the above mentioned issues work to exclude their study as evidence to support the efficacy of Sensory Integration Therapy.

Additional lack of operationalization includes the study done by Ayers,[23] where she reports a sixty percent "good response" versus a forty percent "poor response" to SIT. Here she is measuring the subjects' reaction to stimuli. This does not address the important, measurable deficits and excesses of autism. An additional article by Cook,[24] has a similar flaw in the study in that the checklist used is specific to sensory dysfunction issues, as opposed to language, IQ gains, and behavioral gains which are predictive of functioning. The McClure et al. article (1991)[25] measures the level of self-stimulatory behavior and self-injury in a case study. Behavioral excesses are a problem for many individuals with autism; consequently, it is a very good idea to measure these variables in autism treatment research. Unfortunately, this study also suffers from some of the flaws discussed above; specifically, while the researchers were providing Sensory Integration Therapy with the self-injurious subject, the subject was also given a variety of other treatments including medication. McClure et al.[25] mention that these other treatments may have influenced the behavior of the subject. In short, the experimenters confounded their study (confused it with other variables), which renders the data meaningless. The confounding variable of "medication" is a crucial piece of information because it tells us that we cannot conclude, with confidence, whether or not the treatment was effective. Finally, most of the studies were non-rigorous case studies,[26,27] which may give us insight into those individuals being studied, but cannot be used to make any conclusions whatsoever about efficacy of SIT for the broader population of children afflicted with autism.

Confounding variables seem to be a recurring flaw in the research that has been done on Sensory Integration. The Cook[28] and Ayers et al.[29] studies do not control the variable of education. In other words, what other intervention the child may have experienced prior to the Sensory Integration treatment study is not accounted for. The results of these two case studies are confounded by the enrollment in preschool for both subjects, one for two years and one for more than eighteen months. The first subject received compliance training in the preschool setting, at the same time as that child received Sensory Integration Therapy, which could explain many of the gains he made over the two-year period. Both subjects were taught using structured activities across, "all domains of development,"[30] and the second subject in the study had a one-to-one aide at school. We cannot conclude that the gains achieved by these two subjects were in any way related to the SIT they received. They could just as easily be attributed to structured behavioral intervention.

## What does the therapy actually look like?

Sensory Integration Therapy encourages the child to play using different kinds of gym equipment. Many of the activities that sensory integration specialists do use commonly available playground equipment such as scooters, swings (special bolster swings and typical playground swings), and playground merry-go-rounds. In addition, they often brush and/or rub the child's skin to apply sensory stimuli to the body. Sensory integrationists will use many different kinds of equipment to create the different types of sensation they require the child to experience. Those advocating deep pressure stimulation, use a Hug Machine, designed by Temple Grandin.[31] The child enters this device and is then squeezed.

## What else do I think?

Based on the studies published to date, we cannot reasonably conclude that Sensory Integration Therapy is a science-based form of treatment for autism. Unfortunately, the outcome variables being measured are often irrelevant to the condition of autism and the results are not supported by rigorous experimental designs. Many factors basic to conclusive outcomes, such as a variety of sufficient experimental controls, are simply not present. The observation that some children with autism have sensory sensitivity does not logically lead me to the conclusion that Sensory Integration Therapy would be effective in lessening the sensitivity, or even if it does (which has not been determined), that this somehow ameliorates the many symptoms of autism.

## Would I try it on my child?

I started hearing about Sensory Integration Therapy in 1992, when my child was diagnosed. At that time, there was insufficient evidence for the efficacy of this treatment and the same remains true today. At this point, I do not see enough evidence to use this method on my child and, although I do not see the method as extremely harmful, I do see it as taking time away from other more worthwhile things a child requires. If one day there is firm scientific evidence that Sensory Integration Therapy can indeed improve my child's autism, then I will most probably try the therapy. Until that day, I will not subject her to Sensory Integration Therapy.

## What kind of study would I like to see the Sensory Integration people do?

I would like to see a study with at a minimum the following elements: first, it is critical to create a hypothesis that states that children who undergo sensory integration therapy are more likely to see a decrease in autistic symptoms compared to those who do not receive this treatment. It is imperative that commonly accepted tests to measure autism be widely used, administered by a registered psychologist who has no knowledge of the study. This needs to be done to ensure that all the children in the study do indeed have autism or Pervasive Developmental Disorder-Not Otherwise Specified (PDD-NOS). In addition, each child should be tested on widely accepted psychometric tests, which are administered before and after the treatment. The psychologist who does the pre- and post tests, should not know which children are in the treatment group and which children are in the control group. All the children should be treated at the same site, including those children in the control group. There should be at least twenty children per group in the experiment, with at least forty children total in the study.

The children in the control group could play in the playground for the same amount of time as the children in the treatment group. They could use typical playground equipment, creating a placebo (fake treatment) that mimics the experience of the experimental group in every way aside from the Sensory Integration Therapy. If replicated results demonstrate that the children in the treatment group score significantly better on these commonly accepted measures, then we could conclude that this therapy works to ameliorate autism. At this time we are a very long way from that.

## Who else recommends against Sensory Integration as a method for the treatment of autism?

The New York State Department of Health has the following to say regarding Sensory Integration Therapy: "There is currently no adequate scientific evidence (based on controlled studies using generally accepted scientific methodology) that demonstrates the effectiveness of sensory integration for young children with autism. Therefore, the use of this method cannot be recommended as a primary intervention method for young children with autism."[32]  Since the New York Report was published, there have been several reviews[33,34,35] supporting its original findings.  In addition, the Association for Science  in Autism treatment (ASAT) also supports the view that Sensory Integration does not have sufficient evidence to consider it as an effective treatment for autism.[36]  Quackwatch[37] also lists this therapy as "questionable."

## So you're still on the horns of a dilemma?

Smith, et al.[38] have written a good, in-depth analysis of Sensory Integration Therapy and demonstrate that there is no evidence regarding efficacy for this treatment method.  These researchers have done a great service to the Sensory Integration research community because they have suggested several study designs by which Sensory Integration can be objectively tested for efficacy where decreasing self-injurious behavior is concerned.  These tests desperately need to be conducted because, at this time, there are thousands of children receiving Sensory Integration Therapy, despite the absence of convincing evidence that it works.  In short, if you decide to use this therapy for your child, remember you are engaging in experimentation.  There is no excuse for the proponents of SIT to avoid conducting this research, as other reputable researchers in the field have set out the experimental design required to demonstrate whether or not Sensory Integration Therapy is truly effective.  For a spirited discussion in the literature on this controversial therapy, Goldstein (2003)[39] is worth a read, as is the Smith et al. chapter in *Controversial Therapies for Developmental Disabilities* (2005).[38]

## What's the bottom line?

Based on the scientific research to date, there is not enough evidence to show that Sensory Integration Therapy is an effective treatment for improving the symptoms associated with autism.

## Endnotes for Sensory Integration Therapy

[1.]Ayers, A.J. 1979. *Sensory Integration and The Child.* Los Angeles, CA: Western Psychological Services.

[2]Ayers, A.J., (see n. 1 above).

[3]Ayers, A.J., (see n. 1 above).

[4]Ayers, A.J., (see n. 1 above).

[5]Cook, D.G. 1991. " A Sensory Approach to the Treatment and Management of Children With Autism." *Focus on Autistic Behavior.* Vol. 5, No. 6, pp. 1-19.

[6]Ayers, A.J., (see n. 1 above).

[7]Ayers, A.J., (see n. 1 above).

[8]Stagnitti, K., P. Raison, and P. Ryan. 1999. "Sensory Defensiveness Syndrome: A Paediatric Perspective and Case Study." *Australian Occupational Therapy Journal,* Vol. 4, No. 46, pp. 175-187.

[9]Dawson, G., and R. Watling. 2000. "Interventions to Facilitate Auditory, Visual and Motor Integration in Autism: A Review of the Evidence." *Journal of Autism & Developmental Disorders,* Vol. 30, No. 5, pp. 415-421.

[10]Goldstein, H. 2000. "Commentary: Interventions to Facilitate Auditory, Visual and Motor Integration: 'Show Me The Data'." *Journal of Autism & Developmental Disorders,* Vol. 30, No. 5, pp. 423-425.

[11]Edelson, S.J., B. Rimland, and T. Grandin. 2003. "Commentary: Response to Goldstein's Commentary: Interventions to Facilitate Auditory, Visual and Motor Integration: 'Show Me The Data'." *Journal of Autism and Developmental Disorders,* Vol. 33, No. 5, pp. 551-552.

[12]Cook, D.G., (see n. 5 above).

[13]Ayers, A.J., and L.S. Tickle. 1980. " Hyper-responsivity to Touch and Vestibular Stimuli as a Predictor of Positive Response to Sensory Integration Procedures by Autistic Children." *The American Journal of Occupational Therapy,* Vol. 34, No. 6, pp. 375-381.

[14]Ray, T.C., L.J. King, and T. Grandin. 1988. "The Effectiveness of Self-initiated Vestibular Stimulation in Producing Speech Sounds in an Autistic Child." *The Occupational Therapy Journal of Research,* Vol. 8, No. 3, pp. 186-190.

[15]Ayers, A.J., and L.S. Tickle, (see n. 13 above).

[16]Ayers, A.J., and L.S. Tickle, (see n. 13 above).

[17]Case-Smith, J., and T. Bryan. 1999. "The Effects of Occupational Therapy With Sensory Integration Emphasis on Preschool-Age Children With Autism." *The American Journal of Occupational Therapy,* Vol. 53, No. 5, pp. 489-497.

[18]Case-Smith, J., and T. Bryan, (see n. 17 above).

[19]Case-Smith, J., and T. Bryan, (see n. 17 above).

[20]Grandin, T. 1992. "Calming Effects of Deep Touch Pressure in Patients with Autistic Disorder, College Students and Animals." *Journal of Child and Adolescent Psychopharmacology,* Vol. 2, No. 1, pp. 63-72.

[21]Edelson, S.M., D. Arin, M. Bauman, S.E. Lukas, J. H. Rudy, M. Sholar, and B. Rimland. 1999. "Auditory Integration Training: A Double-Blind Study of Behavioral and Elecrophysiological Effects in People with Autism." *Focus On Autism and Other Developmental Disabilities,* Vol. 14, No. 2, pp. 73-81.

[22]Edelson, S.M. et al., (see n. 21 above).

[23]Ayers, A.J., and L.S. Tickle, (see n. 13 above).

[24]Cook, D.G., (see n. 5 above).

[25]McClure, M.K., and M. Holtz-Yotz. 1991. "The Effects of Sensory Stimulatory Treatment on an Autistic Child." *The American Journal of Occupational Therapy,* Vol. 45, No. 12, pp. 1138-1142.

[26]Larrinton, G.G. 1987. "A Sensory Integration Based Program with a Severely Retarded/Autistic Teenager: An Occupational Therapy Case Report." *Occupational Therapy in Health Care,* Vol. 4, No. 2, pp. 101-107.

[27]Stagnitti, K., P. Raison, and P. Ryan, (see n. 8 above).

[28] Cook, D.G., (see n. 5 above).

[29]Ayers, A.J., and L.S. Tickle, (see n. 13 above).

[30]Cook, D.G., (see n. 5 above).

[31]Grandin, T., (see n. 20 above).

[32]Guralnick, M., ed. 1999. *Clinical Practice Guideline: Report of the Recommendations. Autism/Pervasive Developmental Disorders, Assessment and Intervention for Young Children* (age 0-3 years). Albany, NY: New York State Department of Health, p. IV-60.

[33]Dawson, G., and R. Watling, (see n. 9 above).

[34]Goldstein, H., (see n. 10 above).

[35]Baranek, G.T. 2002. "Efficacy of Sensory and Motor Interventions for Children With Autism." *Journal of Autism and Developmental Disorders,* Vol. 32, No. 5, pp. 391-422.

[36]Association for Science in Autism Treatment (ASAT), www,asatonline.org/about-autism/autism-info12.html, (accessed Feb. 16, 2006).

[37]Quackwatch, www.quackwatch.org, (accessed Feb. 16, 2006).

[38]Smith, T., D.W. Mruzek, and D. Mozzingo. 2005. "Sensory Integrative Therapy."  In: *Controversial Therapies for Developmental Disabilities.* J.W. Jacobson, R.M. Foxx, J.A. Mulick. Mahwah, NJ:  Lawrence Erlbaum Associates, pp. 331-347.

[39]Goldstein, H. 2003. "Response to Edelson, Rimland, and Grandin's Commentary." *Journal of Autism and Developmental Disorders,* Vol. 33, No. 5, pp. 553-555.

# Miscellaneous Therapies:  Vision Therapy

## What is Vision Therapy?

The use of Vision Therapy in autism treatment stems from the concept that people with autism are not social because they experience visual dysfunction.  In other words, their vision is somehow being disturbed.  The "ambient" visual system, which is said to be responsible for the perception of space (and thereby movement, depth perception and position of one's body in space), is thought to be impaired in some persons afflicted with autism.  Symptoms experienced by people with autism, such as toe-walking, abnormal posture, head tilts and abnormal gaze, are claimed by Vision Therapy researchers to result in the person with autism being unable to experience normal vision.  According to these researchers, they do not have, "an integrated visual precept of events and objects in their environment."[1] From this theory, these researchers claim that this impairment results in the individual being unable to recognize the consequences of their actions, due to the inability to track their own position in space.

Vision Therapy is conducted by having the autistic person wear special "ambient lenses" which are thought to improve posture, correct head tilts, and improve coordination in such activities as catching a ball.  According to Kaplan and colleagues, "the symptoms demonstrated by autistic children may be an adaptation to an ambient visual system that has distorted the appearance of the spatial environment."[2] By using these special glasses, the purported distortion of vision is claimed to be lessened or eliminated.

## What evidence do the practitioners have that this really works?

After a comprehensive literature search, eight articles on Vision Therapy relating to autism were found.  Of those eight articles, only two studies involving the use of prism lenses for individuals with autism report any outcome data.  The first study was weak; however, the second study corrected many of the flaws of the first study.

Published in 1996, the first study is a within-subjects design, in which the first author recorded data based on the use of the lenses.  This introduced the possibility of experimenter bias influencing the results, as it is generally accepted that the person who designs the study and predicts the outcome should not be collecting the data; rather, someone who has no knowledge of the research hypothesis should be involved in data collection.  In addition, these researchers did not use a standardized behavioral measure to measure behaviors.  They did not include a measure of behaviors such as self-stimulatory and/or self-injurious behaviors, among others, which are characteristic of the autistic population.  The measures they *did* use are typically not representative of children with autism.  Specifically, they measured behaviors in the first study by observing children watching television with correct or incorrect prisms and describing the head position (erect, slanted backward, slanted forward, or tilted to the side), body posture (erect, slanted backward, slanted forward, or tilted to the side), and facial expression (from hypertense to relaxed).  In addition, they measured how well the children caught a ball when seated.  In short, there was no measurement of behaviors that are typically considered characteristic to autism and define the diagnosis of autism.

The second study conducted by Kaplan and his colleagues (1998), although flawed as well, is a vast improvement over the first study.  The experiment is a double-blind, crossover design with two randomly-assigned groups (see Section Two for a discussion on this type of design). Another improvement was the addition of a dependent variable assessment of behavior, as measured by the Aberrant Behavior Checklist (ABC). This assessment was used before, during and after each of the four phases of the experiment. This improvement provided the researchers with an opportunity to see behavioral differences at different points to be used for comparison. Unfortunately, the ABC measure was used by the child's parents to report behavior (and, by this time, you all know what I think about parental reporting!). Despite my criticisms regarding the ABC measure for autism, these improvements in methodology were necessary in order to better assess the effects of "prism lenses" on autism. The researchers did not use any other traditional autism measurement tool alongside the ABC, and although the Aberrant Behavior Check list is an accepted measurement tool, it was designed to be used on moderately to profoundly retarded people, not children with autism.[3] In short, this measure was not designed to gauge improvement in autism through the application of special eye glass lenses.

The results of the second study found no significant changes in orientation and attention, as measured by their four performance tasks of ball catch, television viewing while seated, television viewing while on a balance board, and visual ball tracking. The results of this second, better-designed study, contradict the results of the first poorly-designed study (although even if they *did* see changes in their measures, these researchers have not established the relevance of their measures as they apply to autism).

In terms of behavioral improvement, the results are quite perplexing and close to meaningless. Based on the ABC scale, behavior showed an interesting trend by decreasing for two months and then increasing![*] In other words, the

---

[*]This result was statistically significant ($p < .05$).

children's behavior improved slightly for two months and then deteriorated for two months. There are several questions that need to be answered in order to interpret these results. First, did the children's behavior improve as a result of the Vision Therapy "prism lenses," or did their behavior improve for another reason that is not readily apparent to us? The researchers claim that the special glasses actually created an improvement in behavior. It is important to state that the improvement was actually quite minuscule, partially because these subjects had very few behavior problems to begin with (scoring at base-line less than one point on a four point scale, with zero indicating no behavioral issues and three indicating severe behavior). The largest difference between research groups was less than one point (0.45 difference). Although statistically significant, it is so small that it is virtually meaningless in terms of improvement for the person with autism. In other words, the five categories of behavior problems – irritability, lethargy, stereotypy, hyperactivity, and excessive speech – improved by a mere 0.45 of a four point scale and this tiny improvement disappeared by the fourth month of the study.

Do we have any alternative explanations for this observed, small, short-term decrease in problematic behaviors? One possible explanation could be that the children in the experimental group were intrigued with the novelty of the glasses as they were somewhat different from the regular glasses (and they perceived the glasses as somehow interesting). In short, the novelty of the glasses may have affected their behavior, but the effect diminished over time. Unfortunately, the researchers do not report the pre-and post scores of the ABC measure for each subject. Therefore, the reader cannot decide whether the difference is meaningful for even one child, in terms of the autism-related problems which affect the child (as we are only presented the average scores per condition and not the score for each child).

An additional flaw with the study is that there were originally twenty-three autistic persons scheduled to participate in the research. Five of the twenty-three (three in the experimental group and two in the control group) did not participate because they refused to wear the glasses or would break the glasses. Those children with the worst behavioral problems may not have participated. This self-selection concern is not terribly problematic because the study is a between-subjects design. However, if the ABC measure is not a sufficiently sensitive instrument to pick up differences in degree of autism, and the five people with the most problematic behaviors are excluded from the study, then the ABC may not accurately assess the effect of the behavior of the persons with autism who remain in the study because they have few behaviors. Ironically, if indeed the prism glasses do have an effect, then the effect would be larger if the children with greater behavioral excesses were included in the study. Unfortunately, they were not, significantly diminishing the value of the study.

## What does the therapy actually look like?

The therapy simply requires that the person wear the "prism lense" glasses much like we wear regular eye glasses for daily living.

## Would I try it on my child?

At this point, I would not try this on my child. There are major flaws in the Vision Therapy study, including the use of parental reporting on the ABC scale to gauge behavioral problems. The results of behavioral regression are unexplained and the social significance of the findings is questionable.

## What else do I think?

Although I was encouraged to see that the vision researchers use a between-subjects research design (rare in the world of autism research), arguably the biggest issue with the use of Vision Therapy for individuals with autism is the lack of connection between improved vision and autism.  Autism cannot be assumed to be a disorder where the cause lies purely in visual dysfunction.  While the cause so far remains unknown, there is insufficient evidence to conclude that vision alone is impaired amongst persons afflicted with autism.  Using dependent measures such as the ability to catch a ball, and the ability to improve posture, do not even begin to address the serious and often debilitating symptoms of autism.  Improved vision in a child with autism may have no relationship whatsoever to improving the degree of autism and common aspects of the disorder, such as self-stimulatory behavior, self-injury, and difficulties in communication.  Other studies observe the ability of a child to better reproduce a grid pattern.[4]  Why the ability to reproduce a grid would in itself be considered relevant to autism is also unclear.

Based on the evidence to this point, I cannot conclude that prism lenses ameliorate the symptoms of autism.  While minimal  improvement in behavior (as measured by the ABC) is temporarily seen for approximately two months, these improvements appear to be diminished at follow up.  It is necessary to provide further research on the longer-term effects of this intervention.

## What kind of study would I like to see the Prism Lenses researchers do?

I would like to see a study that includes the replication of the Kaplan, et al. (1997), with a randomly assigned experimental and control group, much like the one these researchers already have; however, more subjects per condition are necessary, particularly because researchers claim to have observed minimal, short-term results. A larger study would be able to more easily recreate those results, if they are real. In addition, the researchers need to give the subjects pre- and post tests which measure autism more accurately and do not rely on parental reporting. Ideally, a psychologist with no knowledge about the experiment, but with experience in administering a variety of well-accepted, psychometric assessment measures, should administer the tests. Among those tests, ideally there should be some standardized IQ tests to measure improvement in the subjects. Finally, I would like to see this study done over a considerable length of time, to ensure that if, indeed, there is an effect, the effect is measurable. If there is *no* effect, we could make a clear statement discarding this treatment method from the long list of treatment options for autism.

## Who else recommends for or against Vision Therapy as a method for the treatment of autism?

The treatment of autism using prism lenses was never very popular; however, Vision Therapy has been offered for a number of years to people with a variety of ailments and learning disabilities. For a history of Vision Therapy in general, the Scientific Review of Mental Health Practice (SRMHP) presents a summary of the many remarkable claims of vision therapists through the ages. The SRMHP also touch on autism: they do not recommend Vision Therapy as a treatment option for the disorder.[5]

## So you're still on the horns of a dilemma?

Ten years ago there was considerable interest in Vision Therapy among parents of children with a variety of learning disabilities. Consequently, the American Academy of Pediatrics, the American Association for Pediatric Ophthalmology and Strabismus and the American Academy of Ophthalmology joined forces and created a joint policy statement which declares: "No scientific evidence exists for the efficacy of eye exercises ("vision therapy") or the use of special tinted lenses in the remediation of these complex pediatric neurological conditions."[6] Although this was not written for autism, the arguments used by those promoting Vision Therapy are the same as those applied to learning disabilities in general.

## What's the bottom line?

Based on the scientific research available to date, there is insufficient evidence to show that Vision Therapy is an effective treatment for improving the symptoms associated with autism in children.

## Endnotes for Vision Therapy

[1]Kaplan, M., D.P. Carmody, and A. Gaydos. 1996. "Postural Orientation Modifications in Autism in Response to Ambient Lenses" *Child Psychiatry and Human Development,* Vol. 27, No. 2, pp. 81-91.

[2]Kaplan, M., D.P. Carmody, and A. Gaydos, (see n. 1 above), p. 83.

[3]Aman, M.G., N.N. Singh, A.W. Stewart, and C.J. Field. 1985. "The Aberrant Behavioral Checklist: A Behavior Rating Scale for the Assessement of Treatment Effects." *American Journal of Mental Deficiency,* Vol. 89, No. 5, pp. 485-491.

[4]Lovelace, K., H. Rhodes, and C. Chambliss. 2002. "Educational Applications of Vision Therapy: A Pilot Study on Children with Autism." *Resource in Education*, ERIC/DGE 458766.

[5]Scientific Review of Mental Health Practice (SRMHP), http//www.srmhp.org/archives/vision-therapy.html, (accessed Nov. 5, 2006).

[6]American Academy of Pediatrics, American Association for Pediatric Ophthalmology and Strabismus, and American Academy of Ophthalmology. Joint policy statement: Learning Disabilities, Dyslexia and Vision, http//www.aao.org/member/policy/disability.cfm, (accessed Feb. 16, 2006).

# Section Two

## How Do We Know What Works and What Doesn't?

Section Two introduces the reader to the basic rules that the scientific method relies upon to evaluate autism treatments in Section One of this book. This section is written in a straight forward, user-friendly way so everyone can access the knowledge tools necessary for the evaluation of autism treatments. This section talks not only about the scientific method, but also gives the reader an introduction to the process by which science is funded and how bias can easily creep into research if proper precautions are not taken to separate the influence of the funders from the scientists.  Aside from the politics of research, this section describes what comprises the scientific method and how it is different from pseudo-science, which is often relied upon by purveyors of unsubstantiated treatments.  I address the importance of understanding: (1) the role of theory; (2) how theory motivates research, and (3) if you do not understand what a theory is supposed to do, how you can potentially be hoodwinked — convinced that a treatment is effective when there is in fact no data supporting that treatment.  I describe how we use science to move closer to the truth which, in our case, is vital to our children's futures.

Next, I give *you* the tools to be able to analyze a study.  Then, I lay bare the large number of pitfalls with which poor research is plagued, so you will be able to identify those potholes.  Furthermore, once we know what the study shows us about autism, I discuss how, when and whether the results of the study can be generalized to the population of children afflicted with autism. I also discuss the important role of repeating studies (replications) for the goal of applying results to the real world.  That would include your child, which is, presumably, why you are reading this book!  Moreover, you are provided with a list of red-flags to watch out for when evaluating autism treatments.  The goal of this section is basically to inoculate you from incompetent researchers or illegitimate purveyors of autism treatment and, thereby, protect your child with autism from the quackery that runs rampant in the field of autism treatment.  Finally, you will be able to understand the analysis of the science behind all the popular autism treatments presented in the first section and, hopefully, be able to apply principles of the scientific method to the next big autism treatment fad that comes your way.

## 2.1 Why care about science?

The Scientific Method is a solid, time-tested, reliable way to uncover evidence to support or refute an idea.  In practical terms, the scientific method can protect you from wasting your child's time and your money.  Regarding autism, some ineffective treatments are very expensive and many may bankrupt you quickly.  In addition, using science to analyze treatments can protect your child from physical harm.  Some treatments are actually physically invasive, such as experimental brain surgery.  The scientific method can also protect you from wasting your child's opportunity to get effective treatment.  Some  treatments are not intrinsically harmful; however, they waste your child's precious time when they preclude the child from receiving treatment that is truly therapeutic.  Therefore, these treatments are indirectly harmful.  Using science to analyze treatments can also protect you from turning your family's life upside down.  There is a collection of unproven treatments that are not harmful per se, but simply an enormous burden to incorporate into the life of your family.  Science can help you avoid implementing these ineffective treatments on your child.  Another group of treatments are not expensive and burdensome and, therefore, not a serious threat to the well-being of your child; however, they have no science behind them and, therefore, may be of no value whatsoever.  All the above reasons illustrate how important it is to know the effectiveness of a treatment before choosing to implement it with your child.  In other words, in order to truly improve your child's condition, you *need* to know whether there is science behind the method you are considering to use with your child.

# 2.2 Why we can't always rely on experts

There are several reasons why experts (and purported experts) may not always be a good source of knowledge.  There are many experts in the field who are tremendously important for children with autism.  However, the parent is not always in the best position to judge whether the so-called  "expert" truly is an expert or whether the self-anointed expert is simply out to sell a product or service that the expert wants the parent to buy.  Experts may not be a good source of information because: (1) they may not know the state of the science in autism treatment; (2) they may not value science; (3) personal advancement in academe may trump quality concerns, and/or (4) their motives may not be pure as in the case of gold-plated quackery.

### "Experts" do not always know about science

The first question you must ask is: "Who are these so-called experts, and where is their expertise?"  There are many people who work with autistic children who may be experts in their individual fields; however, most of them do not know how to properly evaluate scientific research. Therefore, if a parent asks an autism therapist or consultant about a variety of treatments or cures, most of them will typically not be qualified to tell you about the state of the science in autism treatment.  Put  simply, they do not know how to evaluate knowledge claims and the *studies* supporting those claims.  This is true for most therapists and consultants who provide treatments that are not science-based as well as many of those who actually provide science-based treatment.  They may be intimately familiar with  their subfield, but have not done the research or do not have the skills to evaluate autism treatment in areas where they do not work.

## They may not value science

There is yet another subgroup of treatment professionals who do not think that their method can be scientifically proven because it cannot be measured. This group desperately wants sticklers for science to "compromise" on the science. I recently went to a conference where an experimental treatment was introduced and the accompanying books and videotapes were available for sale. When I challenged the author privately about the fact that there is no evidence regarding this method and that if she really wanted to improve this field, she would try to convince those pushing the treatment to do some research. She asked me this question: "Can't you bend a little on the science?" Clearly, scientific evidence is not important for some autism "experts;" yet their presentations attempt to appear very science-based. This particular lecture was introducing a biomedical treatment and the lecture consisted of a multimedia production supported with many charts, graphs and computer-generated brain animations.

## Advancement trumps quality concerns

In a researcher's life, the cliche "publish or perish" is absolutely true. The more researchers publish, the better for their careers. A long list of academic publications can lead to a permanent position at a university (tenure), more respect in their field, more grants and the likelihood that those researchers will push the field forward. In fact, I am familiar with one department in which there was actually debate about linking salaries to amount published and docking professors if they did not pump out enough publications!

There is obviously something that the "publish or perish" doctrine fails to capture — *quality* of research and *quality* of publication. Every field has its top journals where researchers try to get published in first. When they fail, they attempt to publish in second or third tier journals that may lack the prestige of the preeminent journals. The quality of the journal is based on the quality of the editorial board, which decides the research papers to accept and the ones to reject. Journal quality is tied to academic advancement; researchers understand this point but parents often do not. As parents of children with autism, we must also understand the advancement dynamic within the university; otherwise, we will take any study that has simply been published anywhere and assume that it has been done correctly and reviewed by others who know how to evaluate research properly. Unfortunately, this is often not the case; there are some very low quality journals and newsletters which publish any and all information on autism, accurate or not. Remember, all anyone requires to set up a publication is a computer with publishing software. A researcher does not need a licence, just a lot of "chutzpah." In short, researchers need to publish: consequently, many will try to publish their studies wherever they are able, even if the studies are poorly designed or executed and the publications are of similarly dubious quality.

## Some experts' motives are not always pure

In addition to the serious problem that many treatment professionals lack expertise in the scientific method, we know that some treatment professionals profit from the treatment they recommend; therefore, they are loathe to point out the lack of science regarding their method because then *you* will not buy their product or purchase their services. I have found this to be often the case when treatments are sold with glossy brochures and testimonials from other parents, describing how the treatment purportedly changed their child's life. It is important *not* to be impressed by very well-dressed, articulate, and confident public speakers. The demeanor of the speaker has nothing to do with whether or not there is any bona fide data supporting the treatment being sold.

For the above reasons, you need to be able to evaluate autism treatments by looking at their scientific evidence, or discovering their lack of scientific evidence. In short, please learn the phrase, "Show Me the Data" and know what to do once you see the data. To summarize, you need the power to be able to evaluate the treatment without the editorializing or persuasion of others. Although professional incompetence is not nearly as morally upsetting as professional greed, it is nonetheless equally as dangerous to children with autism. We parents are a desperate bunch who are thirsting for a cure; however, remember the moral of the story — *Bad Data is Worse Than No Data.*

## The scientific method versus pseudo-science

To differentiate between real science and pseudo-science, it is crucial to understand the purpose of science and what rules scientists must follow in order for science to tell us anything meaningful. Put simply, science is the way to uncover facts and genuine relationships. The scientific method is simply a group of rules that, when followed precisely, can help us discover facts about whatever we are studying. In the case of autism, science can help us discover and test treatments for autism, and be able to know whether those treatments work.

Science is the way to test the many claims made by others. In the same way as biologists use the rules of the scientific method to uncover facts about the natural world, so do sociologists and psychologists use the same method to uncover facts about the social world or about aspects of human behavior. In the case of autism treatment, science can test treatments claimed to work by one group of researchers, and see if indeed the claims of those scientists are correct. Put simply, in the same way as the scientific method is the underpinning of western civilization's technological base including modern medicine, researchers in autism must also use the scientific method to acquire (and substantiate) a better understanding of autism. Using the scientific method, researchers can uncover relationships that exist, i.e., treatments that improve or ameliorate autism, and then other researchers can test those relationships to make sure they exist. When others test those relationships, they can replicate the studies to see whether the results the first scientist found will occur again (that the results are real). Noteworthy in this discussion is that experiments are the *only* reliable way to determine whether a treatment really works. Shortly, you will learn much more about how experiments work, as they are *key* to evaluating autism treatments.

The question boils down to this: How can we tell the difference between pseudo-science and the "Real Deal"? The best way to know the difference between science and pseudo-science (or outright fraud) is to look at the rules and how they may have been broken. When researchers are engaged in pseudo-science, there are generally three rules that they breach. Here are the fingerprints:

> Rule 1: The results of an autism treatment study must be observable by someone other than the original researcher(s).

Put another way, an observation needs also to be seen by someone else. Therefore, if a researcher claims that a child with autism has improved, other people need to objectively see the same improvement at the same time. Otherwise, as far as science is concerned, the improvement claimed never happened. *In pseudo-science, only the original researchers can "see" the results.*

> Rule 2: An independent researcher must be able to reproduce results of the original study.

The second rule is a relative to the first rule. Any result observed in research must be reproducable by somebody else. In other words, a different researcher, using the same method as the first researcher, should be able to come up with similar results.  Replication is a "must do" for the scientific method in general, and important for autism treatments in particular, because there is so much fraud being perpetrated against parents and their afflicted children.  *In pseudo-science, no one can replicate the results except the same researchers.*  This is a big red flag.

> Rule 3:  The research question must have a way that it can be disproven.

 All research questions that are being asked must, theoretically, have a way by which they can be proven wrong.  Put simply, the scientist needs to be able to describe a scenario or situation where his or her hypothesis is not supported.  For example, if the theory states that giving vitamin B6 and magnesium to a child with autism will decrease the symptoms of autism (those symptoms measured objectively), then the scientist must also describe what will happen if the theory is wrong.  In other words, what is it going to look like if vitamin B6 and magnesium treatment doesn't work.  *In pseudo-science, every incorrect result is either explained away or simply ignored.*

Every result that does not support the original researcher's prediction is dismissed by delegitimizing a second group of researchers that may have found contrary findings.  It is difficult to dismiss negative findings published in peer-reviewed journals; however, it still occurs on a regular basis because there is a fortune to be made by offering unsubstantiated autism treatment services, even when they have been scientifically discredited.

Pseudo-science is non-science dressed up to look like science.  Pseudo-science uses an impressively large vocabulary; tables and graphs are used, typically by people with MDs and/or PhDs behind their names, often in different fields to the one being researched.  In autism research, there are many examples of dentists, nurses and general practitioners (instead of neurobiologists) doing brain research or providing unsubstantiated autism treatments.  It is important to make sure that those doing the research have an MD or PhD in a field related to the kind of research being conducted.  I have seen very sophisticated presentations by people who have absolutely no background in the area in which they are working, and who also often *do not* understand the scientific method.  These experts will often tell you that, in their professional opinion, a specific treatment is effective. Bona-fide scientists will not pontificate, using only their opinion, without backing up their position with hard data.  In short, pseudo-science breaks the rules of the scientific method but it *cloaks* the research in symbols of legitimacy using persuasive techniques more common to advertising than science.

A typical red flag for quackery is the use of sophisticated multimedia techniques. When  presentations are too slick and  technical, in a showy Hollywood fashion, do not be impressed.  A brain scan tells us nothing about how much data (if any) the researcher has gathered.  In fact, the slicker the graphics and animations, the more money the researcher likely has to waste on expensive animations.  As grant money is hard to come by, bona fide scientists do not usually squander it on glossy brochures and multimedia presentations.  They generally use simple slides and do not appear to be "selling" the treatment.  Academic researchers are also generally tentative in making the claims that they *do* make.  The reason for this is that they follow the scientific method which supports a healthy dose of skepticism. Science can provide evidence that a treatment works (sometimes a small amount of evidence, other times a compelling amount of evidence);  however, scientists do not like to say that they have actually "proven" that a treatment works.  They will generally say that the evidence supporting the treatment is strong or weak, but will not usually refer to their research as "proof."

## Using the scientific method to protect your child

As an intelligent and savvy consumer, you have a right to see any and all scientific evidence which either supports or negates the claim that an autism treatment is effective.  Before starting any treatment, as the parent you should ask for a bibliography of academic journal articles published on the method by the practitioners recommending or providing the service.  If the "experts" on any particular method cannot give you any of the material that you request, chances are there's not scientific evidence available yet to support their claims that the treatment ameliorates autism.  Your answer as to whether this method is scientifically-supported is then easy.  In other words, no data equals no science in support of the so-called treatment method being touted by the so-called expert.  Most fringe treatment methods will not have any science behind them, which makes evaluating them relatively easy.

## What if the treatment method is too new for data collection?

If a treatment method is new, you have the option to wait for supporting evidence. Those practitioners of the method should be working on a study to test the method, prior to offering it to the public.   At this point, you can always sit back, keep your money in the bank and wait for the data.  Occasionally, there are effective treatments that need more scientific scrutiny and the parent may only wait a short time; however, this is rare.  In my personal experience as a parent waiting for good data to substantiate a variety of treatment methods, it is *rare* that after ten or fifteen years of hearing about a treatment method, a scientific study is done, and the treatment method is suddenly supported by quality data.  The opposite is more often true.  More typical is the scenario where a method which is not scientifically supported is used by many parents.  Finally, a reputable researcher will actually test the method and find that there is scientific evidence to show the method is completely *ineffective*.

The lag time between discovering a promising treatment which actually works on children and having that treatment scientifically tested is often short because science moves very quickly when it looks as though there is real possibility for a new discovery.  At this point, many researchers jump in and compete to see who can  find the significant results first.  A good example of this phenomenon is the large number of researchers looking for the gene(s) for autism.  Ten years ago, there were only one or two university research programs targeting autism.  Today, there are research groups around the world competing in this area because the chances that a discovery may occur are good.

What *does* take a considerable amount of time, however, is a treatment that must first be tested on animals in the lab.  This type of research is difficult because it is hard to approximate autism in rats or monkeys (although researchers are working this problem).  Research that uses animal models does not typically suffer the problems of pseudo-science or quackery as, generally, these researchers do not prematurely offer treatments for autism; rather, they painstakingly and responsibly research autism to be able to eventually treat the disorder biochemically.  These researchers do not regularly offer half-baked treatments and, therefore, I address them only in passing.

## What about anecdotes?  Can we use them at all?

What is the role of anecdotal evidence in autism research?  For our purposes, an anecdote is defined as a personal story or observation about how a child purportedly improved when he was given a particular type of treatment.   The question is this:  can we legitimately use anecdotes in scientific research for autism treatment or is it just a waste of time?

One might be surprised to know that anecdotes are actually very useful if used correctly, but disastrous if used incorrectly. Scientists use anecdotes to start thinking about questions to research — that is a good use. In other words, anecdotes can motivate science. Think about all the surprising findings that have been discovered by chance or by scientists simply having hunches. Hunches are great to start scientists thinking. Although the hunch may be caused by an anecdote, that's where its usefulness ends. In short, once the research question is developed, then the role of the anecdote is over. An anecdote gives a scientist an interesting idea to *study*. Researchers do not jump to conclusions the minute they suspect an interesting relationship. On the contrary, they set up a way to *test* their hunch, according the generally-accepted principles of sound research.

Unfortunately, many parents use anecdotes in a disastrous way. We hear a story from a friend, see a news piece or read an autobiography and then start administering the treatment to our child. Children are not well-served through this use of anecdotal evidence, and neither is science. In addition, this *is* the way to create considerable and unnecessary hardship in both the life of the parent and child.

Let's illustrate this point with the following scenario: a scientist goes to Thanksgiving dinner at her friend's house every year, for years, and sees that David, a child with autism at the same thanksgiving dinner, becomes lucid. He is attentive, talks to people, sits appropriately and is the model child. After a few years of observing this interesting change in behavior, the scientist wonders if the improvement in behavior is caused by the food the child is eating, specifically, the tryptophan in the turkey? The scientist proceeds to design an elaborate experiment to test this possibility. She happens to mention this to her friend, David's mother. What do you think David's mother does? I'm sure most of us can guess what she does because we've probably all had this instinct.  The mother runs to the store, starts cooking and feeds this child turkey for breakfast, lunch and dinner, every single day.

Why does the mother go out and specifically buy turkey for the child?  Perhaps it's the pumpkin pie for thankgiving dinner that is responsible for the effect on the child's behavior.  Since we cannot tell what is responsible for the change in the child, we need to do an experiment to test the various possibilities. Put simply, we need to separate the possible influence of the pumpkin pie from the tryptophan in the turkey.  We can easily do this with an experiment.

Herein lies the problem with anecdotal evidence.  As parents, we search for that cure and jump on every hope or idea, regardless of the scant evidence that the treatment will actually make a difference.  In the process, we absorb unnecessary cost and inconvenience in our lives and we waste a child's valuable window of opportunity for effective autism treatment.  In the worst-case scenario, we can actually endanger our children, subjecting them to harmful procedures.  This is how seductive anecdotal evidence can be.  It is important to be skeptical and decide whether you want to spend time, money and endure disruption on a treatment for which support is purely anecdotal.   Unfortunately, in the world of autism treatments, there is an epidemic of anecdotes fueling unsubstantiated treatments. *In short, quackery is alive and well in the world of autism treatment.* The reasons why anecdotal evidence perpetuates itself will become clearer when we discuss how to properly evaluate experiments;  for now,  remember, anecdotes and their cousins, testimonials, are trouble waiting to happen.

## We need to care about theory

I was prepared to ignore the role of theory in autism treatment, because I thought we could get away without it, and I didn't want anyone falling asleep reading this book; however, after speaking to some very intelligent parents who were being swayed by beautiful theories with no data to support those theories, I realized that I have to explicitly define what a theory is and address the role of theory in the evaluation of autism treatments.

Why do we care about theory? I'm bringing up the topic of "theory" for four reasons. First, good research is motivated or driven by theory. Second, beautiful, logical, precise theories can be quite compelling and convincing, and also 100 percent *wrong*! Third, through theory, we can easily generalize our results to the real world and know which treatments to provide to our children. Finally, it is important *not* to trust your "gut" when judging a theory. This is a common trap which parents are snared into on a regular basis.

## What is a theory?

A theory is simply a set of sentences that explain and predict *causal* relationships. In autism research, often a theory is simple with maybe one or two sentences describing the relationship between two statements. An example of a knowledge claim that is the important part of the theory for our purposes is: Treatment A can cure autism.

A theory generally takes the form of sentences that are conditional. So, for example, one theory claims that the reason children have autism is because their blood contains too much lead and other heavy metals. The theory goes on at length as to why these heavy metals injure the brain. Then the theory claims that removing these toxins is going to improve the child's condition. The relationship between autism and heavy metals could be put into the following "If, Then" sentences:

• IF a child has high blood toxicity levels, THEN he will be more likely to develop autism than a child without high blood toxicity.

• IF a child with autism has high blood toxicity levels, THEN removing those toxins will ameliorate the autism.

In addition, a theory will have conditions under which it is believed to hold or be correct.  These conditions are known scope conditions, which tell us under which conditions the theory applies.  I will address scope conditions in more depth later in the book, as it is a very relevant and neglected part of autism research, but for now, we only need to know that scope conditions are part of a theory.

## Good research is motivated or driven by theory

It is crucial to remember that in high quality research, a theory always motivates the research.  In other words, good researchers always have a theory that they are trying to support or refute.  If you come across research with no theory, beware.  These researchers do not understand the way science works and chances are that they are not going about the research process correctly.

There are all kinds of predictive sentences that you could make out of a theory which, to the average person, appear very logical, elegant and even beautiful.  This is where parents often get duped!  Here is the important point to consider: the theory may be right or it may be wrong.  But *the logic of the theory has absolutely nothing to do with whether a theory is right or wrong*.  Thomas Huxley, put it very well when he described the tragedy of science as when we witness "the slaying of a beautiful theory by an ugly little fact."[1]  Good researchers understand this point all too well.  Huxley's point is that the theory may be perfect in every way, except for the unfortunate problem that the facts, or in this case, one ugly little fact, gets in the way by disproving the theory.  In other words, the theory does not mesh with observations or facts that *stubbornly* cannot be explained away.

The concept of theory is very important in autism research because, when done properly with competent researchers, we can know whether there *is* evidence to support the theory, or whether the theory is flat out wrong!  That's how parents should approach the many kooky autism treatment theories out there.  We need theories to motivate research and we need that so researchers can *show us the data*.  Put simply, we just cannot accept a treatment based on its theory alone.  It is important to make sure that the *data* support the idea that the treatment is effective.

Through theory, if we can create the same important conditions that made the treatment effective, we can generalize our results to the real world and know what to do with our children.  In my opinion, autism is such a devastating neurological disorder that it behooves us to attempt to recreate the study conditions which created substantive change in children.  Our children deserve no less than the lucky children in the experimental group of the successful study.  Here is where the concept of scope conditions becomes important.  The question to ask is this:  What are the conditions that must be present in order for the treatment to work?  If those conditions can be recreated, then the treatment should logically work again.  The challenge for parents of children with autism is to replicate the important conditions present in the study so the treatment that worked in the laboratory will also work for them in the real world.

The next point has to do with your intuition about judging whether a theory is true or not. Again, it is important *not* to trust your "gut" when judging the theory that supports an autism treatment. This point may disturb some and, in general, I tell parents to trust their gut, particularly when making decisions about vulnerable children. If you think something is too good to be true, you are most likely correct. But here I must reverse my usual position. When it comes to theory, *do not* trust your gut.

Let us suppose that a researcher develops a seemingly crazy theory. After you stop laughing about the absurdity of the theory, do not dismiss it because of its seemingly bizarre nature. Instead, it is prudent to wait and see whether the data supports the theory. It is important to remain open-minded while awaiting research data because, in science, the strangest theories have, periodically, been supported. Two common illustrations come to mind to help make this point: whether it was the theory that invisible organisms we now know as germs were making people sick, rather than bad smells, or that surgeons washing their hands with soap to kill invisible contagions would result in less people dying in surgery, it becomes clear that we cannot judge a theory based on its initial claims. We must judge a theory purely based on the evidence.

Another example of a seemingly absurd theory at the time was the use of cobwebs to heal wounds. Prior to the discovery of penicillin, people used to actually place cobwebs on their wounds to heal them! If I suggested that today, you'd think I had lost my mind; however, we now know that penicillin can be derived from cobwebs. The lesson here is to avoid discounting a theory because it may sound farfetched or absurd. Instead, the reasonable person waits to see what kind of data are produced to support or refute the theory. If the data demonstrate that the treatment is not effective, then the hypothesis can be said to be falsified. Although positive data cannot *prove* that a treatment works (but rather provides *evidence*), negative data can actually prove that a treatment does *not* work.

## 2.3 How do we generalize results in autism research?

Can we generalize research results from a study to all children with autism, without taking theory into account? Here is where autism researchers engage in much debate. Typically, when medical researchers conduct clinical trials on a treatment (usually a drug), they go to a statistician and ask how large a sample size they will need to ensure that the results of the study will apply to the population at large. In other words, how many people need to be in the study before we can confidently start using the treatment widely for all people who need it. You will notice that often the number of people which medical researchers use is up in the thousands. The statisticians will suggest a number dependent upon the randomness of the sample. In short, if the statistician is convinced that a few people represent the population of those who are ill as a whole, then the number will be low. If the statistician thinks that many people in the study are needed to represent the population, then the number will be high.

Here is where we run into trouble, where autism research is concerned. How can researchers make sure that the children with autism in the study are representative of all children with autism in the population if we can't randomly choose the children? Any statistician who tells the autism researchers that they need hundreds of children in the study in order to provide accurate results, will effectively destroy the study. In my opinion, the creation of very large sample sizes for autism research will occur very rarely if at all (aside from drug trials that are heavily underwritten by pharmaceutical companies). Therefore, the key is to ask how representative the group of children with autism in the study is to the population at large. If you think that these children *are* representative of children with autism, based on the tests that have been done on the children in the study, you can feel more confident with the results than if you think that these children are not representative of the general population of children with autism. This is an area where much of the controversy in autism treatment research occurs.

However, even if you believe that a particular autism treatment study does not have a representative sample of children with autism, there is another way to generalize the results of the study. This way is through the theory behind the study. Theory is of crucial importance if we want to easily generalize the results of autism studies, using a small numbers of children (which is the norm in most autism research). I will address the details of generalizing study results later, but remember for now that we cannot ignore theory, because using theory is a very powerful way to make the results of a study apply to more than simply one child.

# 2.4 Using science to move closer to the truth

What is the next step? We have discussed the concept that a researcher has an idea and then creates an elegant theory. He or she now has to test the theory. The challenge for a researcher is to find a way to take a piece of the theory and structure it so that it is operationally testable. The process of testing theory is where science gets interesting and fraud becomes easier to differentiate and identify.

## Testing theory

If you remember only one thing from this entire book, remember this one simple illustration. For our purposes, this simple question is, in a nut shell, what science is all about:

## Does A cause B?

There are many different ways to pose the same question. Examples include: Does one thing cause something else? Does A cause B to happen? Does A cause a change in B? This question above (in all its various forms) is important because it would be beneficial to know the answer before you provide treatment to your child. This question can be represented in the following equation:

$$A \longrightarrow B$$

For our purposes in the autism research world, **A** in the above schematic is the Treatment and **B** is Autism. Another way of saying this is that **A** (the treatment) **causes B** (autism) to improve, to be ameliorated, or decrease. **B** (autism) is what is called in science, the dependent variable (the D.V.) because how severe or mild the variable is will depend upon **A** (the treatment). **A** (the treatment) is called the independent variable (the I.V.) because it is independent of what happens to the autism. To review: we want to know whether **A** (treatment) has an effect on **B** (autism). We want to find that **A** (the treatment) ---> **B** (the autism) to decrease, improve or in the best case scenario, be cured. So now, our equation looks like this:

## IV (treatment) —> DV (autism)

In science, both the independent variable (A) and the dependent variable (B) can be anything one cares to test. To make this more concrete, we can use examples of how this concept works and purposely not use examples from the world of autism. Instead we can use the following examples (which are used in any introductory class on the scientific method): Does smoking cause cancer? Do miniskirts cause bull markets? Does larger class-size lead to lower student achievement?

In each of these well-known examples, the first variable is the independent variable and the second variable is the dependent variable. The hypothesis in the first example is that whether or not someone gets cancer is *dependent* upon whether they smoke. The hypothesis in the second example is that miniskirts *cause* the stock market to improve. The hypothesis in the third example is that large class sizes *cause* students to underachieve. Put simply, the independent variable can be anything that one believes is causing a *change* in the dependent variable, which is whatever one is measuring or studying.

By the way, occasionally autism is actually the independent variable. An example of this is when researchers study whether autism causes an increase in the divorce rate among parents of children with autism. So, the equation in such an instance would look like this:

## Child's Autism —> Increase in Divorce Rate.

Although I'm sure this is a legitimate topic to study (when autism is the independent variable), this kind of research does not help us protect our children from autism treatment quackery.*

---

*As an aside, although the scientist side of me thinks that the relationship between the child's autism and the increased divorce rate is a legitimate topic, the parental side of me is tired of being student and analyzed. There is nothing wrong with us – the problem is that our child has a neurological condition that needs to be treated and hopefully, with good research, we will eventually find a cure. In my opinion, the limited research dollars for autism treatment should be spent trying to find the cause and cure rather than to fund research analyzing parents' coping mechanisms. That view, however, is a very anti-science view and comes from years of frustration over the poor state of the science in autism treatment. Scientists should not make any value judgments regarding the theory being tested; therefore, I will attempt to control my parental opinions.

## Experiments are not Optional

The bottom line in science is that experiments are truly not optional.  In order to find out whether A really does cause B, or whether a particular treatment *causes* a change in the autism, researchers  need to do a well-designed experiment to lay this question to rest.  In other words, an experiment is the only way to collect legitimate evidence to show that the treatment *does* in fact improve the condition of autism, or that it *does not* improve the condition of autism.  When I use the word "experiment," I'm not referring to gathering data or information from something that has already happened and then, retrospectively, making an argument as to why it has happened.  I am referring to the setting up of a testing situation, taking measurements before the study, taking measurements after the study and then seeing whether there is a change in the autism.  Shortly, we will explore how this is done, but first it must be understood that an experiment must be conducted before any autism treatment can be taken seriously.

Once the experiment is completed and the data analyzed, the next step is for the researcher to have the results published in a peer-reviewed journal.  If the researcher has not yet published his or her results, or is not planning on publishing the results, those results may as well not exist for all practical purposes.  Often researchers say that their results are not published in peer-reviewed journals because the scientific community is "conspiring" against them.  If the results *are* significant and the study is well done, chances are that the article will be published, even if these results go against the prevailing beliefs of the scientific community of the time.

## Peer review — necessary but not sufficient

The publication of an article in an academic journal does not necessarily provide enough evidence to show us that the data collected can actually be trusted.  There is a range of quality in peer-reviewed journals.  Peer review is necessary, but on its own is insufficient, to trust the efficacy of autism treatment.  It is crucial that the study is designed and executed competently prior to trusting the results.

The peer-review process is the way editors of academic journals decide whether or not to publish a study in their journal.  Generally, the editor sends an article that has been submitted to a journal, out to three reviewers.  These three reviewers ideally do not know the name of the author but are in the same academic field and are competent to evaluate the study.  The reviewers critique the study and recommend to the editor to either *accept* the article, to have the author *revise and resubmit* the article based on the reviewers suggestions for more evaluation, or to *reject* the article outright.

 The peer-review process is important because it typically weeds out poorly done studies from well-done studies; however, even studies that are peer-reviewed and not of high quality can end up published in low quality, peer-reviewed journals or journals that have been established by the very people who desire their poor quality research to be published.  In short, peer review helps ensure that very  poorly done studies do not get published; however, it is *certainly* not a fail-safe process.

## Uncover the funding source for the study

Before analyzing the quality of a study, it is *very* important to ask the following three questions: 1)  Are the "money people" a disinterested source? 2) Is the funding source a government department that cares about the outcome? 3) Is the funding source a company whose profit depend on the results of the study?  In short, it is important to uncover who is funding the study and what their agenda may be.  To illustrate, it is a positive sign if the funding source is the *National Science Foundation* or another granting agency, with no vested interest in the outcome of the study. Agencies with no interest in a study's outcome, award the researcher funding because he or she presents an interesting theory and a competent experimental design. It is difficult to receive an arms-length government grant if the study design is flawed or the researcher is unscrupulous or incompetent. The main goal of these agencies is to fund researchers to move science forward in terms of finding the cause, treatment or cure for autism;[*] however, if the funding agency has an agenda, then you must be more critical in terms of the quality (and honesty) of the data. If the granting agency is either a government department that cares about the outcome or a private company trying to sell the treatment they are researching, it is crucial to be careful about trusting the data published about the treatment protocol. Biased data only sets science back; yet it is often difficult to discover whether or not the data is biased. Occasionally, biased data does get published in peer-reviewed journals; however, this is not the norm.

The most important lesson I have learned from my time fighting the autism wars is that there are some very intelligent, talented researchers who produce biased research which they often have published in peer-reviewed journals. These

---

[*]As a shorthand, you should know that if a researcher gets a grant from one of the following U.S. or Canadian agencies, chances are that the research is being done by reputable scientists: National Institute of Health (NIH); National Institute of Mental Health (NIMH); National Science Foundation (NSF); Centers for Disease Control (CDC); Science Research Council of Canada (SRCC); Social Science Research Council of Canada (SSRCC). In addition, chances are that a government granting agency from a democratic country awards grants to its most promising researchers. If you see articles from other countries with government granting agencies from those countries, chances are that this government sponsored research is being done by researchers who know what they are doing. Many researchers in other countries also apply for U.S. grants when they are eligible. Government granting agencies look for researchers with track records of good research or with affiliation to researchers with good research records. In addition, the research idea is generally reviewed by two or three other scientists in that field to determine whether or not the idea is a waste of taxpayer money. *Note that these government grants cannot be connected to specific government departments.* The minute there is any connection directly to a specific governmental department, the consumer must be extremely careful about trusting research that is generated from that type of grant.

competent researchers can legitimately be known as academic mercenaries, good at the peer-review game but quite corrupt where the search for truth is concerned. Therefore, peer review in itself is not a sufficient safeguard. It is prudent to be suspicious if the granting agency is a state or provincial health, education or social services department that actually has to pay for autism treatment; remember, it is in that government's interests to find inexpensive treatment options that are effective and expensive, and, in their view, treatment options that are *somehow* experimental or ineffective. Trusting research paid for by these governmental agencies is dangerous.[*]

Unfortunately, academic corruption occurs all over the world, not only in Canada and the United States. One group which we must be particularly wary of is the academics who evaluate emergent health technologies. They often hide behind the crests of their respective universities, posing as supposedly disinterested scholars, when actually they are paid handsomely by government to help ration expensive health treatments and produce junk science to defeat parents' autism treatment lawsuits against government. For the complete story on how one group of corrupt health technologists discredited a science-based treatment for autism, I encourage you all to read *Science for Sale in the Autism Wars: Medically necessary autism treatment, the court battle for health insurance and why health technology academics are enemy number one*.[4] This book recounts the story of how a group of health technologists succeeded in blocking autism treatment to the entire population of children with autism in Canada. Remember, before

---

[*]The most recent example that comes to mind in the world of autism research is the case where a review of the science conducted by health policy analysts to defend government in court was discredited by the sitting justice as being *obviously biased* and this finding was written into the judgment.[2] These health technologists then proceeded to present their findings at an international health policy conference and their review was given a half-page mention in the *International Journal of Health Technology Assessment*.[3] Since their review of the science was discredited in July 2000, their article has been relied upon by several researchers whose works have subsequently been published in other peer-reviewed journals.

trusting research on autism, it is wise to confirm that the granting agency does not care about, nor have any vested interest in, the ultimate outcome of the research.

## Finding the peer-reviewed journal articles

The most efficient way to research a treatment is through a home computer or in a university library. The major databases can be accessed from home (at times for a fee, but often for free).  The following four databases are worthwhile:  1) MEDLINE – The database "Medline" contains descriptions (also called abstracts) of almost every *medical* journal article published in the last forty years, from 1966.  Through a website called "PubMed" you can search the MEDLINE[5] for free; 2) PSYCHINFO[6] – This database contains descriptions of most *psychology* journal articles published in the last two hundred years, from the 1800s.   For a fee, the articles in PsycINFO can be downloaded through its sister database, PsycARTICLES; 3) ERIC[7] – This database has abstracts of most *education* journal articles published in the last forty years, from 1966.  Often, the journal articles can be downloaded free; 4) COCHRANE[8] – The Cochrane databases are comprised of three different databases that include all systematic reviews and clinical trials on treatments.  They include peer-reviewed and unpublished "fugitive" literature (such as unpublished government reports) so they must be viewed more critically than the Medline or info databases.  However, they are useful because it is important to know what government officials are reading to influence their opinions about funding or not funding research.  If there have been zero reviews on a specific topic, this suggests that the treatment is so experimental that no one in mainstream academe has chosen it for review.

These databases are the most fruitful places to look up topics relating to autism. Additional databases may be suggested by your local university librarian, depending upon the type of treatment you are researching. Once you have logged on to the database, simply type in the treatment you are trying to research. For example, if you were researching Vitamin B6 as a treatment for autism, you could get started by searching "autism Vitamin B6" in any of the databases suggested above.

It is important to limit your search to: (1) the exact treatment you are researching, and (2) articles that actually test the method and present data. In addition, occasionally databases allow your search to be limited to peer-reviewed articles only. Once you identify a manageable number of articles, then a one paragraph abstract of each article can be printed. After reading the abstract, you then must decide if it is worth finding the article to analyze how the research was conducted. In our Vitamin B6 example, you would have found approximately thirty-six articles from the "PubMed" database alone (note that less than half of these articles report any data). Although this sounds like a large number of articles to find and read, it certainly is worth doing the research before you commit your child to an autism treatment.

## Is the journal peer-reviewed?

It is relatively easy to discern whether or not a journal is peer-reviewed. As mentioned above, some databases actually specify whether or not the article is peer-reviewed and allow the search to include *only* the peer-reviewed journals. In addition, every journal has a section (generally on the inside front or back of the journal) describing how to submit an article for publication. Often the journal will tell you that the papers that have been submitted are going to be subjected to a "blind review" (where the reviewers do not know who authored the study). Sometimes the journal will actually describe itself as a peer-reviewed journal.

However, more typically, the indicators of a genuinely peer-reviewed journal are a huge editorial board, and the journal requiring five copies of the article with only the title of the work appearing on the copies that are to be sent to the reviewers (omitting the author's name). This is done so the editor can send the article to a reviewer without the reviewer knowing who wrote the article, i.e., blind review. This procedure prevents a scientist evaluating a colleague's research favorably because they may be friends or related professionally in some way.

# 2.5  Analyzing a study

At this point, I am assuming that you have access to a copy of the study found from an academic journal, available in a university library or for download from the worldwide web.  Here is a list of all the questions you need to ask to discern whether the study would meet minimum criteria to be considered as a well-designed and executed study.  In this section, I go through each of the following questions, in depth, to help you critically analyze any autism treatment study you choose to evaluate.

- How many groups are there in the study?
- How many children are in each experimental group?
- How are these children assigned to the groups?
- What is being measured and how?
- Who collects the data?
- Who administers the treatment?
- Could the results have happened by chance?
- Is the study possibly compromised by bias and how can bias be avoided?

## How many groups are there in the study?

The first question to be asked is this: "How many experimental groups are in the study?"  The answer to this question exposes the design of the study as certain study designs use only one experimental group whereas other studies use two or more.  As parents, it is important to understand experimental design, because the way an experiment is designed is going to provide information on how and whether the results of that design can be generalized to all children afflicted with autism. In addition, the experiment's design provides information about possible bias, and how that bias can creep into the design often without the researchers even knowing.

There are five common experimental design types: between-subjects design; within-subjects design; between-within subjects design; factorial design; single-subject case design.  I will walk you through each design type in detail, to allow you to establish which of the following designs is used for the autism treatment study in which you are interested.  It is important to know the differences among all the research designs, to see whether or not the conclusions presented can legitimately be made based on the design of the study.  Often, researchers in the field of autism make statements about treatment that the study design cannot support.  As a parent, in order to make informed decisions regarding autism treatment for your child, you need to be able to understand the study design and uncover the potential flaws on your own.  Unfortunately, we cannot trust many of the "experts" in this field.  In the next section of this book, I introduce the common study designs you will see in autism treatment research.

## Is it a Between-Subjects Design?

In a between-subjects study design, there are at least two groups, one experimental group (the group that gets the treatment), and at least one other group acting as a control group, which does not receive the treatment that has been hypothesized to work.  The data are generally taken on each subject and averaged in each group.  Then the averages of one group are compared to the averages of the other group.

The best way to explain this process  is through illustration.  In all my examples, I am going to use IQ tests, because most of us are familiar with this measurement tool.  It is important to keep in mind that in autism research, there is a variety of measures used, in addition to IQ scores. The numbers you see in the following specific examples are IQ scores, with the approximate scores of thirty and below indicating severe intellectual impairment, thirty to seventy moderate intellectual impairment, seventy to eighty borderline impairment and eighty to one hundred representing the normal range of intelligence.

**Between-Subject Design: Table 1**

| Treatment Group | | Control Group | |
|---|---|---|---|
| SUBJECT | IQ SCORE | SUBJECT | IQ SCORE |
| 1. Johnny | 71 | 1. Cori | 43 |
| 2. Jim | 63 | 2. Jack | 36 |
| 3. Don | 105 | 3. Greg | 51 |
| | | | |
| | | | |
| | | | |
| 19. Dave | 94 | 19. Jane | 67 |
| 20. Sue | 62 | 20. Ed | 31 |
| Total: 395 | Av. = 79 | Total: 228 | Av. = 45.6 |

Here is a typical between-subjects design. Officially, this is called an "after-only design" as the researcher only measures the group *after* the treatment. Technically, researchers can design this type of study if they are extremely confident that the children in both groups are functionally identical. However, it is preferable in autism research to take measurements of both groups prior to the treatment. This design has twenty children in each group, (twenty in the experimental group and twenty in the control group). The numbers represent the results of the children at the end of the autism treatment experiment, after the treatment has been given to the children in the experimental group only.

Suppose the children in the experimental group have been given a type of therapy for one month and the children in the control group have been in a special education class for that same month. Further, let's suppose that the measure being used is IQ points. In a between-subjects design, one need only compare the IQ scores of one group with the IQ scores of the other group in the treatment experiment. In this example, does it look like the treatment worked? Based on the average of each group, the treatment appears to have worked. But caution is advised! Based on these raw scores, this conclusion cannot be made. A skilled researcher will compare the scores using statistics, to make sure that there truly is a difference between the two groups. There are several comparison tests that researchers can use. It is important to know now that a between-subjects design compares two groups of subjects *after* a treatment has been administered.

Many people question the importance of a control or comparison group, but a control group is very important to ensure that a change due to the treatment actually occurred. The best way to emphasize this point is by example. Let's suppose that you may have started autism treatment with a group of children in September and found within the first week that the behavior of most of these children started to go downhill rapidly. You might logically think that the cause of the slide is the treatment and end the study prematurely. The problem with this thought process is that you do not know whether the treatment created the behavior problems or whether the first week back in school, with new teachers and new routines, may have caused the downhill slide.

This is an obvious error which, hopefully, no competent researcher would make. A control group acts as insurance, guarding against other influences that may render the study meaningless. There are numerous other less obvious influences that occur (far less obvious than the example above), but we may not always be sufficiently savvy to recognize them. These "things" or "influences" are known as variables. In the above example, the variable of "school opening" was an unintended variable and neither controlled for nor eliminated. If there are two groups, and both groups return to school at the same time, then the behavior of both groups should deteriorate at approximately the same rate. The fact that both groups deteriorate or improve concurrently tells us that it is not the treatment that has caused the behavior change, but something else that is affecting both groups equally and, therefore, will not affect the study results (because the results all have to do with comparing one group to the other). In short, a good study design must have at least two groups where one group receives the treatment, the other does not. Each group's results are then measured, averaged and compared in the post-experiment analysis.

## Is it a Within-Subjects Design?

A within-subjects design has no control group. The subject is measured before the treatment and then after the treatment, or at different points in the experiment and then after the experiment. The pre-treatment scores are compared to the post-treatment scores.

**Within-Subject Design: Table 2**

| Child | Pretest | Post-test | Difference |
|---|---|---|---|
| 1. Johnny | 43 | 73 | +30 |
| 2. Jim | 36 | 61 | +25 |
| 3. Don | 51 | 105 | +54 |
|  |  |  |  |
|  |  |  |  |
| 19. Dave | 67 | 94 | +27 |
| 20. Sue | 31 | 62 | +31 |
| **Average:** | **45.6** | **79** | **+33.4** |

In this within-subjects design, note that there is no formal, separate control group. The comparison is between the child's score prior to the treatment and the same child's score after the treatment. In this kind of research design, the child acts as his or her own control. This example is the most simple within-subjects design because the children are only tested once before, and once after the treatment is administered. The main analyses that need to be done in this case are to see whether or not each child improved. The following two analyses could easily be done in this instance: (1) The pre-treatment scores of all the children could be averaged and compared to the posttreatment scores averaged; and (2) each child's pre-treatment score could be compared to that child's post-treatment score so that the improvement could be observed for each child. From what we can see in Table 2, you would think that the treatment looks very good. Keep in mind, however, that we still need to use statistics to make sure this is indeed the case.

The main problem with this type of design is the other variables that may influence the outcome of the study. To illustrate this point, let's consider this example: children with autism are often affected by the seasons. Some of our children do much better in the spring than in the fall (we do not know why, but this has been observed). If the study occurs over a one-year period, we may see behavioral peeks and valleys that correspond with the seasons, rather than with the treatment. Therefore, a researcher may incorrectly conclude that strawberries help autism because during strawberry season, the child improves! As ridiculous as this kind of reasoning may seem, researchers are regularly making logical errors such as this; they confuse correlation with causation. The jargon for this type of error is called a "causal fallacy." The world of autism "treatments" are chock full of these causal fallacies, so please be forewarned that without a control group, researchers must be much more sensitive to external influences than when there is a control group used in an autism treatment experiment. The advantage to a within-subjects design is that the control group is identical to the experimental group because the child acts as his or her control (as we compare the child's own scores prior to and after the treatment is administered).  However, the disadvantage is that there is no control group separate and apart from the children who receive the treatment.

To summarize, a within-subjects design has only one group.  The children are measured against themselves before and after the treatment.  However, there is no separate control group of children who do not receive the treatment.

## Is it a Between-Within Subjects Design?

A between-within subjects design (in my view, the ideal research design), has two groups, an experimental and control group. In this design, the two groups are compared to each other, and each individual child's *pre-treatment* scores are compared to his or her *post-treatment* scores.

In my opinion, this is the best type of research design because it gives researchers more information on what they are studying. To illustrate, if a treatment works on only half of the experimental group, and the scores of the other half of the experimental group do not change, then by analyzing each subject's score before and after the treatment, we can find out which subjects improved and which subjects did not. Then we can ask the question: "What makes those children who improved different from those children who did not?" The next experiment would then use only children with those characteristics indicative of the group that improved in the original experiment. These children would be assigned to either the experimental or control group. This second experiment would then yield better results (if the treatment is indeed effective). A much stronger result would move the field closer to discovering new treatments for a subset of children with autism. In addition, we would know which children benefit most from the treatment and then study the children who do not benefit, and ask ourselves why. We would be able to develop another area of research using the subset of children who *did* respond to the treatment in the experiment.

Below is an example of a between-within-subjects design. There are two groups of children (an experimental group with twenty children and a control group with twenty children). Each child's IQ is measured before the treatment begins and after the treatment has been administered.

**Between-Within Subjects Design:  Table 3**

| Experimental Group D | | | Control Group D | | | Difference btw. groups |
|---|---|---|---|---|---|---|
| Pretest | Post-test | | Pretest | Post-test | | |
| 1.  43 | 73 | +30 | 1. 41 | 44 | +3 | +27 |
| 2.  36 | 61 | +25 | 2. 39 | 38 | -1 | +26 |
| 3.  51 | 105 | +54 | 3. 53 | 57 | +4 | +50 |
| | | | | | | |
| | | | | | | |
| 19.  67 | 94 | +27 | 19. 64 | 66 | +2 | +25 |
| 20.  31 | 62 | +31 | 20. 34 | 37 | +3 | +28 |
| T=45.6 | T = 79 | 33.4 | T=46.2 | T=48.4 | 2.2 | T.D. = 31.2 |

Note that the children in the control group are tested at exactly the same time as those in the treatment group (before and after the study).  The children in the control group do not receive treatment (although, depending upon the study design, they may receive what is typically available for children with autism in the public health or educational system). We analyze the data in the following way: 1) the total scores of each group before the study are compared (to make sure there was no difference between groups) then after the study (to see if the experimental group improved as compared to the control group) and 2) each child's scores before the study are compared to his own scores after the study. Note the "Difference Between Groups" column.  In this design, the researchers also matched a specific child in the experimental group with a child in the control group and then compared these matched children's score as well.  Matching two children before assigning one of them to the experimental group and the other to the control group helps further ensure that the two groups are similar prior to the treatment being administered.  A research claim that the treatment is responsible for the difference can then be concluded with more confidence, as the groups were similar at the beginning of the study.  Matching children is done occasionally in autism studies.

Why would we want to do a within-subjects analysis as well as a between-subjects analysis of an autism treatment study?  As I mentioned above briefly, this design allows us to see if some children in the experimental group benefit more than others.  If there is an effect (or, put simply, the treatment works), then it will show up in the analysis, and will not be drowned out by the data of the children who did not respond to the treatment.  Take the example of secretin.  If one suspects that secretin has an effect on only 5% of the children with autism (the children with compromised gastro-intestinal systems), a good researcher would design a study with an in-depth, sensitive analysis of each subject and his or her scores before and after the treatment.  The researcher would never find the effect of secretin if not for the within-subjects design because the effect would be diluted among the children in the experimental group who did not improve.  However, a quality experiment would also need the control group's influence to make sure that the effect wasn't caused by something else.  We will later discuss other variables that could possibly confuse researchers to think that there is an effect, when in fact there is not.  The important point here is that by measuring children before and after treatment, we can discern: (1) whether the treatment is effective at all, and  (2) if it is effective, for which children.

To summarize, this design has at least two groups of children.  Each group's results are measured and compared, and each child's pre-treatment results are measured and compared to that child's post-treatment results.

## Is it a Factorial Design?

A factorial design is rare in autism research; however, it is important to know about this type of study design if you ever need to evaluate a study which uses this type of design. A factorial design is simply an experiment where two or more treatments are being tested at once, and the groups act as controls for each other. For example, if researchers think they have two treatments that work for autism, but they want to see if each works alone and/or in combination with each other, a factorial design would be the design of choice.

Factorial designs are common in drug trials when researchers test two or more drugs at once. The researcher may want to know whether Drug A works better alone, or in combination with Drug B, and also, whether Drug B works better alone or in combination with Drug A. The more drugs that the researchers need to test together, the bigger the study will be. Factorial designs can use more than two drugs at a time. However, more conditions are required when a larger number of drugs or treatments are tested. A simple two by two (2 x 2) design (using two drugs) will have four conditions.

**Factorial Design: Table 4**

| Condition 1:<br>Drug A Given<br>Drug B Given | Condition 3:<br>Drug B Given Only |
|---|---|
| Condition 2:<br>Drug A Given Only | Condition 4:<br>No Drug Given |

A three by two (3 x 2) design (using three drugs) will have six conditions  (seven conditions if a no drug condition were included or eight conditions if there were a condition in which three drugs were administered at once).

This table illustrates a factorial design with two different drugs tested (the simplest factorial design). Here we can think about our thanksgiving dinner example earlier in this section where we could test the turkey and the pumpkin pie in the same experiment.  Imagine the turkey is A and the pumpkin pie is B.  In a more realistic scenario, in the case of AIDS, for example, where a drug cocktail needs to be tested with more than three drugs, the experiment would have a greater number than four conditions.  The beauty of a factorial design (even a simple one) is that researchers can discern whether: 1) one drug is effective; 2) both drugs are effective; 3) if neither is effective alone but are very effective in combination, or 4) that neither treatment or drug is effective. In the case where two drugs or treatments are more effective together than each one alone, this is known as an *interaction effect* because the results are due to the interaction between the two treatments, rather than each treatment alone.

To summarize, in a factorial design, there are at least four groups and two or more treatments are compared at once.  This is a very good design to compare treatments because the study can tell us whether two or more treatments, given together, are better than only one treatment given at a time.

## Is it a Single-Subject Case Design?

A single-subject case design (SSCD), also referred to as a single-subject research design (SSRD), is simply an experiment that uses a single subject (although many SSCDs may use a small number of subjects rather than one subject). I'm certain almost every parent of a child with autism has seen or heard of this type of research design. It is very common in autism research among *legitimate* clinicians but, unfortunately, among the kooks as well. Due to the overreliance of SSCDs among pseudo-scientists, it is important to recognize the proper use of SSCDs.

The vast majority of studies done in the field of applied behavior analysis and in rehabilitation research (used by occupational therapists and physiotherapists) are single-subject case designs. Single-subject designs are ideally suited for a patient with an injury and the treatment plan for the person is individualized. In this case, the use of SSCDs is to rehabilitate that one patient, not to generalize that treatment plan to another patient or a population of patients with the same diagnosis.

**Single-Subject Case Design: Table 5**

| | |
|---|---|
| A: Treatment | 70 IQ |
| B: Withdrawal of Treatment | 50 IQ |
| A: Treatment | 70 IQ |
| B: Withdrawal of Treatment | 55 IQ |

Before describing this type of research, it is worth mentioning that researchers who legitimately use SSCDs often believe that they are being unfairly attacked by the scientific community; there is ongoing debate about how this kind of research should be properly used. That said, there is consensus in science that single-subject research is useful in clinical settings, but that **it is *not*** appropriate to generalize specifically from one single-subject research design to the population at large, which unfortunately happens in autism research a lot!

There are advantages to single-subject research designs versus other study designs. The first advantage is that the experimenter uses the person as his own control by comparing that person's data before the treatment and immediately after the treatment. Using the same person removes all the possible errors that can occur from random, individual differences among people. When modifying behavior, this design typically observes behavior on a few different occasions prior to introduction of the treatment. Many researchers conducting an SSRD-type study will then use statistical analysis to ensure that there is a true difference between the "before treatment" and "after treatment" data. Other researchers do not use statistics to see the results; they simply look at a graph showing the data points before and after the treatment (those using statistics are often criticized because there is a debate about which statistical tests are appropriate to use). These researchers claim that SSRDs are actually better than the other designs because the internal validity is high - there is no variability between children in the control and experimental groups because the control and the treatment are done on the same person.

The hypothetical design above shows a child who enters treatment for six months and then is given an IQ test. The child is then denied treatment for a year; his IQ is subsequently measured. The child then enters a treatment program for another six months and his IQ is measured once again. The child is once again taken out of the treatment program for another year and his IQ is subsequently measured. From this kind of design, we could clearly see whether the child was benefiting from treatment, and regressing when not in treatment. For that one child, it would appear as though the autism treatment has a very strong effect. For clinical decisions, the single-subject design is very compelling, as we are not generalizing to the population at large; rather, we are simply making a clinical decision about what treatment does or does not work for that specific child. When single-subject designs are used in that manner, they do a true service to the child.

This is particularly true in the case of autistic individuals with self-injurious behaviors. If a clinician uses techniques to eliminate self-injurious behavior, do we really care about the fact that there was only one child in the study? Obviously, we care that this treatment worked for this individual and has now given the child a life with no physical restraints; the individual can go out into the community with the family. When these kinds of studies are published, they are incredibly beneficial to other clinicians, offering new and valuable tools in the kit box for use when the clinician is presented with a similarly self-injurious client.

Single-subject research designs are also very useful because they motivate different kinds of research which attempt to generate causal relationships. In fact, a small SSRD-type study using two children, actually motivated Lovaas to do a large scale between-within subjects design which became the very well-known autism treatment experiment published in 1987.

To summarize, a single-subject research or case design uses one person in the entire study. This design is common in autism research and is useful in clinical settings, but controversial if used improperly by generalizing to the whole population of children with autism.

## What's the problem with Single-Subject Case Designs?

There is no debate regarding the importance of the single-subject case design, when used properly; however, it is used improperly all the time.  Particularly troubling is that the single-subject case design method of research is used heavily by "quacks" because it is cheap and easy to do.  These practitioners only need to find one child to experiment with and a mere anecdote, now dressed-up as genuine research, can quickly morph into a poor single-subject case design.  In addition, case studies often masquerade as single-subject case designs (which is a problem due to the lack of rigor in a case study).

Another problem among some researchers is their claim that single-subject designs show A causes B within the general population of children with autism.  Under certain conditions, it is fine to say that a child improved due to the treatment, if proper experimental controls or safeguards have been put into place.  When this happens, the "Therapeutic Criterion" or the treatment value for the subject has been met.  Unfortunately, from that one child, one cannot make general statements about how effective the treatment would be in general.  In short, the "Experimental Criterion"  has not been met from one or two or even three single-subject research designed experiments.  Single-subject designs are a very valuable way to treat individual clients and probe to see if it is worthwhile creating a between-subjects experiment with a larger number of subjects (as in Lovaas' research mentioned above).  If, indeed, we want to generalize results to the larger  population of children with autism, or in other words, want to meet the experimental criterion, we need to do between-subjects designs with larger numbers of children.  There is no legitimate way to get around that type of necessary scientific heavy lifting in autism treatment research.

Proponents of the single-subject case design argue that the solution to the generalizability problem is to do many replications, and in this way show that the result can be generalized to the population of children with autism. They would argue that their studies are equal to between-subjects designs in terms of generalization as long as both types of studies replicate their results. Theoretically, this is a compelling notion; however, in practice it is rare to see a large number of single subject study designs replicated in the field of autism treatment research.

Researchers who use the SSRD method are also generally proponents of meta-analysis.  In a meta-analysis, the researcher combines the results of a large number of single-subject studies to determine if a given treatment is effective.  This is difficult to do well and has some methodological problems associated with it, but it is a much better way to add to the body of knowledge in autism research than generalizing through one single-subject research design (a definite no-no).

Other critics, such as Furedy,[11] are adamantly in their opposition to the use of this type of design.  Furedy states, "The 'single-subject' design (which really denotes a design that employs too few subjects to allow statistical inferences concerning significance to be made) is useful only for the generation, but not for the testing or evaluation, of hypotheses concerning any psychological functions."  Simply put, critics like Furedy are saying that the problem with single-subject research designs is that there are not enough children in the study to make sure that the effect is real, and that the proper use of the single-subject research design is to generate interesting ideas to test properly.

Although we are not going to end the long-running debate regarding the shortcomings of single-subject designs in autism treatment any time soon, it is safe to say that there are too many methodological problems associated with this type of research design to rely on its results, exclusively, to generalize an autism treatment protocol to the autistic population at large. In my view, single-subject designs are relied upon far too heavily in autism research, often by pseudo-scientists.  The main points to take away from this discussion are that there are legitimate researchers using the SSRD method.  However, make sure they are using the design in the way it was intended and not simply using a single-subject case design for quick and cheap research to hoodwink you into providing a treatment for your child that has not been properly substantiated with sufficient scientific data.  In addition, you can "take it to the bank" that it is not scientifically valid to generalize to the entire population of children with autism from one single-subject design.  Please be careful!

## How many children should there be in each experimental group?

The answer to this question is very important for any consumer checking out autism treatment.  The answer depends upon the goal of the research.  If researchers plan to generalize their results to the population of autistic people or the population of autistic children, then they have to be relatively certain that those children with autism in the study are similar to autistic children in the general population.  The more representative the experimental group is to the population at large, the less children are required in the experiment.  As mentioned previously, autism is a spectrum disorder, and children with autism can be affected to a greater or lesser extent.  Therefore, the degree that children with autism in a study represent the population at large is always a concern for competent researchers.

## What is the ideal number?

As a general rule, the less the children in a study are representative of all children with autism, the larger the number of children will be required in that study.  Put differently, if researchers are not using pretreatment measurements to clarify the type of children with autism in the study, then the larger the group, the more confident we can be that these children represent the population of children with autism as a whole. However, we are still *not* very confident. To avoid this problem, in well-conducted studies, researchers do extensive testing to measure the severity of autism of their subjects before they administer the treatment. If we generalize the results of each study through the theory the researchers are testing, and we use an experimental and control group as we discussed earlier, then we avoid this problem providing the experimental and control group are the same at the outset of the study. In autism research, the number of subjects in each study is so small and generally without a control group. The big question of the ideal number becomes problematic.

## What is acceptable?

The short answer is this: it depends. If you want to generalize autism treatment research results directly from a study to the population at large (like researchers do in drug trials), then you need to have confidence that the children in the study are truly representative of all the children out there who are afflicted with the disorder. However, if one generalizes through a theory, then twenty subjects per condition would be considered a very respectable number. Obviously, thirty subjects would make us even happier; however, the more unrealistic the number of children required for an autism study, the smaller the likelihood that the research will actually be conducted. Even twenty children per condition in an autism study is almost unheard of (unfortunately) and would be a very respectable goal. The results of each study would then be considered an instance (known as "instantiation") where the treatment was deemed effective. On the other hand, a negative finding would have to be explained by the theory. Or the theory would have to be modified to explain the finding. Or the theory would need to be wholly rejected, in which case the treatment based on the rejected theory would properly need to be discarded.

## How are children in a study assigned to the experimental groups?

I am certain many have heard that the most important thing a researcher can do is to randomly assign subjects to experimental groups. The idea behind random assignment is to ensure that the groups (the experimental and control group) are the same at the beginning of the study to guarantee that the treatment indeed has created the differences we may see post-treatment between groups. Random assignment avoids any possible confusion that any post-treatment differences between the groups may have been caused by the group assignment procedure. The easiest way to ensure group equivalence is to randomly assign subjects. This can be done through assigning subjects based on a random numbers table in the back of any statistics book. Today, researchers also use a computer generated random numbers program. Random assignment can be done very easily, with the presumption (ethical caveat) that the treatment is not already well established as being effective. Random assignment is also simple to do with college students who volunteer for a psychology experiment. If our children were laboratory mice, we could always randomly assign them to control and experimental groups. But our children are not animals. They are our *precious* children; not only are they children, but they are disabled children. They are amongst the most vulnerable populations to study and their human rights must be protected at all costs. Therefore, random assignment in autism treatment studies is not always ethically possible.

Here is where we wade into the serious issue of ethics in random assignment for children with autism. To bring this example home to parents, think about the following: if I believe that my child will benefit from a treatment due to preliminary published results from a study, and that treatment is considered more effective the earlier it is started, then I will not allow anyone to randomly assign my child because I refuse to put my child into the control group (the children who do not get the treatment).  The researcher also has an ethical obligation to tell me that there is evidence the treatment is effective.  In addition, that researcher must also provide children in the control group with something equally effective in order to conduct the experiment.  To provide an example of how important ethics is in research, a study on spina bifida comes to mind.  The experiment included pregnant women, who had previously given birth to a child suffering from spina bifida.  The women were separated into a treatment and a control group.  The treatment group received folic acid and the control group did not.  It became very clear that folic acid was preventing spina bifida; therefore, the researchers were compelled to stop halfway through the experiment and give all the women folic acid; otherwise, the women in the control group would have given birth to children with spina bifida at a disproportionately higher rate!

The above example illustrates how difficult random assignment can be, particularly in terms of study replications.  Unfortunately, these ethical rules are breached often with autism.  Reputable researchers are understandably very concerned about this issue.  To avoid the problem of assigning a group of children with autism to a control group, some researchers make due with a treatment group only.   One way to avoid pure random assignment is to use something out of the researcher's control to determine that subjects are assigned randomly; placing children in the treatment group when there is grant money for the experiment and putting children in the control group when there is no money is one example of functional random-assignment without breaching ethical standards. When pure random-assignment cannot be done ethically, many tests need to be conducted to ensure that the groups are functionally the same at the outset of the experiment.

The vast majority of unsubstantiated treatments for autism could easily be tested through random assignment, as there are no preliminary results to suggest that any of these so-called treatments are effective.  It would certainly help parents to better evaluate the effectiveness of many of these experimental treatments. However, in the area of behavioral treatment, it is unethical to randomly assigned children to experimental and control groups because the data showing efficacy of behavioral treatment and applied behavioral analysis is, at this point, very strong and clearly out of the experimental (i.e., research) stage.  In other words, based on our knowledge of the state of science in autism treatment, denying children with autism behavioral treatment to test a completely unsubstantiated treatment is ethically unacceptable.  At the date of this publication, we still have researchers randomly assigning children to experimental and control groups where *neither* group receives behavioral treatment.  Parents do not get full disclosure about the proven effectiveness of behavioral treatment for autism.  Tragically, this is somehow considered to be ethically reasonable by some government-funded researchers.[*]

In sum, researchers tend to compensate for the problem of their inability to randomly assign children to conditions, by matching groups and using quasi-random assignment.  However, even this is ethically questionable in the case of behavioral treatment, as this treatment is already considered best practice. Unfortunately, governments often refuse to accept the science behind this method and refuse to fund this form of treatment.  Therefore, government-funded researchers all too often engage in unethical research practices, and thanks to politics, are able to continue doing so to the exclusion of science.  Until best practices in autism treatment are firmly established amongst policy-makers and government-funded academics, the unethical research practice of assigning children to control groups in studies testing behavioral treatment will regrettably continue.

---

[*]For a discussion on the conduct of government-owned academics and their argument about the ethical justification for assigning children with autism to experimental and control groups, *Science for Sale in the Autism Wars*[9] lays out the case in some detail.

## What is being measured and how?

The next question that must be asked in evaluating any study is this:  "How are the variables being measured?"    The first variable which we spoke about earlier, is the Dependent Variable (DV).   In our case, the DV is almost always autism, which needs to be operationalized.  In other words, for the purposes of the study, the researcher must actually *measure* the degree to which the child is affected by autism, before and after the intervention.

## Autism (the Dependent Variable)

How do we turn autism (which we live with every day) into something that can be measured.  Remember, we need to measure autism in order to know whether the child with autism has improved as a result of the treatment being studied in an experiment.  We also need to be able to measure autism in case the autistic child's condition worsens during any intervention.

We must measure autism in such a way that the amount of autism (or the severity of autism) is the same, whether I measure it, you measure it or a randomly selected researcher measures it.  It cannot be a mysterious kind of measurement that only people with "special" powers can do.  Autism needs to be measured in a standardized way so that regardless of who measures it, the results are the same (as long as the person can be trained to use the measurement tools properly).  Good researchers use a variety of tests that have themselves been tested again and again to ensure that they accurately measure degree of autism.

Unfortunately, autism is more difficult to measure, as compared to many conditions or diseases, because the diagnosis of autism is behavioral and not biomedical.  Put simply, we can't use a blood sample to establish the degree of a person's autism. Therefore, testing autism properly creates some challenges. To meet those challenges, researchers use many well-established IQ tests and developmental measures, as well as autism-rating scales. In addition, researchers often measure the children's behavior using time. For example, some researchers count minutes children are engaged in self-stimulatory behavior and see whether the amount of self-stimulatory behavior diminishes after treatment. Any study that uses a large number of measures (that make sense to you) is one sign of a well-done study. It is a good idea to be skeptical when someone uses a new measure or a biological measure for autism in the study. Many parents are often mislead when someone with a PhD after their name uses a biological measure, lulled in the belief that a "hard" biological measure can somehow measure autism accurately. Suspicion is particularly warranted when a study uses a biological measure without any behavioral measures. In addition, if you see a study that uses a biological measure and a behavioral measure, and no findings are reported for the behavioral measure, but findings have been observed for the biological measure, this discrepancy should be a red flag. How could such a finding occur. Why would the finding be significant in decreasing the level of autism? Peptides used in vitamin research are an example of a way to measure autism that has no science behind it, at least at the time of this publication.

Tests used to measure autism often include the diagnostic criteria from the Diagnostic Statistical Manual (DSM), a number of standardized tests such as (but not limited to) the Autism Behavioral Checklist (ABC) as well as a variety of IQ tests. IQ tests do not diagnose autism; however, used in conjunction with other tests, IQ measures provide researchers with some idea of whether the child is on the autism spectrum. This is done by looking at the child's testing patterns, i.e., whether the child has peaks and valleys in ability or whether the child's scores are all consistent. Peaks and valleys would typically show a pattern indicating autism, whereas flat, consistent scores would typically signify other kinds of disorders (such as mental retardation).  In addition, researchers may try to measure autism by simply counting how often certain symptoms occur, e.g., within a number of twenty-four hour periods or a number of one-hour periods. Behavioral measures are common when a study is looking into techniques to decrease aggression or self-stimulatory behavior, e.g., researchers may count how often a child has tantrums in a twenty-four hour period.

The bottom line is that when reading a study, make sure that you agree with a basic premise:  the way researchers have measured autism.  In technical terms,  evaluate the way the dependent variable has been "operationalized."  If researchers are measuring autism in a novel way, pay special attention to how they justify this new measure.  Measurement of autism is crucial, because if study results do not change any of the measures of autism that make sense, then the positive results based on their novel measurement of degrees of autism are meaningless.  The level of autism has not changed based on the well-established, reliable, observable measurements of autism.  In other words, they can claim that their new treatment improves autism based on the way they have measured it. However, when this treatment is given to children who have autism (measured in the traditional way), the children's behavior remains the same.  If a novel improvement in the way we measure degree of autism were developed,  I would expect that there would be some overlap with the older behavioral approaches. In addition, for any new autism measure to be widely adopted, it is important that it be tested and then published in a peer-reviewed journal, to demonstrate its superiority over other measures.

## Treatment (the Independent Variable)

The next challenge for any researcher is taking the *concept* of the treatment and making it possible to actually administer.  This process is very straightforward when researching vitamins or drugs.  The researcher may spend time on producing the treatment, but once the drug or vitamin is produced, then administering the drug or sugar pill (placebo) is a simple thing to do.  It is much more difficult when the treatment is non-drug or non-vitamin-related. Do not trust treatment professionals who claim that only their special people can provide the treatment and that their technique cannot be taught without buying into the philosophy.  The treatment protocol must be thoroughly documented through treatment manuals and/or videotapes.  That is not to say that people administering the treatment do not need to be highly trained, but rather, there must be an opportunity for others to be highly trained and a documented protocol followed.  Many so-called autism treatments that are unsubstantiated do not have treatment protocols (documented treatment methods), and therefore, do not have an objective way to ensure that the treatment protocol is being followed.  In short, please make sure that the way the treatment is operationalized: (1) makes sense; (2) is objective, and (3) can be evaluated whether or not it is being stringently followed.

It is also important that the various outcome measures for autism used in the study measure the degree of autism consistently.  This criterion is called "internal consistency."  Put simply, if the first measurement shows that the child's autism is severe, the second measure should also come up with similar results.  If one measure indicates that the child has severe autism and the next measure shows that the child is mildly autistic, there is a problem with one of the measures, and the internal consistency of autism (the dependent variable) is problematic.

In addition, the outcome of the measure must be the same, regardless of when the outcome is measured.  In other words, the way we measure autism must always give us the same results, whether the child is measured in the morning, noon or night, or in the winter or summer.  If a researcher uses a rating scale to measure autism, we need to have confidence in the consistency of the child's score (before the treatment is administered).  Obviously, the more consistent the measure, the more confidence we can have about relying upon it.

As mentioned before, a key characteristic regarding the measure of the degree of autism is that the outcome must be the same regardless of who does the measuring. This is called inter-observer reliability. In other words, those observing the behavior must record it in the same way (give it the same score). When inter-observer reliability is high, we can be more confident that the degree of autism is being measured consistently and properly during an autism treatment experiment.

Even if the measure is reliable, we have to then ask ourselves: Is it valid? Another way to look at this is by asking this question: "Does the measure really capture the essence of what autism is and how it has changed as a result of the treatment?" Put simply: Is autism measured accurately throughout the study? This is a significant issue in autism studies because autism is difficult to measure. I'm typically put at ease when I see a study that has used a large number of different ways to measure autism. The use of many measures to establish degree of autism, in the same study, is the way researchers make certain the measurement of autism is as valid as possible, considering that we do not have a biological way to measure autism at this time. To grapple with this problem, autism research uses many autism measurement scales that have been tested and refined to improve the validity of the measurement.

The validity of the Treatment (the Independent Variable) is also important. Here I am referring to the *treatment* actually affecting the degree of autism, and not another variable that has little to do with the treatment, but appears to occur at the same time. For example, Dolphin Therapy is hypothesized to be effective for children with autism because dolphins are thought to communicate (in some mysterious, secret way) with our children. More likely, however, is the thesis that perhaps dolphins are simply reinforcing to most children with autism, and therefore, children are more likely to pay attention and learn a skill when in the pool with a dolphin.  It may be the reinforcement, rather than the intrinsic powers of the dolphin, that is important for researchers to discern.  In short, the validity of the treatment must be considered (and shown to be considered) in every study.

## Who collects the data?

Much of the research done in autism treatment is highly flawed with respect to data collection.  Although as many as 90 percent of autism researchers might disagree with me, I am going to suggest that parents should *never* collect data on their own children.  The reason researchers are going to vehemently disagree with me on this point is that it takes away all their no-cost manpower for the studies.  Despite the manpower issues, I submit that parental reporting is a disastrous research practice.  Scientists know that "no data is better than bad data," because very poor decisions may be based on bad data.  Therefore, if we have bad data, we will make bad decisions.   You may ask why I am so firmly against the notion of parents collecting data.  It's quite simple: parents have many motivations for studies to succeed or fail.  Some parents are so desperate and hopeful for the magic pill or treatment to work that when they collect data, they may inadvertently *influence* the data, without being aware of this.  Conversely, parents can collect biased data and be quite aware that they are doing so, often understanding the personal, economic implications of a positive or negative result when data collection may be associated with government respite or treatment services.

As a parent, I would never trust myself to take treatment data on my own child. I would be completely unable to do so because I am so invested in the outcome (even though I would try to be objective).   I am quite sure, however, that if I were sufficiently trained, I could do a fine job taking data on your child.  This reticence of mine, to take data on my own child, is to avoid creating a self-fulfilling prophecy. A self-fulfilling prophecy occurs when the experimenter unintentionally biases the results of the study to confirm the hypothesis.

If you ever need any justification regarding why parents should never take data on their own children, the following example is but one instance of a parent's self-filling prophesies biasing a study. At a large, prestigious hospital in a major metropolitan area, there was a study done on melatonin (a hormone that is thought to help regulate sleep among children afflicted with autism). In good faith, the researchers gave melatonin to parents of children with autism, to administer thirty minutes before bedtime. The parent was to track the sleep patterns of the child over a two-week period. What's wrong with this study? What if I told you that this was a public hospital? Does that give you any more clues? What if I told you that in the same region, respite monies from the government were tied to amount of time that the child slept, and that sleep problems were the only criterion that would realistically qualify most parents of children with autism for the respite money?

In this type of research design, we have set up the perfect dilemma for the parent. Parents cannot report on their children's improvement in sleep to these researchers because they fear their respite monies may be rescinded. I can guarantee that these researchers had no idea that this was occurring among some of the parents, as the researchers had no intention of passing along the sleep information. In this illustration, it is easy to conclude that melatonin's efficacy was most probably *under*-reported. In the case of melatonin, that is unfortunate, because melatonin is a supplement which pharmaceutical companies will not spend time and money to research because there is no profit to be made from it, (it is inexpensive and widely available from health food stores). Therefore, this rare opportunity to objectively test the efficacy of melatonin has been biased toward the hormone having less positive effect on sleep than it may truly have.

## Who administers the treatment?

Illustrations such as the melatonin example above justify the notion that parents should not administer the treatment nor record the data on the treatment. Unfortunately, a study becomes much more expensive when the parent cannot administer the treatment because the researchers must hire research assistants, rather than use free parent labor. Aside from poor data recording, parents are also not as reliable administering the treatment because they have hectic lives. In addition, I do not trust all parents to provide the proper treatment dosage that is recommended, because if a parent does not see results, he or she may double the dose. Remember, we are dealing with a population of parents who may be chronically sleep-deprived and desperate to see positive treatment results for their children.

It is the researchers from a study (and not the parents) who are best suited to administer the treatment and record its data. In addition, those recording the data should not know which children are in the control group and which children are in the experimental group of an autism treatment study. In other words, *blind is best*. This is particularly important for those taking data at the beginning and upon completion of the study. It is not always possible to hide the experimental condition from those administering the treatment, particularly if the study lasts for years, but this should nevertheless be the goal. The less those taking the data know about the study, the higher the probability that bias will not creep into the study.

Another good example why those recording the data should not know which children are in which group and why parents should never collect data, is a study conducted in Manitoba.[12] The design of this study was well done. Children were randomly assigned to one of two groups, and data was taken on each group before and after the treatment. A psychologist evaluated the children and found that there was no change in the degree of autism of the children in both groups (which means that the intervention or treatment was not successful). The psychologist used a very well-known test to measure autism (the Autism Behavioral Checklist — the ABC). In addition, the parents were asked to evaluate their own child's progress. The parents reported a very different finding from the psychologist: they saw improvement in their child. This was true of the parents whose children were in both the treatment and control groups; however, there was no difference between the children in the treatment and control groups! Parents so desperately want to see improvement in their children's condition that they perceive improvement when it may not actually exist. In contrast, the psychologist in this particular study was blind to which children received the treatment and found no improvement across conditions, which means his conclusions were not biased by group assignment.

## Did research results happen by chance?

Once we are presented with the results of a study which compare the scores of two groups, then we need to know whether those results are meaningful or whether they happened by chance. To answer this question, researchers use statistical measures. They ask themselves: "What are the odds that this effect happened by chance?" In addition, they use something called a "p" value. You may read a study that says, for example, "children in the experimental group increased their IQ by an average of 20 points, (p = .05)." The p value indicates that on the basis of probability, ninety-five times out of one hundred, this result did not happen by chance. Or in other words, five times out of one hundred, this result may have happened by pure chance. Therefore, the lower the p value in a study publication, the better. When a researcher presents a finding supported by a p value of p = .00001, that is fantastic! This means that *the odds* that the outcome of the experiment happened by chance are virtually nil.

Why should we care about p values?  When one evaluates a treatment for autism, and the Between-Subjects Designed Study either does not have p values, or the p values are .07 or higher, one needs to think about whether those findings are sufficiently robust.  In other words, are the findings of the study correct?  In short, the smaller the p value, the more confident one can be that the results of the study do, in fact, reflect reality.  Another statistical term that is reported often with p values is the Standard Deviation (SD).  For our purposes, it is important to know whether the SD is large within the group (meaning that the average score of the group is quite different from each child's individual score).  If the SD is large, that means that the average score does not accurately reflect each child's score, which indicates a less *reliable* finding.

## Is the study biased and how can bias be avoided?

Many designs (such as some Single-Subject and Within-Subject Designs) suffer from flaws that can call into question the entire study.  Bias may be created by the experimental design, yet the experimenter may have no control or may not even know about the bias.  It becomes unclear whether the treatment is causing the result or whether there is something else causing the result.  One of these types of bias is called history.

### Bias Type 1:  History

History refers to something that has happened between the pre-test and post-test, of which the researcher is unaware.  For example, perhaps at the same time as a vitamin experiment was taking place, some of the parents in the study went to a lecture on behavioral treatment and started a behavioral treatment program.  Enrollment of the children into another program was not controlled by the researcher, who did not know that the child received another treatment at the same time as the vitamins were administered.

## Bias Type 2:  Maturation

Another influence that can entirely ruin a study on autism treatment is called maturation.  There are two kinds of maturation that we need to recognize.  The first is simply the amount of time that has passed between the pre-test and post-test.  The more time that has passed, the more likely that the child has matured.  To illustrate, if researchers start a study with two-year olds and the study is over when the child is six years old, that child has matured through the duration of the study.  Cognitive development may be a factor of concern to the researcher.  With autism, development is less of a problem than with typically developing children, since autism is a pervasive *developmental* disorder; however, the researcher still needs to take maturation  into account (the child getting older) and adjust accordingly.

The second kind of maturation refers to fatigue.  A child will often tire over the course of a study, if the study has the child work for long periods of time at once.  Fatigue is a common problem when testing children, as the child may give more accurate answers, for example, in the first hour than in the second hour.  Fatigue must be avoided if the researcher is to obtain accurate results for the study.

## Bias Type 3:  Treatment Contamination

Treatment contamination occurs when a treatment is given and then withdrawn.  Occasionally, the treatment has lasting effects even after withdrawal.  Treatment contamination is a common occurrence when testing drugs that stay in a person's system for some time.  This may be an issue of relevance to autism, as some autistic children do not metabolize drugs in the same manner as non-autistic children. Treatment contamination may or may not be important, depending upon what is being tested and the time period.

A completely different kind of contamination concerns prerequisite skill levels prior to participation in the experiment. The "learning history" (other treatments received prior to the new study) of the child before even being asked to participate in the study, is a possible confounding variable. In other words, the results of the study may be partially influenced by the skills that the child has acquired before the study. Although there will be no effect when comparing a child's pre-score with his post-score, learning history does confound the claim that the treatment under study works for all children with autism, versus a more modest claim that the treatment works mainly for children with autism who already have a certain skill set. An example of this type of bias is a study done in New Jersey on naturalistic learning. Researchers compared children's skill acquisition through a technique called Discrete Trial Training (DTT) versus a technique called Naturalistic Learning, to evaluate which of the two was more effective and efficient. The researchers casually mentioned that in New Jersey it is practically impossible to find children who have not had Discrete Trial Training histories. This significantly complicates autism treatment studies in New Jersey.

These researchers were *not* actually studying which autism treatment type was more effective and efficient, but rather, among children who already had considerable DTT learning histories, which method was more efficient. This is a very different question. The goal of using DTT is to develop sufficient skills and provide enough of a foundation to enable children to learn naturally from their environment. It may be that this research tells us something valuable about naturalistic teaching; however, the scope condition would need to say something along these lines, to validate the study's conclusions: this is based on children who have had discrete trial treatment.  This would need to be added to the theory to be certain that the hypotheses of the researchers will be supported in other autism treatment studies where perhaps the children have not received *any* discrete trial training treatment.

## Confounding Variables in General

The researcher may not be aware of these influences which may affect the outcome of the study in profound and significant ways.  In general, any variable that has not been considered and controlled may confound an experiment and, thereby, render the results meaningless.  The world of autism research suffers from the problem of confounding variables to a very disturbing degree.

As mentioned previously, the effect of season is an important consideration when it comes to research on children with autism.  Apparently, children with autism often fare better in one season rather than another.  The reason for the seasonal effect is not clear.  If the experiment lasts for one year, the results of the study could be skewed unless researchers consider this influence and design their study accordingly.

Another example of a variable that needs to be considered is sensory sensitivity.  Imagine that in the room where the child receives treatment, there is a florescent tube with a buzzing sound emanating from its transformer.  It is possible that the child may be distracted;  the researcher may attribute that distraction to autism rather than to the buzzing light, or perhaps some other sensory interference of which the researcher is unaware.

There are many variables that have nothing whatsoever to do with the treatment which may inadvertently affect the outcome of a study.   Although no study is perfect, without a control group that is having the same experience in every way, aside from being administered the treatment, it is infinitely more difficult to control unknown variables that can confound an experiment. Every researcher must be aware of this issue. Such awareness helps ensure that the scientific method will be used successfully to develop and test effective treatments for children afflicted with autism.

## 2.6 How researchers mistakenly ruin their own well-designed autism treatment studies

The first mistake that I see commonly in autism publications is the faulty interpretation of data. Researchers often mistakenly ruin their own studies by misinterpreting the data. This is why the process of peer review is so crucially important. Perhaps some researchers may err in their interpretation of a study's data; however, their academic peers will use the opportunity to robustly critique the study and expose any errors or misinterpretations. In addition, researchers can also introduce bias by using data collected inaccurately (by parents or untrained others), or by the observation measure being too subjective (yielding different results based on who collects the data). This issue is addressed by ensuring that experimenters standardize their data collection procedures. The accurate measurement of the dependent and independent variables is vitally important.

Although we've spoken about bias that may occur due to type of design chosen, even if the study design is good, there are two other kinds of bias that can creep into research: demand characteristics and experimenter bias. Demand characteristics occur when the subject tries to please the experimenter. The subject attempts to behave to confirm the experimenter's hypothesis. This is not a huge concern in autism research as the autistic child would likely not care or understand the hypothesis, but it is a major influence when the parent is involved in taking and reporting the data, for example. This is why, if possible, the parent should not know the hypothesis of the study, or to which condition the autistic child has been assigned. Unfortunately, this is not always practical or ethical; however, when possible, the parent should not know the purpose of the study and the research group to which their child has been assigned.

The other type of bias, which is a *major* issue in autism research, is the effect of the experimenter's expectations of outcome. Researchers, unfortunately, tend to be very invested in the outcome of their study: this overzealous commitment to their hypothesis is often due to potential monetary benefit. On the other hand, we see some researchers are over-invested because they care profoundly about this population of children, irrespective of personal gain. These researchers also want their hypothesis to be supported; therefore, they must take great care to avoid inadvertently influencing the outcome of the study.

To illustrate this point, I will spotlight a famous study that illustrates the problem of the self-fulfilling prophecy. The researcher, Rosenthal (1968), set up a situation where he told teachers in a classroom that a subset of their students were "late bloomers." The children were actually randomly chosen, without the teacher's knowledge. At the end of the school year, Rosenthal found that the children who were expected to excel, did indeed do very well as measured by IQ scores. The children were actually perceived to be more intellectually gifted and autonomous by their teachers. More alarming was the circumstance that the children who did so in school (as measured by IQ) but were *not* expected to do well by the teachers, were actually perceived by the teachers to be less affectionate, less well-adjusted, and less interesting.[10] The power of the self-fulfilling prophecy should not be discounted by any competent researcher. The experimental design must safeguard against this issue.

# 2.7 How can bias be avoided?

As I have reiterated throughout the book, the goal of every researcher must be to avoid bias. This can be done in the following manner: studies should be designed with a control group; the groups should be the same; subject assignment should be hidden from the researchers taking and evaluating the data; inadvertent parental influence should be avoided; the influence of the person being studied should be eliminated; funding should be received at arms-length, from agencies who have no interest in the research outcome.

A control group to compare results helps eliminate bias. A control group is particularly important for the parent or consumer when the treatment claims made are spectacular. In addition, both groups must have the same characteristics at the beginning of the study, by random assignment when possible or functional or "quasi-random" assignment when random assignment is an ethically questionable practice. Further, the assignment to conditions must be concealed from the experimenter (or at a minimum hidden from those in the research team who administer the treatment). When possible, external evaluators must be used. These evaluators, although part of the experiment, must have no idea which conditions the subjects have been assigned. Moreover, parents must be kept as uninformed as is ethically possible, to avoid inadvertent parental influence and, thereby, confound the experiment. In addition, parents should not be involved in the experimental procedures, including the administration of treatment or data collection. In the case of autism research, it is important not only to eliminate the influence of the autistic person on experimental outcomes, but also to eliminate the influence of the parent or the person who will most likely accompany the child while participating in the study.

# 2.8 When Is It Time To Apply the Results to Children?

When can we trust the results of a study and apply these results to our children? In other words, *when can we generalize the results?* If the children in the study are representative of the greater population of children with autism, then results may be generalized directly from the study to the population at large. However, even if the children are not representative of all children with autism, the results can still be valuable. They simply need to be generalized in a different way. Here I am referring to the generalization of results through theory.

Although the generalization of results through a theory is more time-consuming than directly to the population at large, it is often the only way to do so responsibly. If research results are to be generalized through a theory, to the population of children with autism as a whole, then it is very important to see many studies which report data that supports the theory. Each study acts as an instance of where the theory is supported. The more supported instances of the theory or hypothesis, the more secure we are in the knowledge that the autism treatment in question is truly effective. It is important to keep in mind that Between-Subjects Designs conducted over a long period of time are much more expensive and difficult than Single-Subject Case Designs (SSCDs); therefore, one would expect less of the Between-Subjects Designed studies to be conducted. That said, a few Between-Subjects Designs conducted with a large number of children and supporting the theory would be more valuable than a few SSCDs supporting the theory, because Between-Subjects Designs have a control group to eliminate variables that may confound the results of a study, whereas SSCDs do not have this built-in quality control mechanism. For researchers conducting research using SSCDs, their results are also instances that can support their hypotheses. However, many more replications of their findings are needed in order to generalize confidently through the theory.

At this point in autism research, there are too few studies being conducted on treatment methods; therefore, multiple replications of SSRDs would be quite valuable.  Unfortunately, what often happens is that less-than-scrupulous researchers, who are pushing their latest fad treatment, use perhaps only one single child research study to generalize their treatment *directly* to the population.  For studies that can be done over a short period of time, we should expect more SSRD studies to support the treatments being tested.

In summary, the time to take a treatment seriously is when you see mounting evidence of its efficacy, irrespective of experimental design.  Since SSRDs are much easier to do than Between-Subjects Designs, prior to evaluating the use of a treatment, we should see many more of these study designs which support the method in question. Currently in autism research, the only area where SSRDs are consistently used responsibly is in the field of applied behavior analysis.

## Is the research far enough along?

The question that remains is this: "When should researchers apply the research to children with autism?"  Pure researchers, who are far from utilizing any of their knowledge to create a treatment, are not problematic for parents.  We simply need these  geneticists, neurobiologists and other pure researchers (whose research may one day find a cure) to keep toiling in their laboratories.  They rarely push treatments prematurely out of the lab.  It is the researchers working in clinical settings who are the most problematic for the consumer.  Even reputable researchers may place children into studies much earlier than is warranted due to parental pressure.  These researchers are in an ethical bind, as they see the desperation of parents, and they may need human subjects for their experiments; however, their research may not be ready to be tested. Premature treatment occurs commonly through drugs designed for autistic adults, when they are prescribed to children with autism. Psychiatrists are well aware of the studies on adults and tell the parents that there are no comparable studies on children with autism. Nevertheless, parents are often still given the option to experiment on their children with drugs that have only been properly tested on adults. These ethical issues are difficult and, in my opinion, should be left up to the parent and the psychiatrist to weigh the potential benefits against the potential risks for the child. Less difficult to discern, however, are researchers who have no data on the efficacy of their treatment. They offer the treatment as purportedly effective for autism even though there are no peer-reviewed studies published on their treatment. Here, parents must use their knowledge of the scientific method to make an informed decision. I hope this book will be a valuable part of that process.

## Testing on human subjects

Experimentation on disabled children is a very touchy subject for researchers. It is obviously important that the child not be harmed by the treatment; however, as children with autism cannot give informed consent, their parents do this on their behalf. Unfortunately, there are potentially dangerous treatments that parents allow their children to receive, due only to their faith in the professional pushing the treatment. Section One of the book discusses these treatments in some detail.

Ethical considerations often interfere with experimental design. A good example of this type of interference occurred when parents were to give informed consent to Lovaas for his landmark study. Parents protested against random assignment because every parent wanted their child to be in the treatment rather than the control group. Consequently, with the National Institutes of Health's blessing, Lovaas had to find another way to randomize the assignment of children to groups (functional random assignment discussed earlier) which had a profound effect on the study design.

Parental pressure is a major concern in autism treatment. When studying children with autism, parents pressure researchers on a regular basis.  Parents can motivate research this way; however, they can also pressure researchers to prematurely let a treatment out of lab.  This phenomenon is exemplified in all the studies done on secretin, due to one family's ability to bring out the media in a major way.  The ability of parents to shine a spotlight on treatments is a mixed blessing because it is, theoretically, possible that an effective treatment may be discovered this way; however, more often than not, significant resources are spent on researching a treatment that is proven to be a dead end.

## 2.9  Red flags for quackery

What are the red flags for quackery you may see when you try to separate fraud from true science?  To review, there are five indicators that when taken together can signal scientific quackery (junk science) to the consumer (which in our case is generally the parent of a child with autism).  These red flags are: personal testimonials with no scientific backup; fancy explanations from the articulate, slick public speakers offering the service; logical arguments about why the treatment should work; videotapes showing the treatment working, and famous people using the method.

The red flag most easily observable is one or more personal testimonials without any scientific backup provided by the person selling the treatment.  Often testimonials take the form of autobiographies, wherein the parent describes stories of how he or she employed the treatment in question and the child improved dramatically or was cured of autism.  Watch out.  These testimonials are highlighted as a selling tool. In addition, the red flag should start flapping in the breeze when, in response to your queries about whether there are any peer-reviewed journal articles available on the treatment method, the sales person answers that science is far too close-minded regarding this research because government or big business have somehow captured science. Conspiracy theories which attempt to explain the prevention of publication of science are always suspect.

Another red flag takes the form of fancy explanations, with a large variety of glossy sell sheets and videos. Generally, scientists do not waste grant money on attempting to sell their research, and then take it prematurely out of the lab into the population at large. Genuine scientists are the *least* likely to use marketing tools of persuasion. In all of the treatments that were evaluated in the first section of this book, the treatments with absolutely no scientific evidence tended to have the most well-developed marketing materials.

A third red flag is the presence of several seemingly logical arguments explaining why the treatment works, but no data supporting the theory. Real scientists are very quick to state that they are working on a theory that could be wrong. They will not try to convince you that their unsubstantiated theory is right because it seems so logical. It is a good sign when the consumer hears that a researcher is tentative about the state of the science in autism treatment. When researchers admit that their assumptions regarding the treatment they are studying may be incorrect, the tentative nature of these researchers should be respected.

Another red flag takes the form of videotapes which demonstrate the therapy and show you the instant effect of the treatment, once again without peer-reviewed scientific support. Videotapes are a valuable way to illustrate the treatment; however, they should not be used to convince consumers that the therapy is effective. This practice is particularly disturbing when a major news organization creates a documentary or news piece on a treatment which has no data supporting its efficacy. This been done on a large number of the unsubstantiated treatments discussed in Section One.

A fifth red flag to note is the endorsement of the treatment by celebrities or academics with credentials. Notoriety as a tool of persuasion to convince you to try the treatment, or buy a product, is a common technique that should wake up your quack detector. The use by researchers of their credentials, without presenting any scientific evidence, regretably is a very common problem in autism research. Put simply, data must lead the way for your family and for the whole autism community. Anything else must be ignored; otherwise, a treatment with no data may be marketed in such a way that even the most savvy parent could be convinced that the treatment is effective.

# Conclusion

Now that you have an understanding of the many ways that researchers do, or do not, use the scientific method to study autism, I'll leave you with the following thought. Regardless of how compelling, articulate, and intelligent researchers appear to be, and no matter how tempting, attractive, and elegant theories regarding treatments appear, the buck stops with data. The best way to protect your child from quackery is to say *SHOW ME THE DATA*! Before you try, buy, or attempt to research any treatment "show me the data," should be your mantra. This basic, guiding principle will save you and your child much time, money and grief.

Once you receive the data that you have requested, you now have the tools to analyze the quality of the study upon which the practitioners are basing their practice and offering treatment to your child. I sincerely hope that one day we parents of children with autism will look back on the "bad old days" when there was no cure for autism and parents had to become scientists to protect their children from quackery peddled by the modern snake-oil salesmen of our day.

# Endnotes

[1]Huxley, T.H. 1969.  *Evolution and Ethics*.  New York:  Kraus Reprint.

[2]Auton et al. vs. the Attorney General et al., July 2000.

[3]Bassett K., et al. 2001.  "Autism and Lovaas Treatment:  a systematic review of effectiveness evidence."  *International Journal of Technology Assessment and Health Care*, Vol. 17, No. 2, p. 252.

[4]Freeman, S. 2003.  *Science for Sale in the Autism Wars*.  Langley, B.C.:  SKF Books, Inc.

[5]PubMed, http://pubmed.gov; MEDLINE, http://medline.cos.com.

[6]PsycINFO, APA Online, http://www.PsycINFO.com

[7]ERIC Education Resources Information Center, http://www.eric.ed.gov

[8]Cochrane Database of Systematic Reviews, http://www.cochrane.org

[9]Freeman, S., (see n. 4 above).

[10]Rosenthal, R., and L. Jacobsen. 1968.  *Pygmalion in the Classroom*. N.Y.:  Holt, Rinehart and Winston.

[11]Furedy, J.J.  1999.  "Commentary:  On the limited role of the 'single-subject' design in psychology:  Hypotheses generating but not testing."  *J. Behavior Therapy and Experimental Psychiatry,* Vol. 30, pp. 21-22.

[12]Jocelyn, L.J., O.G. Casiro, D. Beattie, J. Bow, and J. Kneisz. 1998.  "Treatment of children with autism:  a randomized controlled trial to evaluate a caregiver-based intervention program in community day-care centers,"  *J. Dev. Behav. Pediatr.*, Vol. 19, No. 5, pp.  326-34.

# References

---

## Behavioral Treatment

### Home-based Intensive Behavioral Treatment

Anderson, S.R., D.L. Avery, E.K. DiPietro, G.L. Edwards, and W.P. Christian. 1987. Intensive Home-Based Early Intervention With Autistic Children. *Education and Treatment of Children* 10(4): 352-366.

Baer, D.M. 1993. Commentaries on McEachin, Smith and Lovaas: Quasi-Random Assignment Can Be As Convincing As Random Assignment. *American Journal of Mental Retardation* 97(4): 374.

Bibby, P., S. Eikeseth, N.T. Martin, O.C. Mudford, and D. Reeves. 2002. Progress and Outcomes for Children With Autism Receiving Parent-Managed Intensive Interventions. *Research in Developmental Disabilities* 23: 81-104.

Birnbrauer, J.S., and D.J. Leach. 1993. The Murdoch Early Intervention Program After 2 Years. *Behavior Change* 10(2): 63-74.

Cohen, H., M. Amerine-Dickens, and T. Smith. 2006. Early Intensive Behavioral Treatment: Replication of the UCLA Model in a Community Setting. *Journal of Developmental and Behavioral Pediatrics* 27(2S): S145-55.

Connor, M. 1998. A Review of Behavioural Early Intervention Programmes for Children with Autism. *Educational Psychology in Practice* 14(2): 109-117.

Dawson, G., and J. Osterling. 1997. Early Intervention in Autism. In: M.J. Guralnick, ed., *The Effectiveness of early intervention*. Baltimore, (MD): P.J. Brooks, pp 307-326.

Eikeseth, S., T. Smith, E. Jahr, and S. Eldevik. 2002. Intensive Behavioral Treatment at School For 4 to 7 Year-old Children With Autism: A One Year Comparison Controlled Study. *Behavior Modification* 26: 49-68.

Gresham, F.M., M.E. Beebe-Frankenberger, and D.L. MacMillan. 1999. A Selective Review of Treatments for Children with Autism: Description and Methodological Considerations. *School Psycology Review* 28(4): 559-575.

Guralnick, M. (ed). 1999. *Clinical Practice Guideline: Report of the Recommendation. Autism/ Pervasive Developmental Disorders, Assessment and Intervention for Young Children* (age 0-3 years). Albany: New York State Department of Health IV-15.

Howard, J.S., C.R. Sparkman, H.G. Cohen, G. Green, and H. Stanislaw. 2004. A Comparison of Intensive Behavior Analytic and Eclectic Treatments for Young Children With Autism. *Research in Developmental Disabilities* 26: 359-383.

Leaf, R., and J. McEachin. 1999. *A work in Progress: Behavior management strategies and a curriculum for intensive behavioral treatment of autism.* N.Y: Different Road to Learning, L.L.C.

Lovaas, O.I. 1979. Contrasting Illness and Behavioral Models for the Treatment of Autistic Children: A Historical Perspective. *Journal of Autism and Developmental Disorders* 9(4): 315-323.

Lovaas O.I. 1987. Behavioral Treatment and Normal Educational and Intellectual Functioning in Young Autistic Children. *Journal of Consulting and Clinical Psychology* 55(1): 3-9.

Lovaas, O.I. 1993. The Development of a Treatment-Research Project for Developmentally Disabled and Autistic Children. *Journal of Applied Behavior Analysis* 26(4): 617-630.

Lovaas, O.I. 2003. *Teaching individuals with developmental delays: Basic intervention techniques.* Austin, TX: Pro-Ed, Inc.

Lovaas, O.I., and G. Buch. 1997. Intense Behavioral Intervention With Young Children With Autism. In: Nirbhay N. Sing, ed. *Prevention and treatment of severe behavior problems: Models and methods in developmental disabilities.* Pacific Grove (CA): Brooks/Cole Publishing 61-85.

Maurice, C., G. Green, and S.C. Luce. 1996. *Behavioral intervention for young children with autism.* Austin, TX: Pro-Ed, Inc.

McEachin, J.J., T. Smith, and O.I. Lovaas. 1993. Long-Term Outcome for Children With Autism Who Received Early Intensive Behavioral Treatment. *American Journal on Mental Retardation* 97(4): 359-372.

Metz, B., J.A. Mulick, and E.M. Butter. 2005. Autism: A late 20th century fad magnet. In: J.W. Jacobson, R.M. Foxx and J.A. Mulick *Controversial Therapies for Developmental Disabilities: Fad, Fashion and Science in Professional Practice.* Mahwah, NJ: Lawrence Erlbaum Associates, 237-264.

Pomeranz, K. 1999. Home-Based Behavioral Treatment. *Journal of Autism and Developmental Disorders* 29(5): 425-426.

Sallows, G., and T. Graupner. 2002. *Replication of the UCLA Model of Intensive Behavioral Treatment: Results after Three Years.* Early Autism Project Conference, Vancouver, BC.

Sallows, G.O., and T.D. Graupner. 2005. Intensive Behavioral Treatment for Children With Autism: Four-Year Outcome and Predictors. *American Journal on Mental Retardation* 110(6): 417-438.

Satcher, D. 1999. *Mental health: A report of the surgeon general.* US Public Health Service, Bethesda, MD, www.surgeongeneral.gov/library/mentalhealth/chapter3/sec6.html#autism, (accessed Jan 11, 2006).

Sheinkoph, S.J., and B. Siegel. 1998. Home-Based Behavioral Treatment of Young Children With Autism. *Journal of Autism and Developmental Disorders* 28(1): 15-23.

Siegel, B. 1999. Response to Pomeranz. *Journal of Autism and Developmental Disorders* 29(5): 425-427.

Smith, T. 1993. Autism. In: T.R. Giles, ed. *Handbook of Effective Psychotherapy*. New York, (NY): Plenum Press 107-133.

Smith, T., S. Eikeseth, M. Klevstrand, and O.I. Lovaas. 1997. Intensive Behavioral Treatment for Preschoolers With Severe Mental Retardation and Pervasive Developmental Disorder. *American Journal on Mental Retardation* 102(3): 238-24.

Smith, T., A. Groen, and J. Wynn. 2000. Randomized Trial of Intensive Early Intervention for Children With Pervasive Developmental Disorder. *American Journal on Mental Retardation* 105: 269-285.

Volkmar, F., E.H. Cook, J. Pomeroy, G. Realmuto, and P. Tanguay. 1999. Practice Parameters for the Assessment and Treatment of Children, Adolescents and Adults With Autism and Other Pervasive Developmental Disorders. *Journal of the American Academy of Child and Adolescent Psychiatry* 38: 32S-54S.

## Centre Based Intensive Behavioral Treatment

Buffington, D.M. 1998. Procedures for Teaching Appropriate Gestural Communication Skills to Children With Autism. *Journal or Autism and Developmental Disorders* 28(6): 535-545.

Celiberti, D.A. 1997. The Differential and Temporal Effects of Antecedent Exercise on the Self-Stimulatory Behavior of a Child with Autism. *Research in Developmental Disabilities* 18(2): 139-150.

Fenske, E.C., S. Zalenski, P.J. Krants, and L.E. McClannahan. 1985. Age at Intervention and Treatment Outcome for Autistic Children in a Comprehensive Intervention Program. *Analysis and Intervention in Developmental Disabilities* 5: 49-58.

Glasberg, B.Z. 2000. The Development of Siblings' Understanding of Autism Spectrum Disorders. *Journal of Autism and Developmental Disorders* 30(2): 143-156.

Handleman, J.S., and S.L. Harris. 1994. The Douglass Developmental Disabilities Center. In: S.L. Harris, and J.S. Handleman *Preschool Education Programs for Children With Autism*, Austin, TX: Pro-Ed Inc. 71-85.

Handleman, J.S., and S.L. Harris. 2000. Age and IQ at Intake as Predictors of Placement for Young Children with Autism: A Four to Six-Year Follow-Up. *Journal of Autism and Developmental Disorders* 30(2): 137-142.

Handleman, J.S., S.L. Harris, D. Celiberti, E. Lilleleht, and L. Tomchek. 1991. Developmental Changes of Preschool Children with Autism and Normally Developing Peers. *The Transdisciplinary Journal* 1(2): 137-143.

Handleman, J.S., S.L. Harris, B. Kristoff, L Bass, and R. Gordon. 1990. Changes in Language Development Among autistic and Peer Children in Segregated and Integrated Preschool Settings. *Journal of Autism and Developmental Disorders* 20(1): 23-31.

Handleman, J.S., S.L. Harris, B. Kristoff, F. Fuentes, and M. Alessandri. 1991. A Specialized Program for Preschool Children With Autism. *Language, Speech, and Hearing Services in Schools* 22: 107-110.

Harris, S.L., and J.S. Handleman. 1994. The Douglass Development Disabilitites Center. *Preschool education programs for children with autism.* Austin, TX: Pro-Ed Inc.

Harris, S.L., J.S. Handleman, B. Kristoff, L. Bass, and R. Gordon. 1990. Changes in Language Development Among Autistic and Peer Children in Segregated and Integrated Preschool Setting. *Journal of Autism and Developmental Disorders* 20(1): 23-31.

Harris, S.L. 2000. Age and IQ at Intake as Predictors of Placement for Young Children With Autism: A Four-to-Six-Year Follow-Up. *Journal of Autism Developmental Disorders* 30(2): 137-142.

Hoyson, M., B. Jamieson, and P.S. Strain. 1984. Individualized Group Instruction of Normally Developing and Autistic-like Children: The LEAP Curriculum Model. *Journal of the Division for Early Childhood* 8(2): 157-172.

Jennett, H.K. 2003. Commitment to Philosophy, Teacher Efficacy, and Burnout Among Teachers of Children With Autism. *Journal of Autism and Developmental Disorders* 33(6): 583-593.

Kohler, F.W., P.S. Strain, M. Hoyson, L Davis, W.M. Donina, and N. Rapp. 1995. Using a Group-Oriented Contingency to Increase Social Interactions Between Children With Autism and Their Peers. A Preliminary Analysis of Corollary Supportive Behaviors. *Behavior Modification* 19(1): 10-32.

Kohler, F.W., P.S. Strain, M. Hoyson, and B. Jamieson. 1997. Merging Naturalistic Teaching and Peer-Based Strategies to Address the IEP Objectives of Preschoolers with Autism: An Examination of Structural and Child Behavior Outcomes. *Focus on Autism and Other Developmental Disabilities* 12(4): 196-206.

Kohler, F.W., P.S. Strain, and D.D. Shearer. 1992. The Overtures of Preschool Social Skill Intervention Agents- Differential Rates, Forms, and Functions. *Behavior Modification* 16(4): 525-542.

Kohler, F.W., P.S. Strain, and D.D. Shearer. 1996. Examining levels of social inclusion within an integrated preschool for children with autism. In: *Positive behavioral support: Including people with difficult behavior in the community.* Baltimore, MD: Paul H. Brookes Publishing Co., 305-322.

Mclannahan, L.E., and P.J. Krants. 1997. Princeton Child Development Institute. *Behavior and Social Issues* 7(1): 65-68.

McLannahan, L.E., G.S. MacDuff, and P.J. Krantz. 2002. Behavior Analysis and Intervention for Adults With Autism. *Behavior Modification* 26(1): 9-27.

Olley, J.G., F.R. Robbins, and M. Morelli-Robbins. 1993. Current Practices in Early Intervention for Children With Autism. In: E. Schopler, M.E. and Van Bourgondien, *Preschool Issues in Autism*. New York, NY: Plenum Press, 223-245.

Rogers, S.J., J.M. Herblson, H.C. Lewis, J. Pantone, and K. Rels. 1987. An Approach for Enhancing the Symbolic, Communicative, and Interpersonal Functioning of Young Children With Autism or Severe Emotional Handicaps. *Journal of the Division for Early Childhood* 10(2): 135-148.

Strain, P.S. 1981. Modification of Sociometric Status and Social Interaction with Mainstreamed Mild Developmentally Disabled Children. *Analysis and Intervention in Developmental Disabilities* 1: 157-169.

Strain, P.S. 1987. Parent Training With Young Autistic Children: A Report on the LEAP Model. *Zero to Three* 7(3): 7-12.

Strain, P.S. 1983. Generalization of Autistic Children's Social Behavior Change: Effects of Developmentally Integrated and Segregated Settings. *Analysis and Intervention in Developmental Disabilities* 3: 23-34.

Strain, P.S., and L.K. Cordisco. 1994. LEAP Preschool. In: S.L. Harris and J.S. Handleman, eds. *Preschool education programs for children with autism*. Austin, TX: Pro-Ed Inc., 225-244.

Strain, P.S., and M. Hoyson. 2000. The Need for Longitudinal, Intensive Social Skill Intervention: LEAP Follow-Up Outcomes for Children With Autism. *Early Childhood Special Education* 20(2): 116-122.

Strain, P.S., M.M. Kerr, and E.U. Ragland. 1979. Effects of Peer-Mediated Social Initiations and Prompting/Reinforcement Procedures on the Social Behavior of Autistic Children. *Journal of Autism and Developmental Disorders* 9(1): 41-55.

Strain, P.S., F.W. Kohler, and H. Goldstein. 1996. Learning experiences, an alternative program: Peer-mediated interventions for young children with autism. In: *Psychosocial treatments for child and adolescent disorders: Empirically based strategies for clinical practice*. Washington, DC: American Psychological Association, 573-587.

Strain, P.S., R.E. Shores, and M.A. Timm. 1977. Effects of Peer Social Initiations on the Behavior of Withdrawn Preschool Children. *Journal of Applied Behavior Analysis* 10(2): 289-298.

Weiss, M.J. 2002. Hardiness and Social Support as Predictors of Stress in Mothers of Typical Children, Children With Autism, and Children With Mental Retardation. *Autism* 6(1): 115-130.

# Offshoots of Behavioral Treatment

### Pivotal Response Training

Ball, J. 1996. *Increasing social interactions of preschoolers with autism through relationships with typically developing peers*. Practicum Report, Nova Southeastern University. 52.

Benaron, L. 2006. Pivotal Response Intervention Model. *Pediatric Development and Behavior,* www.dbpeds.org, (accessed May 2, 2006).

Bruinsma, Y., R.L. Koegel, and L.K. Koegel, 2004. Joint Attention and Children With Autism: A Review of the Literature. *Mental Retardation and Developmental Disabilities* 10: 169-175.

Burke, J.C., and L. Cerniglia. 1990. Stimulus Complexity and Autistic Children's Responsivity: Assessing and Training a Pivotal Behavior. *Journal of Autism and Developmental Disorders* 20(2): 233-253.

Delprato, D.J. 2001. Comparisons of Discrete-Trial and Normalized Behavioral Language Intervention for Young Children With Autism. *Journal of Autism and Developmental Disorders* 31(3): 315-325.

Koegel, L.K., S.M. Camarata, M. Valdez-Menchaca, and R.L. Koegel. 1998. Setting Generalization of Question-Asking by Children With Autism. *American Journal on Mental Retardation* 102(4): 346-357.

Koegel, L.K., C.M. Carter, and R.L. Koegel. 2003. Teaching Children With Autism Self-Initiations as a Pivotal Response. *Topics in Language Disorders* 23(2): 134-145.

Koegel, L.K., et al. 1996. *Positive Behavioral Support: Including People with Difficult Behavior in the Community.* Baltimore, MD: Paul H. Brookes Publishing Co.

Koegel, L.K., R.L. Koegel, and C.M. Carter. 1998. Pivotal Responses and the Natural Language Teaching Paradigm. *Seminars in Speech and Language* 19(4): 355-371.

Koegel, L.K., R.L. Koegel, J.K. Harrower, and C.M. Carter. 1999. Pivotal Response Intervention I: Overview of Approach. *Journal of the Association for Persons with Severe Handicaps* 24(3): 174-185.

Koegel, L.K., R.L. Koegel, Y. Shoshan, and E. McNerney. 1999. Pivotal Response Intervention II: Preliminary Long-Term Outcome Data. *Journal of the Association for Persons with Severe Handicaps* 24(3): 186-198.

Koegel, R.L., S. Camarata, L.K. Koegel, A. Ben-Tall, and A.E. Smith. 1998. Increasing Speech Intelligibility in Children With Autism. *Journal of Autism and Developmental Disorders* 28(3): 241-251.

Koegel, R.L., et al. 1996. Collateral Effects of Parent Training on Family Interactions. *Journal of Autism and Developmental Disorders,* 26(3): 347-359.

Koegel, R.L., and W.D. Frea. 1993. Treatment of Social Behavior in Autism Through the Modification of Pivotal Social Skills. *Journal of Applied Behavior Analysis,* 26(3): 369-377.

Koegel, R.L., L.K. Koegel, and L.I. Brookman. 2003. Empirically supported pivotal response interventions for children with autism. In: A.E. Kazdin, *Evidence-based Psychotherapies for Children and Adolescents.* New York, NY: Guilford Press, 341-357.

Koegel, R.L., L.K. Koegel, and A. Surratt. 1992. Language Intervention and Disruptive Behavior in Preschool Children With Autism. *Journal of Autism and Developmental Disorders* 22(2): 141-153.

Koegel, R.L., L. Schreibman, A. Good, L. Cerniglia, C. Murphy, and L.K. Koegel. 1989. *How To Teach Pivotal Behaviors to Children With Autism: A Training Manual.* Santa Barbara, CA: University of California.

Koegel, R.L., J.B. Symon, and L.K. Koegel. 2002. Parent Education for Families of Children With Autism Living in Geographically Distant Areas. *Journal of Positive Behavior Interventions* 4(2): 88-103.

Koegel, R.L., G.A. Werner, L.A. Vismara, and L.K. Koegel. 2005. The Effectiveness of Consectually Supported Play Date Interactions Between Children With Autism and Typically Developing Peers. *Research and Practice for Persons With Severe Disabilities* 30(2): 93-102.

Laski, K.E., M.H. Charlop, and L. Schreibman. 1988. Training Parents to Use the Natural Language Pardigm to Increase Their Autistic Children's Speech. *Journal of Applied Behavior Analysis* 21(4): 391-400.

Pierce, K., and L. Schreibman. 1995. Increasing Complex Social Behaviors in Children With Autism: Effects of Peer-Implemented Pivotal Response Training. *Journal of Applied Behavior Analysis* 28(3): 285-295.

Pierce, K., and L. Schreibman. 1997. Using Peer Trainers to Promote Social Behavior in Autism: Are They Effective at Enhancing Multiple Social Modalities? *Focus on Autism and Other Developmental Disabilities* 12(4): 207-218.

Pierce, K., and L. Schreibman. 1997. Multiple Peer Use of Pivotal Response Training to Increase Social Behaviors of Classmates with Autism: Results from Trained and Untrained Peers. *Journal of Applied Behavior Analysis* 30(1): 157-160.

Schreibman, L., W.M. Kaneko, and R.L. Koegel. 1991. Positive Affect of Parents of Autistic Children: A Comparison Across Two Teaching Techniques. *Association for Advancement of Behavior Therapy* 22(4): 479-490.

Schreibman, L., and R.L. Koegel. 1996. Fostering self-management: Parent delivered pivotal response training for children with autistic disorder. In: E.D. Hibbs, and P.S. Jense, *Psychosocial Treatments for Child and Adolescent Disorders: Empirically Based Strategies for Clinical Practice.* Washington, DC: American Psychological Association, 525-552.

Schreibman, L., A.C. Stahmer, and K.L. Pierce. 1996. Alternative applications of pivotal response training: Teaching symbolic play and social interaction skills. In: L.K. Koegel, and R.L. Koegel, *Positive Behavioral Support: Including People With Diffcult Behavior in the Community.* Baltimore, MD: Paul H. Brookes Publishing Co., 353-371.

Stahmer, A.C. 1995. Teaching Symbolic Play Skills to Children With Autism Using Pivotal Response Training. *Journal of Autism and Developmental Disorders* 25(2): 123-141.

Stahmer, A.C. 1999. Using Pivotal Response Training to Facilitate Appropriate Play in Children With Autistic Spectrum Disorders. *Child Language Teaching and Therapy* 15(1): 29-40.

Stahmer, A.C., B. Ingersoll, and C. Carter. 2003. Behavioral Approaches to Promoting Play. *Autism* 7(4): 401-413.

Terpstra, J.E., K. Iggins, and T. Pierce. 2002. Can I Play? Classroom-Based Interventions for Teaching Play Skills to Children With Autism. *Focus on Autism and Other Developmental Disabilities* 17(2): 119-126, 128.

Thorp, D.M., A.C. Stahmer, and L. Schreibman. 1995. Effects of Sociodramatic Play Training on Children With Autism. *Journal of Autism and Developmental Disorders* 25(3): 265-282.

### Verbal Behavior

Braam, S.J., and A. Poling. 1983. Development of Intraverbal Behavior in Mentally Retarded Individuals Through Transfer of Stimulus Control Procedures: Classification of Verbal Responses. *Applied Research in Mental Retardation* (4): 279-301.

Carr, J.E., and A.M. Firth. 2005. The Verbal Behavior Approach to Early and Intensive Behavioral Intervention for Autism: A Call for Additional Empirical Support. *Journal of Early and Intensive Behavioral Intervention* 2(1): 18-27.

Drash, P.W., L.R. High, and R.M. Tudor. 1999. Using Mand Training to Establish an Echoic Repertoire in Young Children With Autism. *The Analysis of Verbal Behavior* 16: 29-44.

Drash, P.W., and R.M. Tudor. 2004. Is Autism a Preventable Disorder of Verbal Behavior? A Response to Five Commentaries. *The Analysis of Verbal Behavior* 20: 55-62.

Drash, P.W., and R.M. Tudor. 2004. An Analysis of Autism as a Contingency-Shaped Disorder of Verbal Behavior. *The Analysis of Verbal Behavior* 20: 5-23.

Miguel, C.F., J.E. Carr, and J. Michael. 2002. The Effects of a Stimulus-Stimulus Pairing Procedure on the Vocal Behavior of Children Diagnosed With Autism. *The Analysis of Verbal Behavior* 18: 3-13.

Oah, S., and A.M. Dickinson. 1989. A Review of Empirical Studies of Verbal Behavior. *The Analysis of Verbal Behavior* 7: 53-68.

Skinner, B.I. 1957. *Verbal Behavior.* New York, NY: Appleton-Centry-Crofts.

Sundberg, M.L. and J.W. Partington. 1998. *Teaching Language to Children With Autism or Other Developmental Disorders.* Danville, CA: Behavior Analysis, Inc.

Sundberg, M.L., M. Loeb, L. Hale, and P. Eigenheer. 2002. Contriving Establishing Operations to Teach Mands for Information. *The Analysis of Verbal Behavior* 18: 15-29.

### Positive Behavior Support

Boettcher, M., R.L. Koegel, E.K. McNerney, and L.K. Koegel. 2003. A Family-Centered Prevention Approach to PBS in a Time of Crisis. *Journal of Positive Behavior Interventions* 5(1): 55-59.

Buschbacher, P.W., and L. Fox. 2003. Understanding and Intervening With the Challenging Behavior of Young Children With Autism Spectrum Disorder. *Language, Speech and Hearing Services in Schools* 34(3): 217-227.

Carr, E.G., G. Dunlap, R.H. Horner, R.L. Koegel, A.P. Turnbull, W. Sailor, et al. 2002. Positive Behavior Support: Evolution of an Applied Science. *Journal of Positive Behavior Interventions* 4: 4-16, 20.

Durand, V.M., and N. Rost. 2005. Does It Matter Who Participates In Our Studies? *Journal of Positive Behavior Interventions* 7(3): 186-188.

Fucilla, R. 2005. Post-crisis Intervention for Individuals With Autism Spectrum Disorder. *Reclaiming Children and Youth* 14(1): 44-51.

Lucyshyn, J.M., and R.W. Albin. 2002. *Families and Positive Behavior Support: Addressing Problem Behavior in Family Contexts.* Baltimore, MD: Paul H. Brookes Publishing.

Marshall, J.K., and P. Mirenda. 2002. Parent Professional Collaboration for Positive Behavior Support in the Home. *Focus on Autism and Other Developmental Disabilities* 17(4): 216-228.

McCurdy, B.L., M.C. Manella, and N. Eldridge. 2003. Positive Behavior Support in Urban Schools: Can We Prevent the Escalation of Antisocial Behavior? *Journal of Positive Behavior Interventions* 5(3): 158-170.

Mulick, J.A., and E.M. Butter. 2005. Positive behavior support: A paternalistic utopian delusion. In: J.W. Jacoson, R.M. Foxx, and J.A. Mulick, *Controversial Therapies for Developmental Disabilities: Fad, Fashion, and Science in Professional Practice.* London, NJ: Lawrence Erlbaum Associates, 385-404.

Wehamn, T., and L. Gilkerson. 1999. Parents of Young Children With Special Needs Speak Out: Perceptions of Early Intervention Services. *Infant-Toddler Intervention: The Transdisciplinary Journal* 9(2): 137-167.

Zane, T. 2005. Fads in special education: An overview. In: J.W. Jacobson, R.M. Foxx, and J.A. Mulick, *Controversial Therapies for Developmental Disabilities: Fad, Fashion, and Science in Professional Practice.* London, NJ: Lawrence Erlbaum Associates, 175-192.

### Fluency Training

Binder, C. 1988. Precision Teaching: Measuring and Attaining Exemplary Academic Achievement. *Youth Policy* 10(7): 12-15.

Binder, C. 1993. Behavioral Fluency: A New Paradigm. *Educational Technology* 33(10): 8-14.

Fabrizio, M.A., S. Pahl, and A. Moors. 2002. Improving Speech Intelligibility Through Precision Teaching. *Journal of Precision Teaching and Celeration* 18(1): 25-27.

Fabrizio, M.A., and K. Schirmer. 2002. Teaching Visual Pattern Imitation to a Child With Autism. *Journal of Precision Teaching and Celeration* 18(1): 80-82.

Fabrizio, M.A., K. Schirmer, and K. Ferris. 2002. Tracking Curricular Progress With Precision. *Journal of Precision Teaching and Celeration* 18(2): 78-79.

Fabrizio, M.A., K. Schirmer, E. Vu, A. Diakite, and M. Yao. 2003. Analog Analysis of Two Variables Related to the Joint Attention of a Toddler With Autism. *Journal of Precision Teaching and Celeration* 19(1): 41-44.

King, A., A.L. Moors, and M.A. Fabrizio. 2003. Concurrently Teaching Multiple Verbal Operants Related to Preposition Use to a Child With Autism. *Journal of Precision Teaching and Celeration* 19(1): 38-40.

Moor, A., and M.A. Fabrizio. 2002. Using Tool Skill Rates to Predict Composite Skill Frequency Aims. *Journal of Precision Teaching and Celeration* 18(1): 28-29.

The Fluency Project, Inc., http://www.fluency.org, (accessed May 2, 2006).

Zambolin, K., M.A. Fabrizio, and S. Isley. 2004. Teaching a Child with Autism to Answer Informational Questions Using Precision Teaching. *Journal of Precision Teaching and Celeration* 20(1): 22-25.

# Other School-based Therapies (non-behavioral)

## TEACCH

Al Saad, S. 2000. Implementation of an Educational Program for Children With Autism: The Case of Kuwait. *International Journal of Mental Health* 29(2): 32-43.

Aoyama, S., 1995. The Efficacy of Structuring the Work System: Individualization of the Work Format and the Use of a 3-level Paper Rack in a Special Education Class. *Japanese Journal of Special Education* 32(5): 1-5.

Cox, R.D., and E. Schopler. 1993. Aggression and Self-injurious Behaviors in Persons with Autism: The TEACCH Approach. *International Journal of Child and Adolescent Psychiatry* 56(2): 85-90.

Durnik, M., J.M. Dougherty, and T. Andersson. 2000. Influence of the TEACCH program in Sweden. *International Journal of Mental Health* 29(1): 72-87.

Durham, C. 2000. Evolution of Services for People with Autism and Their Families in France: Influence of the TEACCH Program. *International Journal of Mental Health* 29(1): 22-34.

Fuentes, J., R. Barinaga, and I. Gallano. 2000. Applying TEACCH in Developing Autism Services in Sapin: The GAUTENA Project. *Internaltional Journal of Mental Health* 29(2):78-88.

Grindstaff, J.P. 2002. Further Evaluation of TEACCH's Experiential Training Programs. Change in Participants' Knowledge, Attributions and Use of Structure. *The Sciences and Engineering, Section B* 62(11-B): 5374.

Haussler, A. 1999. Parents' Attitudes and Experiences Regarding Treatment for Children With Autism: A Cross-national Study. *The Sciences and Engineering, Section B:* 59(7-B): 3734.

Howley, M., D. Preecem, and T. Arnold, 2001. Multidisciplinary Use of "Structured Teaching" to promote Consistency of Approach for Children With Autistic Spectrum Disorder. *Educational and Child Psychology* 18(2): 41-52.

Hungelmann, A.M. 2001. An Analysis of TEACCH-Based Home Programming for Young Children With Autism. *The Sciences and Engineering, Section B:* 61(10-B): 5567.

Jennett, H.K., S.L. Harris, and G.B. Mesibov. 2003. Commitment to Philosophy, Teacher Efficacy and Burnout Among Teachers of Children With Autism. *Journal of Autism and Developmental Disorders* 33(6): 583-593.

Keel, J.H., G. B. Mesibov, and A.V. Woods. 1997. TEACCH-Supported Employment Program. *Journal of Autism and Developmental Disorders* 27(1): 3-9.

Kielinen, M. 2002. Some Aspects of Treatment and Habilitation of Children and Adolescents With Autistic Disorder in Northern Finland. *International Journal of Circumpolar Health* 61(2): 69-79.

Kunce, L, and G.B. Mesibov. 1998. Educational approaches to high-functioning autism and asperger syndrome. In: E. Schopler, and G.B. Mesibov, *Asperger Syndrome or High-Functioning Autism?* New York, NY: Plenum Press, 227-261.

Lansing, M.D. 1989. Educational evaluation. In: Christopher Gillberg, *Diagnosis and Treatment of Autism.* New York, NY: Plenum Press, 151-166.

Lord, C., M.M. Bristol, and E. Schopler. 1993. Early Intervention for Children With Autism and Related Developmental Disorders. In: E. Schopler, and M.E. Van Bourgondien, *Preschool Issues in Autism.* New York, NY: Plenum Press, 199-221.

Lord, C., and E. Schopler. 1994. TEACCH Services for Preschool Children. In: S.L. Harris, and J.S. Handelman, eds. *Preschool Education Programs for Children With Autism.* Austin, TX: Pro-Ed, Inc, 87-105.

Magerotte, G. 2000. From Quality of Services to Quality of Life of Persons With Autism: Contributions to Research, Training and Community Services of the University of Mons-Hainaut. *International Journal of Mental Health* 29(2): 60-77.

Marcus, L.M. 1990. Training of Psychologists in Autism and Related Severe Development Disorders. In: Phyllis R. Magrab, and Paul Wohlford, *Improving Psychological Services for Children and Adolescents With Severe Mental Disorders: Clinical Training in Psychology.* Washington, DC: American Psychological Association, 133-137.

Marcus, L.M., M. Lansing, and E. Schopler. 1993. Assessment of Children With Autism and Pervasive Developmental Disorder. In: J.L. Culbertson, and D.J. Willis, *Testing Young Children: A Reference Guide for Developmental, Psychoeducational and Psychosocial Assessments.* Austin, TX: Pro-Ed, Inc., 319-344.

Marcus, L.M., and G.B. Mesibov. 1987. Comprehensive Services for Adolescents With Autism. *International Journal of Adolescent Medicine and Health* 3(2): 145-154.

Marcus, L.M., and E. Schopler. 1989. Parents as Co-Therapists With Autistic Children. In: Charles E. Schaefer, and James M. Briesmeister, *Handbook of Parent Training: Parents as Co-Therapists for Children's Behavior Problems.* Oxford, England: John Wiley and Sons, 337-360.

Mesibov, G.B. 1988. Diagnosis and Assessment of Autistic Adolescents and Adults. In: Eric Schopler, and Gary B. Mesibov, *Diagnosis and Assessment in Autism.* New York, NY: Plenum Press, 227-238.

Mesibov, G.B. 1994. A Comprehensive Program for Serving People With Autism and Their Families: The TEACCH Model. In: J.L. Matson, *Autism in Children and Adults: Etiology, Assessment and Intervention.* Belmont, CA: Brooks/Cole Publishing Co., 85-97.

Mesibov, G.B. 1997. Formal and Informal Measures on the Effectiveness of the TEACCH programme. *Autism* 1(1): 25-35.

Micheli, E. 2000. Dealing With the Reality of Autism: A Psychoeducational Program in Milan, Italy. *International Journal of Mental Health* 29(1): 50-71.

Mesibov, G.B., E. Schopler, and W. Caison. 1989. The Adolescent and Adult Psychoeducational Profile: Assessment of Adolescents and Adults With Severe Developmental Handicaps. *Journal of Autism and Developmental Disorders* 19(1): 33-39.

Mesibov, G.B., E. Schopler, and K.A. Hearsey. 1994. Structured Teaching. In: Eric Schopler, and Gary B. Mesibov, *Behavioral Issues in Autism*. New York, NY: Plenum Press, 195-207.

Ono, M., 1994. A Trial in Applying the TEACCH Program in a Children's Counseling Service. *Japanese Journal of Special Education* 31(5): 15-22.

Ozonoff, S., and K. Cathcart. 1998. Effectiveness of a Home Program Intervention for Young Children with Autism. *Journal of Autism and Developmental Disorders* 28(1): 25-32.

Panerai, S. J. 2002. Benefits of the Treatment and Education of Autistic and Communication Handicapped Children. *Intellectual Disability Research* 46(4): 318-327.

Panerai, S., L. Ferrante, and V. Caputo. 1997. The TEACCH Strategy in Mentally Retarded Children With Autism: A Multidimensional Assessment. Pilot Study. *Journal of Autism and Developmental Disorders* 27(3): 345-347.

Panerai, S., L. Ferrante, V. Caputo, and C. Impellizzeri. 1998. Use of Structured Teaching for Treatment of Children With Autism and Severe and Profound Mental Retardation. *Education and Training in Mental Retardation and Developmental Disabilities* 33(4): 367-374.

Peeters, T. 2000. The Role of Training in Developing Services for Persons With Autism and Their Families. *International Journal of Mental Health* 29(2):44-59.

Persson, B. 2000. A Longitudinal Study of Quality of Life and Independence Among Adult Men With Autism. Brief Report. *Journal of Autism and Developmental Disorders* 30(1): 61-66.

Porter M.E. 1980. Effect of Vocational Instruction on Academic Achievement. *Exceptional Children* 46(6): 463-464.

Preece, D., K. Lovett, and P. Lovett. 2000. The Adoption of TEACCH in Northamptonshire, UK. A Unique Collaboration Between a Voluntary Organization and a Local Authority. *International Journal of Mental Health* 29(2): 19-31.

Rogé, B. 2000. Meeting the Needs of Persons With Autism: A Regional Network Model. *International Journal of Mental Health* 29(1): 35-49.

Sasaki, M. 2000. Aspects of Autism in Japan Before and After the Introduction of TEACCH. *International Journal of Mental Health* 29(2): 3-18.

Schopler, E. 1986. A New Approach to Autism. *Social Science* 71(2-3): 183-185.

Schopler, E. 1987. Specific and Nonspecific Factors in the Effectiveness of a Treatment System. *American Psychologist* 42(4): 376-383.

Schopler, E. 1989. Principles for Directing Both Educational Treatment and Research. In: Christopher Gillberg, *Diagnosis and Treatment of Autism*. New York, NY: Plenum Press, 167-183.

Schopler, E. 1991. *Current and Past Research on Autistic Children and Their Families*. Conducted by Division TEACCH, Chapel Hill, NC: TEACCH, Research Report, ED 339161.

Schopler, E. 1994. Behavioral Priorities for Autism and Related Developmental Disorders. In: Eric Schopler, and Gary B. Mesibov, *Behavioral Issues in Autism*. New York, NY: Plenum Press, 55-77.

Schopler, E. 1998. Prevention and Management of Behavior Problems: The TEACCH Approach. In: E. Sanavio, *Behavior and Cognitive Therapy Today: Essays in Honor of Hans J. Eysenck*. Oxford, England: Elsevier Science Ltd., 249-259.

Schopler, E., and J.M. Hennike. 1990. Past and Present Trends in Residential Treatment. *Journal of Autism and Developmental Disorders* 20(3): 291-298.

Schopler, E., and G.B. Mesibov. 2000. Cross-Cultural Priorities in Developing Autism Services. *International Journal of Mental Health* 29(1): 3-21.

Schopler, E., G. Mesibov, and A. Baker. 1982. Evaluation of Treatment for Autistic Children and Their Parents. *Journal of the American Academy of Child Psychiatry* 21(3): 262-267.

Schopler, E., G.B. Mesibov, and K. Hearsey. 1995. Structured Teaching in the TEACCH System. In: Eric Schopler, and Gary B. Mesibov, *Learning and Cognition in Autism*. New York, NY: Plenum Press, 243-268.

Short, A.B., and E. Schopler. 1988. Factors Relating to Age of Onset in Autism. *Journal of Autism and Developmental Disorders* 18(2): 207-216.

Schultheis, S.F., B.B. Boswell, and J. Decker, 2000. Successful Physical Activity Programming for Students With Autism. *Focus on Autism and Other Developmental Disabilities* 15(3): 159-162.

Shulman, C. 2000. Services for Persons With Autism in Israel. *International Journal of Mental Health* 29(1): 88-97.

Sloan, J.L., and E. Schopler. 1977. Some Thoughts About Developing Programs for Autistic Adolescents. *Journal of Pediatric Psychology* 2(4): 187-190.

Smith, T. 1999. Outcome of Early Intervention for Children With Autism. *Clinical Psychology: Science and Practice* 6(1): 33-49.

Van Bourgondien, M.E. 1993. Behavior Management in the Preschool Years. In: Eric Schopler, and M. E. Van Bourgondien, *Preschool Issues in Autism*. New York, NY: Plenum Press, 129-145.

Van Bourgondien, M.E., N.C. Reichle, and E. Schopler. 2003. Effects of a Model Treatment Approach on Adults With Autism. *Journal of Autism and Developmental Disorders* 33(2): 131-140.

Van Bourgondien, M.E., and E. Schopler. 1990. Critical Issues in the Residential Care of People with Autism. *Journal of Autism and Developmental Disorders* 20(3): 391-399.

Wall, A.J. 1990. Group Homes in North Carolina for Children and Adults with Autism. *Journal of Autism and Developmental Disorders* 20(3): 353-366.

## The Playschool (Colorado Health Sciences Center)

Rogers, S.J. 1998. Empirically Supported Comprehensive Treatments for Young Children With Autism. *Journal of Clinical Child Psychology* 27(2): 168-179.

Rogers, S.J., and D.L. DiLalla. 1991. A Comparative Study of the Effects of a Developmentally Based Instructional Model on Young Children With Autism and Young Children With Other Disorders of Behavior and Development. *Topics in Early Childhood Special Education* 11(2): 29-47.

Rogers, S.J., J.M Herbison, H.C. Lewis, J. Pantone, and K. Reis. 1986. An Approach for Enchancing the Symbolic, Communicative, and Interpersonal Functioning of Young Children With Autism or Severe Emotional Handicaps. *Journal of the Division for Early Childhood* 10(2): 135-148.

Rogers, S.J., and H. Lewis. 1989. An Effective Day Treatment Model for Young Children With Pervasive Developmental Disorders. *The American Academy of Child and Adolescent Psychiatry* 28(2): 207-214.

Rogers, S., H.C. Lewis, and K. Reis. 1987. An Effective Procedure for Training Early Special Education Teams to Implement a Model Program. *Journal of the Division for Early Childhood* 11(2): 180-188.

Weiss, R.C. 1981. INREAL Intervention for Language Handicapped and Bilingual Children. *Journal of the Division of Early Childhood* 4: 40-51.

## Giant Steps

Kim, S., L. Richardson, G. Yard, M. Cleveand, and K. Keller. 1998. Giant Steps-St. Louis: An Alternative Intervention Model for Children with Autism. *Focus on Autism and Other Developmental Disabilities* 13(2): 101-107.

## Higashi/Daily Life Therapy

Larkin, A.S., and S. Gurry. 1998. Brief Report: Progress Reported in Three Children with Autism Using Daily Life Therapy. *Journal of Autism and Developmental Disorders* 28(4): 339-342.

Quill, K., S. Gurry, and A. Larkin. 1989. Daily Life Therapy: A Japanese Model for Educating Children With Autism. *Journal of Autism and Developmental Disorders* 19(4): 625-635.

Sallows, G. 2000. Educational Interventions for Children With Autism in the UK. *Early Child Development and Care* 163: 25-47.

Saegusa, T. 1991. The Providence of Nature: Teaching Autistic Children. *Educational Forum* 55(2): 139-153.

Smith, Tristram. 1996. Are Other Treatments Effective? In: C. Maurice, G. Green, and S. Luce, *Behavioral Intervention for Young Children With Autism: A Manual for Parents and Professionals.* Austin, TX: Pro-Ed Inc., 45-59.

## Walden Program

Elliott, R.O. Jr., et al. 1991. Analog Language Teaching Versus Natural Language Teaching: Generalization and Retention of Language Learning for Adults With Autism and Mental Retardation. *Journal of Autism and Developmental Disorders* 21(4): 433-447.

Farmer-Dougan, V. 1994. Increasing Requests by Adults With Developmental Disabilities Using Incidental Teaching by Peers. J*ournal of Applied Behavior Analysis* 27(3): 533-544.

Mc Gee, G.G., et al. 1985. The Facilitative Effects of Incidental Teaching on Preposition Use by Autistic Children. *Journal of Applied Behavior Analysis* 18(1): 17-31.

Mc Gee, G.G., et al. 1986. An Extension of Incidental Teaching Procedures to Reading Instruction for Autistic Children. *Journal of Applied Behavior Analysis* 19(2): 147- 157.

McGee, G.G., et al. 1992. Promoting Reciprocal Interactions via Peer Incidental Teaching. *Journal of Applied Behavior Analysis* 25(1): 117-126.

McGee, G.G., T. Daly, and H.A. Jacobs. 1994. The Walden Preschool. In: S. L. Harris, and J.S. Handleman, eds., *Preschool Education Programs for Children With Autism.* Austin, TX: Pro-Ed Inc.

McGee, G.G., M.J. Morrier, T. Daly, 1999. An Incidental Teaching Approach to Early Intervention for Toddlers With Autism. *Journal of the Association for Persons With Severe Handicaps,* 24(3): 133-146.

Miranda-Linne, F., and L. Melin. 1992. Acquisition, Generalization and Spontaneous Use of Color Adjectives: A Comparison of Incidental Teaching and Traditional Discrete-Trial Procedures for Children With Autism. *Research in Developmental Disabilities* 13(3): 191-210.

Parisy, D. 1999. Early Intervention: The View From a Distance. *Journal of the Association for Persons With Severe Handicaps* 24(3): 226-229.

Stahmer, A.C., and B. Ingersoll. 2004. Inclusive Programming for Toddlers With Autism Spectrum Disorders: Outcomes From the Children's Toddler School. *Journal of Positive Behavior Interventions* 6(2): 67-82.

# Child-lead Parent-facilitated Therapies

## Greenspan/ Developmental, Individual Difference Relationship Model (DIR) Floor-Time

Greenspan, S.I. 1992. *Infancy and early childhood: The practice of clinical assessment and intervention with emotional and developmental challenges.* Madison, CT: International Universities Press.

Greenspan S.I. 1993. Autism: AKA Communication Disorder. *Journal of the American Academy of Child and Adolescent Psychiatry* 32(1): 221-222.

Greenspan, S. I. 1997. "Autism": Comment. *New England Journal of Medicine* 337(21): 1556.

Greenspan, S.I. 2000. Children With Autistic Spectrum Disorders: Individual Differences, Affect, Interaction, and Outcomes. *Psychoanalytic Inquiry* 20(5): 675-703.

Greenspan, S. I., and G.A. DeGangi. 1988. The Development of Sensory Functions in Infants. *Physical and Occupational Therapy in Pediatrics* 8(4): 21-33.

Greenspan, S. I., G.A. DeGangi, and R.A. Berk. 1988. The Clinical Measurement of Sensory Functioning in Infants: A Preliminary Study. *Physical and Occupational Therapy in Pediatrics* 8(2-3): 1-23.

Greenspan, S.I., and S. Wieder. 1997. Developmental Patterns and Outcomes in Infants and Children With Disorders in Relating and Communicating: A Chart Review of 200 Cases of Children With Autistic Spectrum Diagnoses. *Journal of Developmental and Learning Disorders* 1(1): 87-141.

Greenspan, S.I., and S. Wieder. 1999. A Functional Developmental Approach to Autism Spectrum Disorders. *Journal of the Association for Persons with Severe Handicaps* 24(3): 147-161.

Greenspan, S.I., and S.Wieder. 2000. A developmental approach to difficulties in relating and communicating in autism spectrum disorders and related syndromes. In: A.M. Wetherby, and B.M. Prizont, *Autism Spectrum Disorders: A Transactional Developmental Perspective.* Baltimore, MD: Paul H. Brookes Publishing Co., 279-306.

Greenspan, S.I., S. Wieder, and R. Simons. 1998. *The child with special needs: Encouraging intellectual and emotional growth.* Reading, MA: Addison-Wesley/Addison Wesley Longman, Inc.

Guralnick, M., ed. 1999. *Clinical practice guideline: Report of the Recommendations. Autism/ Pervasive Developmental Disorders, Assessment and Intervention for Young Children* (age 0-3 years). Albany (NY): New York State Department of Health, IV-15 to 21, IV-24.

Wieder, S., and S.I. Greenspan. 2003. Climbing the Symbolic Ladder in the DIR Model Through Floor Time/Interactive Play. *Autism* 7(4): 425-435.

## Son-Rise /Options Institute

Egan, C.  Personal communication, April 14, 2000.

Kaufman, B.N. 1994. Son-Rise: The Miracle Continues. *SKOLE: The Journal of Alternative Education,* 11(2): 93-104.

Kaufman, N., and S.L. Kaufman. 1997.  The 'HEART" of What We Teach. In: *The Son-Rise Program.*  Sheffield, MA: Option Institute.

Williams, K.R., and J.G. Wishart. 2003. The Son-Rise program intervention for Autism: An investigation into family experiences. *Journal of Intellectual Disbility Research* 47(4-5): 291-299.

## Relationship Development Intervention

Gustein, S.E. 2002. *The Effectiveness of RDI*: *Preliminary Evaluation of the Relationship Development Intervention Program,*  The Connections Center, Houston, TX, 2-14. http://www. rdiconnect.com, (accessed on Apr. 4, 2006).

Gustein, S.E. 2004.  The Effectiveness of Relationship Development Intervention in Remediating Core Deficits of Autism-Spectrum Children. *Journal of Developmental and Behavioral Pediatrics* 25(5): 375.

Gutstein, S.E., and R. Sheely. 2002. *Relationship Development Intervention Activities for Young Children.*  London,UK: Jessica Kingsley Publications.

Gustein, S.E., and R. Sheely. n.d.  *Introductory guide for parents, going to the heart of autism, asperger syndrome and pervasive development disorder,* www.rdiconnect.com, (accessed on Oct. 25, 2005).

Gutstein, S.E., and R. Sheely. 2002 (a).  *Relationship Development Intervention With Young Children, Social and Emotional Development Activities for Asperger Syndrome, Autism, PDD and NLD.*  London, UK: Jessica Kingsley Publications.

Gutstein, S.E., and R. Sheely. 2002 (b). *Relationship Development Intervention With Older Children, Adolescents and Adults: Social and Emotional Development Activities for Asperger Syndrome, Autism, PPD and NLD.*  London, UK: Jessica Kingsley Publications.

## Learning to Speak/Zelazo Program

Zelazo, P.R. 1984. *Learning to Speak: A Manual for Parents.*  Hillsdale, NJ: Lawrence Erlbaum Associates, Inc.

Zelazo, P. R. 1997.  Infant-Toddler Information Processing Treatment of Children with Pervasive Developmental Disorder and Autism: Part II. *Infants and Young Children* 10(2): 1-13

# Biomedical Therapies

## Diet/Nutrition Therapy (Gluten and Casein-Free Diet)

Adams, L., and S. Conn. 1997. Nutrition and Its Relationship to Autism. *Focus on Autism and Other Developmental Disabilities* 12(1): 3-58.

Arnold, G.L. 2003. Plasma Amino Acids Profiles in Children With Autism: Potential Risk of Nutritional Deficiencies. *Journal of Autism and Developmental Disroders* 33(4): 449-454.

Arnold, G.L., S.L. Hyman, and R.A. Mooney. 1998. Amino Acid Profiles in Autism. *American Journal of Human Genetics* (63): A262.

Barrett, S. 1985. Commercial Hair Analysis Science or Scam? *Journal of the American Medical Association* 254(8): 1041-1045.

Bidet, B., M. Leboyer, B. Descours, and M.P. Bouvard. 1993. Allergic Sensitization in Infantile Autism. *Journal of Autism and Developmental Disorders* 23(2): 419-420.

Bird, B. L., D.C. Russo, and M.F. Cataldo. 1977. Considerations in the Analysis and Treatment of Dietary Effects on Behavior: A Case Study. *Journal of Autism Child Schizophrenia* 7(4): 373-382.

Birtwistle, S. 2000. Autism and a Gluten and Casein Free Diet. *Nutritional Perspectives* 23(2): 8-9.

Bliumina, M.G. 1975. A Schizophrenia-like Variant of Phenylketonuria. *Zh Nevropatol Psikhiatr Im S. S. Korsakova* 75(10): 1525-1529.

Bowers, L. 2002. An Audit of Referrals of Children With Autistic Spectrum Disorder to the Dietetic Service. *Journal of Human Nutritional Dietetics* 15: 261-269.

Brudnak, M.A. 2001. Application of Genomeceuticals to the Molecular and Immunological Aspects of Autism. *Medical Hypotheses* 57(2): 186-191.

Cocchi, R. 1996. On Gluten-free and Casein-free Diet in Autism and the Opioids' Excess Theory: Another Perspective. *Italian Journal of Intellective Impairment* 9(2): 139-152, 203-218.

Coleman, M., and J.P. Blass. 1985. Autism and Lactic Acidosis. *Journal of Autism and Developmental Disorders* 15: 1-8.

Cook, R. 1997. Use of Orthomolecular Therapy for Those With Behavioural Problems and Mental Handicap: A Review. *Complementary Therapies in Medicine 5(4): 228-232.*

Cornish, E. 2002. Gluten and Casein Free Diets in Autism: A Study of the Effects on Food Choice and Nutrition. *Journal of Human Nutrition and Dietetics* 15(4): 261-269.

Cunningham, E. 2001. Question of the Month: Is There Any Research to Support a Gluten and Casein-free Diet For a Child That is Diagnosed With Autism? *Journal of the American Dietetic Association* 101(2): 222.

Del Giudice-Asch, G., L. Simon, J. Schmeidler, C. Cunningham-Rundles, and E. Hollander. 1999. Brief Report: A Pilot Open Clinical Trial of Intravenous Immunoglobulin in Childhood Autism. *Journal of Autism and Developmental Disorders* 29(2): 157-160.

Dennis, M. 1999. Intelligence Patterns Among Children With High-functioning Autism, Phenylketonuria, and Childhood Head Injury. *Journal of Autism and Developmental Disorders* 29(1): 5-17.

Desorgher, S. 2000. Autism--Dietary Treatment Options. *Positive Health* 57: 37-40.

Dietary Supplements Seized After Autism Claims. 2003. *FDA Consumer* 37(1): 4.

Dohan, F.C. 1969. Is Celiac Disease a Clue to the Pathogenesis of Schizophrenia? *Mental Hygiene* 53(4): 525-529.

Elder, J.H. 2002. Current Treatments in Autism: Examining Scientific Evidence and Clinical Implications. *Journal of. Neuroscience Nursing* 34(2): 67-73.

Evangeliou, A., J. Vlachonikolis, H. Mihailidou, M. Spilioti, A. Skarpalezou, N. Makaronas, et al. 2003. Application of a Ketogenic Diet in Children With Autistic Behavior: Pilot Study. *Journal of Child Neurology* 18(2): 113-118.

Feingold, B.F. 1979. Dietary Management of Nystagmus. *Journal of Neural Transmission* 45(2): 107-115.

Garvey, J. 2002. Diet In Autism and Associated Disorders. *Journal of Family Health Care* 12(2): 34-38.

Gemmell, M., and C. Chambliss. 1997. Effects of a Gluten-free Diet on Rate of Achievement in Autistic Children in an Applied Behavioral Analysis Program. *Research Report,* ED 406761: 12.

Goldberg, E.A. 2004. The Link Between Gastroenterology and Autism. *Gastroenterology Nursing* 27(1): 16-19.

Guralnick, M. ed. 1999. *Clinical practice guideline: Report of the Recommendations. Autism/ Pervasive Developmental Disorders, Assessment and Intervention for Young Children* (age 0-3 years). Albany (NY): New York State Department of Health, IV-104.

Hansen, C. 2003. Are Our Children What they Eat? *Children's Voice* 12(2): 30-34.

Hecht, M.Z. 2003. Dietary Interventions for Children With Autism. *Exceptional Parent* 33(2): 22-23.

Heflin, L.J., and R.L. Simpson. 1998. Interventions for Children and Youth with Autism: Prudent Choices in a World of Exaggerated Claims and Empty Promises. Part 1: Intervention and Treatment Option Review. *Focus on Autism and Other Developmental Disabilities* 13(4): 194-211.

Horvath, K., J.C. Papadimitriou, A. Rabsztyn, C. Drachenber, and J.T. Tildon. 1999. Gastrointestinal Abnormalities in Children With Autistic Disorder. *Journal of Pediatrics* 135: 559-563.

Howlin, P. 1997. Prognosis in Autism: Do Specialist Treatments Affect Long-term Outcome? *European Child Adolescent Psychiatry* 6(2): 55-72.

Hyman, S.L., and S.E. Levy. 2000. Autism Spectrum Disorders: When Traditional Medicine Is Not Enough. *Contemporary Pediatrics* 17:101-116.

Isaacson, R.H., M.M. Moran, A. Hall, B.J. Harman, and M.S. Prehosovich. 1996. Autism: A Retrospective Outcome Study of Nutrient Therapy. *Journal of Applied Nutrition* 48(4): 110-118.

Israngkun, P.P., H.A.L. Newman, S.T. Patel, V.A. Duruibe, and A. Abuissa. 1986. Potential Biochemical Marks for Infantile Autism. *Neurochemical Pathology* 5: 51-70.

Kane, P.C., and E. Kane. 1997. Peroxisomal Disturbances in Autistic Spectrum Disorder. *Journal of Orthomolecular Medicine* 12: 207-218.

Kane, P. 1997. Ask the Physician. Reversing Autism With Nutrition. *Alternative Medicine Digest* (19): 36-40, 42-44.

Kidd, P.M. 2002. Autism, An Extreme Challenge to Integrative Medicine. Part II: Medical Managment. *Alternative Medicine Review* 7(6): 472-499.

Kidd, P.M. 2003. An Approach to the Nutritional Management of Autism. *Alternative Therapies-Health and Medicine* 9(5): 22-31.

Kirk, S.A., J.J. McCarthy, and W.D. Kirk. 1961. *Illinois Test of Psycholinguistic Abilities (ITPA)*. Urbana, IL: University of Illinois Press.

Knivsberg, A.M. 2001. Reports on Dietary Intervention in Autistic Disorders. *Nutritional Neuroscience* 4(1): 25-37.

Knivsberg, A.M., K.L. Reichelt, T. Hoien, and M. Nodland. 2002. A Randomised, Controlled Study of Dietary Intervention in Autistic Syndromes. *Nutritional Neurosciencen* 5(4): 251-261.

Knivsberg, A.M., K.L. Reichelt, M. Nodland, and T. Hoien. 1995. Autistic Syndromes and Diet: A Follow-up Study. *Scandinavian Journal of Educational Research* 39(3): 223-236.

Knivsberg, A.M., K. Wiig, G. Lind, M. Nodland, et al. 1990. Dietary Intervention in Autisitic Syndromes. *Brain Dysfunction* 3(5-6): 315-327.

Kozlowski, B.W. 1992. Megavitamin Treatment of Mental Retardation in Children: A Review of Effects on Behavior and Cognition. *Journal of Child and Adolescent Psychopharmacology* 2(4): 307-320.

Krueger, A. 2003. Alternative Remedies: They Work for You, But Are They Safe for Your Kids? *Alternative Medicine* 5: 70-74, 121.

LaPerchia, P. 1987. Behavioral Disorders, Learning Disabilities and Megavitamin Therapy. *Adolescence* 22(87): 729-738.

Levy, S.E. 2002. Alternative/Complementary Approaches to Treatment of Children With Autistic Spectrum Disorders. *Infants and Young Children* 14(3): 33-42.

Lovaas, O.I. 1979. Contrasting Illness and Behavioral Models for the Treatment of Autistic Children: A Historical Perspective. *Journal of Autism and Developmental Disorders* 9(4): 315-323.

Lucarelli, S., T. Frediani, A.M. Zingoni, F. Ferruzzi, O. Giardini, F. Quintieri, M. Barbato, P. D'Eufemia, and E. Cardi. 1995. Food Allergy and Infantile Autism. *Panminerva-Medica* 37(3): 137-141.

McCarthy, D.M., and M. Coleman. 1979. Response of Intestinal Mucosa to Gluten Challenge in Autistic Subjects. *Lancet* 27(2)(8148): 877-878.

Millward, C. 2004. Gluten and Casein-free Diets for Autistic Spectrum Disorder. *Cochrane Database of Systematic Reviews* (2): CD003498.

Neil, K. 2003. The Nutrition Practitioner. Nutritional Support for Children With Autism. *Positive Health* 92: 30.

Nickel, R.E. 1996. Controversial Therapies for Young Children With Developmental Disabilities. *Infants and Young Children* 8(4): 29-40.

O'Banion, D., B. Armstrong, R.A. Cummings, and J. Stange. 1978. Disruptive Behavior: A Dietary Approach. *Journal for Autism and Childhood Schizophrenia* 8(3): 325-337.

Parks, S.L. 1983. Psychometric Instruments Available for the Assessment of Autistic Children. *Journal of Autism and Development Disabilities* 9: 255- 267.

Pavone, L., A. Fiumara , G. Bottaro, D. Mazzone, and M. Coleman. 1997. Autism and Celiac Disease: Failure to Validate the Hypothesis That a Link Might Exist. *Biological Psychiatry* 42(1): 72-75.

Pontino, J.L., K. Schaal, and C. Chambliss. 1998. Effects of a Gluten-free Diet on Rate of Learning in Autistic Children in an Applied Behavioral Analysis Program: Summary Analysis. *Research Report* ED 413689: 35.

Position of the American Dietetic Association: Nutrition in Comprehensive Program Planning for Persons with Developmental Disabilities. 1992. *Journal of The American Dietetic Association* 92(5): 613-615.

Raven, J.C. 1958. *Raven Progressive Matrices.* London: H.K. Lewis.

Reichelt, K.L. 1991. Gluten-free Diet in Infantile Autism. Comment on E. Sponheim's Communication in Tidsskriftet. *Tidsskriftfor Norske Laegeforening* 111(11): 1406.

Reichelt, K.L. 1991. Gluten-free Diet in Infantile Autism. *Tidsskriftfor Norske Laegeforening* 111(10): 1286-1287.

Reichelt, K.L., H.K. Hamberfer, and G. Saelid. 1981. Biologically Active Peptide Containing Fractions in Schizophrenia and Childhood Autism. *Advances in Biochemical Psychopharmacology* 28: 627-643.

Reichelt, K.L., A.M. Knivsberg, G. Lind, and M. Nodland. 1991. Probable Etiology and Possible Treatment of Childhood Autism. *Brain Dysfunction* 4(6): 308-319.

Reichelt, K.L., A.M. Knivsberg, M. Nodland, and G. Lind. 1994. Nature and Consequences of Hyperpeptiduria and Bovine Casomorphins Found in Autistic Syndromes. *Developmental Brain Dysfunction* 7:71-85.

Reichelt, K.L. and Y. Liu. 1997. Exorphins, Serotonin Uptake Stimulatory Peptides and Autism. *Italian Journal of Intellectual Impairment* 10(2): 107-114, 161-169.

Reichelt, K.L., G. Saelid, T. Lindback, et al. 1986. Childhood Autism: A Complex Disorder. *Biological Psychiatry* (21): 1279-1290.

Reichelt, K.L., H. Scott, A.M Knivsberg, K. Wiig, G. Lind, and M. Nodland. 1990. Childhood autism: A group of hyperpeptidergic disorders. Possible etiology and tentative treatment. In: F. Nyberg, and V. Brandtl, eds., *Beta-Casomorphins and Related Peptides*. Uppsala: Fyrris Tryck, 163- 173.

Reid, J.S. 2004. Can Enzymes help Your Child With Autism? *Exceptional Parent* 34(2): 25-27.

Risebro B. 1991. Gluten-free Diet in Infantile Autism. *Tidsskriftfor Norske Laegeforening* 111(15): 1885-1886.

Seroussi, K. 2000. *Unraveling the Mystery of Autism and Pervasive Developmental Disorder: A Mother's Story of Research and Recovery.* New York: Simon and Shuster.

Seroussi, K. 2000. We Cured Our Son's Autism. *Parents* 75(2):118-120, 123-125.

Smith, T., J., and M. Antlovich. 2000. Parental Perceptions of Supplemental Interventions Received by Young Children With Autism in Intensive Behavior Analytic Treatment. *Behavioral Interventions* 15: 83-97.

Sponheim, E. 1991. Gluten-free Diet in Infantile Autism. A Therapeutic Trial. *Tidsskriftfor Norske Laegeforening* 111(6):704-707.

Tafjord, M. 1982. *Obevasjon av fornutsetnnninger for lek og aktivitet, observasjonsskjema.* [Observation of prerequisites for play and activity: Observation schedule]. Oslo: College for Special Education Training.

Taylor, D. 2000. Essential Fatty Acids, Diet and Developmental Disorders. *Positive Health* (52): 37-40.

Torisky, D.M., C.V. Torisky, S. Kaplan, and C. Spelcher. 1993. The NAC Pilot Project: A Model for Nutrition Screening and Intervention for Developmentally Disabled Children with Behavior Disorders. *Journal of Orthomolecular Medicine* 8(1): 25-42.

Whiteley, P., R. Jacqui, D. Savery, and P. Shatock. 1999. A Gluten-free Diet as an Intervention for Autism and Associated Spectrum Disorders: Preliminary Findings. *Autism* 3(1): 45-65.

Whiteley, P. 2001. Autism Unravelled Conference: The Biology of Autism Unravelled. *Expert Opinion on Pharmacotherapy* 2(7): 1191-1193.

## Chelation Therapy

Committee on Children With Disabilities. 2001. Technical Report. The Pediatrician's Role in the Diagnosis and Management of Autistic Spectrum Disorder in Children. *Pediatrics* 107(5): 1-18.

Gentile, P.S., M.J. Trentalange, W. Zamichek, and M. Coleman. 1983. Brief Report: Trace Elements in the Hair of Autistic and Control Children. *Journal of Autism and Developmental Disorders* 13(2): 205-206.

Hallaway, N., and Z. Strauts. 1995. *Turning Lead into Gold: How Heavy Metal Poisoning Can Affect Your Child and How to Prevent and Treat It*. Vancouver, BC: New Star Books.

Heath, A. 1979. Psychiatric Drug Treatment in Children. *Journal of the Maine Medical Association* 70(5): 181-189.

Hurd, L. 2002. PCA-Rx: Restoring Health and Detoxifying Your Body. *Total Health Magazine* 24(4): 38-40.

Kidd, P.M., 2002. Autism, An Extreme Challenge to Integrative Medicine. Part II: Medical Management. *Alternative Medicine Review,* 7(6): 472-499.

Kimhi, R, Y, Barak, T. Schlezinger, P. Sirota, and A. Elizur. 1999. Vanadium Concentrations in Autistic Subjects. *New Trends in Experimental and Clinical Psychiatry* 15(4): 205-207.

Lane, W.G. 2001. Screening for Elevated Blood Lead Levels in Children. *American Journal of Preventative Medicine* 20(1): 78-82, www.acpm.org/pol_practice.htm#several (accessed Feb. 16, 2006).

Lelord, G., J.P. Muh, C. Barthelemy, and J. Martineau. 1981, Effects of Pyridoxine and Magnesium on Autistic Symptoms--Initial Observations. *Journal of Autism and Developmental Disorders* 11(2): 219-230.

Levy, S.E. 2002. Alternative/Complementary Approaches to Treatment of Children With Autistic Spectrum Disorders. *Infants and Young Children* 14(3): 33-42.

Massaro ,T.F., D.J. Raiten, and C.H. Zuckerman. 1983. Trace Element Concentrations and Behavior: Clinical Utility in the Assessment of Developmental Disabilities. *Topics in Early Childhood Special Education* 3(2): 55-61.

Porterm C. 2003. Heavy Metal Toxicity and Mercury Detoxification: The Secret Life of Mercury. *Informed Choice* 1(2): 18-22.

Raiten, D.J., T.F. Massaro, and C. Zuckerman. 1984. Vitamin and Trace Element Assessment of Autistic and Learning Disabled Children. *Nutrition and Development Disabilities* 2: 9-17.

Rimland, B. 1988. Controversies in the Treatment of Autistic Children; Vitamin and Drug Therapy. *Journal of Child Neurology* 3: S68-72.

Rimland, B., and G.E. Larson. 1983. Hair Mineral Analysis and Behavior: An Analysis of 51 Studies. *Journal of Learning Disabilities* 16(5): 279-285.

Shannon, M. 2003. Children's Environmental Health: One Year In A Pediatric Environmental Health Specialty Unit. *Ambulatory Pediatrics* 3(1): 53-56.

Shearer, T.R., K. Larson, J. Neuschwander, and B. Gedney. 1982. Minerals in the Hair and Nutrient Intake of Autistic Children. *Journal of Autism and Developmental Disorders* 12(1): 25-34.

Sohler, A., M. Kruesi, and C.C. Pfeiffer. 1977. Blood Lead Levels in Psychiatric Outpatients Reduced by Zinc and Vitamin C. *Journal of Orthomolecular Psychiatry* 6(3): 272-276.

Tolbert, L, T. Haigler, M.M. Waits, and T. Dennis. 1993. Brief Report: Lack of Response in an Autistic Population to a Low Dose Clinical Trial of Pyridozine Plus Magnesium. *Journal of Autism and Developmental Disorders* 23(1): 193-199.

Wecker, L., S.B. Miller, S.R. Cochran, and D.L. Dugger. 1985. Trace Element Concentrations in Hair From Autistic Children. *Journal of Mental Deficiency Research* 29(1): 15-22.

Yung, C.Y. 1984. A Synopsis on Metals in Medicine and Psychiatry. *Pharmacology, Biochemistry and Behavior* 21(1): 41-47.

# Intervenous Immunoglobulin Therapy

AAP Policy Statement. 2005. Counseling Families Who Choose Complementary and Alternative Medicare for Their Child With Chronic Illness or Disability. *Pediatrics* 107(3): 598-601, http.//aappolicy/aappublications.org, (accessed aug. 17, 2005).

Bristol-Powers, M. 2001. The etiology of autism and NICHD research. National Institute of Child Health and Human Development. Washington, DC: National Academy of Sciences.

DelGiudice-Asch, G., L. Simon, J. Schmeidler, C. Cunningham-Rundles, and E. Hollander. 1999. Brief Report: A Pilot Open Clinical Trial of Intravenous Immunoglobulin in Childhood Autism. *Journal of Autism and Developmental Disorders* 29(2): 157-160.

Gupta, S. 1999. Treatment of Children With Autism With Intravenous Immunoglobulin [letter; comment]. *Journal of Child Neurology* 14(3): 203-205.

Gupta, S., S. Aggarwal, and C. Heads. 1996. Dysregulated Immune System in Children With Autism: Beneficial Effects of Intravenous Immune Globulin on Autistic Characteristics. *Journal of Autism and Developmental Disorders* 26(4): 439-452.

Guralnick, M., ed., 1999. *Clinical Practice Guideline: Report of the Recommendations. Autism/ Pervasive Developmental Disorders, Assessment and Intervention for Young Children* (age 0-3 years). Albany (NY): New York State Department of Health, IV-91.

Hyman, S., and S. Lery. 2000. Autism Spectrum Disorders: When Traditional Medicine is Not Enough. *Contemporary Pediatrics* 10:101.

Piloplys, A.V. 1998. Intravenous Immunoglobulin Treatment of Children With Autism [see comments]. *Journal of Child Neurology* 13(2): 79-82.

Piloplys, A.V. 1999. Response to Letter by Dr. Gupta Concerning The Treatment of Autistic Children With Intravenous Immunoglobulin. *Journal of Child Neurology* 14(3): 203-205.

Singh, V.K., H.H. Fudenberg, D. Emerson, and M. Coleman. 1998. Immunodiagnosis and Immuotherapy in Autistic Children. *Annual. New.York Academy of Science* 540: 602-604.

## Secretin

Carey, T., K. Ratliff-Schaub, J. Funk, C. Weinle, M. Myers, and J. Jenks. 2002. Double-Blind Placebo-Controlled Trial of Secretin: Effects on Aberrant Behavior in Children With Autism. *Journal of Autism and Developmental Disorders* 32(30): 161-167.

Chez, M.G., and C.P. Buchanan. 2000. Reply to B. Rimland's "Comments on Secretin and Autism: A Two-Part Clinical Investigation." *Journal of Autism and Developmental Disorders* 30(2).

Chez, M.G., C.P. Buchanan, B.T. Bagan, M.S. Hammer, K.S. McCarthy, I. Ovrutskaya, C.V. Nowinski, and Z.S. Cohen. 2000. Secretin and Autism: A Two-part Clinical Investigation. *Journal of Autism and Developmental Disorders* 30(2):87-94.

Committee on Children With Disabilities, Technical Report. 2001. The Pediatrician's Role in the Diagnosis and Management of Autistic Spectrum Disorder in Children. *Pediatrics* 107(5): 1-18.

Coniglio, S.J., J.D. Lewis, C. Lang, T.G. Burns, R. Subhani-Siddique, A. Weintraub, H. Schub, and E.W. Holden. 2001. A Randomized, Double-blind, Placebo-controlled Trial of Single-dose Intravenous Secretin as Treatment for Children With Autism. *Journal of Pediatrics* 138(5): 649-655.

Coplan, J., M.C. Souders, A.E. Mulberg, J.K. Belchic, J. Wray, A.F. Jawad, P.R. Gallagher, R. Mitchell, M. Gerdes, and S.E. Levy. 2003. Children With Autistic Spectrum Disorders. II: Parents Are Unable to Distinguish Secretin from Placebo Under Double-blind Conditions. *Archives of Disease in Childhood* 88(8): 737-739.

Corbett, B., K. Khan, D. Czapansky-Beilman, N. Brady, P. Dropik, D.Z. Goldman, K. Delany, H. Sharp, I. Mueller, E. Shapiro, and R. Ziegler. 2001. A Double-blind, Placebo-controlled Crossover Study Investigating the Effect of Pocine Secretin in Children With Autism. *Clinical Pediatrics* 40(6): 327-331.

Dunn-Geier, J., H.H. Ho, E. Auersperg, D. Doyle, L. Eaves, C. Matsuba, E. Orrbine, B. Pham, and S. Whiting. 2000. Effect of Secretin on Children With Autism: A Randomized Controlled Trial. *Developmental Medicine and Child Neurology* 42(12): 796-802.

Guralnick, M., ed., 1999. *Clinical Practice Guideline: Report of the Recommendations. Autism/ Pervasive Developmental Disorders, Assessment and Intervention for Young Children* (age 0-3 years). Albany (NY): New York State Department of Health, IV-87.

Herlihy, W.C. 2000. Secretin: Cure or Snake Oil for Autism in the New Millennium? (response) [letter: comment]. *Journal of Pediatric Gastroenterology and Nutritition* 30(2):112-113; discussion 113-114.

Honomichl, R.D., B.L. Goodlin-Jones, M.M. Burnham, R.L. Hanse, and T.F. Anders. 2002. Secretin and Sleep in Children With Autism. *Child Psychatry and Human Development* 33(2): 107-123.

Horvath, K., G. Stefanatos, K.N. Sokolski, R. Wachtel, L. Nabors, and J.T. Tildon. 1998. Improved Social and Language Skills After Secretin Administration in Patients With Autistic Spectrum Disorders. *Journal of the Association for Academic Minority Physicians* 9(1):9-15.

Jun, S.S., P.C.H. Kao, and Y.C. Lee. 2000. Double Blind Crossover Study of Secretin/Secrepan Treatment for Children With Autistic Symptoms. *Tzu Chi Medical Journal* 12(3): 173-181.

Kern, J.K., S. Van Miller, P.A. Evans, and M.H. Trivedi. 2002. Efficacy of Porcine Secretin in Children With Autism and Pervasive Developmental Disorder. *Journal of Autism and Developmental Disorders* 32(3): 153-160.

Levy, S.E., M.C. Souders, J. Wray, A.F. Jawad, P.R. Gallagher, J. Coplan, J.K. Belchic, M. Gerdes, R. Michell, and A.E. Mulberg. 2003. Children With Autistic Spectrum Disorders. I: Comparison of Placebo and Single Dose of Human Synthetic Secretin. *Archives of Disease in Childhood* 88(8): 731-736.

Lonsdale, D., and R.J. Schamberger. 2000. A Clinical Study of Secretin in Autism and Pervasive Developmental Delay. *Journal of Nutritional and Environmental Medicicne* 10(4): 271-280.

Molloy, C.A., P. Manning-Courtney, S. Swayne, J. Bean, J.M. Brown, D.S. Murray, A.M. Kinsman, M. Brasington, and C.D. Ulrich. 2002. Lack of Benefit of Intravenous Synthetic Human Secretin in the Treatment of Autism. *Journal of Autism and Developmental Disorders* 32(6): 545-551.

Owley, T., W. McMahon, E.H. Cook, T. Laulhere, M. South, L.Z. Mays, E.S. Shernoff, I. Lainhart, C.B. Modahl, C. Corsello, S. Ozonoff, S. Risi, C. Lord, B.L. Leventhal, and P.A. Filipek. 2001. Multisite, Double-blind, Placebo-Controlled Trial of Porcine Secretin in Autism. *Journal of the American Academy of Child and Adolescent Psychiatry* 40(11): 1293-1299.

Policy Statement. 2005. American Academy of Child and Adolescent Psychiatry, www.aacap. org/publications/policy/ps39.htm #top, (accessed Aug. 16, 2005).

Posey, D.J., and C.I. McDougle. 2000. The Pharmacotherapy of Target Symptoms Associated With Autistic Disorder and Other Pervasive Developmental Disorders. *Harvard Review of Psychiatry* 8(2): 45-63.

Richman, D. M., R.M. Reese, and D. Daniels. 1999. Use of Evidence-based Practice as a Method for Evaluating the Effects of Secretin on a Child With Autism. *Focus on Autism and Other Developmental Disabilities* 14(4): 204-211.

Rimland, B. 2000. Comments on " Secretin and Autism: A Two-Part Clinical Investigation" by M.G. Chez, et al. *Journal of Autism and Developmental Disorders* 30(2): 95.

Roberts, W., L. Weaver, J. Brian, S. Bryson, S. Emelianova, A.M. Griffiths, B. MacKinnon, C. Yim, J. Wolpin, and G. Koren. 2001. Repeated Doses of Porcine Secretin in the Treatment of Autism: A Randomized, Placebo-controlled Trial. *Pediatrics* 107(5): E71.

Robinson, T.W. 2001. Homeophathic Secretin in Autism: A Clinical Pilot Study. *The British Homeopathic Journal* 90(2): 86-91.

Sandler, A.D., K.A. Sutton, J. DeWeese, M.A. Girardi, V. Sheppard, and J.W. Bodfish. 1999. Lack of Benefit of a Single Dose of Synthetic Human Secretin in the Treatment of Autism and Pervasive Developmental Disorder. *New England Journal of Medicine* 341(24):1801-1806.

Sponheim, E., G. Oftedal, and S.B. Helverschou. 2002. Multiple Doses of Secretin in the Treatment of Autism: A Controlled Study. *Acta Paediatrica* 91(5): 540-545.

Sturmey, P. 2005. Secretin is an Ineffective Treatment for Pervasive Developmental Disabilities: A Review of 15 Double-blind Randomized Controlled Trials. *Research of Developmental Disabilities* 26(1):87-97.

Unis, A.S., J.A. Munson, S.J. Rogers, E. Goldson, J. Osterling, R. Gabriels, R.D. Abbott, and G. Dawson. 2002. A Randomized, Double-Blind, Placebo-Controlled Trial of Porcine Versus Synthetic Secretin for Reducing Symptoms of Autism. *Journal of the American Academy of Child and Adolescent Psychiatry* 41(11): 1315-1321.

Wilienfeld, S.O. 2005. Scientifically Unsupported and Supported Interventions for Childhood Psychopathology: A summary. *Pediatrics* 5(3): 761-764.

## Vitamin B6 and Magnesium

Adams, L., and S. Conn. 1997. Nutrition and Its Relationship to Autism. *Focus on Autism and Other Developmental Disabilities* 12(1): 53-58.

Barthelemy, C. 1983. Value of Behavior Scales and Urinary Homovanillic Acid Determinations in Monitoring the Combined Treatment With Vitamin B6 and Magnesium of Children Displaying Autistic Behavior. *Neuropsychiatrie de l' Enfance et de Adolescence* 31(5-6): 289-301.

Barthelemy, C., B. Garreau, N. Bruneau, J. Martineau, J. Jouve, S. Roux, and G. Lelord. 1998. Biological and Behavioural Effects of Magnesium + Vtamin B6, Folates and Fenfluramine in Autistic Children. In: L. Wing, ed., *Aspects of Autism; Biological Research.* Gaskell Psychiatry Series, College of Psychiatrists, 59-73.

Barthelemy, C., B. Garreau, I. Leddet, D. Ernoug, J.P. Muh, and G. Lelord. 1981. Behavioral and Biological Effects of Oral Magnesium, Vitamin B6 and Combined Magnesium - Vitamin B6 Administration in Autistic Children. *Magnesium - Bulletin* 2: 150-153.

Barthelemy, C., B. Garreau, I. Leddet, D. Sauvage, J. Domenech, J.P. Muh, and G. Lelord. 1980. Biological and Clinical Effects of Oral Magnesium and Associated Magnesium-Vitamin B6 Administration on Certain Disorders Observed in Infantile Autism (author's transl). *Therapie* 35(5): 627-632.

Campbell, M., and M. Palij. 1985. Behavioral and Cognitive Measures Used in Psychopharmacologic Studies of Infantile Autism. *Psychopharmacology Bulletin* 21: 1047-1053.

Clark, J.H. 1993. Symptomatic Vitamin A and D Deficiencies in an Eight-Year-Old With Autism... Intake Consisting of Only French Fried Potatoes and Water for Several Years. *Journal of Parenteral and Enteral Nutrition* 17(3): 284-286.

Committee on Children with Disabilities. 2001. Technical Report: The Pediatrician's Role in the Diagnosis and Management of Autism Spectrum Disorders in Children. *Pediatrics* 107(5): e85.

DiLalla, D.L., and S.J. Rogers. 1994. Domains of the Childhood Autism Rating Scale: Relevance for Diagnosis and Treatment. *Journal of Autism and Developmental Disorders* 2: 115-128.

Dolske, M.C., J. Spollen, S. McKay, E. Lancashire, et al. 1993. A Preliminary Trial of Ascorbic Acid as Supplemental Therapy for Autism. *Progress in Neuro Psychopharmacology and Biological Psychiatry* 17(5): 765-774.

Findling, R.L., K. Maxwell, L. Scotese-Wojtila, J. Huan, T. Yamashita, and M. Wiznitzer. 1997. High-Dose Pyridoxine and Magnesium Administration in Children With Autistic Disorder: An Absence of Salutary Effects in a Double-Blind, Placebo-Controlled Study. *Journal of Autism and Developmental Disorders* 27(4): 467-478.

Goyette, C.H., C.K. Conners, and R.F. Ulrich. 1978. Normative Data on Revised Conners Parent and Teacher Rating Scales. *Journal of Abnormal Child Psychology* 6: 221-236.

Guralnick, M., ed. 1999. *Clinical Practice Guideline: Report of the Recommendations. Autism/ Pervasive Developmental Disorders, Assessment and Intervention for Young Children* (0-3 years). Albany (NY): New York State Department of Health, IV-99.

Insel, T.R., D.L. Murphy, R.M. Cohen, I. Alterman, C. Kilts, and M. Linnoila. 1983. Obsessive-compulsive Disorder: A Double-Blind Trial of Clomipramine and Clorgyline. *Archives of General Psychiatry* 4: 605-612.

Jonas, C., T. Etienne, C. Barthelemy, and J. Jouve. 1984. Clinical and Biochemical Value of Magnesium + Vitamin B6 Combination in the Treatment of Residual Autism in Adults. *Therapie* 39(6): 661-669.

Kleijnen, J., and P. Knipschild. 1991. Niacin and Vitamin B6 in Mental Functioning: A Review of Controlled Trials in Humans. *Biological Psychiatry* 29: 931-941.

LaPerchia, P. 1987. Behavioral Disorders, Learning Disabilities and Megavitamin Therapy. *Adolescence* 22(87): 729-738.

Lelord, G., E. Callaway, and J.P. Muh. 1982. Clinical and Biological Effect of High Doses of Vitamin B6 and Magnesium on Autistic Children. *Acta Vitaminologica et Enzymologica* 4(1-2): 27-44.

Lelord, G., E. Dallawy, J.P. Mu, J.C. Arlot, D. Sauvage, B. Garreau, and J. Domenech. 1978. Modifications in Urinary Homovanillic Acid After Ingestion of Vitamin B6; Functional Study in Autistic Children (author's transl). *Revista Neurologica (Paris)* 134(12): 797-801.

Lelord, G., J.P. Muh, C. Barthelemy, J. Martineau, B. Garreau, and E. Callaway. 1981. Effects of Pyridoxine and Magnesium on Autistic Symptoms - Initial Observations. *Journal of Autism and Developmental Disorders* 11(2): 219-230.

Lerner, B., C. Miodownik, A. Kaptsan, H. Cohen, U Loewenthal, and M. Kotler. 2002. Vitamin B6 as Add-on Treatment in Chronic Schizophrenic and Schizoaffective Patients: A Double-Blind, Placebo-Controlled Study. *Journal of Clinical Psychiatry* 63(1): 54-58.

Martineau, J., C. Barthelemy, C. Cheliakine, and G. Lelord. 1988. Brief Report: An Open Middle-Term Study of Combined Vitamin B6-Magnesium in a Subgroup of Autistic Children Selected on Their Sensitivity to This Treatment. *Journal of Autism and Developmental Disorders* 18(3): 435-447.

Martineau, J., C. Barthelemy, B. Garreau, and G. Lelord. 1985. Vitamin B6, Magnesium and Combined B6-MG: Therapeutic Effects in Childhood Autism. *Biological Psychiatry* 20(5): 467-478.

Martineau, J., C. Barthelemy, and G. Lelord. 1986. Long-Term Effects of Combined Vitamin B6-Magnesium Administration in an Autistic Child. *Biological Psychiatry* 21(5-6): 511-518.

Martineau, J., C. Barthelemy, S. Rux, and B. Gareau. 1989. Electrophysiological Effects of Fenfluramine or Combined Vitamin B6 and Magnesium on Children With Autistic Behaviour. *Development of Medicine and Child Neurology* 31(6): 721-727.

Martineau, J., B. Garreau, C. Barthelemy, E. Callaway, and G. Lelord. 1981. Effects of Vitamin B6 on Averaged Evoked Potentials in Infantile Autism. *Biological Psychiatry* 16(7): 627-641.

Menage, P., G. Thibault, C. Berthelemy, and G. Lelord. 1992. CD4 + CD45RA + T Lymphocyte Deficiency in Autistic Children: Effect of a Pyridoxine-Magnesium Treatment. *Brain Dysfunction* 5(5-6): 326-333.

Moreno, H. 1992. Clinical Heterogeneity of the Autistic Syndrome: A Study of 60 Families. *Invesitigacion Clinice* 33(1): 13-31.

Nye C. 2005. Combined Vitamin B6-Magnesium Treatment in Autism Spectrum Disorders. *The Cochrane Database of Systematic Reviews* Issue 2, Art. No. CD 003497.

Overall, J.E., and M. Campbell. 1988. Behavioral Assessment of Psychopathology in Children: Infantile Autism. *Journal of Clinical Psychology* 44: 708-716.

Page, T. 2000. Metabolic Approaches to the Treatment of Autism Spectrum Disorders. *Journal of Autism and Developmental Disorders* 30(5): 463-469.

Pheiffer, S.I., J. Norton, L. Nelson, and S. Shott. 1995. Efficacy of Vitamin B6 and Magnesium in the Treatment of Autism: A Methodology review and Summary of outcomes. *Journal of Autism and Developmental Disorders* 25(5): 481-493.

Rimland, B. 1974. An Orthomolecular Study of Psychotic Children. *Child Behavior Research* 3(4): 371-377.

Rimland, B. 1988. Controversies in the Treatment of Autistic Children: Vitamin and Drug Therapy. *Journal of Child Neurology* 3 (Suppl): S68-72.

Rimland, B. 2005. Dimethylglycine for Autism. www.autismwebsite.com/ari/newsletter/dmg2.htm (accessed Dec. 28, 2006).

Rimland, B. 1996. Form Letter Regarding High Dosage Vitamin B6 and Magnesium Therapy for Autism and Related Disorders: *ARI Publication*. San Diego (CA): Autism Research Institute.

Rimland, B. 1997. What is the Right 'Dosage' for Vitamin B6, DMG, and Other Nutrients Useful in Autism? *Autism Research Review International* 11(4): 3.

Rimland, B. 1998. High Dose Vitamin B6 and Magnesium in Treating Autism: Response to Study by Findling, et al. *Journal of Autism and Developmental Disorders* 28(6): 581-582.

Rimland, B., and S.M. Baker. 1996. Brief Report: Alternative Approaches to the Development of Effective Treatments for Autism. *Journal of Autism and Developmental Disorders* 26(2): 237-240.

Rimland, B., E. Callaway, and P. Dreyfus. 1978. The Effect of High Doses of Vitamin B6 on Autistic Children: A Double-Blind Crossover Study. *American Journal of Psychiatry* 135(4): 472-475.

Sankar, D.V.S. 1979. Plasma Levels of Folates, Riboflavin, Vitamin B6 and Ascorbate in Severely Disturbed Children. *Journal of Autism and Developmental Disorders* 9(1): 73-83.

Schopler, E., R. Reichler, R. DeVellis, and K. Daly. 1980. Toward Objective Classification of Childhood Autism: Childhood Autism Rating Scale (CARS). *Journal of Autism and Developmental Disorders* 1: 91-103.

Szymanski, L., and B.H. King. 1999. Summary of the Practice Parameters for the Assessment and Treatment of Children, Adolescents and Adults With Mental Retardation and Comorbid Mental Disorders. *Journal of the American Academy of Child and Adolescent Psychiatry* 38(1): 1606-1610.

Tolbert, L., T. Haigler, M.M. Waits, and T. Dennis. 1993. Brief Report: Lack of Response in an Autistic Population to a Low Dose Clinical Trial of Pyridoxine Plus Magnesium. *Journal of Autism and Developmental Disorders* 23(1):193-199.

# Speech and Language Therapies

## Fast Forward

Bolton, S. 1998. Auditory Processing and Fast Forward. *Curriculum/Technology Quarterly* 7(2): 2-4.

Earle, J. 1998. Fast Forward: Is the Hype Justified? *Technology, Educators, and Children With Disabilities* (TECH-N) New Jersey College 9(1): 8-9.

Tallal, P., and M. Merzenich. 1997. *Fast forward training for children with language learning problems: Results from a national field study by 35 independent facilities.* Unpublished paper presented at the annual meeting of the American Speech-Language-Hearing Association. Boston, MA. 11/21/97.

Tallal, P., and M.L. Rice. 1997. Evaluating New Training Programs for Language Impairment. *American Speech Language Hearing Association* 39(3): 12-13.

Tallal, P., G. Saunders, S. Miller, W.M. Jenkins, A. Protopapa, and M.M. Merzenich. 1997. Rapid Training-Driven Improvement in Language Ability in Autistic and Other PDD Children. *Society for Neuroscience, Scientific Learning Corporation* 23: 490.

## Hannan Method

Bebko, J.M., A. Perry, and S. Bryson. 1996. Multiple Method Validation Study of Facilitated Communication: II Individual Differences and Subgroup Results. *Journal of Autism Development Disorders* 26(1):19-42.

Bomba, C., L O'Donnell, C. Markowitz, and D.L. Homes. 1996. Evaluating the Impact of Facilitated Communication on the Communicative Competence of Fourteen Students With Autism. *Journal of Autism and Development Disorders* 26(1): 43-58.

Girolametto, L. 1997. Development of a Parent Report Measure for Profiling the Conversational Skills of Preschool Children. *American Journal of Speech-Language Pathology* 6(4): 25-27.

Girolametto, L.E. 1988. Improving The Social-Conversational Skills of Developmentally Delayed Children: An Intervention Study. *Journal of Speech and Hearing Disorders* 53:156-167.

Girolametto, L., P.S. Pearce, and E. Weitzman. 1996. The Effects of Focused Stimulation for Promoting Vocabulary in Young Children with Delays: A Pilot Study. *Journal of Children's Communication Development* 17(2): 39-49.

Manolson, A. 1992. *It takes two to talk*. Toronto, ON: Hanen Centre Publication.

Tannock, R., L. Girolametto, and L. Siegel. 1992. Language Intervention With Children Who Have Developmental Delays: Effects of an Interactive Approach. *American Journal on Mental Retardation* 97(2): 145-160.

## Lindamood-Bell

Koegel, R.L., K. Dyer, and L.K. Bell. 1997. The Influence of Child-Preferred Activities on Autistic Children's Social Behavior. *Journal of Applied Behavior Analysis* 20(3): 243-252.

*Lindamood-Bell Learning Processes* (n.d). San Luis Obispo, CA.

## The SCERTS Model

Prizant, B.M. 1982. Speech-Language pathologists and autistic children: What is our role? Part I. Assessment and intervention considerations. Part II. Working with parents and professionals. *American Speech Language Hearing Association Journal* 24: 463-468; 531-437.

Prizant, B.M., A.M. Wetherby, E. Rubin, and A.C. Laurent. 2003. The SCERTS Model, A Transactional Family-Centered Approach to Enhancing Communication and Socioemotional Abilities of Children With Autism Spectrum Disorder. *Infants and Young Children* 16(4): 296-316.

# Miscellaneous Therapies

## Art Therapy

Bentivegna, S., L. Schwartz, and D. Deschner. 1983. The Use of Art With an Autistic Child in Residential Care – Case Study. *American Journal of Art Therapy* 22: 51-56.

Blasco, S.P. 1978. Art Expression as a Guide to Music Therapy – Case Study. *American Journal of Art Therapy* 17: 51-56. .

Buck, L., F. Goldstein, and E. Kardeman. 1984. Art as a Means of Interpersonal Communication in Autistic Young Adults. *Journal of Psychology and Christianity* 3(3): 73-84.

Golomb, C., and J. Schmeling. 1996. Drawing Development in Autistic and Mentally Retarded Children. *Visual Arts Research* 22(44): 5-18.

Ishii, T., A. Ishii, T. Ishii, and T. Sugiyama. 1996. Drawings by an Autistic Adult Chronicling a Day in His Childhood. *Visual Arts Research* 22(44): 47-55.

Judge, C., and M. Hilgendorf. 1979. Art and the Mentally Retarded. *Australian Journal of Mental Retardation* 5(7): 282-288.

Kellman, J. 1996. Making Sense of Seeing: Autism and David Marr. *Visual Arts Research* 2(44): 76-89.

Kellman, J. 1999. Drawing With Peter: Autobiography, Narrative, and the Art of A Child With Autism. *Studies in Art Education* 40(3): 258-274.

Milbrath, C., and B. Siegel. 1996. Perspective Taking in the Drawings of a Talented Autistic Child. *Visual Arts Research* 22(44): 56-75.

Quill, K. 1989. Daily Life Therapy: A Japanese Model for Educating Children With Autism. *Journal of Autism and Developmental Disorders* 19(4): 625-635.

Scanlon, K. 1993. Art therapy with autistic children. *Creative Arts Therapy Review* 14: 34-42.

Schleien, S.J., T. Mustonen, and J.E. Rynders. 1995. Participation of Children with Autism and Nondisabled Peers in a Cooperatively Structured Community Art Program. *Journal of Autism and Developmental Disorders* 25(4): 397-412.

## Auditory Integration Therapy

Baranek, Grace T. 2002. Efficacy of Sensory and Motor Interventions for Children With Autism. *Journal of Autism and Developmental Disorders* 32(5): 397- 422.

Berard, G. 1993. *Hearing equals behavior.* New Canaan, CT: Keats.

Berkell, D.E., E. S. Malgeri, and M.K. Streit. 1996. Auditory Integration Training for Individuals With Autism. *Education and Training in Mental Retardation and Developmental Disabilities* 31(1): 66-70.

Bettison, S. 1996. The Long-Term Effects of Auditory Training On Children With Autism. *Journal of Autism and Developmental Disorders* 26(3): 361-374.

Brown, M.M. 1999. Auditory Integration Training and Autism: Two Case Studies. *British Journal of Occupational Therapy* 62(1): 13-18.

Committee on Children with Disabilities. 1998. Auditory Integration Training and Facilitated Communication for Autism. *Pediatrics* 102(2): 431-433.

Dawson, G. 2000. Interventions to Facilitate Auditory, Visual and Motor Integration in Autism: A Review of the Evidence. *Journal of Autism and Developmental Disorders* 30 (5): 415-421.

Dempsey, I., and P. Foreman. 2001. A Review of Educational Approaches for Individuals With Autism. *International Journal of Disability, Development and Education* 48(1): 103-116.

Edelson, S.M. 2003. Response to Goldstein's Commentary: Interventions to Facilitate Auditory, Visual, and Motor Integration: "Show Me The Data". *Journal of Autism and Developmental Disorders* 33(5): 551-552.

Edelson, S.M., D. Arin, M. Bauman, S.E. Lukas, J. Rudy, H. Jane, M. Sholar, and B. Rimland. 1999. Auditory Integration Training: A Double-Blind Study of Behavioral and Electrophysiological Effects in People with Autism. *Focus on Autism and Other Developmental Disabilities* 14 (2):73-81.

Frankel F., J.Q. Simmons, M. Fichter, and B.J. Freeman. 1984. Stimulus Overselectivity in Autistic and Mentally Retarded Children – A Research Note. *Journal of Child Psychology and Psychiatry* 25: 147-155.

Gillberg, C., M. Johansson, and S. Steffenburg. 1997. Auditory Integration Training in Children With Autism. *Autism* 1(1): 97-100.

Gillberg, C., M. Johansson, and S. Steffenbur. 1998. Auditory Integration Training in Children With Autism: Reply to Rimland and Edelson. *Autism* 2(1): 93-94.

Goldstein, H. 2000. Commentary: Interventions To Facilitate Auditory, Visual and Motor Integration: "Show Me The Data". *Journal of Autism and Developmental Disorders* 30(5): 423-425.

Goldstein, H. 2003. Response to Edelson, Rimland, and Grandin's Commentary. *Journal of Autism and Developmental Disorders,* 33(5): 553-555.

Guralnick, M. 1999., ed. *Clinical Practice Guideline: Report of the Recommendations. Autism/ Pervasive Developmental Disorders, Assessment and Intervention for Young Children* (age 0-3 years), Albany (NY): New York State Department of Health, IV-63.

Harris, S.L. 1998. Behavioural and Educational Approaches to the Pervasive Developmental Disorders. In: Fred R. Volkmar, *Autism and Pervasive Developmental Disorders.* New York, NY: Cambridge University Press, 195-208.

Howlin, P. 1997. When Is A Significant Change Not Significant? *Journal of Autism and Developmental Disorders* 27(3): 347-348.

Link, H. M. 1997. Auditory Integration Training (AIT): Sound Therapy: Case Studies of Three Boys With Autism Who Received AIT. *British Journal of Learning Disabilities* 25(3): 106-110.

Madell, J.R., and D.E. Rose. 1994. Auditory Integration Training: Face to Face. *Journal of Audiology* 3(1): 14-18.

Monville, D., and N. Nelson. 1994. *Parental perceptions of change following AIT for autism.* Presentation. American Speech-Language-Hearing Conference, New Orleans, MS.

Mudford, O.C., B.A. Cross, S. Breen, C. Cullen, D. Reeves, J. Gould, and J. Douglas. 2000. Cockrane Developmental, Psychosocial and Learning Problems Group, Cochrane Complementary Medicine. Auditory Integration Training for Children With Autism: No Behavioral Benefits Detected. *American Journal of Mental Retardation* 10(2): 118-129.

Rimland, B., and S.M. Edleson. 1991. Improving the Auditory Functioning of Autistic Persons: A Comparison of the Berard Auditory Training Approach With the Tomatis Audio-Psychophonology Approach, *Technical. Report. 111.* San Diego: Autism Research Institute.

Rimland, B., and S.M. Edelson. 1994. The Effects of Auditory Integration Training on Autism. *American Journal of Speech Pathology* 3: 16-24.

Rimland, B., and S.M. Edelson. 1995. Brief Report: A Pilot Study of Auditory Integration Training in Autism. *Journal of Autism and Developmental Disorders* 25(1): 62-69.

Rimland, B., and S.M. Edelson. 1998. Auditory Integration Training in Children With Autism: Commentary. *Autism* 2(1): 91-92.

Schreibman, L. B.S. Kohlenerg, and K.R. Britten. 1986. Differential Responding to Content and Intonation Components of a Complex Auditory Stimulus by Nonverbal and Echolalic Autistic Children. Special Issue: Stimulus Control Research and Developmental Disabilities. *Analysis and Intervention in Developmental Disabilitites* (2): 109-125.

Siegel, B., and B. Zimnitzky. 1998. Assessing 'Alternative' Therapies for Communication Disorders in Children With Autistic Spectrum Disorders: Facilitated Communication and Auditory Integration Training. *Journal of Speech-Language Pathology and Audiology* 22 (2): 61-70.

Sinha, Y. 2004. Auditory Integration Training and Other Sound Therapies for Autism Spectrum Disorders. *Cochrane Database Systematic Review* (1): CD003681; OMID: 14974028.

Smith, I.M. 1998. Complex Choices: Commentary on Assessing 'Alternative' Therapies for Communication Disorders in Children With Autistic Spectrum Disorders: Failitated Communication and Auditory Integration Training. *Journal of Speech-Language Pathology and Audiology* 22(2): 71-73.

Stehli, A. 1991. *The sound of a miracle: A child's triumph over autism.* NY: Doubleday.

Tharpe, A.M. 1999. Auditory Integration Training: The Magical Mystery Cure. *Language, Speech, and Hearing Services in Schools* 30(4): 378-382.

Ziring, P.R., D. Brazdziunas, W.C. Cooley, T.A. Kastner, M.E. Kummer, L.G. De Pijem, R.D. Quint, E.S. Ruppert, A.D. Sandler, W.C. Anderson, P. Arango, P. Brgan, C. Garner, M. McPherson, A.M. Yeargin, C. Johnson, L.S.M. Wheeler, and R.C. Wachtel. 1998. Auditory Integration Training and Facilitated Communication For Autism. *Pediatrics* 102(2): 431-433.

Zollweg, W., D. Palm, and V. Vance. 1997. The Efficacy of Auditory Integration Training: A Double Blind Study. *American Journal of Audiology* 6(3): 39-47.

## Craniosacral Therapy

Barrett, S. 2004. Craniosacral Therapy, http:// www. quackwatch.org, (accessed May 5, 2006).

Continuing Education, Continuing Care. 1999. Palm Beach Gardens, FL: The Upledger Institute, Inc.

## Dolphin Therapy

Hulme, P. 1995. Historical Overview of Nonstandard Treatment. ED384156, p. 149.

Lukina, L.N. 1999. The Effect of Dolphin-Assisted Therapy Sessions on the Functional Status of Children with Psychoneurological Disease Symptoms. *Psychological Information* 25(6): 56-60.

Reppuk, E., and H. Koll. 1989. Structurally Assimilative Therapy for Autistic Disorders. *Frühförderung Interdisziplinär* 8(1): 33-36.

Servais, V. 1999. Some Comments On Context Embodiment in Zootherapy: The Case of the Autidolfin Project. *Anthrozoos* 12(1): 5-15.

Tak-Cho, L.L. Quantec and the Dolphin - Effect, http:// www.mtec-aq.de/autismus_und-intrumentelle-biokommunikation.asp?lang=eng, (accessed April 21, 2005).

Walker, L.A. 1999. These Dolphins Help Families Heal. *Parade Magazine* Key Largo, FL.

## Exercise Therapy

Allison, D.B., V.C. Basile, and R.B. MacDonald. 1991. Brief Report: Comparative Effects of Antecedent Exercise and Lorazepam in the Aggressive Behavior of an Autistic Man. *Journal of Autism and Developmental Disorders* 21(1): 89-95.

Celiberti, D.A., et al. 1997. The Differential and Temporal Effects of Antecedent Exercise on the Self-Stimulatory Behavior of a Child With Autism. *Research in Developmental Disabilities* 18(2):139-150.

Cowden, J.E., L.K. Sayers, and C.C. Torrey. 1998. *Pediatric Adapted Motor Development and Exercise: An Innovative, Multisystem Approach for Professionals and Families.* Springfield, IL: Charles C. Thomas Publisher, Ltd.

Davidson-Gooch, L. 1980. Autism Reversal: A Method for Reducing Aggressive-Disruptive Behavior. *Behavior Therapist* 3(2): 21-23.

Elliott, R.O, A.R. Dobbin, G.D. Rose, and H.V. Soper. 1994. Vigorous, Aerobic Exercise Versus General Motor Training Activities: Effects on Maladaptive and Stereotypic Behaviors of Adults With Both Autism and Mental Retardation. *Journal of Autism and Developmental Disorders* 24(5): 565-576.

Farrar-Schneider, D. 1994. Aggression and Noncompliance: Behavior Modification. In J.L. Matson, *Autism in Children and Adults: Etiology, Assessment and Intervention.* Belmont, CA: Brooks/Cole Publishing Co., 181-191.

Gutstein, S.E., and R.K. Sheely. 2002. *Relationship Development Intervention With Young Children: Social and Emotional Development Activities for Asperger Syndrome, Autism, PPD and NLD.* Philadelphia, PA: Jessica Kingsley Publishers, Ltd.

Hellings, J.A., J.R. Zarcone, and K. Crandall. 2001. Weight Gain in a Controlled Study of Risperidone in Children, Adolescents, and Adults with Mental Retardation and Autism. *Journal of Child and Adolescent Psychopharmacology* 11(3): 229-238.

Hinerman, P.S., W.R. Jenson, and G.R. Walker. 1982. Positive Practice Overcorrection Combined With Additional Procedures to Teach Signed Words to An Autistic Child. *Journal of Autism and Developmental Disorders* 12(3): 253-263.

Kay, B.R. 1990. Bittersweet Farms, *Journal of Autism and Developmental Disorders* 20(3): 309-321.

Kern, L, R.L. Koegel, and G. Dunlap. 1984. The Influence of Vigorous Versus Mild Exercise on Autistic Stereotyped Behaviors. *Journal of Autism and Developmental Disorders* 14(1): 57-67.

Kern, L, R.L. Koegel, K. Dyer, P.A. Blew, and L.R. Fenton. 1982. The effects of Physical Exercise on Self-Stimulation and Appropriate Responding in Autistic Children. *Journal of Autism and Developmental Disorders* 12(4): 399-419.

Levinson, L.J., and G. Reid. 1993. The Effects of Exercise Intensity on the Stereotypic Behaviors of Individuals With Autism. *Adapted Physical Activity Quarterly* 10(3): 255-268.

Powers, S., S. Thibadeau, and K. Rose. 1992. Antecedent Exercise and its Effects on Self-Stimulation. *Behavioral Residential Treatment* 7(1): 15-22.

Quill, K., S. Gurry, and A. Larkin. 1989. Daily Life Therapy: A Japanese Model for Educating Children With Autism. *Journal of Autism and Developmental Disorders* 19(4): 625-635.

Rosenthal, M.A., and M. Stella. 1997. Brief Report: The Effects of Exercise on the Self-Stimulatory Behaviors and Positive Responding of Adolescents With Autism. *Journal of Autism and Developmental Disorders* 27(2): 193-202.

Szot, Z. 1997. The Method of Stimulated Serial Repetitions of Gymnastic Exercises in Therapy of Autistic Children. *Journal of Autism and Developmental Disorders* 27(3): 341-342.

Watters, R.G., and W.E. Watters. 1980. Decreasing Self-Stimulatory Behavior With Physical Exercise in a Group of Autistic Boys. *Journal of Autism and Developmental Disorders* 10(4): 379-387.

Wunderlich, R.C. 1978. The Phenomenon of Peering. *Academic Therapy* 14(1): 49-54.

# Faciliated Communication

Bebko, J.M., A. Perry, and S. Bryson. 1996. Multiple Method Validation Study of Facilitated Communication: II. Individual Differences and Subgroup Results. *Journal of Autism and Developmental Disorders* 26(1): 19-42.

Beck, A.R., and C.M. Pirovano. 1996. Facilitated Communicators' Performance on a Task of Receptive Language. *Journal of Autism and Developmental Disorders* 26(5): 497-512.

Biklen, D., and D.N. Cardinal. 1997. *Contested Words, Contested Science: Unraveling the Facilitated Communication Controversy.* Special Education Series, New York, NY: Teachers College Press.

Biklen, D., M.W. Morton, D. Gold, C. Berrigan, and S. Swaminathan. 1992. Facilitated Communication: Implication for Individuals With Autism. *Topics in Language Disorders* 12(4): 1-28.

Biklen, D., and A. Schubert. 1991. New words: The Communication of Students With Autism. *Remedial and Special Education* 12(6): 46-57.

Bligh, S., and P. Kupperman. 1993. Brief Report: Facilitated Communication Evaluation Procedure Accepted in a Court Case. *Journal of Autism and Developmental Disorders* 23(3): 553-557.

Bomba, C., L. O'Donnell, C. Markowitz, and D.L. Homes. 1996. Evaluating the Impact of Facilitated Communication on the Communicative Competence of Fourteen Students with Autism. *Journal of Autism and Developmental Disorders* 26(1): 43-58.

Boomer, L.W., and L. Garrison-Harrell. 1995. Legal Issues Concerning Children With Autism and Pervasive Developmental Disabilities. *Behavioral Disorders* 21(1): 53-61.

Borthwick, C., and R. Crossley. 1999. Language and Retardation. *Psycoloquy* (10): 38, http://psycprints.ecs.soton.ac.uk/archive/00000673/html, (accessed May 5, 2006).

Braman, B.J., et al. 1995. Facilitated Communication for Children With Autism: An Examination of Face Validity. *Behavioral Disorders* 21(1): 110-119.

Brandl, C. 2001. The Education of A Teacher. *Focus on Autism and Other Developmental Disabilities* 16(1): 36-40.

Broderick, A.A., and C. Kasa-Hendrickson. 2001. "Say Just One Word at First": The Emergence of Reliable Speech in a Student Labeled with Autism. *Journal of the Association for Persons with Severe Handicaps* 26(1): 13-24.

Burgess, C.A., I. Kirsch, H. Shane, K.L. Niederauer, S.M. Graham, and A. Bacon. 1998. Facilitated Communication as an Ideomotor Reponse. *American Psychological Society* 9(1): 71-74.

Cabay, M. 1994. Brief Report: A Controlled Evaluation of Facilitated Communication Using Open-ended and Fill-in Questions. *Journal of Autism and Developmental Disorders* 24: 517-527.

Calculator, S.N., and K. Singer. 1992. Preliminary Validation of Facilitated Communication. *Topics in Language Disorders* 12(1): 9-16.

Cardinal, D.M., D. Hanson, and J. Wakeham. 1996. Investigation of Authorship in Facilitated Communication. *Mental Retardation* 34: 231-242.

Clarkson, G. 1994. Creative Music Therapy and Facilitated Communication: New Ways of Reaching Students With Autism. *Preventing School Failure* 38(2): 31-33.

Cohen, S. 1998. *Targeting Autism: What We Know, Don't Know, and Can Do to Help Young Children with Autism and Related Disorders.* Berkeley, CA: University of California Press.

Committee on Children With Disabilitites. 1998. Auditory Integration Training and Facilitated Communication for Autism. *Pediatrics* 102(2): 431-433.

Crossley, R. 1988. Unexpected communication attainments by persons diagnosed as autistic and intellectually impaired. Unpublished paper presented at The International Society for Augmentative and Alternative Communication, Los Angeles, CA.

Crossley, R. 1997. *Speechless: Facilitating Communication for People Without Voices.* New York, NY: Signet/Dutton.

Crossley, R., and J.R. Gurney. 1992. Getting the Words Out: Case Studies in Facilitated Communication Training. *Topics in Language Disorders* 12(4): 29-45.

Crossley, R., and A. Macdonald. 1984. *Annie's coming out.* New York, NY: Viking Penguin.

Delmolino, L., and R.G. Romanczyk. 1995. Facilitated Communication: A Critical Review. *The Bahavior Therapist* 18: 27-30.

Dillon, K.M., J.E. Fenlason, and D.J. Vogel. 1994. Belief In and Use of a Questionable Technique, Facilitated Communication, for Children With Autism. *Psychological Reports* 75: 459-464.

Duchan, J.F. 1999. Views of Facilitated Communication. What's the point? *Language, Speech and Hearing Services in Schools* 3: 401-407.

Eberlin, M., G. McConnachie, S. Ibel, and L. Volpe. 1993. Facilitated Communication: A Failure to Replicate the Phenomenon. *Journal of Autism and Developmental Disorders* 23(3): 507-529.

Edelson, S.M., B. Rimland, C.L. Berger, and D. Billings. 1998. Evaluation of a Mechanical Hand Support for Facilitated Communication. *Journal of Autism and Developmental Disorders* 28(2): 153-157.

Erevelle, N. 2002. Voices of Silence: Foucault, Disability and the Question of Self-determination. *Studies in Philosophy and Education* 21(1): 17-35.

Guralnick, M., ed. 1999. *Clinical Practice Guideline: Report of the Recommendation. Autism/ Pervasive Developmental Disorders, Assessment and Intervention for Young Children* (age 0-3 years). Albany (NY): New York State Department of Health, IV-65.

Heckler, S. 1994. Facilitated Communication: A Response by Child Protection [see comments]. *Child Abuse and Neglect* 18: 495-503.

Hirshorn, A., and J. Gregory. 1995. Further Negative Findings on Facilitated Communications. *Psychology in the Schools* 32(2): 109-113.

Howlin, P. 1998. Facilitated Communication: A Response by Child Protection. *Child Abuse and Neglect* 18: 529-530.

Howlin, P., and D.P.H. Jones. 1996. An Assessment Approach to Abuse Allegations Made Through Facilitated Communication. *Child Abuse and Neglect: The International Journal* 20(2): 103-110.

Hulme, P. 1995. Historical Overview of Nonstandard Treatments. ED384156.

Jacobson, J.W., J.A. Mulick, and A.A. Schwartz. 1995. A History of Facilitated Communication: Science, Pseudoscience and Antiscience: Science Working Group on Facilitated Communication. *American Psychologist* 50(9):750-765.

Jones, D.P. 1994. Autism, Facilitated Communication and Allegations of Child Abuse and Neglect. *Child Abuse and Neglect* 18: 491-493.

Jordon, R. 1997. Education of Children and Young People With Autism. *Guides for Special Education No. 10,* United Nations Educational, Scientific, and Cultural Organization. UNESCO, Special Needs Education, ED420130.

Katsiyannis, A., and J.W. Maag. 2001. Educational Methodologies: Legal and Practical Considerations. *Preventing School Failure* 46(1): 31-36.

Kerrin, R.G., J.Y. Murdock, W.R. Sharpton, and N. Jones. 1998. Who's Doing the Pointing? Investigating Facilitated Communication in a Classroom Setting with Students with Autism. *Focus on Autism and Other Developmental Disabilities* 13(2): 73-79.

Kezuka, E. 1998. The Role of Touch in Facilitated Communication. *Journal of Autism and Developmental Disorders* 27: 571-593.

Konstantareas, M.M. 1998. Allegations of Sexual Abuse by Nonverbal Autistic People via Facilitated Communication: Testing of Validity. *Child Abuse and Neglect: The International Journal* 22(10): 1027-1041.

Margolin, K.N. 1994. How shall facilitated communication be judged? Facilitated communication and the legal system. In: H.C. Shane, *Facilitated Communication: The Clinical and Social Phenomenon.* San Diego, CA: Singular Press, 227-258.

Mesibov, G. 1995. Commentary: Facilitated Communication: A Warning For Pediatric Psychologists. *Journal of Pediatric Psychology* 20(1): 127-130.

Mirenda, P. 2003. "He's Not Really a Reader...": Perspectives on Supporting Literacy Development in Individuals With Autism. *Topics in Language Disorders* 23(4): 271-282.

Montee, B.B., and R.G. Miltenberger. 1995. An Experimental Analysis of Facilitated Communication. *Journal of Applied Behavior Analysis* 28(2): 189-200.

Moore, S., B. Donavan, and A. Hudson. 1993. Brief Report: Facilitator-Suggested Conversational Evaluation of Facilitated Communication. *Journal of Autism and Developmental Disorders* 23(3): 541-553.

Moore, S., B. Donavan, A. Hudson, J. Dykstra, and J. Lawrence. 1993. Brief Report: Evaluation of Eight Case Studies of Facilitated Communication. *Journal of Autism and Developmental Disorders* 23(3): 531-538.

Moster, M.P. 2001. Facilitated Communication Since 1995: A Review of Published Studies. *Journal of Autism and Developmental Disorders* 31(3): 287-313.

Myers, J.E.B. 1994. The Tendency of the Legal System to Distort Scientific and Clinical Innovations: Facilitated Communication as a Case Study. *Child Abuse and Neglect* 18(6): 505-513.

Myles, B.S., and R.L. Simpson. 1994. Facilitated Communication With Children Diagnosed as Autistic in Public School Settings. *Psychiatry in the Schools* 31: 208-221.

Myles, B.S., and R.L. Simpson. 1996. Impact of Facilitated Communication Combined with Direct Instruction on Academic Performance of Individuals with Autism. *Focus on Autism and Other Developmental Disabilities* 11(1): 37-44.

Myles, B.S., R.L. Simpson, and S.M. Smith. 1996. Collateral Behavioral and Social Effects of Using Facilitated Communication with Individuals with Autism. *Focus on Autism and Other Developmental Disabilities* 11(3): 163-169, 190.

Niemi, J., and E. Kâenâ-Lin. 2002. Grammar and Lexicon in Facilitated Communication: A Linguistic Authorship Analysis of a Finnish Case. *Mental Retardation* 40(5): 347-357.

Ogletree, B.T., A. Hamtil. 1993. Facilitated Communication: Illustration of a Naturalistic Validation Method. *Focus on Autistic Behavior* 8(4): 1-10.

Olney, M.F. 1995. Time and Task Sampling Approach to Validation: A Quantitative Evaluation of Facilitated Communication Using Educational Computer Games, ED390244.

Olney, M. 1997. Contested Words, Contested Science: Unraveling the Facilitated Communication Controversy. In: D. Biklen and D.N. Cardinal, eds. *A Controlled Study of Facilitated Communication Using Computer Games*. New York, NY: Teachers College Press, 96-114.

Olney, M. 2001. Evidence of Literacy in Individuals Labeled With Mental Retardation. *Disability Studies Quarterly* 21(2), http://dsq-sds.org/_articles_pdf/2001/Spring/dsq_2001_Spring_10.pdf, (accessed Dec. 28, 2006).

Oswald, D.P. 1994. Facilitator Influence in Facilitated Communication. *Journal of Behavioral Education* 4(2):191-200.

Perry, A., S. Bryson, and J. Bebko. 1993. Multiple Method Validation Study of Facilitated Communication: Preliminary Group Results. *Journal of Developmental Disabilities* 2(2): 1-19.

Perry, A., S. Bryson, and J. Bebko. 1998. Degree of Facilitator Influence in Facilitated Communication as a Function of Facilitator Characteristics, Attitudes and Beliefs. *Journal of Autism and Developmental Disorders* 28(1): 87-90.

Pontino, J.L., K. Schaal, and C. Chambliss. 1999. Changes in Rate of Learning in Autistic Children Following 9 Months on a Gluten Free Diet, ED437782.

Regal, R.A., J.E. Rooney, and T. Wandas. 1994. Facilitated Communication: An Experimental Evaluation. *Journal of Autism and Developmental Disorders* 24(3): 345-354.

Rubin, S., D. Biklen, C. Kasa-Hendrickson, P. Kluth, D.N. Cardinal, and A. Broderick. 2001. Independence, Participation and the Meaning of Intellectual Ability. *Disability and Society* 16(3): 415-429.

Schubert, A. 1997. "I Want To Talk Like Everyone": On the Use of Multiple Means of Communication. *Mental Retardation* 35(5): 347-354.

Sheehan, C.M., and R.T. Matuozzi. 1996. Investigation of the Validity of Facilitated Communication Through the Disclosure of Unknown Information. *Mental Retardation* 34(2): 94-107.

Siegel, B. 1995. Assessing Allegations of Sexual Molestation Made Through Facilitated Communication. *Journal of Autism and Developmental Disorders* 25(3): 319-326.

Simon, E.W., D.M. Toll, and P.M. Whitehair. 1994. A Naturalistic Approach to the Validation of Facilitated Communication. *Journal of Autism and Developmental Disorders* 24(5): 647-657.

Simpson, R.L., and B.Smith Myles. 1995. Effectiveness of Facilitated Communication With Children and Youth With Autism. *Journal of Special Education* 28(4): 424-439.

Simpson, R.L., and B. Smith Myles. 1995. Facilitated Communication and Children With Disabilities: An Enigma in Search of a Perspective. *Focus on Exceptional Children* 27(9): 1-16.

Smith, M.D., and R.G. Belcher. 1993. Brief Report: Facilitated Communication With Adults With Autism. *Journal of Autism and Developmental Disorders* 23(1): 175-183.

Smith, M.D., P.J. Haas, and R.G. Belcher. 1994. Facilitated Communication: The Effects of Facilitator Knowledge and Level of Assistance on Output. *Journal of Autism and Developmental Disorders* 24(3): 357-367.

Starr E. 1994. Facilitated Communication: A Response by Child Protection. *Child Abuse and Neglect* 18(6): 515-527.

Szempruch, J., and J.W. Jacobson. 1993. Evaluating Facilitated Communications of People With Developmental Disabilities. *Research in Developmental Disabilities* 14: 253-264.

Vásquez, C.A. 1994. Brief Report: A Multitask Controlled Evaluation of Facilitated Communication. *Journal of Autism and Developmental Disorders* 24(3): 369-379.

Vásquez, C.A. 1995. Failure to Confirm the Word-Retrieval Problem Hypothesis in Facilitated Communication. *Journal of Autism and Developmental Disorders* 25(6): 597-610.

Weiss, M.J., S.H. Wagner, and M.L. Bauman. 1996. A Validated Case Study of Facilitated Communication. *Mental Retardation* 34(4): 220-230.

Wheeler, D.L., J.W. Jacobson, R.A. Paglieri, and A.A. Schwartz. 1993. An Experimental Assessment of Facilitated Communication. *Mental Retardation* 11(1): 49-60.

Williams, D. 1994. In the Real World. *Journal of the Association for Persons With Severe Handicaps* 19(3): 196-199.

## Holding Therapy

Burcard, F. 1988. Follow Up Study of Holding Therapy – Initial Results in 85 Children. *Prax Kindepsychol Kinderpsychiatr* 37(3): 89-98.

Linderman, T.M., and K.B. Stewart. 1999. Sensory Integrative-based Occupational Therapy and Functional Outcomes in Young Children With Pervasive Developmental Disorders: A Single-Subject Study. *The American Journal of Occupational Therapy* 53: 207-213.

Rohmann, U.H., and H. Hartmann. 1985. Modified Holding Therapy. A Basic Therapy in the Treatment of Autistic Children. *Z Kinder Jugendpsychiatr* 13(3):182-198.

Stades-Veth, J. 1988. Autism/Broken symbiosis: Persistent avoidance of eye contact with the mother. Causes, consequences, prevention and cure of autistiform behavior in babies through mother-child holding. ED 294344.

Welch, M.G. 1983. Autistic children – New hope for a cure. In: E.A. and N. Tinbergen. *Autism Through Mother-Child Holding Therapy*. London, UK: George Allen and Unwin Ltd., Appendix I., 323-335.

Welch, M.G. 1989. Toward Prevention of Developmental Disorders. *Pre and Peri Natal Psychology Journal* 3(4): 319-328.

Welch, M.G., and P. Chaput. 1988. Mother Child Holding Therapy and Autism. *Pennsylvania Medicine* 91(10): 33-38.

## Music Therapy

Aigen, K. 1995. Cognitive and Affective Processes in Music Therapy With Individuals With Developmental Delays: A Preliminary Model for Contemporary Nordoff-Robbins Practice. *Music Therapy* 13(1): 13-45.

Baker, F. 2003. Music Therapy, Sensory Integration and the Autistic Child. *Journal of Disability, Development and Education* 50(3): 351-353.

Barber, C.F. 1999. The Use of Music and Colour Theory as a Behaviour Modifier. *British Journal of Nursing* 8(7): 443-448.

Benenzon, R.O. 1976. Music Therapy in Infantile Autism. *Vie Medicale au Canada Francais* 5(12): 1257-1264.

Blasco, S. P. 1978. Case Study: Art Expression as a Guide to Music Therapy. *American Journal of Art Therapy* 17(2): 51-56.

Boxill, E. H. 1976. Developing Communication With the Autistic Child Through Music Therapy, ED149534.

Brauner, A., and F. Brauner. 1976. Musical Aids to Assist Therapy in Mentally Retarded and Autistic Children. *Vie Medicale au Canada Francais* 5(10): 1024-1026, 1037-1039.

Brown, S. 1994. Autism and Music therapy – Is Change Possible, and Why Music? *Journal of British Music Therapy* (8): 15-25.

Brown, S. 2002. "Hello Object! I Destroyed You" In: L. Bunt, and S. Hoskyns *Handbook of Music Therapy*. New York, NY: Brunner-Routledge, 84-96.

Brownell, M.D. 2002. Musically Adapted Social Stories to Modify Behaviors in Students With Autism: Four Case Studies. *Journal of Music Therapy* 39(2): 117-144.

Brunk, B.K. and K.A. Coleman. 2000. Development of a Special Education Music Therapy Assessment Process. *Music Therapy* 18(1): 59-68.

Buday, E.M. 1995. The Effects of Signed and Spoken Words Taught with Music on Sign and Speech Imitation by Children with Autism. *Journal of Music Therapy* 32(3):189-202.

Bunt, Leslie, and S. Hoskyns. 2002. *The Handbook of Music Therapy*. New York, NY: Brunner-Routledge.

Burleson, S.J., D.B. Center, and H. Reeves. 1989. The Effect of Background Music on Task Performance in Psychotic Children. *Journal of Music Therapy* 26(4): 198-205.

Clarkson, G. 1998-1999. The Spiritual Insights of a Guided Imagery and Music Client With Autism. *Journal of the Association for Music and Imagery* 6: 87-103.

Darrow, A.A., and T. Armstrong. 1999. Research on Music and Autism: Implications for Music Educators. *Application of Research in Music Education* 18(1): 15-20.

Decuir, A. 1991. Trends in Music and Family therapy. *Arts in Psychotherapy* 18(3): 195-199.

Dellaton, A.K. 2003. The Use of Music With Chronic Food Refusal: A Case Study. *Music Therapy Perspectives* 21(2): 105-109.

Dott, L.P. 1995. Aesthetic Listening: Contributions of Dance/Movement Therapy to the Psychic Understanding of Motor Stereotypes and Distortions in Autism and Psychosis in Childhood and Adolescence. *The Arts in Psychotherapy* 22(3): 241-247.

Durand, V.M., and E. Mapstone. 1998. Influence of "Mood-Inducing" Music on Challenging Behavior. *American Journal on Mental Retardation* 102(4): 367-378.

Edgerton, C.L. 1994. The Effect of Improvisational Music Therapy on the Communicative Behaviors of Autistic Children. *Journal of Music Therapy* 31(1): 31-62.

Griggs-Drane, E.R., and J.J. Wheeler. 1997. The Use of Functional Assessment Procedures and Individualized Schedules in the Treatment of Autism: Recommendations for Music Therapists. *Music Therapy Perspectives* 15(2): 87-93.

Guralnick, M., ed. 1999. *Clinical Practice Guideline: Report of the Recommendations. Autism/ Pervasive Developmental Disorders, Assessment and Intervention for Young Children* (age 0-3 years). Albany (NY): New York State Department of Health, IV-15 to 21, IV-24.

Hairston, M.P. 1990. Analyses of Responses of Mentally Retarded Autistic and Mentally Retarded Nonautistic Children to Art Therapy and Music Therapy. *Journal of Music Therapy* 27(3):137-150.

Hollander, F.M., and P.D. Juhrs. 1974. Orff-Schulwerk: An Effective Treatment Tool With Autistic Children, *Journal of Music Therapy* 11(1): 1-12.

Hudson, W.C. 1973. Music: A Physiologic Language. *Journal of Music Therapy* 10(3): 137-140.

Keats, L. 1995. Doug: The Rhythm in His World. *Canadian Journal of Music Therapy* 3(1): 53-69.

Koffer-Ullrich, E., 1967. Music Therapy in the Group Therapy Rehabilitation Program. *Psychotherapy and Psychosomatics* 15(1): 35.

Kostka, M.J. 1993. A Comparison of Selected Behaviors of a Student with Autism in Special Education and Regular Music Classes. *Music Therapy Perspectives* 11: 57-60.

Mahlberg, M. 1973. Music Therapy in the Treatment of An Autistic Child. *Journal of Music Therapy* 10(4): 189-193.

Martin, A.J. 2000. A Research Project, *Journal of Music Therapy* 9(1): 50-59.

Miller, L. K., and G. Orsmond. 1994. Assessing Structure in the Musical Explorations of Children With Disabilities. *Journal of Music Therapy* 31(4): 248-265.

Monti R. 1985. Music Therapy in a Therapeutic Nursery. *Music Therapy* 5(1): 22-27.

Müller, P., and A. Warwick. 1993. Autistic Children and Music Therapy: The Effects of Maternal Involvement in Therapy. In: M.H. Heal, and T. Wigram, *Music Therapy in Health and Education.* Philadelphia, PA: Jessica Kingsley Publishers, Ltd., 214-234.

Myskja, A. 2000. Examples of the Use of Music in Clinical Medicine. *Tidsskr Nor Laegeforen* 120(10): 1186-1190.

Nelson, D.L., V.G. Anderson, and A.D. Gonzales. 1984. Music Activities as Therapy for Children With Autism and Other Pervasive Developmental Disorders. *Journal of Music Therapy* 21(3): 100-116.

Orr, T. J., B.S. Myles, and J.K. Carlson. 1998. The Impact of Rhythmic Entrainment on a Person With Autism. *Focus on Autism and Other Developmental Disabilities* 13(3): 163-166.

Parteli, L. 1995. Aesthetic Listening Contributions of Dance/Movement Therapy to the Psychic Understanding of Motor Stereotypes and Distortions in Autism and Psychosis in Childhood and Adolescents. Special Issue: *European Consortium for Arts Therapy Education (ECATE). The Arts in Psychotherapy* 22(3): 241-247.

Rider, M.S., and C.T. Eagle. 1986. Rhythmic Entrainment as a Mechanism for Learning in Music Therapy. In: J.R. Evan, and M. Clynes, *Rhythm in Psychological, Linguistic and Musical Processes*. Springfield, IL: Charles C. Thomas., 225-248.

Schleien, S.J., T. Mustonen, and J.E. Rynders. 1995. Participation of children with Autism and Nondisabled peers in a Cooperatively Structured Community Art Program. *Journal of Autism and Developmental Disorders* 25(4): 397-413.

Skille, O. 1989. VibroAccoustic Therapy. *Music Therapy* 8(1): 61-77.

Starr, E., and K. Zenker. 1998. Understanding Autism in the Context of Music Therapy: Bridging Theory and Practice. *Canadian Journal of Music Therapy* 6(1): 1-19.

Stevens, E., and F. Clark. 1969. Music Therapy in the Treatment of Autistic Children. *Journal of Music Therapy* 6(4): 98-104.

Sydenstricker, T. 1991. Music Therapy: An Alternative for Psychosis Treatment. *Jornal Brasileiro de Psiquiatria* 40(10): 509-513.

Thaut, M.H. 1987. Visual Versus Auditory (Musical) Stimulus Preferences in 5. The Effect of Occupational Therapy on the Motor Proficiency of Children With Motor/Learning Difficulties: A Pilot Study Autistic Children: A Pilot Study. *Journal of Autism and Developmental Disorders* 17(3):425 - 431.

Toigo, D.A., 1992. Autism: Integrating a Personal Perspective with Music Therapy Practice. *Music Therapy Perspectives,* 10: 13 - 20.

Toolan, P.G., and S.Y. Coleman. 1994. Music Therapy; A Description of Process: Engagement and Avoidance in Five People With Learning Disabilities. *Journal of Intellectual Disability Research* 38(4):433-444.

Trevarthen, C. 2002. Autism, Sympathy of Motives and Music Therapy. *Enfance* 54(1): 86-99.

Turry, A., and D. Marcus. 2003. Using the Nordoff-Robbins Approach to Music Therapy With Adults Diagnosed With Autism. In: Daniel J. Wiener, and Linda K. Oxford, *Action Therapy With Families and Groups: Using Creative Arts Improvisation in Clinical Practice*. Washington, DC: American Psychological Association, 197-228.

Wager, K.M. 2000. The Effects of Music Therapy Upon an Adult Male With Autism and Mental Retardation: A Four-Year Case Study. *Music Therapy* 18(2): 131-140.

Watson, D. 1979. Music as Reinforcement in Increasing Spontaneous Speech Among Autistic Children. *Missouri Journal of Research in Music Education* 4: 8-20.

Whipple, J. 2004. Music in Intervention for Children and Adolescents With Autism: A Meta-Analysis. *Journal of Music Therapy* 41(2): 90-106.

Wigram, T. 1995. A Model of Assessment and Differential Diagnosis of Handicap in Children through the Medium of Music Therapy. In: Tony Wigram, and Bruce Saperston, *Art and Science of Music Therapy: A Handbook*. Langhorne, PA: Harwood Academic Publishers/Gordon, 181-193.

Wigram, T. 1995. The Psychological and Physiological Effects of Low Frequency Sound and Music. *Music Therapy Perspectives* 13(1): 16-23.

Wigram, T. 2000. A Method of Music Therapy Assessment for the Diagnosis of Autism and Communications Disorders in Children. *Music Therapy Perspectives* 18(1): 13-22.

Wilson, B.L. 2000. Music Therapy Assessment in School Settings: A Preliminary Investigation. *Journal of Music Therapy* 37(2): 95-117.

Wimpory, D., P. Chadwick, and S. Nash. 1995. Brief Report: Musical Interaction Therapy for Children with Autism: An Evaluative Case Study With Two-Year Follow-Up. *Journal of Autism and Developmental Disorders* 25(5): 541-553.

Wimpory, D.C., and S. Nash, 1999. Musical Interaction Therapy: Therapeutic Play for Children With Autism. *Child Language Teaching and Therapy* 15(1): 17-28.

Yeaw, J.D.A., 2001. Music Therapy With Children: A Review of Clinical Utility and Application to Special Populations, ED457635.

Zárate, P. 2001. Application of Music Therapy in Medicine. *Revista Medica Chile* 129(2): 219-223.

## Pet Therapy

Hulme, P. 1995. Historical Overview of Nonstandard Treatments, ED384156.

Law, S., and S. Scott. 1995. Tips for Practitioners: Pet Care: A Vehicle for Learning. *Focus on Autistic Behavior* 10(2): 17-18.

Martin, F., and J. Farnum. 2002. Animal-assisted Therapy For Children With P.D.D. *Western Journal of Nursing Research* 24(6): 657-670.

Redefer, L.A., and J.F. Goodman. 1989. Brief Report: Pet-Facilitated Therapy With Autistic Children. *Journal of Autism and Developmental Disorders* 19(3) : 461-467.

## Sensory Integration Therapy

Allen, S., and M. Donald. 1995. The Effect of Occupational Therapy on the Motor Proficiency of Children With Motor/Learning Difficulties: A Pilot Study. *British Journal of Occupational Therapy* 58(9): 385-391.

Arendt, R.E., W.E. MacLean, and A.A. Baumeister. 1988. Critique of Sensory Integration Therapy and its Application in Mental Retardation. *American Journal on Mental Retardation* 92:401-411.

Ayers, A.J. 1979. *Sensory Integration and The Child.* Los Angeles, CA: Western Psychological Services.

Ayres, A.J., and Z.K. Mailloux. 1983. Possible Pubertal Effect on Therapeutic Gains in an Autistic Girl. *American Journal of Occupational Therapy* 37(8): 535-540.

Ayres, A.J., and L.S. Tickle. 1980. Hyper-responsivity to Touch and Vestibular Stimuli as a Predictor of Positive Response to Sensory Integration Procedures by Autistic Children. *The American Journal of Occupational Therapy* 34(6):375-381.

Baker, F. 2003. Music Therapy, Sensory Integration and the Autistic Child. *International Journal of Disability, Development and Education* 50(3): 351-353.

Baranek, G.T. 2002. Efficacy of Sensory and Motor Interventions for Children With Autism. *Journal of Autism and Developmental Disorders* 32(5): 397-422.

Case-Smith, J., and T. Bryan. 1999. The Effects of Occupational Therapy With Sensory Integration Emphasis on Preschool-Age Children With Autism. *The American Journal of Occupational Therapy* 53(5):489-497.

Cohen, S. 1998. *Targeting Autism: What We Know, Don't Know, and Can Do to Help Young Children with Autism and Related Disorders.* Berkeley, CA: University of California Press.

Cook, D.G. 1990. A Sensory Approach to the Treatment and Management of Children with Autism. *Focus on Autistic Behavior* 5(6):1-19.

Dawson, G., and R. Watling. 2000. Interventions to Facilitate Auditory, Visual and Motor Integration in Autism: A Review of the Evidence. *Journal of Autism and Developmental Disorders* 30(5): 415-421.

Dempsey, I., and P. Foreman. 2001. A Review of Educational Approaches for Individuals With Autism. *International Journal of Disability, Development and Education* 48(1): 103-116.

Edelson, S.M. 1984. Implications of Sensory Stimulation in Self-Destructive Behavior. *American Journal of Mental Deficiency* 89(2): 140-145.

Edelson, S.M., D. Arin, M. Bauman, S.E. Lukas, J.H. Rudy, M. Sholar, and R. Rimland. 1999. Auditory Integration Training: A Double-Blind Study of Behavioral and Elecrophysiological Effects in People With Autism. *Focus on Autism and Other Developmental Disabilities,* 14(2): 73-81.

Edelson, S.M, M. Goldbert-Edelson, D.C.R. Kerr, and T. Grandin. 1999. Behavioral and Physiological Effects of Deep Pressure on Children With Autism: A Pilot Study Evaluating the Efficacy of Grandin's Hug Machine. *The American Journal of Occupational Therapy* 53(2): 145-152.

Edelson, S., B. Rimland, and T. Grandin. 2003. Commentary: Response to Goldstein's Commentary: Interventions to Facilitate Auditory, Visual and Motor Integration: "Show Me the Data". *Journal of Autism and Developmental Disorders* 33(5): 551-552.

Edelson, S.M., M.T. Taubman, and O.I. Lovaas. 1983. Some Social Contexts of Self-Destructive Behavior. *Journal of Abnormal Child Psychology* 11(2): 299-312.

Field, T., D. Lasko, P. Mundy, et al. 1997. Brief Report: Autistic Children's Attentiveness and Responsivity Improve After Touch Therapy. *Journal of Autism and Developmental Disorders* 27: 333-338.

Gillberg, C., M. Johansson, and S. Steffenburg. 1997. Auditory Integration Training in Children With Autism. *Autism* 1(1): 97-100.

Goldstein, H. 2000. Commentary: Interventions to Facilitate auditory, Visual and Motor Integration: "Show me the data". *Journal of Autism and Developmental Disorders* 30(5): 423-425.

Goldstein, H. 2003. Response to Edelson, Rimland, and Grandin's Commentary. *Journal of Autism and Developmental Disorders* 33(5): 553-555.

Grandin, T. 1992. Calming Effects of Deep Touch Pressure in Patients with Autistic Disorder, College Students, and Animals. *Journal of Child and Adolescent Psychopharmacology* 2(1): 63-72.

Grandin, T. 1996. Brief Report: Response to National Institutes of Health Report. *Journal of Autism and Developmental Disorders* 26(2): 185-187.

Grimwood, L.M., and E.M. Rutherford. 1980. Sensory Integrative Therapy as an Intervention Procedure With Grade One "at risk" Readers – a Three Year Study. *Exceptional Children* 27: 52-61.

Guralnick, M., ed. 1999. *Clinical Practice Guideline: Report of the Recommendations. Autism/ Pervasive Developmental Disorders, Assessment and Intervention for Young Children* (age 0-3 years). Albany (NY): New York State Department of Health, 1V-60.

King, L.J. 1987. A Sensory Integrative Approach to the Education of the Autistic Child. *Occupation Therapy in Health Care* 4(2): 77-85.

Larrington, G.G. 1987. A Sensory Integration Based Program With a Severely Retarded/Autistic Teenager: An Occupation Therapy Case Report. *Occupational Therapy in Health Care* 4(2): 101-107.

Link, H.M. 1997. Auditory Integration Training (AIT): Sound Therapy? Case Studies of Three Boys with Autism Who Received AIT. *British Journal of Learning Disabilities* 25(3): 106-110.

Magrun, W.M., K. Ottenbacher, S. McCue, and R. Keefe. 1981. Effects of Vestibular Stimulation on Spontaneous Use of Verbal Language in Developmentally Delayed Children. *American Journal of Occupational Therapy* 35:101-104.

Mason, S.A., and B.A. Iwata. 1990. Artifactual Effets of Sensory-Integrative Therapy on Self-Injurious Behavior *Journal of Applied Behavior Analysis,* 23(3): 361-370.

McClure, M.K. and M. Holtz-Yotz. 1991. The Effects of Sensory Stimulatory Treatment on an Autistic Child . *The American Journal of Occupational Therapy* 45(12): 1138-1142.

Norwood, K.W. 1999. Reliability of "the Motor Observations With Regards to Sensory Integration": A Pilot Study. *British Journal of Occupatioal Therapy* 62(2): 80-88.

Olson, L.J. 2004. Use of Weighted Vests in Pediatric Occupational Therapy Practice. *Physical Occupational Therapy Pediatrics* 24(3): 45-60.

Ornitz, E.M. 1974. The Modulation of Sensory Input and Motor Output in Autistic Children. *Journal of Autism and Childhood Schizophrenia* 4(3): 197-215.

Peterson, T.W. 1986. Recent Studies in Autism: A Review of the Literature. *Occupational Therapy in Mental Health* 6(4): 63-75.

Ramirez, J. 1998. Sensory Integration and Its Effects on Young Children. ED432071.

Ray, T.C., L.J. King, and T. Grandin. 1988. The Effectiveness of Self-Initiated Vestigular Stimulation in Producing Speech Sounds in an Autistic Child. *The Occupational Therapy Journal of Research* 8(3): 186-190.

Reilly, C., D.L. Nelson, and A.C. Bundy. 1983. Sensori Motor Versus Fine Motor Activities in Eliciting Vocalizations in Autistic Children. *The Occupational Therapy Journal of Research* 3(4):200-211.

Rimland, B., and S.M. Edelson. 1995. A Pilot Study of Auditory Integration Training in Autism. *Journal of Autism and Developmental Disorders* 25(1): 61-70.

Rinner, L. 2002. Sensory Assessment for Children and Youth With Autism Spectrum Disorders. *Assessment for Effective Intervention* 27(1-2): 37-46.

Slavik, B.A., L.J. Kitsuwa, P.T. Danner, J. Green, and A.J. Ayres. 1984. Vestibular Stimulation and Eye Contact In Autistic Children. *Neuropediatrics* 15: 33-36.

Smith, T. 1996. Are Other Treatments Effective? In: C. Maurice, and G. Green, *Behavioral Intervention for Young Children With Autism: A Manual for Parents and Professionals.* Austin, TX: Pro-Ed, Inc., 45-99.

Smith, T., D.W. Mruzek, and D. Mozzingo. 2005. Sensory Integrative Therapy. In: J.W. Jacobson, R.M. Foxx, and J.A. Mulick, *Controversial Therapies for Developmental Disabilities.* Mahwah, NJ: Lawrence Erlbaum Associates, 331-347.

Stagnitti, K., P. Raison, and P. Ryan. 1999. Sensory Defensiveness Syndrome: A Paediatric Perspective and Case Study. *Australian Occupational Therapy Journal* (46)4: 175-187.

Watling, R., J. Deitz, and E.M. Kanny. 1999. Current Practice of Occupational Therapy for Children With Autism. *American Journal of Occupational Therapy* 53(5): 498-505.

Watson, L.R., G.T. Baranek, and P. DiLavore. 2003. Toddlers With Autism: Developmental Perspectives. *Infants and Young Children* 16(3): 201-214.

Wokowicz, R., J. Fish, and R. Schaffer. 1977. Sensory Integration With Autistic Children. *Canadian Journal of Occupational Therapy* 44(4):171-175.

Zissermann, L. 1992. The Effects of Deep Pressure on Self-Stimulating Behaviors in a Child With Autism and Other Disabilities. *American Journal of Occupation Therapy* 46(6): 547-551.

# Vision Therapy

Aman, M.G., N.N. Singh, A.W. Steart, and C.J. Field. 1985. The Aberrant Behavioral Checklist: A Behavior Rating Scale for the Assessment of Treatment Effects. *American Journal of Mental Deficiency* 89(5): 485-491.

Bondy, A.S., and L.A. Frost. 1994. The Picture Exchange Communication System. *Focus on Autistic Behavior* 9(3): 1-19

Groffman, S. 1998. The Power of Eye Gaze. *Journal of Optometric Vision Development* 29(3): 95-97.

Kaplan, M., D.P. Carmody, and A. Gaydos. 1996. Postural Orientation Modifications in Autism in Response to Ambient Lenses. *Child Psychiatry and Human Development* 27(2): 81-91.

Kaplan, M., S.M. Edelson, and B. Rimland. 1999. Strabismus in Autism Spectrum Disorder. *Focus on Autism and Other Developmental Disabilities* 14(2): 101-105.

Kaplan, M., S.M. Edelson, and J.L. Seip. 1998. Behavioral Changes in Autistic Individuals as a Result of Wearing Ambient Transitional Prism Lenses. *Child Psychiatry and Human Development* 29(1): 65-76.

Lovelace, K., H. Rhodes, and C. Chambliss. 2002. Educational Applications of Vision Therapy: A Pilot Study on Children with Autism. ED458766.

Missouri Autism Resource Guide. 1998. Missouri State Department of Elementary and Secondary Education, Jefferson City, MO: ED434466.

Rose, M., and N.G. Torgerson. 1994. A Behavioral Approach to Vision and Autism. *Journal of Optometric Vision Development* 25(4): 269-275.

Schulman, R.L. 1994. Optometry's Role in the Treatment of Autism. *Journal of Optometric Vision Development* 25: 259-268.

Streff, J.W. 1975. Optometric Care for a Child Manifesting Qualitites of Autism. *Journal of the American Optometry Association* 46(6): 592-597.

# Web Sites

AAP Policy Statement. 2005. Counseling Families Who Choose Complementary and Alternative Medicare for Their Child With Chronic Illness or Disability. *Pediatrics,* 107(3): 598-601, http.// aappolicy/aappublications.org (accessed Aug. 17, 2005).

American Academy of Child and Adolescent Psychiatry. http//www.aacap.org/publications/ policy/ps30.htm#TOP (accessed May 5, 2006).

American Academy of Pediatrics. 2001. The Pediatricians Role in the Diagnosis and Management of Autistic Spectrum Disorder in Children. Policy Statement. In *Pediatrics* 107: 1221-1226, www.aap.org/policy/re060018.html (accessed Dec. 28, 2006).

American Academy of Pediatrics, American Association for Pediatric Ophthalmology and Strabismus, and American Academy of Ophthalmology. Joint policy statement: Learning Disabilities, Dyslexia and Vision, www.aao.org/member/policy/diability.cfm (accessed Feb. 16, 2006).

American Speech Language Hearing Association. 1994. Facilitated Communication III-113, 12, http://www.asha.org (accessed Oct. 3, 2005).

Autism-Watch, www.autism-watch.org (accessed April 18, 2005).

Barrett, S. 2004. Carniosacral therapy, http://www.quackwatch.org (accessed May 5, 2006).

Behavioral Analyst Certification Board. www.bacb.com/consum_frame.html (accessed June 13, 2006).

Benaron, L. 2006. Pivotal Response Intervention Model. *Pediatric Development and Behavior,* www.dbpeds.org (accessed May 2, 2006).

Cambridge Center for Behavioral Studies (CCBS), http://store.ccbsstore.com/default.asp (accessed Dec. 28, 2006).

Committee on Children with Disabilities. Technical Report. 2001. The Pediatrican's Role in the Diagnosis and Management of Autistic Spectrum Disorder in Children. *Pediatrics* 107(5): e85, www.aacap.org/clinical/parameters/summaries/autism.htm (accessed Feb. 21, 2006).

Consumer Health Digest #05-07, www.ncaf.org/digest05/05-07.html (accessed Feb. 8, 2006).

Gustein, S.E., 2002. *The Effectiveness of RDI*: *Preliminary Evaluation of the Relationship Development Intervention Program*, Houston, TX: The Connections Center, 2-14. http://www. rdiconnect.com (accessed April 5, 2006).

Gutstein, S.E., R. Sheely. *Introductory Guide for Parents. Going to the Heart of Autism, Asperger's Syndrome and Pervasive Development Disorder*, www.rdiconnect.com (accessed Oct. 25, 2005).

Lane, W.G. 2002. Screening For Elevated Blood Lead Levels in Children. *American Journal of Preventive Medicine* 20(1): 78-82, www.acpm.org/pol_practice.htm#several (accessed Feb. 16, 2005).

Maine Administrators of Services for Children with Disabilities (MADSEC).1999. [Report of the MADSEC Autism Task Force]. Manchester, ME, www.madsec.org/docs/ATFreport.pdf (accessed May 20, 2006).

National Council Against Health Fraud. (NCAHF). Policy Statement on Chelation Therapy, www.ncahf.org (accessedAug. 9, 2005).

Commission on educational interventions for children with autism, division of behavioral and social sciences and education. 2001. *Educating Children With Autism,* Washington, DC: National Academy Press, http://books.nap.edu/books/0309072697/html/index.html (accessed May 5, 2005).

Public Health Service. 1999. *Mental health: A report of the Surgeon General,* www.surgeongeneral.gov/library/mentalhealth/chapter3/sec6.html#autism (accessed Jan. 11, 2006).

Quackwatch, www.quackwatch.org (accessed Feb. 16, 2005).

Scientific Review of Mental Health Practice (SRMHP), www.srmhp.orgarchives/vision-therapy.html (accessed Nov. 11, 2005).

Tak-Cho,L.L. Quantec and the Dolphin Effect, http://www.mtec-aq.de/autismus_und_instrumentelle-biokommunikation.asp?lang=eng (accessed April 21, 2005).

The American Academy of Child and Adolescent Psychiatry in Their Practice. http://www.aacap.org/AACAPsearch/SearchResults.cfm (accessed Feb. 21, 2005).

The American Academy of Child and Adolescent Psychiatry. Policy Statement. 2005. http://www.aacap.org/publications/policy/ps39.htm#top (accessed Aug. 16, 2005).

The Consolidated Standard of Reporting Trials (CONSORT). www.consort-statement.org/downloads/download.htm (accessed Feb. 13, 2005).

The Hanen Centre, www.hanen.org (accessed Feb. 21, 2005).

The Scientific Review of Mental Health Practice, www.srmhp.org/0101/autism.html (accessed Jan 11, 2005).

National Institute of Child Health and Human Development, www.nichd.nih.gov/presentations/etiology1.cfm (accessed Dec. 28, 2006).

Washington State University College of Veterinary Medicines People-Pet Partnership (PPP) Program, www.vetmed.wsu.edudepts-pppp (accessed Feb. 21, 2006).

# Index

## D

Toddler Center Model  121
toe-walking  349
touch  267, 269, 298, 303, 311, 335, 346-347, 355
toy play  12, 25, 44
transition  27
treatment contamination  423-424
treatment efficacy  14, 88
treatment gains  14, 23, 135
treatment protocol  11, 13, 19-22, 97, 99, 101, 146, 253, 386, 407, 416
Tudor  64, 79
typically developing  17, 19, 25, 34-35, 43-44, 55-56, 76, 98, 113, 121, 125, 268, 275, 284, 423

## U

U.S. Surgeon General  22
UCLA model  64, 73
unbiased measure  48
unbiased research  147
unproven treatment  262, 278, 362
unsubstantiated method  148
unsubstantiated treatment  301, 412

## V

validation  147, 293, 303-306
Verbal Behavior  58, 69-73, 86-87
Verbal Behavior Therapy  61-65, 79
video modeling  26
Vineland Adaptive Behavioral Scales  87
Vision Therapy  349-350, 352-257
visual dysfunction  349, 354
visual schedules  26, 83
visual strengths  84
visual-motor  113, 235
Vitamin B6  170, 173, 205-207, 209-212, 214-215, 368
vocabulary  30, 69, 233, 257, 338, 368
vocal tone  135

## W

Walden  121-129
Weiss  103, 292, 306
Welch  309-311, 315